AF477004

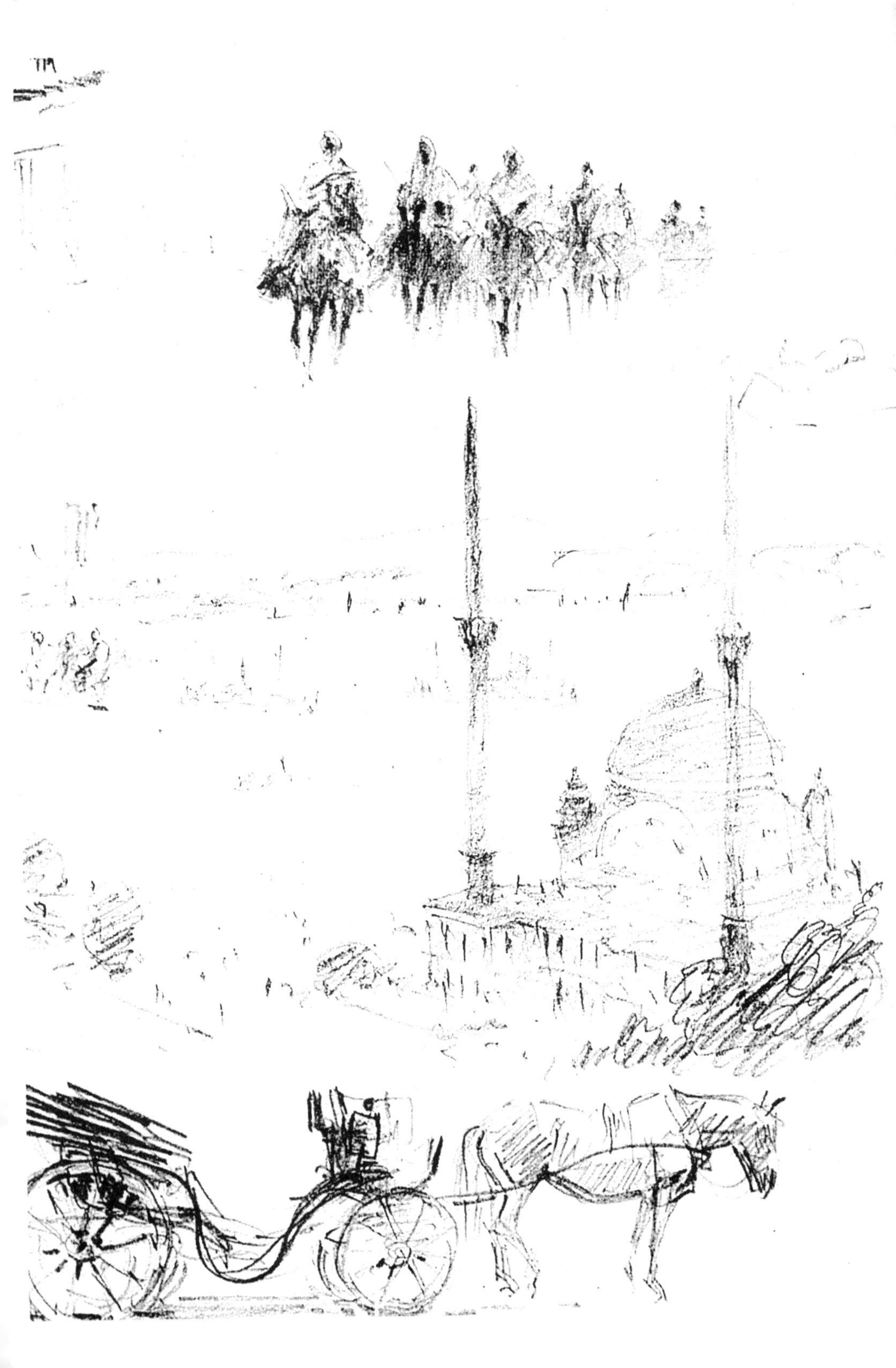

Seago

A Wider Canvas

THE LIFE OF EDWARD SEAGO
with
WRITINGS BY HIS BROTHER, JOHN

By the Same Author

Anything But Housework: An Autobiography
Edward Seago: The Other Side of the Canvas
AJ The Life of Alfred Munnings 1898–1959
The Mond Legacy: A Family Saga
Royal Scotland (in collaboration with
Sir Iain Moncreiffe of that Ilk, Bart)
With Love from Bunty: A Biography
Debrett's books of the Engagement
and Marriage of the Duke and Duchess of York

Seago
A Wider Canvas

THE LIFE OF EDWARD SEAGO
with
WRITINGS BY HIS BROTHER, JOHN

―――――――――

by

Jean Goodman

THE ERSKINE PRESS
2002

SEAGO
A WIDER CANVAS
The Life of Edward Seago
with
writings by his brother, John

Published in 2002 by
The Erskine Press, The Old Bakery, Banham, Norwich, Norfolk NR16 2HW

Text © Jean Goodman, 1978 and 2002

ISBN 1 85297 068 5

The right of Jean Goodman to be identified as the author
of this work has been asserted by her in accordance
with the Copyright, Designs & Patents Act, 1988

First published as EDWARD SEAGO, The Other Side of the Canvas
in 1978 by William Collins & Co Ltd
This revised edition © The Erskine Press 2002

Printed and bound by Athenaeum Press, Gateshead

For my eldest grandson
James

CONTENTS

LIST OF ILLUSTRATIONS

COLOUR PLATES

BLACK AND WHITE PLATES

Between pages 141/142

FOREWORD
by
H.R.H. The Prince of Wales

Essentially my memories of Ted Seago are childhood ones. I have vivid and happy recollections of almost annual January visits with my father to the Dutch House at Ludham where the rather special atmosphere of the place – the cosy, paint-smelling, picture-crammed studio, the delicious food, the garden leading down to a branch of the broads, *Capricorn* sitting invitingly on the water – all this was imprinted joyfully on my mind, never to be forgotten.

Seago's pictures, too, are a part of that childhood. Not only was my grandmother surrounded by glorious visions of that limitless East Anglian landscape, but my father had a huge collection of Seago's paintings of the Antarctic islands in the South Atlantic and West Africa, some of which hung in my room and provided me with wonderfully exciting and contrasting images of icebergs and the heat and colour of Africa.

It is possible, I suppose, that with so much 'Seago' around I could have been put off for ever. But the opposite was the case and I found myself totally captivated by the unique way in which he could convey atmosphere on canvas and by the living texture of his pictures. Perhaps one of the reasons that Ted Seago inspired such a devoted and 'regular' following, and correspondingly goaded his critics and detractors to scorn and deride his style, was precisely because if you knew and loved the sort of places that Seago painted, then his pictures conveyed in an uncanny way the *actual* sound of the wind in a lone Norfolk tree or the smell of cows and plough or the soaring, twisting movements of a seagull in a windy, storm-filled sky.

I can only say that I was powerfully influenced by the impression his pictures made on me and eventually I could no longer resist the temptation to experiment with water-colours myself. I drove myself mad with frustration because it was so incredibly difficult and because I could never achieve the effect I wanted! In the end I wrote to the expert himself and asked if I could come over to visit him from Sandringham and pick up a few useful hints. The result was even more frustrating because, in the same way that my father discovered, I felt exactly as though I were riding a bicycle extremely badly on the ground while the painter was on another on a high wire above. Ted Seago never gave lessons, but he agreed to 'talk me through' a painting. He simply sat down and, talking as he painted, he produced within a very short time a beautiful water-colour of a pair of Thames barges on a Norfolk broad. Watching the picture grow out of the paper was one of the most impressive demonstrations of sheer creativity that I have ever seen. I asked how he managed, with just a few strokes of his brush, to convey the impression of a cow in the distance, or a stormy sky or a ploughed field. His answer was most revealing. He told me that it was simply because he had spent such a long time observing things. He was fascinated by the weather, for instance, and its characteristic cloud formations, he knew the play of light and shadow on cows and trees and, what is more, having studied for a time as a vet, he knew about anatomy. All this hard work and study enabled him to paint with economy and with that distinctive skill that he had. On top of that, of course, he had the gift of what Laurens van der Post has described as 'man's mysterious communion with Nature which the visual artists of East Anglia achieved'.

Whatever the so-called experts may say, Ted Seago's gifts will long be remembered, valued and loved. His work was in the best tradition of that peculiarly English school of landscape artists with which few others can compare.

I, certainly, will always miss those visits to the Norfolk studio, but the pictures I have will be a constant inspiration and a happy memory of an intriguing person – as, indeed, will this excellent book.

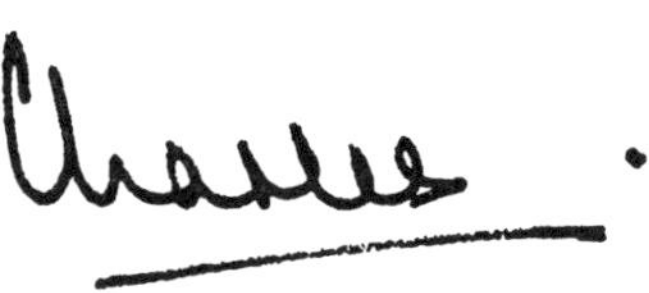

'... How can I know myself, and prevent that genuine atom from being strangled by theories and known facts? I want to see nature for myself; I want to feel for myself, and to know that what I feel is mine, and only mine. I cannot do this. I am sure that what I feel has been felt before, that what I see has been seen before. I can only persevere and hope that, gradually, I shall reveal myself.'

Edward Seago – *A Canvas to Cover*

ACKNOWLEDGEMENTS

So many people have helped me with this biography, which was first commissioned by the late Sir William Collins, that it is impossible to mention everyone individually although I most sincerely express my thanks to them all.

In particular, I am immeasurably indebted to two men: Peter Seymour, the friend whose loyalty to Edward Seago extended to an insistence that I found my own way to an unbiased conclusion about the man he knew better than any living person; and John Seago who, for two years, communicated with me regularly from Kenya about his brother, in letters and on tape recordings and who allowed me access to all the family papers in his possession.

Edward Seago's story indicates that he was a microcosm of his time and the generous co-operation I received from whoever I approached testifies to the affection and admiration he engendered in many walks of life. I am most grateful to Her Majesty Queen Elizabeth the Queen Mother for permission to quote one of her letters to Edward Seago; to His Royal Highness the Duke of Edinburgh who has allowed me to reproduce paintings and photographs; to His Royal Highness the Prince of Wales; and to the Earl of Harewood for permission to quote from a letter from his late father.

I must record my particular gratitude to Margaret Countess Alexander of Tunis for permission to quote extensively from the letters of her late husband; to Mr Nigel Nicolson for his generosity in allowing me to quote from the tape recordings he made with the late Field-Marshal Earl Alexander of Tunis in connection with his biography *Alex*; to Lady Pearce for permission to quote from the letters of her father, the late Mr Bertram Priestman; and to Mr John Gregory for generously allowing me access to his letters from

Edward Seago and permitting me to quote from his diary as did Mr John Hill to whom I am also indebted. I would also like to thank the following for their help: Mr Christopher Alston, Mr Derek Ancil, General Sir John and Lady Anderson. Mr Dennis Arundell, Field-Marshal Sir Claude Auchinleck, the late Earl of Avon, Mrs Stevens Baird, Mr Pat Baker, Mr Richard Baker, Mr Freddy Bantoft, Mr A. M. Baptista Fernandes, The Hon. Mrs John Baring, Mr John Baskett, Mr Leslie Bell, Lieut.-Colonel Alfred Beddington, Dr Ronald Bennett, Colonel J. H. Bevan, Mr Reg Bloom, Mrs Anne Boardman, Mrs Jeanne Bridge, Mr Ben Burgess, Mr Cyril Butcher, Miss Iris Butler, Lord Butler, Mr Jimmy Chipperfield, Mrs Mary Clay, Mr Jack Clegg, Mr Harold Colmer, Miss Evelyn Cooke, Mrs Ada Cubitt, Mr William Cunningham, Mr Peter Cushing, Mrs Mary Pyne Cutting, Miss Constance Daniels, Mr and Mrs Michael Denison, Mr Anton Dolin, Dr Otto Edholm, Mr John Erle-Drax, Mr Joe Fairhurst, The Hon. Julian Fane, Mr Cyril Fletcher, Mrs Penty Fraser, Dr Stefan Galeski, Mrs Evelyn Gowing, Mrs Elizabeth Haldin, Field-Marshal Lord Harding, Mr Richard Hearne, Mr Charles Hobbis, Mrs Caroline Horejsi, Mr and Mrs Michael Hornby, Mr Simon Hornby, Miss Joyce Howell, Mr Jeremy Jamieson, Mr Fred Jarvis, Lieut.-Colonel James Langley, Mr Peter Leighton, Mrs Dorothy Lemon, Mr Cole Lesley, Sir Christopher Lever, Mr James Longstaffe, Dame Alicia Markova, Miss Judith Masefield, Mr Henry Maxwell, Lady McCreery, Mr Frew McMillan, Sonia Lady Melchett, Lord Melchett, Mr Cyril Mills, Mr John Morgan, Mr Alexander Parker, Mr Arthur Parkinson, Lord Pearce, Dr Maurice Perlzweig, Mr Colin Preston, The Marquis of Reading, Mrs Yvonne Rowe, Mr Vernon Russell Smith, Mr Donald Sewell, Miss Athene Seyler, Mr Peter Shaw, Mrs Violet Showell, Mr Donald Sinden, Mr Paul Smythe, Mr Ralph Snagge, Mr David Spenser, the late Mr Victor Stiebel, Mr John Kidston Swire, Mr John Taunton, Field-Marshal Sir Gerald Templer, Miss Annie Thompson, Mrs Laurie Thompson Hancock, Mrs Monica Topham, Mr Monty Trethowan, Mr Raleigh Trevelyan, Mr Laurens van der Post, Mr Peter Vanzeller, The Hon. Mrs Brian Wallace, Mr John Wright, Mrs Jock Youngs, Lord and Lady Zuckerman.

I have also received help from the British Broadcasting Corporation, Eastern Counties Newspapers Limited, Castle Museum

Norwich, Institute of Contemporary History and Wiener Library London, Imperial War Museum, Norwich Central Library, Royal Academy of Arts, University of Texas.

I should also like to thank the Society of Authors as the Literary Representative of the estate of John Masefield for permission to quote letters and poetry of John Masefield, the Trustees of the Sir Alfred Munnings Art Museum for permitting me to quote from letters and memoirs and the Noël Coward Estate for permission to quote from letters.

On a personal level I should like to express my gratitude to my husband and two sons who, for nearly three years, accepted uncomplainingly that Edward Seago took precedence as 'the other man in my life'. Also to Pat White my agent for her unfailing support. And to Mrs Suzanne Huff and Mrs Jill Little for typing the book.

Finally, I am tremendously grateful to Adrian House and Alan Delgado for their encouragement and practical help. Both men had, at different times, worked with Edward Seago on his own books and there was a strange inevitability when, as editors, they came to advise me in a similar way. By helping me 'to set the record straight', I know they would have earned Seago's gratitude even more than my own.

For help in compiling the writings of John Seago I am grateful to my publisher Crispin de Boos and to Mr Peter Boardman, Mr Alan Haigh, Mrs Thelma Manning, Mr Tony Parkinson and Mr Oliver Prior. Also to Vickie Brown for secretarial help.

J.G.

Prelude to a Portrait

It was a bleak winter's day, with the east wind whipping in over the marshes from the North Sea, when I sat for my portrait in a small Tudor house in the heart of Norfolk. Broken branches from the trees flung against the car windscreen as I drove past the flat brown fields and wide landscapes that Gainsborough and Constable, Cotman and Crome and, in his own time, Edward Seago, painted again and again.

I left my car in the narrow lane near a small iron gate let into a wall, with stone sea-horses surmounting the two brick pillars on either side. I opened the gate and went in. As it clanged behind me there was a sense of entering a private world of enchantment. Seago's secretary, a young man with a puckish face and laughing eyes, let me in to the small square hall where a conglomeration of personal treasures jostled for attention. A sculpture of a bronze horse and winged rider, the model for the wartime insignia of the Airborne Forces, stood on an oak table which had once belonged to the painter's sculptor friend, the late Charles Sargeant Jagger; a Georgian pine corner-cupboard displayed Italian and Portuguese china; there were hand-painted hessian curtains, an Orpen self-portrait, some Augustus John drawings and, through the open doorway into the drawing-room, a glimpse of an ancient clavichord, elegant silk curtains and velvet and damask-covered chairs.

Inside Seago's studio a giant Parliament Clock on the wall ticked solemnly and the crackling of a log fire mingled with the soft wail of the wind. A pair of dachshunds snuffled around their two-tier dog basket. There were well-worn armchairs, rug-covered settees, shelves of books, model aeroplanes and souvenirs of working holidays spent abroad. It was a homely place more like a sitting-room than a studio. One expected to see family portraits on the walls instead of the paintings of recognizable celebrities, including a field-marshal, an actor and a king in RAF uniform.

'I rarely paint women,' Seago had volunteered at our first meeting. 'If I have to do portraits, I prefer to paint men. They have better bone structure and the head gives far more scope, in terms of colouring and skin tones . . .' He had learnt to his cost, he added ruefully, that every woman has a preconceived idea of her own appearance and a fairly definite image of how she should appear in her portrait. Usually there was a world of difference between her own idea and what he saw, as a painter.

I was more than willing to be the exception for this was an artist whose work had always held a strange magic for me. But there was a sudden misgiving and I was momentarily on the defensive when I enthroned myself on the sheeted armchair on a raised dais in the centre of his studio. He ignored me and busied himself mixing the paints. It seemed as if he would never stop. I studied him, a tall lean man in his early forties; an attractive man who held himself strictly even in an old corduroy sports jacket over a well-worn cardigan. He had long, beautiful hands but on the middle finger of the left hand an ornate gold ring seemed as out-of-place as his bow tie. The fine, deep-set eyes under the thick eyebrows were an unusual shade of clear grey. Coolly they met mine, appraising and enquiring, but without emotion. What type of woman, if any, did it require to arouse emotion in him? I wondered.

'Just relax a bit,' he said, and from somewhere produced, un-opened, a small box of chocolates and placed it on my knee. It was for his sake, rather than mine – to preclude conversation. The concession to my taste, I suspected, came from the radio playing in the background for it was tuned to dance music. Its owner would have preferred Chopin.

This I knew, and a good deal more, for a few months earlier I had been commissioned to write an article about him. Then, very courteously and patiently, he had answered all the predictable and rather factual questions. He had told me everything – and nothing! I realized this as I studied him studying me and I sensed that already he knew all he needed to know about me and, with an occasional look, was transferring it to canvas. In less than three hours it was caught for ever, as large as life. But writers need time to do that amount of justice to their subjects.

'It's like,' he said, even before I had been invited to see the portrait, and I detected the relief and satisfaction in his voice. So he too had been apprehensive about the result!

It was 'like'. As I studied the mirror-image of a slightly windswept girl in a faded red shirt, my hand automatically went up to straighten my hair. 'I shall paint a picture,' he had said, 'not just a likeness.' But how had he sensed that, given different opportunities, I could have been the outdoor type?

'Do you like her?' he asked, suddenly diffident before his canvas.

'I don't know,' I said honestly, studying the likeness, conscious only of relief that I had been let off so lightly. 'I don't dislike her though and one day I feel I may be a little jealous of her.'

'You needn't worry,' he said. 'I'll re-touch her, now and again, and paint in the crow's feet, to keep her up to date.' But he never did and neither, over the years, have I grown jealous of my other self.

Over the years too, I acquired other Seago paintings: ships and scenes of far-away places, oils and water-colours and little pen-and-ink sketches. But always, the portrait held pride of place in the sitting-room; or it did until recently.

Last year it was supplanted and moved over to make way for one of his last canvases. It is a picture of a place where we once walked together, a place he loved as much as anywhere in the world. It is a near-secret place at the bottom of his garden where a little wood gives way to a dyke leading to a secluded stretch of water where he kept the blue-hulled boat that bore him on painting trips, across the seas.

This clearing in the trees was both home and a place of promise, but in the picture, he painted it as a place of fulfilment rather than of anticipation, where journeys end rather than wanderings begin. To study it was, for me, to know I should write about him again. But this time it would be a portrait in depth of the painter I had once studied from the other side of a canvas.

When I started the book I had misgivings until I came across a letter written, by pure coincidence, to someone with my own initials. It was a wartime letter Seago had written to his friend John Gregory and in it he expressed many of his own ideals. In one passage it seemed as if the painter could have been exonerating his own biographer when he wrote:

'I have known painters who have gone too far in trying to perfect their technique so that they have finally lost the power of creating a good picture. Another painter may say "I know my drawing is at fault and the painting of the picture is far from perfect. For the moment, I will bear with these imperfections. The picture is saying something which I might otherwise lose altogether." For instance, Keats says of Endymion; ". . . It is as good as I had the power to make it. Had I been nervous about it being a perfect piece then it would not have been written." '

March, 1977

I

The Elder Brother

It must be hard being the over-shadowed elder brother of a successful painter, particularly a very charismatic one around whom family life revolved and whose friendship was sought by some of the most interesting and influential personalities of the time. Moreover difficulties increase when siblings share many fundamental qualities – inherited or acquired, good or bad – as John and Edward Seago did. These included courage, disposition to ill health and a preference for the company of young men although, in John's case not for sexual reasons.

Basically the brother's relationship was warm and friendly in a close-knit family and always John's admiration and respect for Edward's talent remained unqualified. But gradually his frustration at his younger brother's preferential treatment in the household intruded. This was perhaps matched by Edward's irritation at John's submissive attitude to chronic ill health which was in marked contrast to his own.

John, in due course, realised that neither his brother nor his parents considered his ultimate career, working with animals in Africa, of any importance. For nearly half his life he organized the humane catching and shipping of wildlife from Nigeria, Kenya and Rwanda to British and other zoos. Before he intervened trappers were a tough cheerful lot of hunters who saw their quarry as something to chase and capture for financial reward. They never considered animals could feel pain but kept and shipped them in inadequate cages, often with fatal results.

John was different. Working alongside the natives he learnt to understand animals as they did. He also learnt about native customs, religion, philosophy and witchcraft and the use of telepathy as a means of communication. He found the chief difference between African and European thinking was that Africans lived in the present and the past with little thought of the future which, they argued, could not be considered because it had not been experienced.

The cause for John's unlikely career lay in his late teens when he contracted TB with lesions in both lungs and never really recovered from the effects. After a spell boarding at Oakham School he returned to a Norwich day school so he 'could be with Ted'. He then studied theology for a time at London University but returned to Norwich to paint designs on furniture under Ted's supervision. At that time he also worked with the famous producer Nugent Monck at the Maddermarket Theatre. This experience helped him to get a job as an assistant film producer at Ealing Studios and in that capacity he went to West Africa to make background shots for several films including 'High Command' and 'Where No Vultures Fly'.

He immediately fell in love with the country and his health began to improve. He also felt an affinity with the natives. This was endorsed by meeting the legendary Welshman Taffy Jones who had worked there since the turn of the century for the Department of Public Works but who was more respected for his ability to restore order between tribes and for opening up new territories. The natives adored him.

When John learned that Taffy Jones lived just a day's journey away from his camp he felt a compelling and inexplicable urge to see him. Accompanied by his English driver, and a group of natives who just attached themselves to him, he turned up uninvited at Jones's bungalow where, to his amazement, tea was waiting for him and a bedroom prepared.

Jones said he had been awaiting John's arrival for a very long time and knew through thought transference that he was coming. John told him of his feeling of certainty that he had been in Africa before; Jones said that he believed quite definitely that John's spirit belonged to Africa. He described the natives' belief that spirits can lead a series of lives in different bodies and from different races, dwelling near to The Great Spirit between each incarnation. Africans recognized this and it would make no difference to them whether John did or not and he should just enjoy the close association it would bring.

'How did an African recognize an African spirit in someone of a different race?' John asked.

'How does a dog know a friend immediately' was the reply. 'After some years you will return here,' Jones said 'and finally settle and find peace for your restless spirit and will die somewhere on this continent.'

For the next five years John worked in Africa with the film company and his health improved dramatically. But he had a serious relapse during the Second World War when he spent five years in the Royal Navy doing coastal service in small armed fishing vessels. His condition became critical during the severe winter of 1947 and an operation or a long stay in a sanatorium was suggested.

'I was really unemployable and my illness gave me a feeling of being unable to contribute and therefore overshadowed by Ted,' he wrote to a friend. It was his first public acknowledgement of any sibling rivalry. He felt that only in Africa he might be able to live out his few remaining years in comfort. At the same time he knew that he had to have some occupation and purpose in life and not just go abroad 'to rot in comfort'.

On impulse he contacted an old friend, Geoffrey De Vevers, Director of the London Zoo who suggested he went to the semi-desert area of Kenya to collect a shipment of zebra waiting in Mombasa for the zoo. They had been caught and left there by an experienced game warden. It was an inspired suggestion and it was arranged that as soon as he felt strong enough he and an old friend, Reg Bloom, should go out and supervise the shipment of the animals back to England to make sure they arrived in prime condition.

John's friendship with Reg Bloom dated from 1929 when, after a bout of illness, John was advised to convalesce by the sea. He went to Walton-on-the-Naze on the Harwich estuary where Reg's father was coxswain of the lifeboat. A sailing friendship developed between the two boys who shared a natural affinity with the wild life which flourished by the lovely salt marshes. There could be no better partner for John's new adventure.

The men found the zebra in an appalling state; they had been brought many miles from the hunting grounds where they were captured. One was dead, others were severely cut and bruised and all were terrified. All their crates had been extensively damaged by the animals' frantic attempts to free themselves after they were captured. This, John knew, had been quite unnecessary because zebra, like most wild animals, soon responded to human company and would often seek it out for protection against other predators.

The local Government veterinary officer confirmed that consignments of animals were usually in poor condition when they arrived for shipment. He had made strong protests but no-one seemed to care and he readily agreed to John's suggestion that in this case shipping should be delayed until the animals were fit to travel.

John remembered from his boyhood experience with the Royal Zoological Society that animals were not afraid of people and often established a close relationship with their keepers. So he and Reg set about making friends with their new charges.

At first the zebra were even afraid of the bowls of water which were pushed into their crates and either kicked or pushed them to the back. They did not know that hay was good food so the veterinary officer drove John to a place outside Mombasa to cut some good grass to mix with hay and feed it to them while fussing about talking to them. Within four days the zebra had lost their fear and a week later they could be fed by hand. They were sleek and glossy-coated, their wounds had healed and they seemed to have realized that their crates were their stalls and not their prison.

On board ship they were kept snug and warm under canvas when the wind blew and in the heat of the Red Sea awnings were rigged up to give them shade. During the voyage they grew more friendly and relaxed. They had been treated like domestic animals and had responded as individuals so that with some it was possible to achieve a wide range of communication. The experience showed that if wild animals were properly prepared for shipment the voyage need not be a serious hazard. That first consignment John transported at the suggestion of Geoffrey Vevers achieved a standard of well being that would benefit zoos and wildlife parks across the world.

He had, however, one regret:

'Ted doesn't approve of this business,' he wrote to a friend. 'I'm not sure if he really knows what I do but he is very against it largely because he doesn't like zoos and that's understandable. I never got a chance to explain how we lived.

'Sometimes, visitors to Ted's studio would ask me what I was doing and I would explain rather quietly if he was there and try and gloss it over. Meanwhile Ted's face would get stonier and stonier and the atmosphere more and more icy. At last the friend would say "Understood" and fade away in a sort of embarrassed silence.

'Usually at least once during a visit home I would get a little lecture from Ted telling me what a bad thing he thought I'd embarked on and that I'd be much wiser to try and find something in England. I used to just accept it and, having said his piece, he would then drop it. It used to irritate Dad a bit. Afterwards I learnt that Ted was intensely interested in racial problems and we might have done a great deal together.'

There were so many things they might have done together but Edward's arrogance and John's humility intervened. Nevertheless John enjoyed his visits home immensely and his admiration for Ted was unbounded.

'One of the great pleasures of going home,' he wrote 'was to see Ted's pictures, to find out what development there'd been. There was always something new, always some new departure. He was slowly turning from the more detailed impressionist to what Turner became towards the end of his life. And I felt Ted was, more or less, in his middle season and working with tremendous intensity. We were likely to see some very startling things.

'I remember once saying to Dad that I did not think Ted would live to a very old age and Dad asked why? I said because he seemed to paint and work as if his time was limited. He paints and works almost with desperation. Dad puffed his pipe and shook his head and said it was a lot of nonsense, so that was that. Nevertheless it continued to worry me a bit and was always at the back of my mind. I think that was probably a reason why I treasured so much the time we spent together and sought every opportunity of doing so.'

There were all too few opportunities. John and Reg, after their first assignment for Geoffrey Vever had shown that there was a genuine need for a team like theirs among the animal collectors in Africa, established a small animal catching unit at Kabete on the outskirts of Nairobi.

They were soon joined by John's sixteen-year-old godson from Norfolk, Tony Parkinson, whose father had been the first man to fly a light aircraft between England and Australia. He stayed with John for twenty-six years, subsequently marrying and building his own house nearby. Reg Bloom worked with them for two years and then left to become Curator of Mammals and Birds at Chester Zoo.

It was the time when Mau Mau activity was at its height but they were undeterred. Their unit was manned by both Africans and whites whose humane method of catching and transporting wild animals from Africa to zoos wherever they were needed was based on John's and Reg's basic knowledge that wild animals in captivity rarely showed fear of human beings, and on their one experience of transforming a severely damaged cargo of zebra into sleek glossy-coated friendly animals in less than three weeks.

Their first problem had been to find a trapper willing to share his own knowledge with them. Gilbert Sauvage was recommended as 'one of the best'. He lived on a farm near Nairobi when he was not collecting animals but he preferred animals – particularly wild ones – to humans and whenever he had the chance he abandoned his wife and two daughters and went up country after them.

A retired farmer friend drove John and Reg fifteen miles to the stone farm house Gilbert had inherited from his father. They found him working at a bench in his compound surrounded by dismantled cars and lorries, old crates and lengths of netting. He nodded briefly to his visitors and continued working on a carburettor. The travellers were hot, sticky and thirsty and badly wanted a cup of tea. Finally John broke the silence and asked for one.

'Reluctantly Gilbert put down his work,' John recalled. 'Tea was brought out to a table shaded by a large tree in his garden and we were able to get down to business. We explained how many and what kind of animals we were seeking. Could he help us? He could but first he must clear a consignment of giraffes ordered by another client and which still had to be caught. Could we help him? This was just what we had hoped for. His catching camp was some three hundred miles to the north beyond the town of Isiolo so we needed a permit to get into the Northern Frontier district where he'd be operating.' There was no difficulty.

'Gilbert's camp,' John wrote, 'lay at the end of a small track some twenty miles beyond the barrier where we presented our permits. We approached it across a great plain scattered with bushes and trees. The late afternoon sun cast blue-grey shadows on the fawn-coloured grass lighting the steady cloud of dust that rose behind us. Ahead lay a small Somali village that Gilbert told us indicated we were nearing his camp. It hid behind a thorn bush fence and a huge herd of cattle moving towards us from across the plain told us our journey was near its end. Some four hundred of the beasts crossed the road in front of us at a leisurely pace, followed unhurriedly by the herdsmen. This was how each night they were collected from their grazing place and brought to the safety of the compound.

'Gilbert's camp was in a shallow depression at the edge of the village. We parked our Chevrolet beside his truck and climbed out stretching our stiff legs while a group of Africans nearby gazed at us expressionlessly. Gilbert emerged from behind his truck to acknowledge our arrival but showed little pleasure at seeing us. His displeasure increased when he saw that we had brought two tents along – one for our African helpers, Kaha the cook and Maina our handyman. As they pitched their tent he snorted and asked how could we expect to keep an African's respect by providing him with accommodation normally reserved for Europeans? I bottled up my anger and did what I always did in such a situation; called to Kaha to provide us with a pot of Earl Grey tea. I am convinced that by providing a tent for my Africans I not only maintained their respect and affection but built up one of the most willing set of helpers in Kenya.

'During supper round Gilbert's fire we encouraged him to talk about himself and his life in Africa. That evening established a rapport between us that was to last for fifteen years.

'Before supper three bearded men with cushion-like turbans and coloured ankle length shirts had walked over from the village to talk with Gilbert. Earlier in the evening we had noticed them eyeing us with suspicion as we waited for the herd of cattle to cross the road. Now Gilbert introduced them. They were the village headsman with two of his henchmen and at once their suspicion vanished.

'Africa was still so wondrously new to us with its constantly changing scenery, its wealth of wild life and the many and varied people. Before settling down for the night we stood in the darkness before the camp and stared into the vast clear sky so different from the sky we had known back home and far more brilliant even than the skies we had seen from the deck of our boat during the war.

'From where we stood it was impossible to glimpse the Pole star but we knew that it must be just below the northern horizon and probably visible from a rise in the ground. Reg made for a large anthill but I was not fit enough to walk the short distance although my health had already vastly improved in the benign climate of Kenya. I waited while Reg climbed the hill. Yes, he could just see the Pole star almost touching the northern horizon.

'As I watched the stars that night I recalled what my brother Edward once said about the people and places he went to paint; each was a new and exciting experience, too exciting, too confusing in its mass of possible subjects for him to select immediately what to paint; he had to digest what he was looking at before he could decide where to set up his easel and start work. Here in Africa I knew exactly what he meant. There was far too much beauty and colour and much more to take in before one could hope to understand this wonderful country and its people.

'We turned back towards our tent, Reg enthusing with excitement: "Just listen to those night jars!" he exclaimed. "If this is Kenya it's just what those wheezy old bellows of yours need. You'll be a different man by the end of the year."

'As I puffed away in the starlight I was just beginning to believe it.

'We were up early the next morning anxious to be off with Gilbert on his giraffe hunt. There was a lowing of cattle and through the hedge came the first of the huge herd we had seen arriving home the previous evening and now returning to their pasture. We drank our tea and watched until Gilbert emerged, still figuratively rubbing his eyes, to join us at breakfast. Meanwhile, we had yet to learn something of how he collected his animals.

'With two black helpers in the back of his beloved pick-up he would cruise along until he sighted a likely victim. Immediately it began its startled flight he would be away, swinging the truck this way and that until the animal was manoeuvred close enough to be grabbed by the helpers. The truck, he told us, had superb turning ability and it would take a clever animal to beat her. With breakfast over Reg decided to offer him the sort of challenge that a man like Gilbert could never resist; "How about a demonstration?" he asked and within minutes we were clambering aboard.

'For some reason I never discovered – unless it was to remind him of a lost love – Gilbert called his curious little catching truck "Caroline". She had no door, the windscreen had been removed, there were holes in the bodywork and the passenger seat had a great gap in its back. Many parts were held together by wire. But it was a powerful little machine capable, according to Gilbert, of swinging rapidly through the terrain.

'I sat in the passenger seat beside Gilbert who wore a little round hat and had the inevitable cigarette dangling between his lips. Reg and two helpers were in the back. Nonchalantly, Gilbert swung the steering wheel in a series of turns across the dusty sunswept plain missing minor and major obstacles by inches. Travelling fast and parallel to the fence surrounding the village his luck ran out: He turned sharply. The front wheels struck a soft patch. The truck skidded and there was a bump that almost threw me through the space where the door should have been.

'Through a cloud of dust I saw the huts of the village. Gilbert cursed and spun the wheel but Caroline failed to respond. She went straight ahead, through the boundary fence and into the garden of the henchman Aldi.

'Chickens and goats scattered as we slid on through a line of gaily-coloured washing hanging on the line and stopped with a bounce against the wall of Aldi's hut leaving a large hole and the truck and its occupants festooned in brightly-coloured frocks and underwear. Miraculously, except for a few bruises, no-one was hurt and no-one seemed at all put out except Gilbert who had to set to work repairing his truck.

'The entire village including the Aldi family thought it was the funniest thing that had happened for years and there were sly digs at Gilbert and his driving ability. Then willing hands set to work to make Aldi's hut whole again. It only needed some sand and a bag of cement to make the place as good as new.'

John's home at Kabete, five miles west of Nairobi, was very different from Gilbert's. It was an old colonial-type wooden house with a tin roof surrounded by fifteen acres of land with a separate guest house and huts for his willing army of natives. The animals they had caught which were awaiting transport were kept in enclosures and cages in the grounds. It was a very comfortable set-up. However, they spent months at a time on safari often two or three hundred miles away.

Peter Boardman, a farmer from Norfolk, was an occasional visitor.

'John led a very enjoyable life,' he said. 'He just had to flick his fingers for anything he wanted. He was his own boss with plenty of people to look after him and the animals. Wherever he went one or two of the Africans went with him to prepare the food. It was Colonial Life – or what I thought Colonial Life ought to be like. He was a friendly chap and would talk to anybody and he was very socially minded and a wonderful storyteller.'

Another visitor to John Seago's home was the traveller and explorer Wilfred Thesiger, 'There were several other animal trappers in Kenya,' he wrote in his book *My Kenya Days*, 'but Seago and Parkinson (his partner) had a reputation that was quite outstanding. I went with them to the Aberdares where Tony Parkinson was trapping bongo, a species of forest antelope. Previously the few bongo that had been captured had been bayed with dogs but they had devised an ingenious method by which bongo followed one of their well-used trails until it ended in a carefully concealed enclosure from which they could not escape. John Seago and Tony Parkinson had already captured four which I saw among their animals in Nairobi. From then on John Seago's house became my base whenever I visited Kenya.'

John Seago's home was a visiting place for many newcomers to Kenya. He was very hospitable and the animals, some with babies, were quite a tourist attraction. Members of the Diplomatic Corps and the British High Commission often brought their guests including visiting personalities such as Imelda Marcos, wife of the President of the Philippines and John delighted in arranging tea parties under the rose-covered pergola. He felt that, at last, his social life was pretty much on a level with Ted's and here he was not known as 'the brother of the painter'.

In another respect his life mirrored that of his brother's; he invariably had a younger and usually well-educated young man living in his house although in his case, with them there was no sexual involvement. It was purely for companionship. He may perhaps, in his early days, have struggled with his emotions towards men but at that time it was heavily frowned upon to be gay and he probably suppressed his feelings and kept them under strict control.

Over the years he invited a stream of young men out from England to join him and Tony Parkinson and gain experience of working with animals. He gave them pocket money and occasional gifts and relished the feeling of being their mentor and becoming completely involved in their lives. During that time he felt he was being looked up to.

There was Julian Tong the son of a Director of Whipsnade Zoo, Barney Hopkinson a parson's son, Barry White who stayed for more than ten years, Andrew Pledger from Norfolk, Nick Gosse and others. One recalled: 'Whenever he was excluded from our plans, as when Tony Parkinson married his childhood sweetheart Thelma from Norfolk, he was liable to suffer one of his "turns" and, if he felt at all neglected, remind us of his "poor old ticker".'

There was a stern streak beneath the slow lop-sided smile. An elderly neighbour, Howard Archer, called on him one day with a gift of some avocado pears from his garden. A small elephant and a young ostrich who had the freedom of John's house came out and the elephant, in an exuberant attempt to get hold of the avocados, knocked the visitor over. John snatched a rope and beat the little animal hard until it shrieked and squealed. He told the visitor this was the only way to ensure the elephant would not do it again.

Eventually John sold his home and with Tony, who had recently become divorced from Thelma, bought a smaller one nearby. Soon afterwards Tony went to the Philippines at the invitation of Imelda Marcos and established a game park for her family on one of the islands and stocked it with game from Kenya. He married a local girl and eventually settled there. John, in return for his half of their house in Kenya, gave him his home in Norfolk which he had inherited from his parents. He lived alone in the house in Kenya for the rest of his life.

I knew nothing of this when I first contacted John in Kenya two years after Edward's death and some eighteen months after I had started working on the painter's biography. John was Edward's only living relative and I should have got in touch with him earlier but soon after the book was commissioned I heard through the bush telegraph that he deeply resented me as the chosen biographer.

I did not blame him. I was a journalist with just one book to my credit and was a completely inexperienced biographer. A great painter deserved better. Moreover John would certainly have appreciated that a homosexual might well resent having a woman prying through his papers and into his innermost secrets.

Yet there was a strange inevitability about the way I came to write it. Considering this and my subsequent biographies I feel that it was not so much a case of my choosing my subjects to write about as that they chose me. Moreover writing these books has convinced me that there are more things in heaven and earth than many of us dream about. John Seago with his experience of African mysticism would doubtless have shared this belief.

For a long time it had been arranged that Edward Seago's friend, the writer and philosopher, Laurens Van der Post, should be his biographer. A few months after Seago's premature death I happened to visit Van der Post at his holiday home in Aldeburgh to interview him about his latest book. Suddenly, a vivid Seago seascape hanging by the door caught my eye.

'How are you getting on with Seago's biography?' I asked conversationally. He clapped his hand to his forehead.

'Don't mention it' he groaned. 'I never dreamt it would be a posthumous one. I've three more books on African mythology to write before I can even start it and all the time I can feel Ted touching me on the shoulder and saying "Do get on with it". He closed his eyes wearily. Suddenly he opened them and stared at me in a rather bemused way.

'Why don't you write it' he said 'and I'll help you?'

Stunned with disbelief it was impossible to take his suggestion seriously. It was a dream and any minute I'd wake up.

'There's nothing I'd like better' I mumbled when I'd collected my thoughts, 'but who'd let me?'

'I'll arrange it with my publisher' he said. And he did.

He may have salved his own conscience in this way but for a long time I felt riddled with guilt for reasons which perhaps would trouble John Seago.

Laurens Van der Post was true to his promise to help me and we met every few months to discuss the book. At every meeting I told him how guilty I felt about writing it. After I had been working on it for about a year he said to me:

'We've been talking for an hour and you've never once mentioned feeling guilty.'

'I'd forgotten all about it,' I said.

'Good' he nodded sagely and pronounced convincingly, 'that just means that Ted's happy about the way the book's going.' And who was I to argue with such an acknowledged intellect? It was my first experience of accepting that there are more things in heaven and earth than many of us dream about.

Meanwhile I decided for the time being not to approach the disgruntled John Seago. Six months later I heard, again on the bush telegraph, that he was upset because his brother's biographer had not even bothered to consult him. I let him sweat for a little longer, then I wrote to him.

His neat reply on flimsy blue airmail notepaper arrived almost by return. Methodically and meticulously he began the task of laboriously detailing his and his brother's lives:

'Dear Jean,' he wrote,

'Our great grandfather William Rix Seago was probably the first Seago to establish himself as a country gentleman with background and money. He married quite well, Sarah Hook of Blakeney whose father was reputed to have been an Admiral.

They lived at Oulton Hall surrounded by a great deal of land where part of Lowestoft is now situated and were quite well off ...'

John was a born story-teller with a marvellous memory and after a few weeks he suggested he should communicate by tape recordings instead of letters. These grew longer and longer as he became immersed in his own life story as well as his brother's. He obviously warmed to the task and soon he was starting each tape with a description of the setting where he was recording;

'Dear Jean, –

'It's a wet day and rather chilly and Karanga has made a nice fire so I've tucked myself up for the afternoon and it will be nice and fun to talk to you. I don't anticipate any interruptions ...

'I'm sorry if I speak slowly, but do remember, Jean, I'm not reading a script, I'm talking as I think ...'

'Morning Jean, –

'The sun has just risen behind the camp, the air is pleasantly cool and the morning tea tastes very good. Weaver birds are busy building in the acacia tree overhead. The distant hills are pale blue and the sky is flecked with little white puffy clouds. I'm sorry for all you people who've got to rush into your offices in trains and buses … Sorry Jean, I must leave you for a minute, it seems there is a giraffe walking about in the garden!

'Thankfully giraffes walking about in the garden are not so serious as they sound because they are tame and used to captivity. But they also eat the flowers which is a nuisance. Although we have double gates on the pens to prevent this sort of thing there is a time when somebody absentmindedly leaves open the whole bloody lot.'

His actor's voice was mesmeric and I could see the scene as he spoke:

'The noise you hear in the background is the lads talking. We're a small group gathered round the fire near my tent. The darkness beyond the circle of lamplight encloses us and hides the grand and rather overpowering scenery. There is a light breeze and the men have brought their bathtub to the fire and have begun their evening ritual. One boy is finished and is drying by the fire, his body, patches of light and dark, changing as he moves. His eyes and teeth are bright in his laughing face. Nbokwe is bending over the bath on the other side washing his sandals, always the last act of the ritual. His dark body only dimly seen. Their dark skins don't reflect the light in the same way as ours. Hasan's wearing a Kokoi – a piece of cloth wrapped around the waist and dropping to the ankles. He's bare-chested and I only really see the cloth. Jay has begun bathing and the soapsuds catch the light. Nbokwe's moved to the far side holding his hands out to the warmth and the firelight's making flickering patterns on his slim body.

'Mbo's still laughing over a story. It seems a Somali caravan with some camels came to the camp at midday for water and rest. Later they moved on and Mbo directed them past a tree where he knew two old elephants were resting. As he hoped, the camels woke up the elephants who trumpeted and stamped to show their annoyance. The camels scattered in fright dropping some of their bundles, the women screamed and the men shouted. Once everyone had left the place the elephants returned to sleep.

'Really, Jean, I think I'd also better sleep and I'll have another bash at this in the morning. Goodnight to you.'

The vividness of his writing reminded me of some of Ted's African paintings and as the tapes progressed John seemed to lose any inhibitions and spoke to me freely of other intimacies:

There was Ted's love for Bernard Clegg, for instance, the young flight-lieutenant who was killed in the Second World War.

'You may be right,' John said. 'He may have been the one real love for Ted. I remember the very sympathetic understanding letter Mother wrote telling me that Bernard had been killed. I wish I'd kept it. She referred to this love as something very special and a great gift to them both. The parents talked about him with the same affection and love they would have talked about another son. There's no doubt that the parents and I adored him.

'Ted and I have been very lucky. We've always had people to love and we've had a lot of love given to us in return. So although we've been a couple of old bachelors don't think either of us has ever felt the loneliness some bachelors feel. Would I have liked a family? I suppose I would but I can't complain that I've been alone and I don't think Ted could either.'

I felt very close at times to this man I had never met and I hoped our friendship would continue after the book was finished. He had reservations:

'I will certainly continue to write to you although my interests and life here with the Africans may not be as appealing to you as to me,' he wrote.

'Looking back, I think it is as well we did not meet while you were writing; we seem to get on very well with the tapes ...'

When the book was published in 1978 he was fulsome in its praise, privately and publicly, when he reviewed it on worldwide radio for the BBC. I doubt he ever realised the effect his writing for it had had on his own life.

II

The Colours are Mixed

Edward Seago's story begins, appropriately enough, in the house where he was born on 31 March 1910. It was No. 13 Christchurch Road, Norwich, a grey stucco semi–detached three–storey villa well set back from the quiet road.

By the time Edward was eight, a row of yew bushes, less than a foot high and evenly spaced like a line of green soldiers, marked the boundary between the parents' and the children's garden at the back of the house. To Edward's mind, his and his older brother John's garden really only began beyond this hedge. Here the rough grass and trees took over, there was a nest of blue-tits and, first thing in the morning and in the evening, rabbits bounded about, introducing an illusion of real country living into the residential part of the thriving city. Like his father, Edward would dearly have loved to live in the real country.

The yew hedge claimed for the boys' part of the garden the biggest prize of all, the huge walnut tree, sole survivor of a stalwart line which had stretched across the flat Norfolk fields, before the houses and the roads were built. On winter days, when Edward lay sick in bed, he could see from his window the twisted branches weaving against the sky. Every spring he was surprised by the warm, spicy smell of the rising sap as the catkins burst their buds signalling the start of another summer when, once again, he would try, and fail, to climb to the highest branches of the walnut. For although he was tall for his age and very wiry, as a tree-climber he was not much good; not nearly as agile as John whose whoops of triumph signalled to the younger brother crouching half-way up, the delights of the view from the top. Even in those days it was rare for John to excel over Edward, two years younger and labelled 'delicate', so that when he did it was hardly surprising that he made the most of it.

Never once did Edward manage to climb above a thick branch growing at right angles to the trunk, which made the perfect bar from which to hang the swing. When he tired of sitting there, hearing John rustling and swaying far above, he could slide down the rope and console himself that swinging was far better than climbing. It was more like flying. One day he would fly, the boy promised himself, as he swung higher and higher, tilting at the clouds with his feet.

The boys' father, Brian Seago, had never considered the superstitious implications of living in a house numbered thirteen. He was a matter-of-fact businessman and had his more imaginative and highly-strung wife, Mabel, raised the question he would, as always, have jockeyed her out of her irrational fears.

Mabel was the fourth of five daughters of Thomas Augustus Woodroffe, a hard-working third-generation Suffolk joiner and boat-builder and she had one brother, Thomas. Her mother, Margaret Reeve, one of nine children, came from solid Norfolk farming stock and in her comfortable modest home in Northgate Street, Beccles, where the boat-building business was also conducted, made the well-being of the family breadwinners, her husband and son, the first consideration.

At the turn of the century when Mabel was twenty-one, she took a job as a governess. This coincided with her eldest sister's marriage. The event may have brought home to Mabel the fact that the only semblance of romance in her own life were the bi-weekly letters from eighteen-year-old Brian Seago, a local boy who had gone to London to acquire a business grounding. Writing to him was a pleasant way of spending the long evenings and it was not unflattering to correspond with the grandson of the wealthy William Rix Seago, JP of nearby Oulton Hall.

Mabel and Brian had met for the first time in Beccles when he was fourteen and she was nearly eighteen and could not have dreamt that the boy had, at that first meeting, firmly resolved to marry her. He was the younger son of a solicitor but he had inherited the tough tenacity of generations of Seago(e) mariners who could be traced back to the seventeenth century. It was his grandfather, William Rix Seago who had broken the seafaring tradition and become a successful lawyer and although, in the next generation, Frank Seago, Brian's father, also took up law he was by no means as successful. He was a lazy, sport-loving charmer who spent his days shooting, fishing and discharging his obligations as a Major in the Militia. He also showed every sign of drinking himself to death while dissipating in advance the money he would one day inherit and also the considerable fortune brought into the family by his bride, Mary Locke Wollaston. Significantly perhaps, this lady introduced a measure of artistic talent into the family. Among her ancestors were two painters represented in the National Portrait Gallery: J. Wollaston, born in London about 1672 and a John Wollaston, born about 1717 who emigrated to the United States and included George Washington's mother among his sitters.

Brian Seago was probably oblivious to any artistic elements in his maternal ancestry. He longed for an outdoor life such as he had enjoyed on the small farm in which his grandfather, the much-respected 'Lawyer Seago' had invested some of his capital, but he sensed the need to get down to the business of earning a living as soon as possible. While his handsome brother, Ralph, revelled in student life at Cologne University where he cut a dashing figure driving behind a handsome bay in a black dog-cart with yellow wheels, Brian found lodgings in London and became an articled clerk. But most evenings he mentally escaped from the drab world of Muswell Hill to write warm, informative letters, recounting the day's happenings to the Suffolk girl who, at the beginning of their four years' correspondence, neither recognized nor reciprocated the profound devotion of her short, bluff and rather unprepossessing young suitor. Nevertheless, she too was a good letter-writer and over the years they grew to understand each other's hopes and fears.

Brian Seago appreciated Mabel's wish for independence and he seized the opportunity to encourage her for, at eighteen years of age, it suited him that his 'Dearest-but-three', as he boldly and somewhat inexplicably addressed her, should be fully occupied for a few years until he was in a position to declare his intention. It was with his full approval that she went as governess, for £2 a term, to the elder daughters of Mr Nicholas Bacon of Raveningham Hall. Five days a week she cycled to and from the fine Georgian mansion, standing in two hundred acres of Norfolk farmland. One day, long after her employer and his descendants had succeeded to the title of Premier Baronet of all England, paintings by her own son would rate a place in its rooms alongside the nineteenth-century water-colours and fine pictures the governess glimpsed on her way to the schoolroom. Imaginative dreamer that she was, Mabel might not have scoffed at the suggestion. On summer mornings she took her charges out under the great elms for painting lessons for, like her brother Thomas, she was a pretty water-colourist and her pictures were much in demand by her family. The little country scene she sent Brian Seago for his bed-sitting room in Muswell Hill was his constant pride. He saw it as only a beginning.

'I want you to please me and try your hand at a big river scene,' he wrote encouragingly in 1903. 'You did that little one very well and I believe you would do water scenes very well, if you tried hard. Don't take in any buildings, simply the water and the marshes or whatever land is in sight and give it a stormy sky. You want to take time over it. Choose a spot up at the locks or anywhere you want to go, several days running. Don't do it all in one day, dearie.'

The letter-writer's business prospects improved rapidly as his employer recognized his enthusiasm and sustained capacity for work. Later that year he made bold enough to ask Mabel to become privately engaged until he was twenty-one, although clearly he sensed that she did not reciprocate his affection.

'We can be engaged for years to come, for I will never attempt to hurry you, love. We will be quite happy engaged and grow more and more fond of one another, until we both wish to have a little house of our own, somewhere in the country. I should be quite happy engaged to you and we can remain so for years, if you wish, old girl. We will go about together, read each other's favourite books, grow up together as sworn comrades. My life-long task will be to make you happy.'

His terrier-like persistence was undeterred by periodic bouts of depression reflected in some of her letters. With a mature understanding and an unfailing buoyancy, he jockeyed her out of them. By twenty-four and with no other suitors, she was no match for his determination and eventually she agreed to their becoming 'privately engaged'. A year later she allowed the engagement to become official.

Neither of their families was enthusiastic about the announcement. The couple were regarded as rather ill-assorted; the sensitive, introspective, softly-spoken governess from generations of hard-working artisans and down-to-earth farming stock, and the ebullient young man with a rough country accent, whose cheerful, unprepossessing appearance gave no indication of his more affluent childhood or distinguished ancestry. There is evidence that three times before the wedding the bridegroom's mother, the well-bred heiress, schooled herself to ask the bride-to-be if she would like to call the whole thing off, with no recriminations on either side. But Mabel had long since come to terms with her decision and the marriage took place quietly in Norwich Parish Church on 29 September 1905.

By that time the bridegroom was the Norfolk Area Manager for a large firm of coal merchants with offices in the centre of Norwich where the great shire horses, used for pulling the coal carts, were stabled. The newly-weds' first home, in Chapelfield Road, was a flat over the stables where the sweet smell of hay and the sound of hooves on the cobbles, morning and evening, were heady bonuses to the young husband's happiness. On 13 June 1908 their first son, John Woodroffe Wollaston Seago was born.

When the baby was a year old, Mabel found she was expecting a second child and the flat over the stables was too small for the growing family. Brian would have liked to move out into the country but for Mabel a gentleman's dwelling in the best residential part of the city represented everything she had ever desired. The move to No. 13 Christchurch Road meant that, at long last, the builder's daughter was freed from the stigma of living over the shop. It resolved her last, lingering misgivings about the marriage and when on 31 March 1910, her second son was born in the fine new house, her happiness, for the first time, matched that of her husband.

The boy was named Edward after the Norfolk-loving King who died that year, and Brian after his father. For the next five years the Seagos' home was a happy one. There was a servant to help with the housework and a nursery maid to look after the children so that the mistress of the house had plenty of time to paint her delicate little water-colours; landscapes and animal studies for the sitting-room and farmyard scenes to hang in the boys' nursery.

They were fine-looking boys and the only times their parents had cause to worry were on two occasions when Edward, without warning and for no apparent reason, turned pale and his heart beat unusually rapidly for a few hours. The family doctor was reassuring. The boy was as tall as John and it was more than likely that he had outgrown his strength. For a week or so after each attack, he was kept at home from Miss Chittock's private kindergarten, ten minutes' walk from their home, which both boys had attended since they were three years old.

Sometimes, on summer afternoons, Mabel Seago collected them from school in her pony and cart and they drove out for picnics or to visit friends. The pony was eventually exchanged for a spirited, high-stepping cob called Beauty Boy and on Sundays the family rode in an elegant dog-cart, the boys sitting between their parents, two heads peeping out over a thick rug, striped in red, yellow and black. Trips further afield to relations in Woodbridge or Lowestoft entailed a drive in the new Singer car with the boys in the little dicky-seat behind their parents, well wrapped up against the wind because the car rushed along at a break-neck speed of forty miles an hour.

The war, as with most families, interrupted their pleasant way of life. Brian Seago went off to become a driver in the Horse Artillery and Mabel tried to ensure their sons continued to lead full and stimulating lives. Both boys had dancing and music lessons; John learned the piano, Edward the violin and when their father was home on leave the family would gather round the piano for an evening's sing-song. Edward had a clear, true voice and his rendering of 'Big Lady Moon' was one of the highlights of the concerts which their dancing teacher, Mrs Barwell, arranged to entertain the wounded soldiers in the local hospital and to raise money for comforts for 'the boys in blue'.

Edward also went to children's art classes because, whenever his mother took out her paint-box he, unlike John, insisted on being allowed to join in and, standing beside her, would daub away with his brushes, completely happy. His lessons however, proved more costly than expected because the teacher, Miss Starmer, raised his fees every term on the grounds that he worked harder and learned faster than any other pupil.

One way and another the boys were kept busy and home became an exciting place when a series of officers from the Royal Flying Corps were billeted with them. A kindly colonel gave the boys small, fur-lined helmets and goggles and took them to sit inside a bi-plane at the nearby airfield. From that moment Edward, bursting with patriotism, attached himself to the nearest group of soldiers or airmen in the neighbourhood and as their self-appointed messenger, tore about on his tiny bicycle, glowing with importance and the heat from his beloved flying helmet and goggles. He was a handsome, friendly child and acquired the habit of chatting to any soldier in hospital blue he met in the neighbourhood and taking him home to tea to meet his mother.

School holidays were usually spent with the grandparents who by then had moved to Woodbridge. The little market town beside the salt-water estuary offered endless delights to two small boys. Grandfather Woodroffe gave them sailing lessons in his small lugsail boat or walked with them along the bank of the estuary to search for sea treasure washed in by the tide. Often he left them in the care of the old waterman 'Peg' Grey, so-called because of his wooden leg.

Peg Grey quanted them up the river in his duck punt or rowed them out to sea in his fishing boat. He taught them about the wild-fowl and how to recognize them both by their cries and by their footprints in the wet sand of the mudflats. The old waterman sang as he rowed and told tales of the old sailing wherries that once carried corn down the east coast. A boy who discovers the romance of the wide expanses where sea meets sky will, for the rest of his life, long to return, to recapture time and time again the joy of that first discovery.

Despite the fact that the war inevitably emphasized the maternal domination of the household it was a secure and stimulating up-bringing for a couple of lively youngsters. Both boys then attended the local grammar school in the precincts of Norwich Cathedral. But by the time he was eight, Edward's heart 'turns' meant that he was more often at home in bed than at school. There was no physiological cause for the attacks and the doctors were baffled by their sudden onset and alarming severity when the boy lay, nearly unconscious and in great discomfort while his respiration dropped to five breaths a minute and the sound of his heart beating at twice its normal rate could be heard outside his bedroom door. The only treatment they suggested was complete sedation until the attack ceased as abruptly and unpredictably as it had started. Then, after a few days' rest in bed, the patient became impatient to resume the life of an apparently normal schoolboy.

Famous physicians including Sir Thomas Horder were consulted, but to no avail. No comparable case of paroxysmal tachycardia was known in this country. The local doctors communicated with medical experts in Switzerland and America where similar cases had been reported, but with little effect. Mabel Seago kept a diary of the 'attacks' and ensured that everything Edward had been doing or eating prior to their onset was, by a process of elimination, systematically excluded as a possible cause which left the doctors nothing else to suggest but rest, care and no violent exercise or excitement.

The patient's interest in painting was a godsend. At ten years old one heart 'turn' lasted for three weeks, according to the diary and was followed by an 'odd nervous attack of oblivion'. The shorter attacks lasted from two to four days and left him so exhausted that afterwards, for a day or two, he could only lie in bed resting while his mother read to him. As soon as he was strong enough to be propped up on pillows he busied himself with his paints and brushes and made water-colours of skies and birds, completely absorbed while the hours slipped away.

He wanted no better companion than his mother. She shared his interest in painting and her approval of his work was the only accolade he needed. During the course of an attack, completely distraught, she was rarely out of earshot and afterwards, fervently grateful to see him resting normally, she made his bedroom the centre of her world where the rest of the family, when they were at home, had perforce to join her. So she read aloud to all of them and

John, who loved listening to her soft, expressive voice, also took turns at reading.

Only Brian Seago, solicitous father though he was, grew impatient at the recurrent shift of emphasis in his home but he concealed any subconscious resentment by staying late at the office and throwing himself even more fervently into his work. He also immersed himself in fund-raising ideas for charities as a new outlet for his energy and initiative. As often as not when he was at home, Mabel's anxiety at their son's illness and her divided loyalties to the boy who needed her and the husband she had never really loved, found their outlet in hysterical outbursts followed by days of moody silence terminated usually by Edward or John bursting into tears and begging her to speak to their father. It was a pattern of behaviour that, once established, was to last over many years.

In the early 1920s Edward suffered heart turns every few weeks but gradually, the fear that came with the rapid, deafening heartbeats and pain and the feeling of helpless exhaustion, faded. Years later he recalled this change in attitude.

'I grew to accept these bouts of illness as ordinary events,' he wrote. 'Although they always depressed me, I came not to resent them.' It was the first essential step towards leading a normal life and in making it and coming to terms with his illness, the son was stronger than the mother.

There was an inherent danger however, in his acceptance of illness and for a time it seemed as if he might slip into the passive role of an invalid son dependent on his mother to sustain him. Both parents were firm believers in the benefits of country air and every other Sunday with remorseless regularity, the family drove out of Norwich to take afternoon tea with a distant cousin of Mabel Seago's. Uncle Ben Burgess and his wife Auntie Nancy had a lively young family of three boys and a girl who were scathingly indifferent to their Norwich contemporaries.

'We just didn't bother with those boys,' the son Ben recalled. 'Ted never left his mother's side. He didn't play any games and it was made quite clear that he couldn't be left alone in case he had one of his turns. John just hung around, doing nothing in particular. They couldn't even cope with Sunday tea. There was usually a rich cream syllabub and it was just too much for them. But they always ate it and, more often than not, were sick before they went home.'

The strain on Mabel Seago of Edward's illness was becoming unendurable. Perhaps the doctors sensed the growing tensions when they suggested that if country air was beneficial, sea air might be even more so and after much deliberation both boys were entered as boarders at South Lodge Preparatory School in Lowestoft. The tall bleak building overlooking the sea was surrounded by a small gravelled playground where not a tree or a bush had survived the unremitting force of the east wind. The forty pupils aged between eight and fourteen slept on the two top floors, facing the sea, while the staff bedrooms were on the sheltered side. 'We almost lived in the sea,' a fellow pupil, Ben Stimpson said half a century later. 'God it was cold! Sea spray came in through the bedroom windows which we were made to keep open and sometimes we put our floor mats on the beds to try and keep warm.'

The headmaster, the Reverend W. Richmond Phillips, MA, was a frightening figure, according to another old boy, Bobby Britten, who was there with his composer brother, Benjamin and recalled: 'He beat the boys, laying into them good and proper and drew blood if he'd a mind to.' The headmaster's wife, Emily, a kindly, plain woman, responsible for the domestic arrangements of the school, also taught art.

For the first few weeks John, according to his letters home, was dreadfully homesick but Edward revelled in the new life and wrote enthusiastically about playing hockey, going fishing and catching three whiting, two crabs and a dab and learning to play chess. 'I do love being at school. It is topping,' he wrote. '(It is good of you to spend the money.) I feel what a good thing it is for me to be at school . . . I am so sory I keep on sending such short letters but I am so exsited.'

Thrilled from the start with his new environment, he did his best to help his brother over his homesickness. 'I am trying to make John happy but it is a hard job but I think I shall suckceed,' he reported. And again, 'Please right and tell me that you are coming on Sunday for that will sherr John up for I have got him in a very good perzishen.'

That first term only one letter referred to his being in the sanatorium, but in the spring term it was a different story and he had only three weeks' schooling. First he had mumps and after he had recovered, a frightened note from John alerted his parents. It read: 'Dear Mum, – Will you come over on Wensday Edward is not well, his heart is beating very fast, he has not been down yet. It seems as if he has got the same thing as he had last time, he may be in bed, but come. I feel rather *nervous* he is as white as a *sheet*. Matron is not to pleased as you can be sure. Much love to all. John.'

Meanwhile, from the sick room the invalid wrote reporting his first public recognition in the art world. He won a prize of half a crown's worth of stamps in a competition run by a Norwich painting club and he was so delighted that after he had used the stamps he stuck the stamp-paper on the wall near his bed, as a memento.

During the third term the pattern of illness reasserted itself but in his letters Edward never complained and once more it was left to John to enlighten his parents. 'Ted is not happy,' he wrote. 'I tell him he cant go through school life without a certain amount of teasing. He cant stand it. He has just been teased. It is natural for boys to tease him. I often get it and I think he would be happier if he could do more. It is worse because he cant do much. I have been talking to a friend. He thinks he would be better at home. He has cryed twice today. I am doing my best. I feel it is my place to tell you. From John.'

In the middle of that term Edward was called out of class and told he was going home for good. It would be a long time before there would be another bid for independence. At the end of the term John also left South Lodge for he was to go to Oakham School in the autumn. Edward pleaded also to be allowed to go to school again but it was decided to be less ambitious and settle for a small private preparatory school just around the corner from their home. This was Winton House, a day-school run by a Mr and Mrs Brabham for forty pupils aged between eight and thirteen. There Edward Seago shared with another new boy, Alexander Parker, who was also labelled delicate on account of persistent headaches, the doubtful distinction of being one of the oldest of the new boys and, in scholastic terms, one of the most backward. The two boys came from dissimilar backgrounds and apart from their respective health handicaps had little in common. But they formed an immediate friendship which was to last a lifetime, apart from a ten-year estrangement after a thoughtless action on Seago's part.

From the first meeting, the inevitably over-protected boy found in 'Tim' Parker the ideal companion. Tim's slight build eventually earned him the nickname 'Tubby' and contributed to his spectacular success as a leading amateur jockey entitled to ride at almost bottom weight although nearly six foot tall. He was one of five children of an eccentric local land-agent and, for all his reputedly frail constitution, he was up at dawn on summer mornings to exercise his father's horses in training. Every day he drove his pony and trap the five miles from his home, into Norwich, stabled his conveyance in the city and caught a tram out to within walking distance of the school.

Sometimes on Fridays, Edward drove home with him to spend a blissful week-end riding or shooting or trying to train young kestrels to fly. As Tim's visitor he was a very different person from the boy who 'never left his mother's side', when he visited the Burgess family.

'I was bottom of the class and Ted was next to bottom,' Tim Parker recalled and conceded with admiration that Ted had the added distinction of almost being expelled for demonstrating his artistic ability in caricatures of the staff and in the cruder kind of schoolboy humour which circulated among his form-mates. According to Parker he was a very popular boy who was always ready to join in any fun that was going, although he was forbidden to play games. But he accepted his heart trouble in such a matter-of-fact way that his friends did not feel shy or embarrassed. 'Oh God!' he would say, 'I'm going to have one of those attacks,' and he would disappear for two or three days. On one occasion he willingly capitalized on his reputation and pretended to faint at the crucial moment to distract a master from discovering that Parker and another friend had not done their homework.

Another time there was no pretence about the faint. It happened when with pupils from the school he took part in a charity performance of a Chester mystery play, *Paradyse*, given in the garden of an old house in Norwich by an amateur group known as the *Norwich Players*. Edward, in a non-speaking part of an attendant angel robed in white and with wings of cheesecloth, was waiting with the other angels to make his first entrance when he suddenly announced that he was going to faint. The next thing he knew was the producer throwing cold water on his face and telling him in no uncertain terms not to be such a damn fool, but to pull himself together and get on stage.

It was the boy's first encounter with the legendary Nugent Monck, a gnome-like theatrical genius. Twelve years previously this actor, author, poet, artist and scholar had come to Norwich 'sick of failure in London' where, following the traditions of William Poel he had tried to revive the classics and also introduce good, modern work to a theatre thriving on dramatic rubbish in its Victorian heyday. The struggle to work out his ideas using professional actors had proved too costly so he turned to amateurs and in the large sitting-room of his Elizabethan home founded the *Norwich Players* with seven boys, all in their late teens. Ten years later he was to design, as a home for them, the famous little Maddermarket Theatre, the first Elizabethan-style theatre to be constructed in England since Cromwell had ordered the closure of the playhouses. There, in due course, Edward Seago, as one of 'Moncklet's boys', would play to audiences of two hundred or so from its apron stage and after the performances, maybe still in his greasepaint, join the favoured ones invited back to the producer's starkly beautiful house where candles flickered on white-washed walls as the company drank hot soup round the peat fire and smoked and talked and amused themselves until dawn.

Meanwhile, by the time he was ten years old, Edward had decided that he could never be anything but a painter. When, at the age of twelve, quite fortuitously he came upon his first 'real artist' holding a large palette on his arm and working at a canvas, he had no hesitation in bombarding him with questions. Fortunately, Ernest Chance, a member of a local art society called *The Woodpecker's Club*, was not annoyed by the interruption.

'He must have thought me a cheeky young scamp and I can imagine the stupid kind of questions I was likely to ask,' Seago recalled, more than twenty years later. 'But I remember he answered them all in a friendly fashion and smiled at me and explained what he was doing.'

Ernest Chance did more than just explain his technique. The Christmas after that first meeting he lent his young friend a copy of a book on landscape painting by Sir Alfred East, RA, a former President of the Royal Society of British Artists which, he said, had taught him more than he could ever have learned at any art school. It was called *Landscape Painting* and there, written simply in student's language, were the guide lines for a receptive young boy eager to learn and whose mind was virtually untrammelled by the formalities of conventional schooling. He absorbed them avidly from the first book on art he had ever read and, like an imprint at the moment of birth, they were with him for the rest of his life.

It was the philosophy of the painter that first caught his imagination. At last it brought reassurance to a youngster, cut off from normal activities and, perhaps, sensing potential loneliness. 'Nature is for you, as it is for all men . . . Do not grovel before her – be a man whose attitude should be respectful, but at the same time confident. Do not go to your work as a task, but as a labour of love.' The stirring words, written with the flamboyant vigour of the Tennysonian age, struck a chord in a romantic whose physical vigour was so often denied. And there was more to come: '. . . if you knew the innermost feelings of the hearts of others you might find that you are envied by those who cannot purchase the pleasure you have, in following the calling you love best in life.' At that moment it was exactly what Edward Seago needed to hear and eagerly he set out to follow the instructions to the letter.

He drew a tree every day for a month until, like a student of human anatomy, he knew what its limbs would do in a given set of circumstances so that he could then alter the tree's form to suit the composition of a picture without losing even one of its characteristics. The technical advice on composition, colour and form was all there but again and again it was the expression of the overall motive that excited him.

'Although we know there are a million years behind Nature's simplest development, yet the result is one of apparent ease, a spontaneous and direct effort. So should art be.' And again: 'There is no harm in studying the reflection in a dewdrop . . . but don't do it until you learn more of the earth and the sky, for you do not want the pretty little things of nature. You want the big, strong essentials, which stir the heart.'

After six months of imbibing the philosophy and practising

techniques as laid down by a master who had died a decade before, Edward Seago wanted a professional opinion of his efforts. His opportunity came in June 1923. The timing was perfect – as it would be over and over again – or perhaps it represented the start of a lifetime's habit of recognizing, rather than contriving, every opportunity to further the cause of his art and seizing it with no thought of compromise. On 27 June the morning newspapers announced that Bertram Priestman, born in Bradford, had been elected one of the youngest Royal Academicians of the time. He was fifty-five, his chief work was landscape painting and East Anglia was his favourite hunting ground.

A few days later Priestman fulfilled a long-standing engagement and opened the Annual Exhibition at the Ipswich School of Art and, as reported in the local newspaper, advised his audience to take full advantage of their county of great skies, seen in their entirety from horizon to horizon. 'Go out with your sketch-book and paint and gather in this harvest,' he told the students.

To thirteen-year-old Edward Seago there was a familiar stirring ring about the words. He read that Priestman had recently made his home at Walberswick which meant that a mere thirty miles away was first-class professional help which never for a moment did he doubt was his for the asking. He asked by letter written with a single-mindedness born of half a young lifetime dedicated to painting. The letter in handwriting large, round and with the inevitable spelling mistakes was given to the maid to post and because it concerned something so deeply personal he could not bring himself to tell anyone about it.

The reply, addressed to him in an easy flowing hand, could hardly be kept secret. It precipitated his mother into one of her hysterical outbursts while, for once, his father backed her up. Their conventional, middle-class propriety was shocked because their shy little son had presumed, without even consulting them, to approach a great painter who must certainly have far more important claims on his time. Obviously, all the attention Edward's illness had earned him had turned his head. Such brazen behaviour could not be condoned and the boy, delicate though he was, must be taught a lesson. He should accept Mr Priestman's invitation to visit him, but the journey to Walberswick would be only to enable him to apologize in person for troubling such a distinguished man. The culprit, after his initial shock when his mother seemingly renounced in one short moment all her long professed faith in his work, listened without comment to the plans for the reparation he would make. But his grey eyes stared, cold as steel, with hard determination.

Bertram Priestman, strictly brought up and descended from an old Quaker family, had no time for disobedient children. Patiently and sympathetically he heard out Mabel Seago's explanation for the irresponsible behaviour of her invalid son whose only pastime had seemingly got out of hand. Priestman had five children of his own, two of whom were about the same age as the tall, pale-faced youngster standing proud and strangely aloof while his mother talked and who, at her cue, made his token apology. Priestman might well have recalled that he himself could only have been a couple of years older than the lad when, contrary to his parents' wishes, he had left the Friends' School, Bootham, to become a full-time art student.

'Well,' he said to the boy, 'now you've come all this way, why don't you show me some of your work?'

'Oh yes, sir. Thank you sir,' Edward burst out and, confident of the outcome, pressed home his claim: 'And then, sir, can I come over and see you again soon?'

Before they left, a bewildered Mabel Seago had agreed that Bertram Priestman should make himself entirely responsible for Edward's drawing and painting tuition. She had also seen the beginning of a life-long friendship.

Edward Seago had chosen soundly. In his teacher he found a man with whom he had so much in common, even discounting their mutual passionate love of painting, that it can only be a matter of conjecture how much of the teacher's approach was absorbed by the pupil and how much was inherent in the boy or evolved spontaneously over the years. For instance, Priestman refused to be influenced by fashion in art, believing that great art outlived fashion. 'Be true to your own convictions,' he told his students. 'Do not mind being considered out-of-date or be as modern as you like providing your inspiration is nature and you are trying to give some vision of it as it appeals to you. Remember that nature is the ideal and, whilst art is not a copy of nature, it is best translated by one who realizes the beauty of its colouring and the subtleties of its drawing.'

Bertram Priestman gave Edward Seago more than painting lessons. Recalling his own childhood in a house full of fine pictures collected by a father who also spent hours sketching from nature, he sensed the need in the sickly, mother-dominated boy for something more than practical instruction. So he provided the young companionship of the Priestman family and their friends at Windy Haugh, his three-storey thatched house a mile from the sea, with glorious views of the water or marshes from every window. It was a house that was often full of students for Priestman held summer art classes, to help with the family finances.

Edward Seago never joined the classes but usually turned up unannounced carrying a batch of new paintings which he and Priestman would discuss in the wooden studio built on to the side of the house. The boy was shown how to look at his subjects, to select and compose and prepare his paints and canvases. Always he was encouraged to paint quickly.

Sometimes master and pupil went off for picnics across the salt marshes or to the sea to paint one picture in the morning and another in the afternoon. Occasionally, they were joined by another keen young painter, Edward Holroyd Pearce (later a law lord), who was to become Priestman's son-in-law. Skies and clouds were their obsessions and as the boy worked alongside the artist he saw the philosophy first expounded to him in Sir Alfred East's book, put into practice. Priestman aimed not to copy but rather to get inspiration from nature and convey his vision on to a canvas as a translation, not as a reproduction.

All his life Seago admired Priestman. He confirmed it in a letter written in the year before his death to a personal admirer, the South African tennis player Frew McMillan. He wrote that, at first, when he was a boy, he considered his teacher's work was masterly but that eventually, he modified this impression and came to see Priestman as 'a sound and sincere painter whose pictures were like the man – gentle, sincere and completely honest'. Seago qualified this in the letter by recalling that Monet had once said that painting a picture was like falling into a swimming bath at the deep end – you'd no idea which way you'd come up. 'Priestman felt his way from the beginning to the end of a picture with no sudden surprises,' Seago explained.

At thirteen years old, however, the experience of working with a fine painter and absorbing his ideas was a tremendously exciting experience, and by that time the boy had an understanding companion with whom to share his new horizons. She was his governess, Miss Dora Daniels, who lived nearby and who over the years became his devoted support and a staunch friend to his mother on whom she was a calming influence when the quick temper and moody silences increasingly registered the tensions.

Miss Daniels was small, neat and unfailingly cheerful. She was Edward's ageless ally on all the adventures he could cope with and on fine days, when he was well enough, she would shoulder his easel, take their lunch and they would tramp miles out into the country for a day's painting. There were days when he was too ill to see her but afterwards, when he lay resting in bed she would take turns with his mother in reading to him, often from the book by Sir Alfred East of which he never tired, and also poetry including the works of Byron and Shelley and, time and again, the poems of John Masefield.

Whereas Mabel Seago had, as a matter of expedience, seized on her younger son's talent with his paints as a means of keeping him happily occupied and had, no doubt, humoured him when he announced at the age of ten that he had decided to be a painter, Dora Daniels the romantic idealist, had a genuine faith in him. She sensed immediately that the sketches and drawings crowding every spare corner of his exercise books represented a remarkable ability. Hers, for a time, was the impartial encouragement he needed although perhaps as someone who wrote poetry, she indulged her imagination in a letter written to him in a moment of either naïve wishful thinking or extraordinary clairvoyance: 'I dreamed last night that Lord Somebody had written to you to take some of your pictures to show him. He said he would send the luggage cart to meet you! So I don't know how many pictures he thought you could produce! But, no doubt, before you have finished, Kings will be sending for you and, one day, one of them will say "Arise, Sir Edward, Knight of the Paint Brush".'

Despite Dora Daniels's calming influence in the household, the family doctor was concerned at the mounting tensions which increased with the frequency of Edward's heart turns. Once again he suggested that a complete change of environment might be worth trying and farming friends, Harry and Katie Cook, who lived a few miles away, invited the boy to visit them for a few months.

He loved every moment of his stay. The bluff, Norfolk farm workers took over from the Suffolk fishermen and extended his knowledge of wild life. During long, sunny days, he worked with them in the fields or went off on his own with his sketch-book to follow Priestman's advice and try to catch an impression of sunlight on the trees in a leafy lane or the light as it struck the pond in the low meadows where, every morning, he drove on the water cart to collect the day's supply. He painted pictures of the farm animals, discovered his first flycatcher's nest in a moss-grown wall and schooled himself to watch, with no show of emotion, the bloody sight of pigs being slaughtered. On a diet of sweet farm milk, a little home-brewed cider, good country air and no maternal pressures, he put on weight and there were no heart turns.

Encouraged by the success of the holiday the doctor suggested that Edward's health might benefit from living permanently in the country where he would certainly be able to lead a less restricted life. Brian Seago, the countryman at heart, was delighted with the idea and pushed home his advantage. Mabel Seago was not enthusiastic but, as usual, she was willing to subordinate her own feelings for her son's good when in 1924 her husband raised the money for the country house of his dreams.

Brooke Lodge was a handsome, red-brick Elizabethan-style house about six miles from Norwich. It was surrounded by lawns and pasture, an orchard, a tennis court, a rose garden and a kitchen garden. Previously it had been the home of the great Jack Cooke, the legendary Master of the Norwich Staghounds of which Alfred Munnings was an enthusiastic member, when he lived five miles away at Church Farm, Swainsthorpe. Munnings was a friend of Cooke's and often visited Brooke Lodge and painted the horses in the sweet, warm atmosphere of the stables. So for Edward Seago, a delicate, gawky teenager, the new home represented an intangible link with the famous painter.

The boy may not have known that fact, but no aspiring painter could be unaware that he was in the heart of Munnings's country. Here the hard-living artist had revelled in the full flavour of Norfolk and painted fine horses to the accompaniment of the Hound Master's booming homilies such as 'Good hay is a luxury. You can always buy good oats; but a good piece of hay is what a horse likes and he'll eat it all night!'* Even if Edward Seago did not know that Munnings had painted at Brooke he too would find his vision sharpened by 'bright winter sunlight on clipped horses and scarlet coats; bare trees; stacks; on farmhouse gables; the riding out after a slight frost; the riding home with a frost beginning and a young moon in the sky; puddles already crisping over . . .'*

His distraught mother would have dearly loved to know that one day it would all come about for, soon after the move to Brooke Lodge, a friend of the family, the Norwich surgeon Mr Joseph Burfield, felt the time had come to warn her: 'You'll never rear the boy.'

* Quoted from Munnings's Memoirs.

III

Parents, Priestman and Patronage

During the first Christmas at Brooke, in 1924, the family moved about their new home stealthily, hardly talking above a whisper, while for twelve days Edward lay in bed under sedation in the throes of his worst heart attack. A trained nurse was installed but his mother hardly left his room as if to reassure herself that, through constant devoted attention, she might prove the doctors wrong.

In those days when psychiatry was in its infancy, no doctor had suggested there might be a subconscious motive for the baffling illness such as the desperate need of a boy who, from childhood, had sensed the overwhelming burden of a great talent but was unable to free himself from his day-to-day obligations in order to allow that talent its full development. Edward's illness allowed him to step outside the routine of living so that for long periods he was alone with his art. Once that pattern had been firmly established it was with him for life, long after a possible reason for it had disappeared.

Psychosomatic illness or no, because of the pattern of illness, life in the fine new home, from the beginning, described itself around the younger son while John escaped to the servants' quarters which was the one place where he could make as much noise as he wanted. Brian Seago meanwhile refused to contemplate the possibility of his son becoming a painter. As an astute businessman the idea was impractical. Moreover he was a man whose cultural horizons were limited as evidenced by his admission that only on the rarest occasions did he open a book and it was his great hope that one day Edward would be a farmer.

In the first summer at the new house it looked unlikely that the boy would ever be able to earn any sort of a living. His heart turns occurred at least once a fortnight and only on warm days was he allowed to leave his bed and lie on the long wicker chair which his mother arranged under the elm tree. There, however, he was far from idle. In his book Sir Alfred East had advised that a student should paint a sky every morning at the same time, and date the sketches with the hour and the direction and the strength of the wind, so that at the end of a few weeks he would have learned more of the sky than he could have by reading the latest scientific books.

Edward did better than that. Lying flat on his back, the sky was the one thing he could really see and he painted it day in and day out, on small wooden panels. Often he painted as many as six panels in one day and on the back of each, just as East had prescribed, he noted the weather and atmospheric conditions so that by the end of a day he had a complete weather picture from morning to sunset. Years afterwards he learned that over a century before another East Anglian painter, John Constable, had at the age of thirty on the advice of the Ipswich painter and drawing-master George Frost, annotated his sketches in a similar way.

Gradually, the boy found that to observe and paint what he saw was not enough to make his clouds 'float with the luminosity of that wondrous ocean overhead'. He studied books on cloud formations and combinations and, like the scientist-painter Leonardo da Vinci, he learned that clouds were composed of minute particles of water or ice and that the answer to their colours lay in the refraction of light by atmosphere. 'Then the real fun began,' he recalled. 'Each day taught me more and each day I saw something of reality in what I had been reading.'

Slowly, frustration at the enforced physical restriction gave way to a positive enjoyment of life. 'Mealtimes were fun in the garden,' he said, 'and during the long afternoons I would lie and listen to my mother reading aloud. I think I liked that best of all – the dreamy, half-awareness of what my mother was reading, mingled with all the pleasant out-of-door sights and sounds.'

His mother anticipated his every wish. The summer house where the wicker chair was kept, was John's workshop where he had made a small lathe. One day John came home to find his mother had collected up all his tools and flung them into a corner of an old harness room and the workshop had been taken over for Edward's studio. Many years later John recalled his resentment at losing his workshop and also his annoyance when family treats were suddenly cancelled or his mother was too preoccupied to do anything more than caution him to be extra quiet about the house and never, on any account, do anything to upset Edward. At the time John's was an unspoken grievance but in the end it coloured both brothers' lives.

As time went by, Edward was considered well enough to go for short walks. The garden gate opened into the pasture where, with the minimum of exertion, he could follow a bullock for a whole day, recording its every movement in his sketch-book.

'Suddenly, everything was at hand,' he wrote. 'All the things I so wanted to draw were within a stone's throw of the house; a farmyard with its wealth of subjects – the binder and the ploughs, the wagon shed, the stack yard, the cow-house and the stables.' He was intoxicated in his new-found happiness and probably still unaware that it was the stable where Munnings had loved to paint.

'Try and go on working out any ideas and information you have got so you will have more to show me next time you come over,' Priestman wrote to him. The fifteen-year-old needed no second telling. 'A bit at a time, I drew them all,' he remembered. 'Looking back it seems that I always worked a bit at a time; the hind legs of cattle, the wheel of a wagon or the horse-collars hanging in the harness room.'

There was one more token attempt at formal education when, on the mornings when he was well enough, he cycled over to the Rectory at the neighbouring parish of Kirstead for lessons with the benevolent Reverend William Stutter, an elderly gentleman who much preferred gardening to tutoring and was as eager as his pupil for the clock to strike twelve so that history and Euclid could give way to the more important demands of the garden and the paint-box.

But if the mornings had dragged, the afternoons passed all too quickly at the new home which, to both father and son, seemed little less than paradise. Brooke Lodge restored Brian Seago, in his own mind, to the sort of place where he really belonged and it was an ideal place for his sons to grow up. Their friends were Charley Attmore, the village carpenter who drove a little donkey cart and preached in chapel on Sundays; Lijah, the poacher who took them on nocturnal escapades and taught them to run home to his cottage backwards so that only their out-going footprints were left in the sandy lane; Reggy Utting, the bus driver who picked up passengers or parcels for Norwich at people's front doors, even if such un-scheduled stops made a nonsense of his time-table; and Mrs Cutbush who kept the grocer's shop where, for regular customers, aniseed balls were twenty a penny plus two for luck.

Once or twice a week during the hunting season, everyone who had a horse or could borrow one, rode to hounds while the others followed on foot or on bicycles. The Norwich Staghounds resumed their old habit of holding the Boxing Day Meet at Brooke Lodge which provided an excellent opportunity for the new owners to get to know the 'right people'. Later, when Mabel Seago had accepted the inevitability of Edward being a painter, she made sure that everyone who came indoors for the hot rum punch and light refreshments noticed his latest pictures on the walls.

But in the early years at Brooke, when his parents discounted the possibility of the boy becoming a professional artist, his father gave him a 4.10 gun and for a few weeks listened with satisfaction as it was fired off at stray rabbits and pigeons in the meadow. Dora Daniels was invited over for an afternoon's shooting and replied with her usual staunch enthusiasm for any activity of her former pupil: 'If you shoulder the gun,' she wrote, 'I will carry the bag and it won't be our fault if we come back empty-handed!' But the novelty of the new sport did not last and the marksman was soon back at his paints and brushes, all day and every day.

When he was well enough his mother often took him to Norwich to see the civic art collection in the Castle where the galleries were dominated by a comprehensive collection of the Norwich School. He studied for hours John Crome's paintings of familiar fields on the city outskirts where the artist, unlike most of his predecessors, had dispensed with formal arrangements so characteristic of the landscapes of the past. There were also the supreme water-colours of John Sell Cotman who, Edward considered, was the first landscape painter to succeed in 'getting air into his pictures', and who captured the cloud shadows on the marsh just as he tried to do. It was sad to think that such work had, at the time, been almost unnoticed and the influence of the two great painters not felt until long after their deaths. Not so with Arnesby Brown and Munnings. Invariably the boy's visits to the Castle ended with a close study of four pictures by Munnings that hung there – three oils and the vigorous water-colour 'The Horse Sale'. So this, it seemed, was what made an artist popular in his own lifetime.

Like Munnings, Edward Seago bought his painting equipment at Hallam's Art Shop in the Royal Arcade and there, when he was fifteen, he made his first sale. It was a little oil painting of a group of cows on the marsh, bought for the princely sum of fifteen shillings by the kindly proprietor, Mr John Hallam, who was always ready to encourage a youngster he thought showed real talent. The plywood panel measured 20″ × 16″ and the purchaser did not consider it was good enough to hang on the wall. He kept it in a portfolio, but forty years later it paid his daughter good dividends when, out of sentiment, the painter invited her to exchange it for a recent oil painting of a Norfolk scene.

Gradually, for Edward Seago life in the country fell into a more relaxed pattern, just as the doctor had hoped. Other than the persistent heart turns the only flaw in his happiness concerned the gift of a talent that had become his very reason for living. He noticed that although his mother never failed to encourage him to paint, neither she nor his father commented – favourably or otherwise – on his finished pictures. Always he waited in perplexed disappointment for the criticism or approval that never came.

Perhaps Mabel Seago kept silent in tactful deference to her husband's ill-concealed impatience whenever Edward mentioned painting as a career. Brian Seago worried about how his younger son would one day earn a living, but in Mabel's mind this problem belonged to a future which, in view of the doctor's prognosis, she probably tried to avoid thinking about. In self-protection against losing her very purpose in life she may, subconsciously, have tended to focus her long-term hopes on her elder boy. Eventually it would

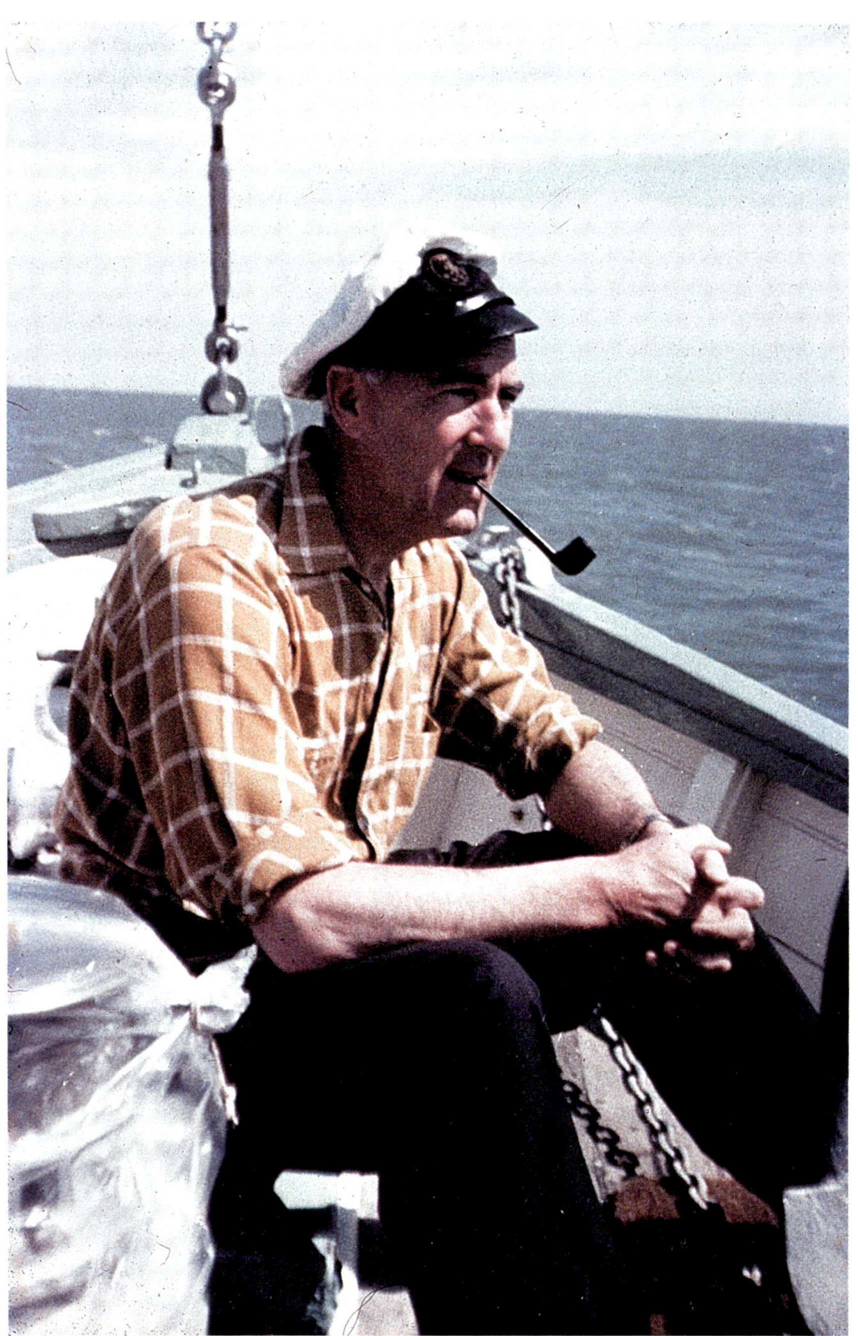

1. Seago aboard his boat, *Capricorn*

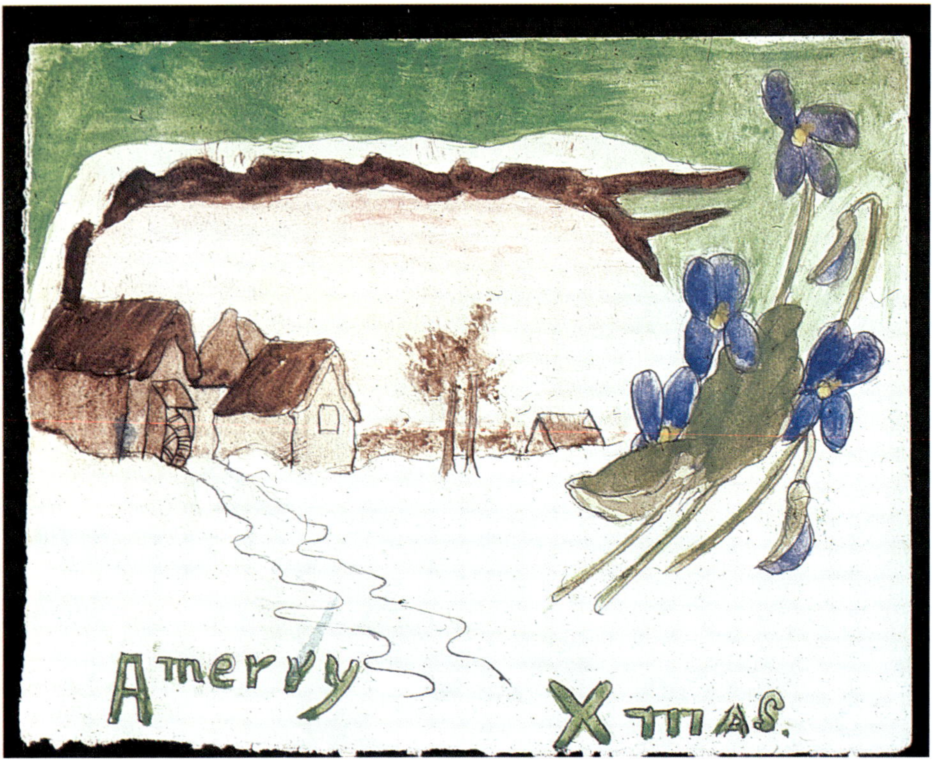

2. Christmas card to his parents – at age 6

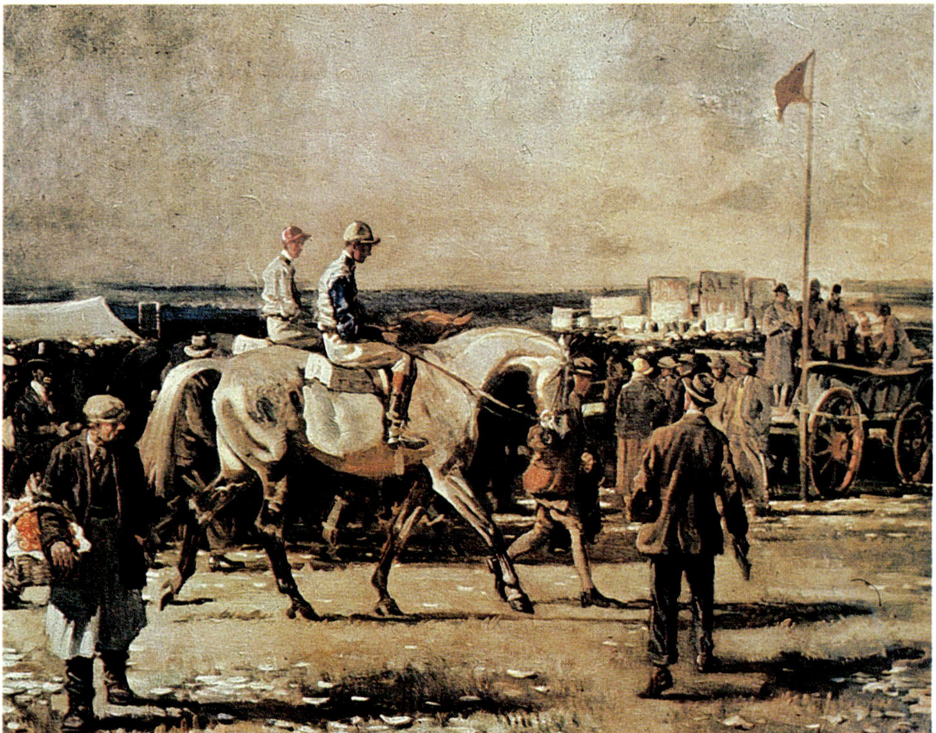

3. A racing study

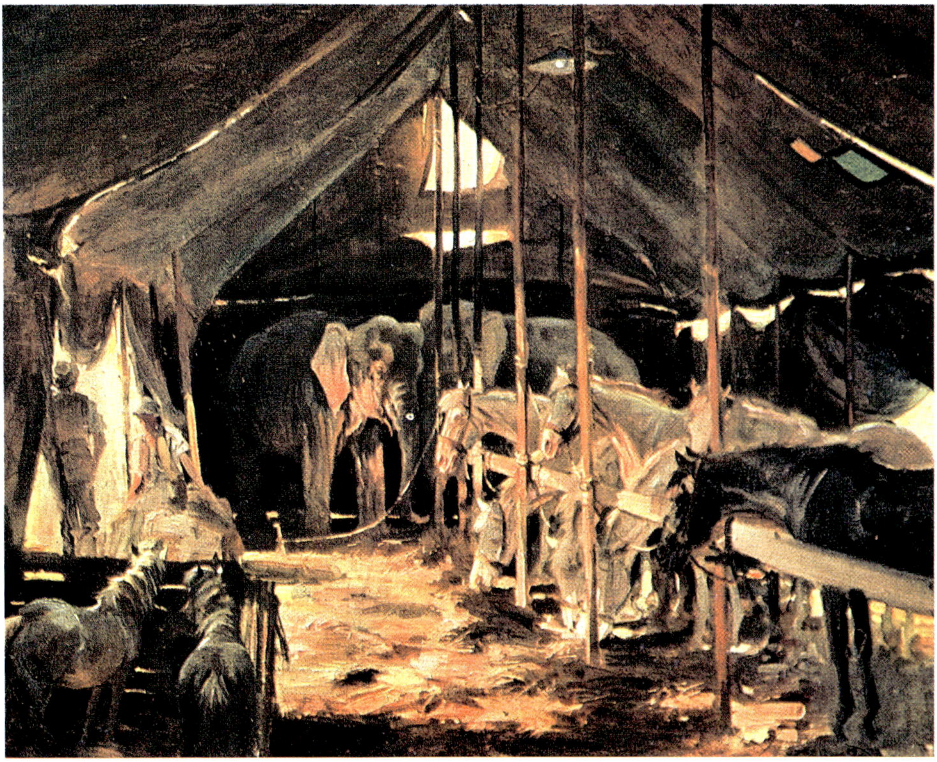

4. Travelling Circus

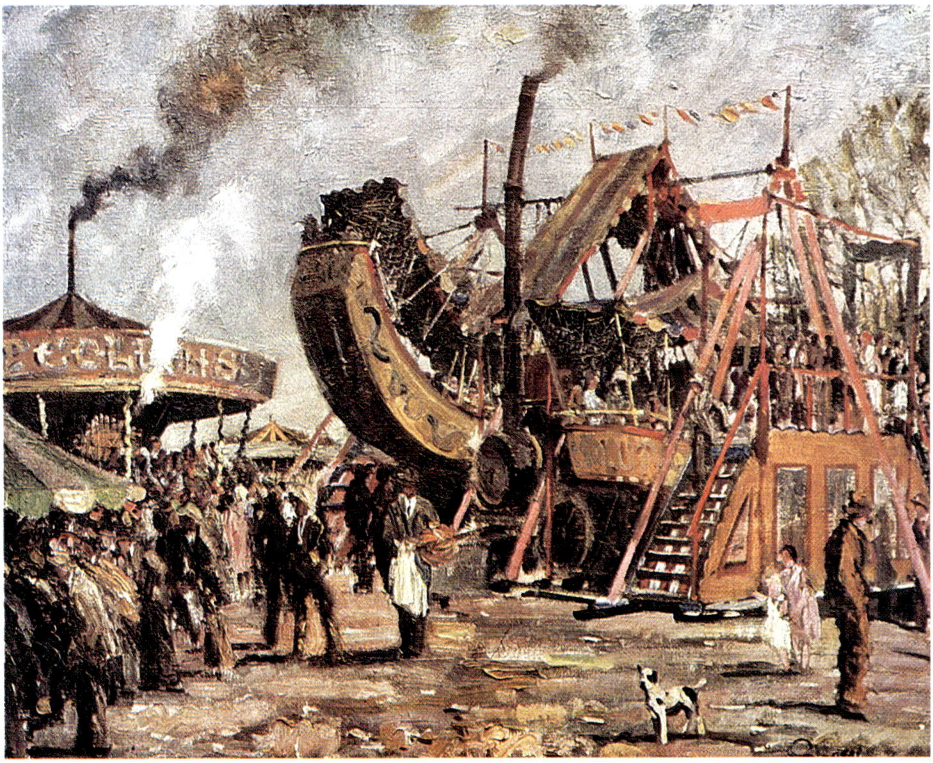

5. Swings & Roundabouts

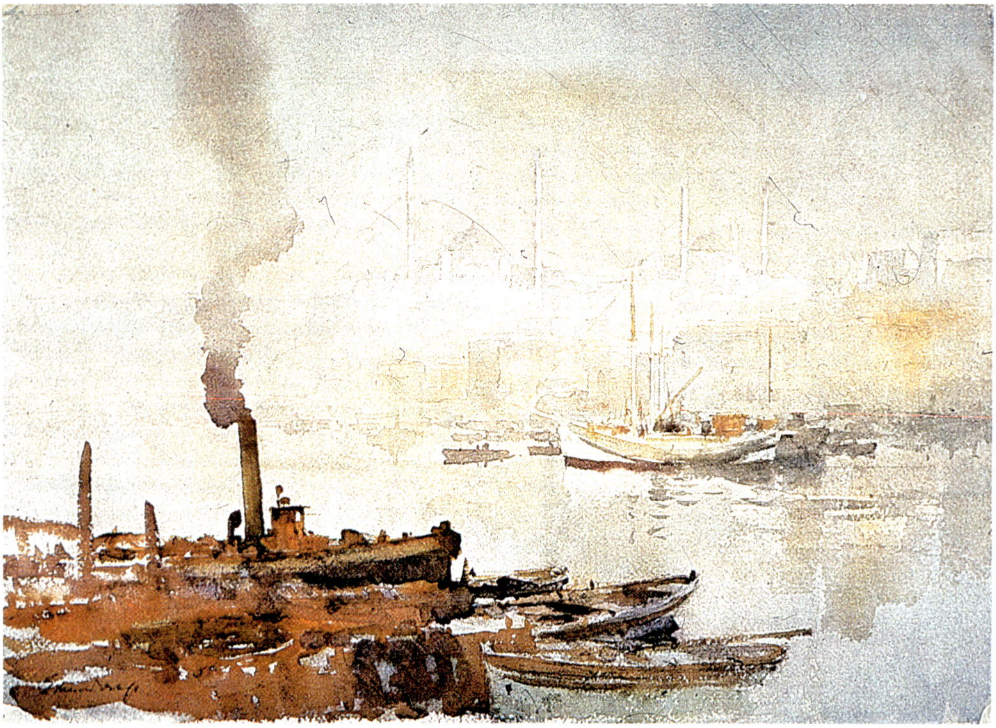

6. The Golden Horn, Istanbul

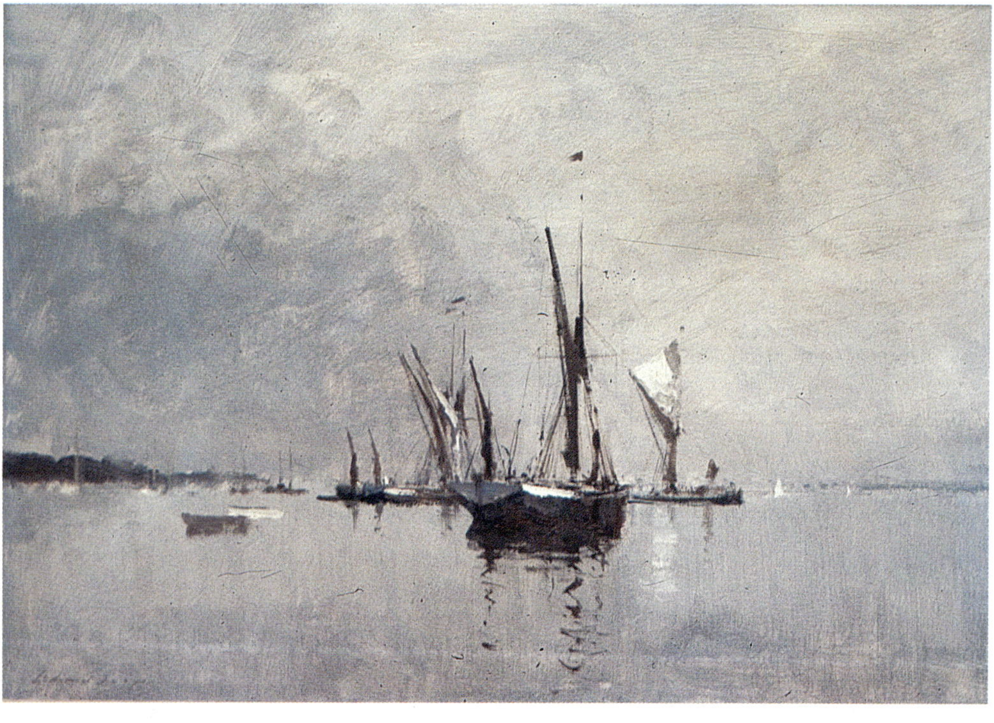

7. Thames barges on the River Orwell

have been impossible for the sensitive Edward, over-dependent on a dominant mother, not to sense her unspoken rejection of himself and his art.

Moreover, because of illness and his parents' unsatisfactory relationship, the adolescent had never successfully identified with his father, a fact which could only have magnified the effect of his mother's bewildering rejection. Hurt again by her seeming betrayal, he never attempted to form a permanent and meaningful relationship with a woman. In addition, years later, his parents' early and inexplicable reluctance to recognize the gift in him grew in his mind until he saw it as a sustained and determined effort on their part to deny him as an artist. Such an exaggerated impression in later years could well have indicated the deep sense of deprivation the boy must have felt. But not for a moment was his irresistible urge to paint diminished. His persistence demonstrated courage, a great strength of character and the overriding determination to follow what he had long recognized as a profound calling.

The clarity with which he saw his purpose is underlined by a boyhood essay in which he visualized himself as an old, white-bearded gentleman, sitting in an armchair looking through the window at a country scene. He called it 'When I am Old'.

'I shall, perhaps, have painted such a scene,' he wrote, 'for God gave me this way of expressing Nature and I have done my best to be worthy of that gift. I have taken from her that which I love best. I have chosen simple landscape and, of landscape, I have also chosen that which I love best. If I have failed in my purpose, I am sorry, and I may not do better were I to try again. But all I ask is that my work shall not be forgotten. I shall be forgotten and I would wish to be. But my work stays behind me . . .'

The essay was, eventually, included in an unpublished set of illuminated manuscripts entitled 'Sketches from Nature – Written for my Mother – July 1926'.

Despite his loneliness and his pleasantly diffident manner, Edward Seago was not shy, and on his way to visit Priestman he often stopped to 'talk shop' with painters who, from early spring, frequented the little seaside village. One day he struck up a conversation with a tall, angular-looking, middle-aged lady, Miss Fanny Louisa Coles, a Bournemouth art mistress and visiting teacher at several schools in Dorset who, in the summer of 1925, was on holiday there with her friend Miss Blanche Baker. The boy invited the ladies home to tea to meet his parents and after the holiday his friendship with Fanny Louisa Coles blossomed through correspondence.

Edward Seago always chose to maintain that, apart from Priestman, as a painter he was completely self-taught. Nevertheless, starting with Miss Coles, there is evidence that in the formative years several able artists were generous with their advice. 'F. L. Coles' (as she invariably signed herself) loved teaching. She said so in an early letter in which she wrote:

'My favourite subjects are, as you know, evening or early morning. The effects are so much more beautiful in the half lights because things are so much more massed and details do not disturb so much. It is so difficult not to get a picture "spotty". I tell my pupils that they must look at the *whole* thing, with eyes half shut, when they are painting *any* part. This is the secret though I, so often, do not succeed in doing it myself.'

Water-colours were her strength. She described her method of keeping her paper damp from the back and running the colours in while it was wet to get a misty, atmospheric effect before allowing it to dry sufficiently to be finished with small washes to leave the hard edges, '– so helpful in water-colours!' and one sensed her delight in his eagerness to learn when she complained: 'Some of my pupils are sketching but they are not keen enough to be *very* interesting!'

Soon, Edward Seago was sending her his work to criticize and the born teacher responded in no uncertain terms, returning his pictures with comments and copious explanatory notes:

'You did not tell me whether you did the sketch of horses from memory,' she wrote. 'I quite understand that you cannot remember lots of things when you try from imagination, but that very fact makes you notice, the next time and so you learn and train your painting memory . . . You are not afraid of making the black manes blue if they *look* it. That is good! . . . The foreground is too *spotty* – that is too equally spotty all over. Both in the landscape and the horses it would help so much if some of the masses were *flat*, that is absolutely *free from detail*. Take special note of this, as it means so much and makes so much difference. Some parts of any picture must be restful (free from detail), and often, this restful part will occur *in the shadow*. Anyway, you must find it *somewhere* . . . I want you to notice the unmeaning touches all over your foreground. Try to let each mass and touch *mean* something. I know this is asking a lot but it is worth while to try . . . Chickens will be useful to put in a picture. They help the composition so much, as figures and any animals do. If you can put them in as *blobs* by half-shutting your eyes and looking at *spaces* instead of *lines*, you will find that your drawing will improve in character and speed.'

Briskly she overrode all his excuses:

'Of course the weather is not fit for sitting out, but you can always carry a small sketch-book and take a scribble of some effect that pleases you and try to work it out at home from *memory* . . . Whatever the weather and however many ankles you twist, you can find something to work at indoors if you cultivate memory and imagination . . . Why do you not teach yourself Italian? You will want to go to Italy when you are grown up – it is so beautiful.'

For Edward Seago, concerned exclusively in proving the talent he sensed within, it was a time for correspondence and Priestman was a constant source of encouragement. At last came the suggestion his pupil had been longing to hear. It was contained in a letter punctuated by numerous little sketches illustrating ideas about technique and composition:

'Altogether, you have done very well,' Priestman wrote. 'You might try and get one better in all respects and send to the RA in March. The size is quite large enough and put the energy into the *quality*. You might make a picture from the material in No. 1 and No. 2. The cottage, for instance, added to No. 1 and a little water, as I suggested, showing in the ditch. If you like to make some charcoal studies of composition and send them before you actually start, I will advise you *which is best,* or of improvements. You might do horses and background of No. 1, for instance, but get the tones and colour of animals *carefully from Nature in relation to background.*'

His pupil needed no second telling.

Meanwhile, Fanny Coles's dogmatic authority exuding through her letters elicited in the boy a desire to confide in her so that she became one of the few women to know of his depressions. He wrote to her unashamedly about them, perhaps because he felt it was unlikely that they would ever meet again. In a characteristic reply her briskness, for once, was tempered with sympathy. '. . . As for being depressed, you must outgrow all your weakness and the more you believe this, the quicker will the weakness be in taking its departure, so there! The price all painters have to pay for the visions we get that other people do not get is the hump, occasionally. But is it not worth it? Think of the joys of form and colour which thrill us and leave so many untouched.' With her encouragement he submitted two paintings to the Norwich Art Circle for their annual exhibition.

Once again his timing could not have been more perfect. Until 1926 the group of amateur and professional painters had shown their work on the top floor of the old Norwich Public Library where only a few determined members of the public could find their way up the tortuous stone stairway. For their 74th Annual Exhibition, the group, under the Presidency of the internationally-known local watercolourist, Geoffrey Birkbeck, took the unprecedented step of hiring the elegant well-situated Stuart Hall and, as a new attraction, included a loan collection of works of famous local artists including Arnesby Brown and Munnings. Sixteen-year-old Edward Seago had arrived in good company.

His debut in the local art world did not go unnoticed. His two exhibits, 'Haysel' and 'Lakenham Viaduct' won favourable comments in the local press and a Norwich dealer, Roy Nightingale, enquired about buying his work. 'Lakenham Viaduct' was bought by his old friend Ernest Chance for two guineas, probably as a token of encouragement. But having obtained a vested interest in the young painter, Mr Chance felt entitled to offer a little friendly advice. 'Some of the members of the Art Circle told me they liked your pictures,' he wrote, 'but you could not draw. Please don't mind me telling you this. It is just as well to hear what people say. If you went to the School of Art in Norwich for the winter months it would do your drawing a great deal of good.' Five years later, Seago enrolled there for one term's evening classes but that was after Munnings had endorsed the suggestion in no uncertain terms.

In the meantime, nothing could have more impressed Brian Seago than the arrival on his doorstep of Geoffrey Birkbeck to take tea and talk painting with his son. The visit from the dashing fifty-two-year-old landowner, a leading representative of the exclusive county set, represented the breaking down of a social barrier whereby country landowners rarely deigned to fraternize with city dwellers or those who earned a living through trade. For the first time, the country-loving coal merchant wondered if there might be something to 'the painting business' after all. Certainly he agreed with Edward that the little summer house was no longer big enough for a studio.

An alternative presented itself in a sadly dilapidated Elizabethan manor house, Kirstead Old Hall, opposite the Rectory where Edward went for morning lessons. It was the home of the Barmby family with three children about the same ages as Edward. They occupied only part of the house and the farmer, John Barmby, was willing for the Rector's pupil to take over the beautiful unused large front drawing-room as a studio. Edward white-washed the walls and Mabel Seago made muslin curtains for the long, diamond-paned windows. The south light was quite wrong for a studio but in summer the sun streamed in and honeysuckle straggled over the window sills. On winter afternoons, John and the young Barmbys often called in to make tea and toast in the open hearth.

At first, Edward was supremely happy there. But John was given a motor bike. Edward thought enviously about the splendid machine as he pedalled his push-bike to the new studio. There had been no suggestion that in a year or two he might be given a similar present, and the ominous silence when he had admired it hopefully was as non-committal as when he showed his paintings to his mother and waited in vain for some sign of approval. Had his parents kept silent about the bike because they had no intention of buying him one in case riding it brought on one of his wretched heart turns? If so, why didn't they say as much? He was sick of the secrecy surrounding his health, seemingly because his parents assumed he was unaware of their fear that he would die at any moment.

He knew fear – but it was for a different reason. Walking home alone through the woods in the late evening he often stopped and listened, feeling a companionship in the sound of the trees and an awareness of a wider range of thought; a perception so nearly within his understanding that suddenly he felt afraid because it seemed as if the woodland were closing in. The many tiny sounds followed faster and faster upon each other and lost their form. At that moment, the sense of companionship was gone.

'There is a desolate loneliness then, which becomes almost unbearable,' he wrote. 'This feeling of something between exultation and fear is, I think, a sense of reverence and awe; reverence for what it portends, awe of the un-understandable. I am afraid of myself, and the loneliness is that of a mind incapable of comprehension.' It was perhaps the nearest he came to formulating a religion.

The daily walk or cycle ride to the studio took him past a gypsy encampment and he got to know the easy-going men and their cheery womenfolk who whittled away at their wooden clothes-pegs and fashioned paper flowers to hawk to the village housewives. Perhaps with the memory of Munnings's 'The Horse Sale' he sketched their ponies and the brightly-painted wagons and the brown-eyed dark-skinned children who crowded round his easel. He found the contented people who lived so close to nature as easy to talk to as the fishermen and the farm workers. They were an ageless people with whom he felt neither old nor young, inadequate nor self-conscious. Throughout the summer he painted them and the following year he invited them to make their encampment on his father's meadow.

To his parents' credit they tried their utmost to welcome the visitors, the first of an unconventional cavalcade that, through the years, Edward, with sublime selfishness, assumed his parents were happy to entertain. For Mabel and Brian Seago who led a simple life, such informal hospitality must have been unprecedented and difficult to accept. Yet they managed to conceal their bewilderment when the rich and the poor, the lame dogs and the famous arrived on their doorstep, often without warning, at their son's invitation. For whatever his sense of deprivation, Edward always assumed that his friends were welcome in his home – even if he were not there to receive them. For Mabel Seago it was sometimes a strain. She was often depressed and sought refuge in her bedroom for days at a time, but she felt that anything that ensured that she had a part in her son's life justified making a supreme effort. Her husband however, with unfailing ebullience, revelled in every opportunity for new companionships. For both of them and for John, because of the enforced hospitality, life grew richer as gradually, for positive reasons rather than through his illness, the younger son introduced his family to new experiences and consolidated his position as the pivot of the household.

At that time virtually the only interest shared by father and son was a love of horses and it was to Brian Seago's regret that he could not afford to keep a mount at Brooke. However, in business he maintained a dozen handsome shires, long after they were not an economic proposition, and used them for carting coal and hauling the railway trucks into sidings. He insisted they were a good advertisement for his firm and they certainly made a fine sight, drawing the civic coach on ceremonial occasions and pulling wagonloads of children out to the country for annual school treats. They afforded Brian Seago the excuse to attend horse sales and agricultural shows where he prided himself on being an excellent judge of horse-flesh and as such was well qualified to assess his son's equestrian pictures. They were the only pictures which interested him and, encouraged by his earthy comments that a painting showed the animal 'too flat in the fetlock' or 'rather broad in the barrel', Edward concentrated on equestrian pictures more than ever.

With the thoroughness with which he had studied the sky, encouraged by Priestman, he set himself to learn about the horse. '. . . The more you know of anatomy the better,' Priestman wrote, 'though you want to keep it as knowledge to help you and not to come out all over an animal to show knowledge as some have done.' So his pupil read books on anatomy, collected bones from a slaughterhouse, built a skeleton and made drawings and plaster casts of bones and muscles until no veterinary student could have known more about the limbs of the horse. Suddenly he realized that to familiarize himself even more, he should learn to ride.

He and John approached a neighbouring farmer, George Cross, a horse-breaker of Woodton who, like Munnings, followed the harriers and the staghounds. He agreed to let the boys ride his horses and give them instruction in return for mucking out his stables. So most days they hacked round the field after him and trailed over small ditches and little broken places in the fences.

Edward was soon the better rider of the two and George Cross entered him at local point-to-points where, as owner, he usually positioned himself conspicuously at the steepest water jump, ready to whip his horse over at the first sign of a refusal. The boy loved riding and only his recurrent heart turns kept him away from George Cross's farm. He was setting off one morning when he felt the usual advance warning of a heart turn. Invariably this was the signal for him to go to bed and allow it to take its course but, for the first time in his life and despite his parents' protests, he refused to change his plans and forgo the ride. After he had left for the stables John telephoned George Cross to say that Edward was not feeling well and asked if he would try and keep an eye on him. That day the young horseman could not understand why he was told to confine himself to trotting and cantering round one large field where the farmer walked backwards and forwards behind a horse harrow, insisting he kept the rider in view so that he could watch his seat.

It proved a significant ride for although Edward went home to bed and stayed there while the familiar heart turn took over, it was not unduly prolonged and was no more nor less severe because he had chosen to discount medical advice. It was a turning point in his attitude because from that day he and the family saw that life might be lived according to his own rules rather than those of the doctors.

Another new interest was the Maddermarket Theatre where Edward hung about, helped to paint scenery and made himself generally useful. He was sixteen years old when in a Christmas letter to Fanny Coles's friend Blanche Baker, he explained that he had been ill and very delirious and they could not steady his heart. He added, 'I have made a great friend of Mr Nugent Monck who is a famous producer and writer. Tagore, the Indian writer, paid him to go over and produce his plays . . .'

The heart turns – such as the one he referred to – were so frequent and severe that a trained nurse was often in the house because Mabel Seago's nerves were stretched to breaking point and she could not endure seeing her son's distress in the worst of an attack. 'As usual the attacks occur every ten or fourteen days,' she wrote in her diary. 'Several times after the heart has steadied he has suffered from a nervous attack when he could not keep still and often has got up and walked about for an hour. At times he seemed quite to lose control of himself.'

Sometimes while Edward was in bed, Priestman drove over from Walberswick to give him a lesson – always with oils rather than water-colours which the teacher considered a far more difficult medium and one which should be left until later. During the winter when Priestman moved back to his London home, he wrote long constructive criticisms of work his pupil sent to him. He was not enthusiastic when Edward suggested spending some of his time writing about nature as well as painting. 'If you feel you can express something you wish to best that way, it can do no harm but don't divide your interest too much. Concentration and specialization are good things,' was his comment.

In the diminishing intervals between the attacks there was little opportunity for many interests. Edward took up conjuring but he gave up playing a musical instrument. He read avidly and painted hard. His mother had been warned by the doctors not to allow him to go far on his own and she was always willing to cycle around the countryside with him so that he could paint landscapes or to drive him over to Walberswick to visit Priestman. For a few weeks she rented rooms in a cottage there for them both and he painted with Priestman every day. Geoffrey Birkbeck also took his young friend out for painting picnics and, in view of Priestman's insistence that it was too soon for water-colours, encouraged him to try his hand with poster paints.

In 1927, as a result of Priestman's suggestion, Edward Seago submitted a painting to the Royal Academy. It was rejected. Priestman, with memories of six consecutive rejections after two early successes, was quick to sympathize. 'As far as you are concerned, there is no need for the *least* discouragement,' he wrote. 'If I had been on the hanging committee this year, I should have considered it well worth placing. A lot of good work was not hung. You see, tastes differ among painters and the men who happen to be hanging, naturally hang the work that appeals to them. Go ahead and better luck next time.'

In the same letter he suggested rather diffidently that for·the sake of his health Edward should perhaps consider homeopathic treatment, a practice which he and his family had often followed. The outcome of the suggestion was that through Priestman's introduction, the boy was treated free of charge but to no apparent benefit by the brother-in-law of the writer John Galsworthy.

The rejection by the Academy had reawakened his parents' misgivings about the advisability of anyone without private means hoping to earn a living as an artist. To reassure them, their son was desperate for real recognition in addition to the modest commissions he was getting, mostly through the dealer Roy Nightingale. Here again, Fate played straight into his hands through the timing of Geoffrey Birkbeck's interest in him since the summer of 1926. The previous year Birkbeck's wife and his nineteen-year-old daughter had died of typhoid after a holiday in Italy and, soon afterwards, his elder son William, three years older than Edward Seago, had been injured in a motor-cycle accident and left mentally impaired. Birkbeck no longer wanted to live in the family home, Stoke Hall, full of memories. He would have told his painting companion that he had leased it for a year to Sir Lawrence and Lady Evelyn Jones while the West Norfolk seat, Cranmer Hall they had recently inherited, was restored and renovated. In the guise of a new neighbour, Edward Seago at last came face to face with his first important patron.

She was Lady Evelyn Jones, daughter of the 4th Earl Grey, a former Governor-General of South Africa and Canada and she and her brilliantly witty husband who was a partner in a firm of City bankers and also an author, were great social assets to the Norfolk scene. Lady Evelyn was artistic and a great activist who loved people and could never resist helping the underdogs and encouraging them to achieve their potential. Edward Seago could not have known as much but the instinct which five years before had motivated him to write to Bertram Priestman, once again asserted itself and, with an unswerving singleness of purpose he cycled over to Stoke Hall.

Again his instinct had been right. Lady Evelyn herself opened the door to the pale, good-looking youth with a stack of pictures under his arm. 'I'm a painter,' he introduced himself with a disarming directness. 'I live near here and I'm trying to find someone who'll help me to earn a living because my parents refuse to give me any encouragement.' The unconventional intrusion convinced Lady Evelyn that here indeed was a painter and one worth helping. She would introduce him to people with fine horses who might well like to have their portraits painted.

Her cousin and her cousin's husband, Brigadier-General Sir Hereward Wake, Master of Dover Castle, were staying with her and they invited the boy to visit their home, Courteenhall, Northampton. There and then ideas for a picture were discussed and Edward said he would like to paint Sir Hereward in his pink coat riding across the park after a day's hunting. A date was fixed for the sittings but once again the boy's illness intervened and the visit was delayed which was fortunate for he had much to learn. When the visit materialized three years later Sir Hereward absolutely refused to put on his pink coat before November and so the original conception of the portrait never materialized. But the alternative, a portrait of the family in the grounds of Courteenhall, proved to be one of the young artist's most successful pictures.

Meanwhile, once Lady Evelyn became interested in a person there was no end to the lengths she was prepared to go on their behalf. She wrote to her aunts, the Countess of Antrim and the Countess of Minto, both Ladies in Waiting to Queen Mary, and also thought of local friends to whom she would introduce him.

Archibald Jamieson, the City financier and Chairman of such diverse companies as Vickers and the Ottoman Bank was one. The tall, lean philanthropist lived at nearby Thornham and, backed by financial security and a beautiful and adoring wife with a keen artistic sense who had studied at the Slade with Professor Tonks, he was an ideal patron. He and his wife took an immediate liking to the young painter whose pictures they considered reflected a great appreciation of living. It was a perceptive judgement of the work of a boy who, although he never admitted it, had learned to live and paint with the knowledge that he might be existing on borrowed time and that each day might prove to be his last.

Moreover, in practical terms, the extremely personable young man rode and sailed and fitted in admirably with the Jamieson family of two boys and two girls. He soon showed that he had an ability to make people laugh and at holiday times he was welcomed into a family who invariably returned to their London home in Smith Square with one or two of his paintings to hang there and be suitably admired by their city friends.

At the Jamieson table Edward Seago first encountered the cut and thrust of sophisticated conversation which later would form an important part of his own life. The talk there was very different from the serious discussions that went on in Priestman's home where all alcohol was barred. Edward Seago revelled in both worlds but decided it might be better to keep them apart. He was painting diligently whenever he was well enough, but in 1928 he spent so much time in bed that he was unable to prepare any suitable work to submit to the Academy and wrote, very despondently, to tell Priestman.

'I think you are wise in not going to the exertion this year,' Priestman replied. 'You are fortunately young and you will not lose anything by not sending for another year.' Priestman by then had moved from Walberswick and taken another Suffolk house, Snape Hall near Saxmundham, for the summers. In September when his pupil drove over for the day he presented him with a portable water-colour table which he had designed and made for him. It was one of Seago's most prized possessions which he used until the end of his life.

That summer Seago, who had learnt to drive his mother's Austin Seven, visited an exhibition of the work of Alfred Munnings in the Castle Museum, Norwich. The walls were alive with landscapes, woodland scenes, paintings of gypsies, race-horses, jockeys in glowing silks, portraits of the famous on horseback, early drawings for designs for cracker-box lids and advertisements for Norwich firms. Several large canvases had been sent over from Canada and during the next six weeks Edward Seago returned many times to study and to admire. 'The qualities of Munnings's art are not dissimilar from those to be found in the poetry of Masefield,' he read in the foreword to the exhibition catalogue. 'The poem "The Everlasting Mercy" comes to mind more than once as we wander round these galleries.' It was a poem Dora Daniels would often have read to him and doubtless he filed away Masefield's association with paintings of the countryside.

Meanwhile, since the day when he had ignored the warning of a heart turn to ride at George Cross's farm, he had been seriously considering his future and he felt the time had come for a frank discussion with his parents. One evening after dinner, he told them of his plans. 'I know that the doctors have warned you that I may not have a long life,' he said quietly and unemotionally, 'but if it is to be a short one, I have decided that it shall be a full one.'

There was relief in, at last, bringing the unspoken fear into the open. His parents, in accepting his decision, matched his courage with their own and their only request was that, in setting out to lead a fuller life, he should neither be rash nor foolish. He promised but, as a first expression of his hard-won independence, he hunted just as Munnings had done, two or three times a week. It was a justifiable gesture of victory as well as a demonstration of the tremendous physical strength that invariably reasserted itself as soon as he had had a few days in which to recover from his exhaustive heart turns.

On emotional terms it had required great power at eighteen years of age to confront his parents and get them to accept his determination to discard the restrictions imposed by them and by his illness. It demanded particular strength because he had had little opportunity to discard the passive relationship with his mother, or to identify successfully with his father. That he found the courage to cut free was to his parents' advantage as well as his own because afterwards he was able to achieve an apparently normal and (to all outward appearances) an enviable relationship with them. Nevertheless, he himself never recovered from the crippling psychological effect of his early upbringing. The result was that he remained emotionally immature, extremely vulnerable and acutely sensitive and receptive. He was always fundamentally unsure of himself and sought constant reassurance – particularly where his work was concerned. In addition, from the day when he had accepted the burden of his talent, he had vowed to put that talent before everything in his life at whatever the cost to himself or to anyone else. Such a calculated decision at times made him intolerably self-centred.

One result of his new relationship with his parents was that soon after he had formally discarded the role of invalid he discovered another interest in common with his father. Both father and son had a genuine aptitude for tennis. They practised together in every spare moment, entered as a doubles pair in local tournaments and organized bi-weekly parties for their friends. These were so popular that they felt one tennis court was not enough and with the enthusiasm for any new project which was characteristic of each of them, they mustered all available voluntary help to make a second.

They were happy days at Brooke Lodge with a sense of real family comradeship again. Brian Seago revelled in the role of host and his wife was proud and happy to provide tea for a dozen or so guests most Sundays and Thursdays. John was on hand to help with the entertaining for strangely, and as the psychiatrists might suggest, significantly, just at the time when Edward was intent on proving he was capable of leading a more normal life, John's health began to show the first signs of deterioration. He developed chest trouble and eventually decided to give up his job as a clerk in a Norwich office to study for the Church.

For both young men the Maddermarket Theatre figured prominently in the new scheme of things. Edward took part in crowd scenes in an ambitious pageant portraying the life of King Henry VIII which Nugent Monck produced in the grounds of the Bishop's Palace with two hundred performers, some mounted on horses supplied by Brian Seago. Five months later Edward made his debut on the stage of Monck's little theatre as a labourer in Chekhov's *Uncle Vanya* and soon afterwards was on stage again in the part of Raleigh in Sheridan's *The Critics* when he shared with the actor playing Leicester the distinction of being commended in the press for, in costume terms, 'looking almost right'! From then on he was content to remain active only off stage where he painted a couple of back-cloths and for a few months became secretary to Nugent Monck.

Alongside his new activities he was painting feverishly and, possibly as an expression of his new relationship with his father, called himself 'Edward Brian Seago' and signed many of his pictures 'E.B.S.' or 'B.S.'. With such a full life he grudged the time it took to cycle to and from the Kirstead studio and persuaded his father to let him take over two unused loose boxes at the back of the house and, with the money he had saved from selling his paintings, convert them into a large studio with a north-facing window overlooking the farmyard. It was the stable where, less than a decade before, Munnings had loved to paint.

It was completed shortly before his nineteenth birthday when Priestman, writing to wish him well in it, tried to counteract the effect of the sustained parental misgiving with which he knew his pupil was having to contend. '. . . You may be sure,' he wrote, 'I would not give my time to trying to give you any little help I do, if I did not believe in you. If not now, one day, your people will be proud of your work.' He reminded his pupil of God's words to Joshua: '. . . only be strong and of good courage.'

Priestman's prophecy materialized sooner than he could have visualized, for a few weeks later Lady Evelyn Jones suggested that Edward should have a one-man exhibition in London for which she and Archibald Jamieson would underwrite any expense. However, Brian Seago, fiercely independent and deeply impressed by the interest the 'county' set were taking in his son, insisted that the financial responsibility was his. The Arlington Gallery in Old Bond Street was chosen and on 25 November 1929, Sir Hereward Wake performed the official opening before a distinguished gathering mustered by Lady Evelyn, for which the press turned out in force.

They saw fifty-seven paintings, priced from £4 to £150 and ranging in subject from landscape to horse paintings and equestrian portraits. Twenty-three pictures were sold on the first day, representing takings of £184 18s. which was enough to send Brian Seago, the astute businessman, rushing back to Brooke in a fever of excitement to collect more pictures and to encourage Edward, when he returned from London after the first few days of the exhibition, to produce others to replace the diminishing stock.

But the painter, exhausted by the strain of a London debut, retired to bed suffering from pains in the head and contented himself with sending a couple of scribbled cartoons to John, one portraying himself in his studio painting with one hand and with the other passing a finished canvas through the door to his father's outstretched hand. The second cartoon showed him in bed languishing against the pillows with a bandage round his head. It was captioned, 'He that holdeth exhibitions in London, is not only in danger of hell-fire, but of Neuralgia!'

As far as the critics were concerned, there was no sign of 'hell-fire'. On the contrary, unanimously, they commented on the nineteen-year-old's 'extraordinary promise and natural instinct as a painter' while, almost unanimously, they decried his drawing ability. After the first notices he anticipated the adverse criticism and fore-stalled it when he glibly confessed to a reporter, 'Of course I must learn to draw. I have colour and technique but my horses are all wrong. Any critic would pull them to pieces.' And, as if to condone such a shortcoming, he admitted disarmingly, 'I cannot add up; my education has been terribly neglected.'

Only *The Morning Post* detected the echo of Munnings's 'Horse Fair' in canvases like 'Michaelmas' and 'Selling the Chestnut Gelding' and, while its critic recognized 'most encouraging signs of future development', he also came up with some constructive advice: 'His drawing is, at times, uncertain,' he wrote, 'and, as yet he is influenced by the art of the elder men, for instance, of Mr A. J. Munnings and Mr Wilson Steer. He could not seek advice from better painters.'

Edward Seago never hesitated to act where any possible benefit to his work was concerned and it seemed but a logical step for him to approach Munnings. In the small world of East Anglian horse-lovers, an introduction to the popular painter presented no problem and a loan portrait in Seago's exhibition of 'Richard Bullard, MH on Lord Rowland', represented the key. Bullard often entertained Mr and Mrs Munnings at his home at Stoke Holy Cross and it was most probably he who arranged the introduction. Soon after the exhibition Seago was driving over regularly to Suffolk, where Munnings then lived. In the Dedham studio he was face to face with the personality who, from his early painting days, had been a name to conjure with, a horseman whose hard-riding life-style was a local legend, a presence which could even have left a half-sensed aura in his new studio at Brooke Lodge. The influence of the jovial, big-hearted man who generously dispensed practical advice to the young painter, must have been overwhelming. Its effect, consciously or subconsciously, for a time not only became even more apparent in Seago's work but, in the years to come, before he fought free of it, could even have threatened him with a permanent physical dis-ability.

In the agricultural world of East Anglia, Munnings was so firmly established as the supreme painter of horses that comparisons were inevitable.

'See, he's even put in Mr Munnings's buttercups,' was a scathing comment Mabel Seago overheard about a painting of her son's at an exhibition.

'Since when has Alfred Munnings had the monopoly of buttercups?' was her sharp rejoinder.

Edward, when he heard of the incident, was very concerned and mentioned it to Munnings on his next visit.

'Don't listen to such damn nonsense,' was the reaction. 'If I can't drum some of my ideas into that foolish head of yours what on earth's the good of your coming here?' It was benevolent advice but the donor would be sorely tried when before long, the recipient was painting portraits of some of Munnings's distinguished sitters and charging a considerably lower price.

Meanwhile, with growing independence, on Saturday evenings Seago often joined half a dozen or so of the young 'horsey set' at the Beaufort Hotel for a pint or two of beer before moving on to the Old Café Royal for a snack and then to a Norwich dance hall where there was no shortage of girls waiting to partner the young county 'bloods', unmistakable in their tweed sports jackets. Usually the evening ended with a return to the Beaufort for a final drink served by the publican's daughter Ada Cannell. 'Ted Seago,' she recalled, 'was the quiet, good-looking one who just sat in the corner and watched and said nothing.' Nevertheless, while learning to rid himself of the label of 'semi-invalid' he was glad to be there as 'one of the boys' and quite a leader when it came to persuading a girl to slip out of the dance hall for a petting session in a dark corner. Writing to John who by then had gone to London to study for the Church, he described a visit to a boxing match in the Corn Hall where he and his crowd cheered and barracked from the ring-side. Afterwards they marched through the street with linked arms singing 'Three Blind Mice' and danced 'Ring-a-Roses' round a policeman who, after a moment of bland astonishment, joined in. Then on to a fish restaurant where, according to his letter, 'we re-arranged the tables and a tall, dark girl came to attend our needs. But would we have her? No! We wanted a fair girl and a fair girl we must have and when she came, Ben Stimpson told her he would like to kiss her.'

He was riding feverishly. 'Riding every day and sometimes all day. Hunting about twice a week,' he boasted to John in a letter, early in 1930. 'Someone from West Norfolk has got a racing four-year-old which they can do nothing with and sent it to Lee Bussey to see if he can do anything with it. The first morning it arrived I got on to it and found that I could do anything I wanted with it. I jumped it without a refusal; I galloped it, got off and on, made it stop to open gates, etc., and never once had any trouble.'

While the twenty-year-old revelled in leading a fully active life there was evidence that the heart turns were just as persistent despite the satisfaction, in May 1930, of having a picture hung in the Royal Academy's Summer Exhibition. It was a small oil called 'Over the Sticks' showing a country point-to-point meeting. The critic of the *Eastern Daily Press* commented rather disparagingly, 'It shows a bleak day, overhung by heavy clouds and three cold-looking people watching two spiritless horses jumping the sticks. The sky is a curious navy blue colour.'

Priestman too was unimpressed. 'It is not what I should call a good example,' he wrote. 'However, I hope you will have something good ready for next year.' Sympathizing about a recent heart attack he added, 'It certainly is a mysterious affair. You will probably grow out of it altogether soon.' But Edward was already accepting the fact that this was most unlikely.

One Saturday evening he and Tubby Parker visited Bertram Mills' travelling circus in Norwich. It was not the first circus that Seago had seen but suddenly, in the tradition of Laura Knight and Munnings, the colour and movement under the strange luminosity of the Big Top, caught his painter's eye. More than that, in a single moment, he saw incorporated under one roof the worlds that fascinated him. There was the romance of the theatre combined with, as he recalled it, '. . . horse-flesh of the purest blood, in a setting of poetic splendour'. Scenes of nomad life had a new glamour in the circus ring. 'What a world,' he wrote, 'for one who loved such things! What freedom! What romance!'

In addition, his admiration as well as his imagination was stirred when three men rode bare-backed into the ring on a galloping horse.

Two wore white and the third, an extraordinarily fine horseman, was dressed as a clown and danced about on the mare's back with apparent unconcern. When, to end the performance, the mount jumped a wooden gate, the clown leapt almost twice as high as the horse, his legs spreadeagled on either side. In the programme the act was billed as 'The Baker Brothers'.

Edward Seago could not wait to see it all again. The next day the show packed up and moved on to Ipswich and he went too and stayed with an aunt for a week and saw the circus every night. When Bertram Mills arrived on his weekly visit, Seago asked him if he would allow him to follow the circus for a time and paint. Mills was delighted. He was extremely sympathetic to painters. Alfred Munnings who had often followed his circus had been a childhood friend of his wife and had passed her some of his sketches across the schoolroom.

But to Munnings, as to Laura Knight, the circus had been nothing more than a marvellous source of inspiration for his canvases. 'Art is long – life is short . . . So many things to see besides circuses. A river even!' So Munnings recalled in his memoirs. Not so for a twenty-year-old who had hardly spent a night away from home. To him a group of talented individuals who came by night, stayed a while and then packed up and left without trace to display their talents elsewhere the next night, represented a way of life he had scarcely even dreamed of and to which, with all his heart, he wanted to belong.

IV

Circus Company

Edward Seago's decision to follow the circus raised no opposition from his parents. His father, who had retrieved all the money he had laid out for the London exhibition, had a new-found confidence in him and agreed to make him a small allowance to be repaid from the sale of pictures. His mother, eager to be involved in the venture, offered to do any washing he sent home and, with memories of the 'tuck' parcels sent to John at boarding school, promised to supplement Edward's supply of food.

Indeed when John drove his brother to join the circus at Colchester there was almost an air of going off to boarding school about the adventure which underlined the extent of the twenty-year-old's late development in worldly affairs. In a letter acknowledging a cheque he had sent to his father, Mabel Seago wrote: 'Dad thinks it would be jolly for you to pay it in yourself, dear, into your bank. He wants you to understand about money as he feels you'll earn big sums sometimes and you'll have to save. See dear?'

The inhibiting relationship between mother and son was underlined when the perplexed country woman who had done her best to nurse her boy through his years of illness and who was inadequately equipped to recognize the demands of his talent, instinctively went through the motions of an ineffectual release.

'Good luck to you dear,' Mabel Seago wrote during his first

weeks with the circus. 'Don't work too hard. You've got out of your mother's clutches at last, haven't you? Quite out! You've been doing it gradually for a long time. And you have my very best wishes and my very best love. I miss you old darling.'

But his letters home showed that the damage done in the early years was irrevocable. He wrote to consult his parents about every decision, shared his hopes, deferred to their wishes and indicated that as well as being grateful for their financial help he was pathetically anxious to preserve the strong family ties and needed their constant reassurance. Discounting his inherent generosity, the way he invariably included them in his plans whenever it was feasible indicated his irresistible urge to display to them, over and over again, the talent they had once rejected.

At first it seemed he was too unhappy to write more than brief letters. The circus folk did not like mixing with outsiders and made no attempt to conceal their mistrust of the pale, well-spoken youth who hung around their tents and caravans. They showed no interest in his work and hardly bothered to hide their disdain when he summoned up courage to ask if they would allow him to sketch them. All his attempts at starting a conversation were met with surly grunts and foiled by slang words which he did not understand. Determined to win their confidence he invested some of his precious allowance in cigarettes which they accepted with curt nods and occasional remarks about the weather. But afterwards he often caught them looking at each other with broad grins as he passed by.

'How I hated those early weeks of my circus life,' he remembered, 'hated almost everything in the circus, and still more the wretched lodgings which gave me shelter for the night.' He had never before felt so timid of his fellow men and so entirely cut off from the life around him. In town after town, where the circus people pitched their tents, he wandered about a new ground exchanging nods with unapproachable familiar faces, watched the work that went on behind the scenes and made endless sketches of circus horses which he posed by tethering to stakes in the ground. Only when a drum-roll heralded it was time for the next performance did the magic under the Big Top once again confirm that, somehow, one day he would become a part of it all.

He particularly longed to get to know the brilliant young horseman who clowned in the Baker Boys' riding act. He was Tommy Baker, the eldest of four sons of a widowed Irish showman who travelled with the circus acting as manager for the three elder boys. The youngest, eight-year-old Pat, was too young to be part of the act.

One morning Seago forced himself to ask Tommy Baker if he could make a drawing of his grey mare.

'Sure,' was the decision after long deliberation.

'That's awfully good of you,' Seago replied. 'I suppose I could find someone to hold her for me?'

'Sure.' There was a long pause. It was the most fruitful conversation Seago had had for weeks. He waited. He sensed it was important to be patient. The fair-haired rider's face was expressionless as he busied himself with his task of whitening a horse girth. Suddenly he looked up; he had come to a decision.

'I'll hold her myself,' he volunteered. So the first of many studies of Kitty, the old mare, became Seago's passport to circus life.

Gradually the circus folk's initial distrust gave way to genuine interest when they recognized that the intruder was a man who knew his job. One morning he was working on the painting of the mare when Tommy Baker invited him back to the family wagon for a meal after the show. There 'Pop' Baker, with an innate 'gift of the gab', told tales of the hardship and struggles in Ireland with his small family circus in a trail of wagons with the name 'Baker' gilded on the sides. Seago pictured squalid vans and muddy fields, battered props and tarnished costumes and horses with broken hooves and bedraggled plumes. He heard of living hand to mouth in remote parts for weeks on end, not knowing where the next penny would come from. There were memories of sickness and sorrow, love and old feuds, tales of wily beggars who knew all the tricks of the trade, of knife-throwers and lion tamers and the 'hobos' who followed the show from town to town hoping for a chance to work as tent men. That night Seago wrote the tales down, to the delight of the story-teller who although he knew the shortest route to every market town in Great Britain and Ireland, had never had a day's schooling in his life. Similarly, his sons' early success in the circus ring had been at the expense of their education. This meant that Seago had at last found companions of his own age with whom, scholastically, he

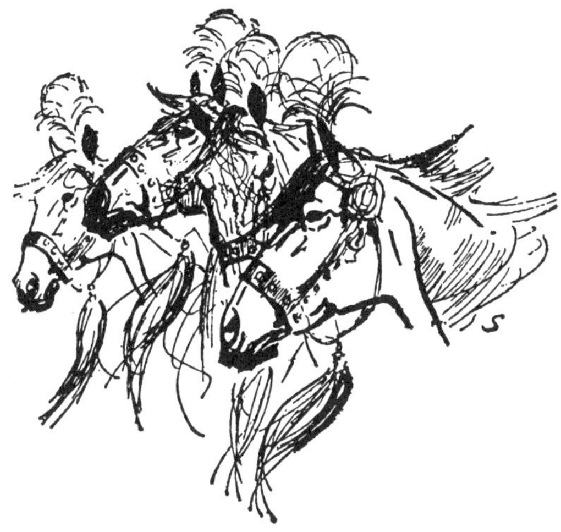

was at no disadvantage so that with them he felt neither strange nor inhibited as he often did with his contemporaries.

He was soon having all his meals with the Bakers and using his lodgings only at night. As a matter of course, he helped with the packing up after the last performance of the week and with two of the brothers rode the Bakers' five horses to the railway station to load them on to the circus train for the next town. Unlike his companions he was not used to riding bare-backed so he strapped a saddle on to his mount. But even in the darkness his new friends noted he rode competently.

At the next town he painted a picture of his piebald mount, Barley and, from imagination, added a lady rider. 'Pop' Baker was delighted. After a private family discussion, tentatively and with some embarrassment, he invited Seago to give up his lodgings and move in with the family. From then on the painter was treated as one of the Bakers by everyone in the circus.

In the crowded wagon he shared one of the two bunks with Tommy, 'Pop' and another brother had the other bunk and the two younger boys and the dog slept in the small bell-tent. Tommy was Ted's particular friend. They were the same age, had a mutual passion for horses, a complete disregard for physical danger and each admired the other for his mastery of widely differing skills. For these and a multitude of indefinable reasons the circus boy stirred the painter's emotions as none of the pleasant girls he met ever did. In addition, Tommy Baker offered him the security of belonging to a family as close-knit as his own, and introduced him to the pleasures of a new life in which each day, from the early morning swill in a pail of cold water and a brisk rub down with the family towel, was packed with fascinating revelations.

It was a magic of which Seago never tired. 'Sometimes it seemed to me that I was living through a dream from which I should eventually awaken,' he wrote. 'I was perplexed sometimes by the oddity of it all and yet, as each day passed, I was acutely aware that I was being captured by the charm of the circus people and the glorious freedom of their healthy, unrestricted life.'

He tried to capture the magic on canvas in paintings of circus encampments, portraits of the knife-throwers; Carl Hess, the German horse trainer in the ring with his white Arab; dwarfs and clowns and acrobats; trapeze artists and Adolphe, the animal tamer. He sketched them on small panels to translate on to big canvases which, he told his parents, he thought might be suitable for the Academy.

He sent home the fullest details of everything he was doing and as soon as he had attained a general effect on a big canvas, he railed it to Brooke to work on in the studio in the winter. But he was always impatient to hear his parents' first reaction. It seemed that, because at long last they had accepted him as a painter he needed them to comment on his work over and over again to compensate for the years when they had maintained their bewildering silence about his pictures.

'It is so difficult doing these things entirely on my own,' he wrote to his father and, wiping away the memory of the lonely years, it appeared as if he had not only convinced himself that they had never happened, but was intent on reminding his parents of the part he had once longed for them to play.

'I am so used to discussing all my pictures with you and mother and having them criticized as I go along,' he wrote. 'However, I shall have to paint on my own some day so I might as well start – but I expect there will be many alterations to make when I get home. I am now really getting some good pictures here and I can work all winter from these and also paint pictures from memory.'

His repeated appeal for their support also coincided with a deliberate attempt to find his own painting identity. 'What I want to do,' he wrote, 'is to get away from Munnings and paint something quite different. I am now painting things which even Laura Knight has not done . . . I can't tell you how grateful I am to you for giving me this chance but I want you to know exactly what I am doing and tell me exactly what you think. I hope when I bring my stuff home you will think it has been worthwhile.'

'I can come home at any time,' he assured them in another letter and, with the dependency of a schoolboy added, 'Do you think you could possibly send me a little drop of cream? We have had quite a lot of fruit at dinner time and we have that rotten condensed milk with it . . . The cake was awfully good but it's no use sending anything like that as it all goes in one. There are eight of us in all and they nearly all like two pieces.'

Probably the two extra at the Bakers' table were lady friends for, once the show was over, an interest in the opposite sex was the natural preoccupation of 'Pop' Baker and Tommy. They were surprised at Seago's disinterest in the all-important business of 'dating' but attributed it to the fact that he was an artist and therefore allowed to be exceptionally particular. Occasionally, perhaps because he felt it was expected of him, he indulged in a little flirtation with a pretty dancer from Lancashire but usually he refused Tommy's invitation to join him for a night on the town. Possibly, as Wyndham Lewis suggested was often the case with artists, the painter was beginning to school himself to find in his work much that other men sought in women. At the same time, it was probable that when he was emotionally involved with a man physical satisfaction with a woman was unappealing.

He had plenty of excuses to stay behind. He found he could paint perfectly well by gas light and he often worked until midnight and left his pictures in the tent to dry, ready to work on again the next morning. He was inundated by the circus people to write letters for the illiterate, give driving lessons, touch up coloured photographs, read to the children and advise on money matters. The last task was splendidly ironic in view of his own financial embarrassment. This was emphasized by an appeal to his father to increase his meagre allowance a little for August Bank Holiday because the prices in

Margate, where the circus was playing, rose during that week.

Often he was blissfully happy. He revived his old conjuring tricks and almost succeeded in teaching a monkey to paint so that it sat on a stool, held a palette and daubed away at a board most convincingly. His boyhood training with old Lijah was turned to good account on occasional nocturnal poaching escapades with eight-year-old Pat Baker. Secure in his hard-won friendships, he realized that even in the strange world of spectacular individualists, he was admired as something of a personality.

At the end of August his parents suggested it was time for him to come home and paint subjects other than the circus. 'I have no wish to drop painting my other stuff,' he assured them when he appealed to them to finance him a little longer, 'but I think the two can go very well together . . . I can paint hunting, sporting and horse pictures during the winter, as it won't take me all the winter to work up these pictures and when I come home I shall have September, October and a little bit of November to paint landscapes. There are some fine skies and outdoor effects to be painted in late September and October . . .' He described four more 'outstanding' circus subjects he badly wanted to paint, apologized for the financial worry he was causing and assured them that he felt he had the field to himself and as an animal and landscape painter could get some good stuff. Having put his case he added, somewhat naïvely, 'I am awfully grateful for what you have done and I should be absolutely content if you told me to come home tomorrow.' But had they done so it is doubtful if he would have stayed there for long.

Finally, a tragic accident made it easy for him to get away. In Hastings early in September, he was working on a sketch of the German animal trainer, Adolphe Cosmeyer. Painter and sitter had breakfasted together in Adolphe's caravan and afterwards Seago worked on the painting while the trainer gave his bears a hosedown because of the heat. Suddenly, one of the bears turned on Adolphe and killed him before Seago's eyes. In a terrifying flash he had a mental picture of a scene from boyhood, when he had been sickened by the bloody sight of pigs being slaughtered. Months later he was able to write about the tragedy but at the time, in a letter to his parents, all he could say was 'It was too terrible to write about. I almost feel that I would like to come home straight away.'

His allowance was so small that he had to ask for a supplement to subscribe for the wreaths for Adolphe's funeral in Germany and the memorial service in Brighton. He painted a notice to hang outside the ground saying that all performances were cancelled and his last days with the circus were spent consoling Adolphe's brother Alfonse, and finishing the dead man's portrait to give to him. It was the only painting he could bring himself to do.

It had been arranged that John would collect him from the circus but after the accident, the painter could not face the intrusion of anyone from outside into the private grief of his new world. 'Would you please ask John if he would mind not coming here?' he wrote to his father. 'I would honestly rather he did not come.' When Tommy Baker drove him to the station on the first stage of his journey home he promised that he would be back with the circus before very long.

He stayed away for just over two months during which time the long-postponed commission materialized to paint Brigadier-General Sir Hereward and Lady Wake and their four children riding in the grounds of their country seat, Courteenhall. There, in contrast to a circus tent, his studio was a Louis XVI drawing-room and Lady Wake borrowed a large easel from the painter Simon Elwes who lived nearby, to hold the ambitious picture intended for the banqueting hall at Dover Castle. 'It is without doubt the best I have ever done,' Seago wrote home. 'Sir Hereward is particularly keen that it should go to the Academy.'

The Wakes showed him around the countryside, took him to Towcester Races, to the theatre, to luncheon and dinner parties and to tea with Lord and Lady Spencer Churchill at Castle Ashby. He wrote to his parents that on one of their drives he and Lady Wake had discussed the price he should ask for his pictures. 'I have now arrived at quite definite ideas,' he wrote, when as a matter of course he invited their opinion. 'While it is a great mistake to make your prices exorbitant, it is just as foolish to make them too small. If you start by adopting a low standard you will never be more than a second-rate painter. On the other hand, if your prices are excessive, you become a first-rate painter and, at the same time, a painter which few people can afford.' At the height of his success when everything at his exhibitions was sold on the opening day, he firmly resisted the suggestion that he could easily charge more and, perhaps partly due to Lady Wake, 'a fair price' was all he ever asked.

At Courteenhall there was mention of just one heart turn which lasted only a short time. 'As a matter of fact, I think I am really having rather a good time,' he admitted in a letter to his parents. Gradually, it seemed he was learning to forget the circus. Then, uncannily 'on cue', in one of the peculiar quirks of timing which always seemed to direct his life, he learned that at the end of the week Bertram Mills' tenting circus was to open in Oxford, just a few miles away. From Courteenhall he drove there on his way back to Norfolk.

The Bakers were delighted to see him again and everyone came to shake him by the hand as if he had been to the ends of the earth which, in terms of environment, he certainly had. His happiness was so great at being back that, for once, he did not unpack his paint-box. Instead he helped with the horses and sat in the unlit Big Top watching rehearsals as if he could never have enough of the smells and sounds and sight of the sawdust ring. 'I am not ashamed to admit that I came back with mixed feelings,' he wrote long afterwards. 'Maybe it was the obvious pleasure they showed to see me again – for I don't think I might fall for flattery. Maybe it was the music which came from the full-bellied canvas dome; but whatever it may have been my heart seemed to swell to double the size and I realized how glad, very, very glad, I was to be back again.'

It was the last week of the tour before the show disbanded for the winter. Most of the clowns and tumblers, the acrobats and jugglers had jobs in variety shows until pantomime time while the equestrian acts hoped to join one of the big Continental circuses that toured all the year round. The Bakers were to join the Cirque Palisse in Belgium and invited Seago to go with them. He needed little persuasion and when he drove to Brooke to collect his clothes he took with him the Bakers' old greyhound, Spring, to live there for the rest of its life.

Before he left England he called at the London offices of *The Field* magazine. In the glossy publication he had noticed reproductions of paintings by Alfred Munnings and recognized them as just the sort of advertisements he needed. As a result of his visit, reproductions of his two most successful paintings appeared in the Christmas issue headed 'From the Brush of a Young Artist'. They were the stylized portrait of the Wake family and a horse-racing scene at a Fakenham meeting. By the time they appeared the painter had spent several weeks travelling through Belgium with hardly any money and writing brief assurances to his parents that he was well and happy and very busy.

In Brussels after the evening show, there were suppers in cheap little bars and restaurants where easy friendships were formed and the conversation lasted until dawn. It was an intoxicating existence for any young man with a streak of adventure. After a time a Belgian dancer joined up with them and although she was Tommy's preserve she took charge of all the housekeeping, laundry and mending and often cooked their meals in the rather sordid lodgings. 'This trip has really been wonderful,' Seago wrote. 'I must say I am very pleased with the work I have done. It is an experience that many fellows would give a good deal for.'

They were all back in London by early December living in two rooms in Islington. Seago had painted nearly a score of circus studies in Belgium but a letter waiting for him from Bertram Priestman indicated the teacher's misgivings.

'I can understand the charm of the natural life in such surrounding,' he wrote, 'but don't in the charm of it and the newness, forget that it has its disadvantages as well and that, in time, you will miss the lack of education which unfortunately exists with most simple and natural people. When young, one is apt to go to extremes and, as a friend, there can be no harm in putting forth a caution against getting too tied up with people, however delightful and good in their own sphere of life, who cannot, in the very nature of things, enter into the high ideals which a man in your position should naturally strive after.'

The caution had come too late. By then Seago's friendship with Tommy was, apart from painting, the most important thing in his life.

The Baker Boys were in Bertram Mills' Christmas Circus at

Olympia and Seago was at the opening night to see the three-hour spectacle, the largest of its kind in Britain, which began with the pomp and glory of a procession of all the artists. As it swung into the ring to the strains of the brass band punctuated by shrieks of delight and applause, mingled with the noise of the funfair outside, the painter was mentally translating it all into a glowing seven-foot canvas.

He went home to Brooke for Christmas but in his pocket was the special pass Bertram Mills issued to a limited number of painters and writers giving them the freedom of Olympia. On his return, he found he had been allocated a dressing-room in the gallery for a studio and in it was a long table specially bought for him from Harrods. The dressing-room was high above the circus ring so he kept one easel there and another in the stables to use when he painted animals or circus scenes. Such recognition more than justified the sordid rooms in Islington where there were often no shillings for the small gas cooker which was the only means of heating.

On New Year's Eve he and Tommy went to the cinema and bought two meat pies from a tea stall to eat in their room and shared a bottle of wine provided by 'Pop' Baker. It was not a romantic start to the year and their winter existence could not be compared to the freedom and romance of life in a travelling circus. No doubt Seago wished himself out of it at times and at the beginning of January he was confined to bed with the worst heart turn he had experienced since he had joined the circus.

For ten days Tommy and the Belgian dancer nursed him through the worst of the attack. They called a doctor, and often he was delirious, but one or other of the family never left his bedside. As soon as he was strong enough he wired his parents explaining why he had not written to them. His mother's reply was exemplary in its non-possessiveness. 'I felt so vexed for you, dear, and wondered if you were *really* all right,' she wrote. 'It did not sound an attractive room to be in bed in. You have got over it well old boy.' For once she was over-optimistic for as soon as he could travel John drove him home to Brooke where he was still so ill that a nurse was engaged to look after him.

Priestman wrote to say he had called to see him at Olympia

several times and had seen his large picture there which he thought looked very well indeed.

'It seemed full of life and well composed and I think from the slight look I had, that it is as good, if not better, than any circus picture I have seen,' he wrote. 'When you can work again, I should advise making a lot of serious studies and drawings. I think you draw well in the big sense of line and proportion but you can't do too much actual study in fine drawing and you have missed that which many people get at art school. Draw heads and portraits; then you know whether they are correct by the likeness you get.'

For once, Seago hardly felt like working. 'Really the last five weeks have been Hell,' he wrote to John in early February. 'I am very shaky and of course, not allowed out, but am living in hopes. I am very grateful for all your letters, as letters are now the only interest. The weather is dull and cold and only adds to one's depression . . . Nurse suggested that I should go away for a change – me, who have hardly seen Brooke for eight months!'

When he left, a few weeks later, it was to join the Bakers in Paris. As usual, after he had recovered from a heart turn he was more eager than ever to paint, but not at that time the 'serious studies and drawing' suggested by Priestman. It was the effects of light and movement that drew him like a moth to the Nouveau Cirque de Gand where the Bakers were riding and also to the Circus Medrano and the Cirque d'Hiver. Paris, for him, revolved only around the circus rings and his great satisfaction on that trip was his portrait of the famous clown Grock. 'His head is the most extraordinary shape I have ever seen,' he wrote to his mother at a time when, it so happened, two finer examples of his early work were on show in the Paris Salon. They were 'A Sultry Summer Day', the highest priced picture from his London exhibition which, at £150, had remained unsold, and a race-course scene 'Easter Holiday'. Priestman's fears were far from groundless.

Seago's return to England coincided with the arrival of a telegram from Munnings of tantalizing uncertainty. It concerned two paintings Seago had submitted to the Royal Academy; one a large circus picture and the other a portrait of Sir Hereward and Lady Wake's children. The telegram read:

'Wrote you today to say your picture children and ponies was out at last moment it has been put up instead of another will write again.'

The letter eventually arrived to explain the initial rejection:

'When we had got everything settled, at the last moment we tried your large picture up again with children and ponies and as none of the others were so fond of it as I was it had to go out,' Munnings had written. 'This one we tried to hang all the time but it was not good enough for so large a picture. You'll now *have* to study seriously somewhere because all the hanging committee are sorry about your work not being in and they all see that you have the *courage* and will work. Your father must let you have a year up in town. Try the Academy Schools and you'll be well seen after there. When you have learned more you'll be a great artist. Don't let this defeat worry you. Both the pictures were beaten by their size and *utter* lack of knowledge and you were at *sea* when you tried to paint the children's faces. Now you get started and no more playing about and we shall be seeing you in great places one day.

'The composition of that picture of the children was good. The circus a tremendous effort but a picture that size has to be better to get hung. Never mind.'

It transpired that after the letter had been posted, the committee had had second thoughts, as confirmed in a second letter which followed the telegram:

'Mind you come up to town on Monday for Varnishing Day,' Munnings wrote. 'Walk right in to the Academy with your ticket and don't faint when you see how awful your picture looks.

'Munnings seems to have taken an interest in you which is all to the good,' Priestman wrote in his letter of congratulation.

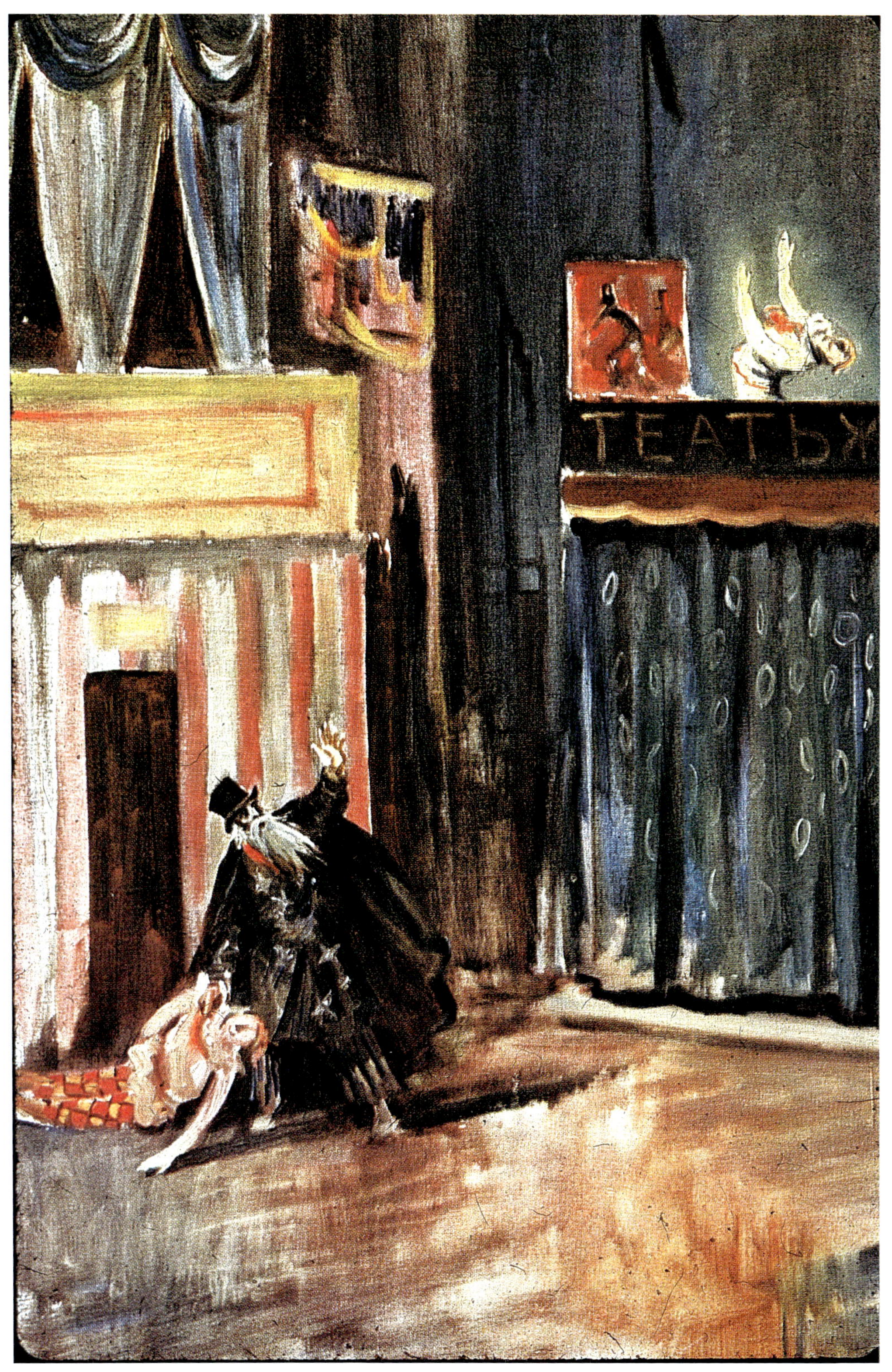

8. Petrouschka

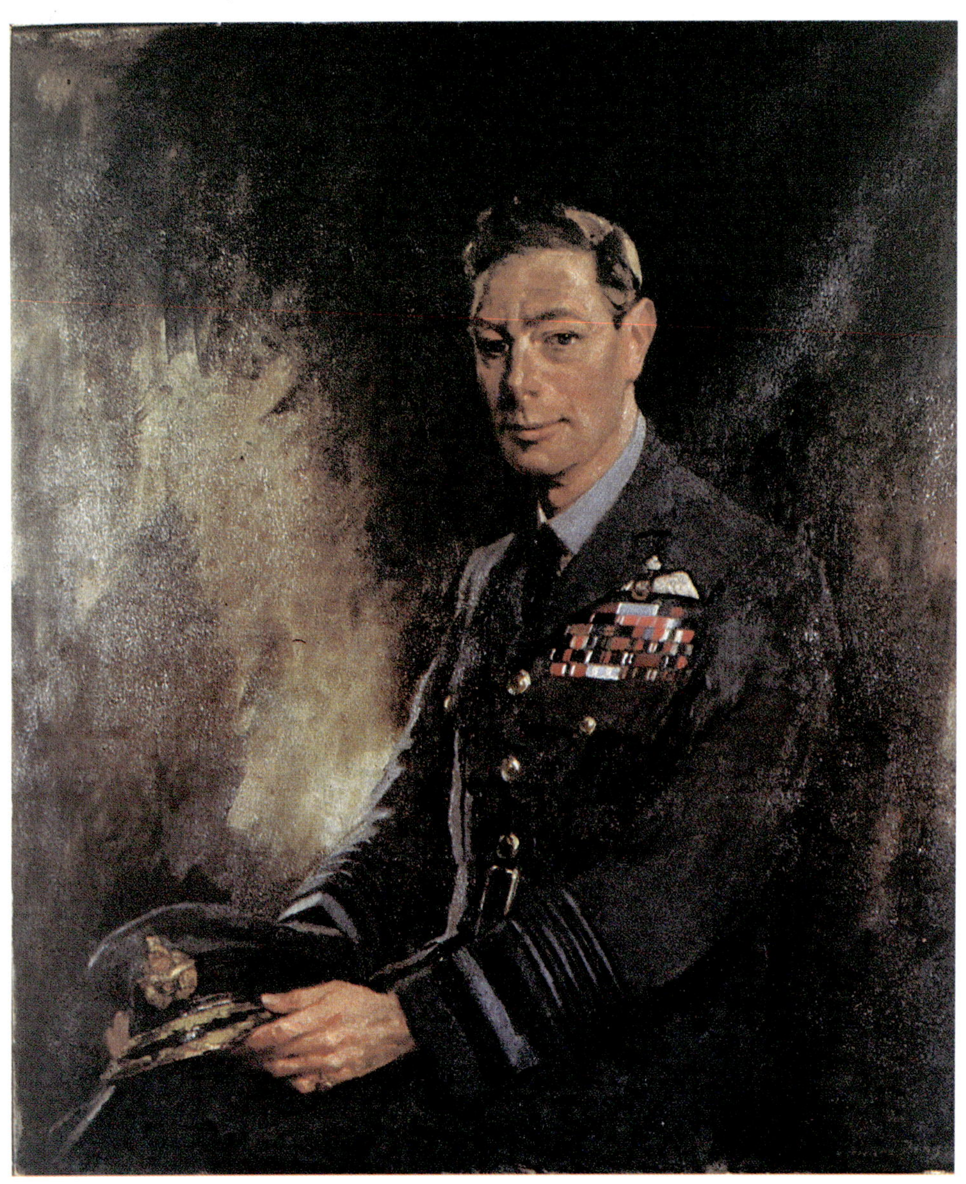

9. King George VI

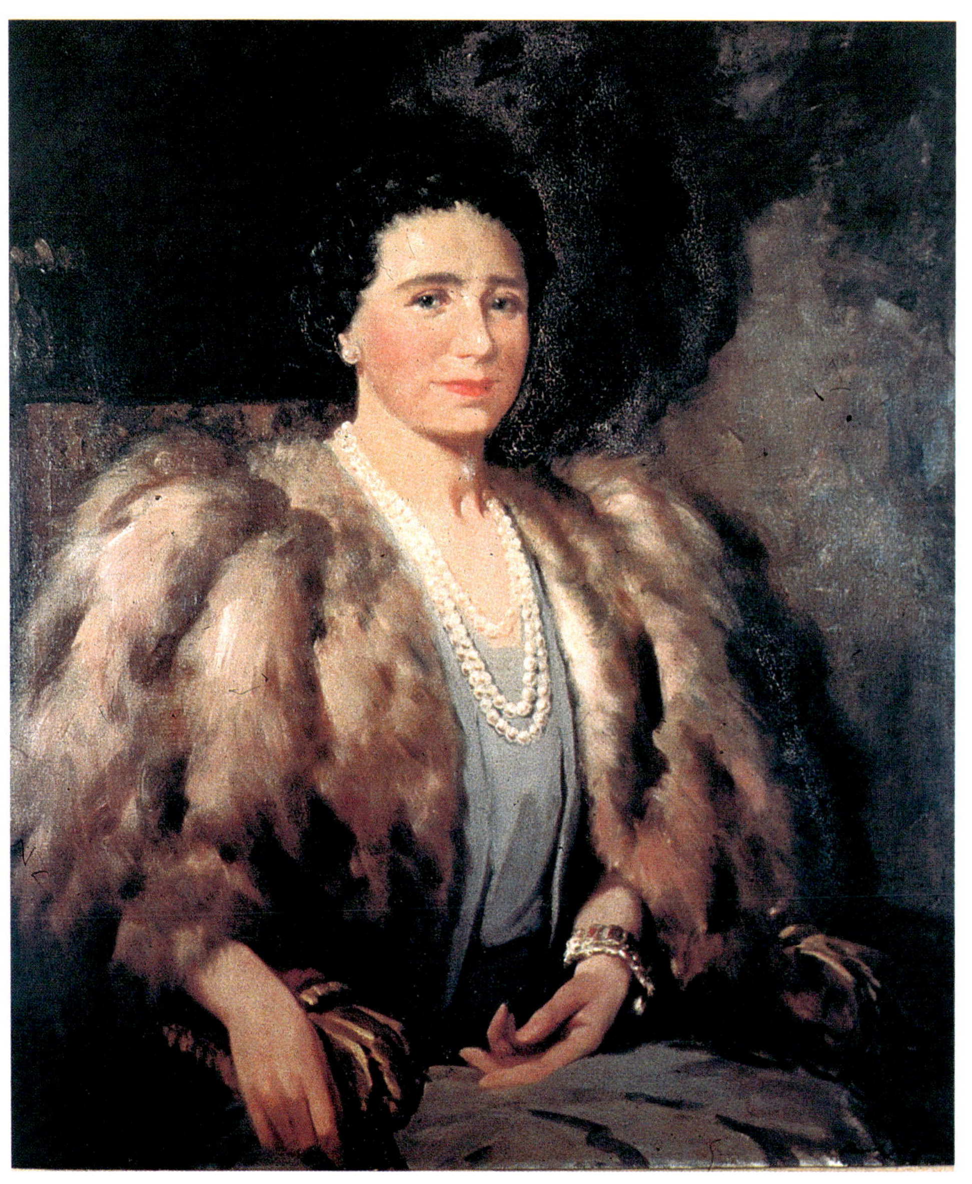

10. Queen Elizabeth

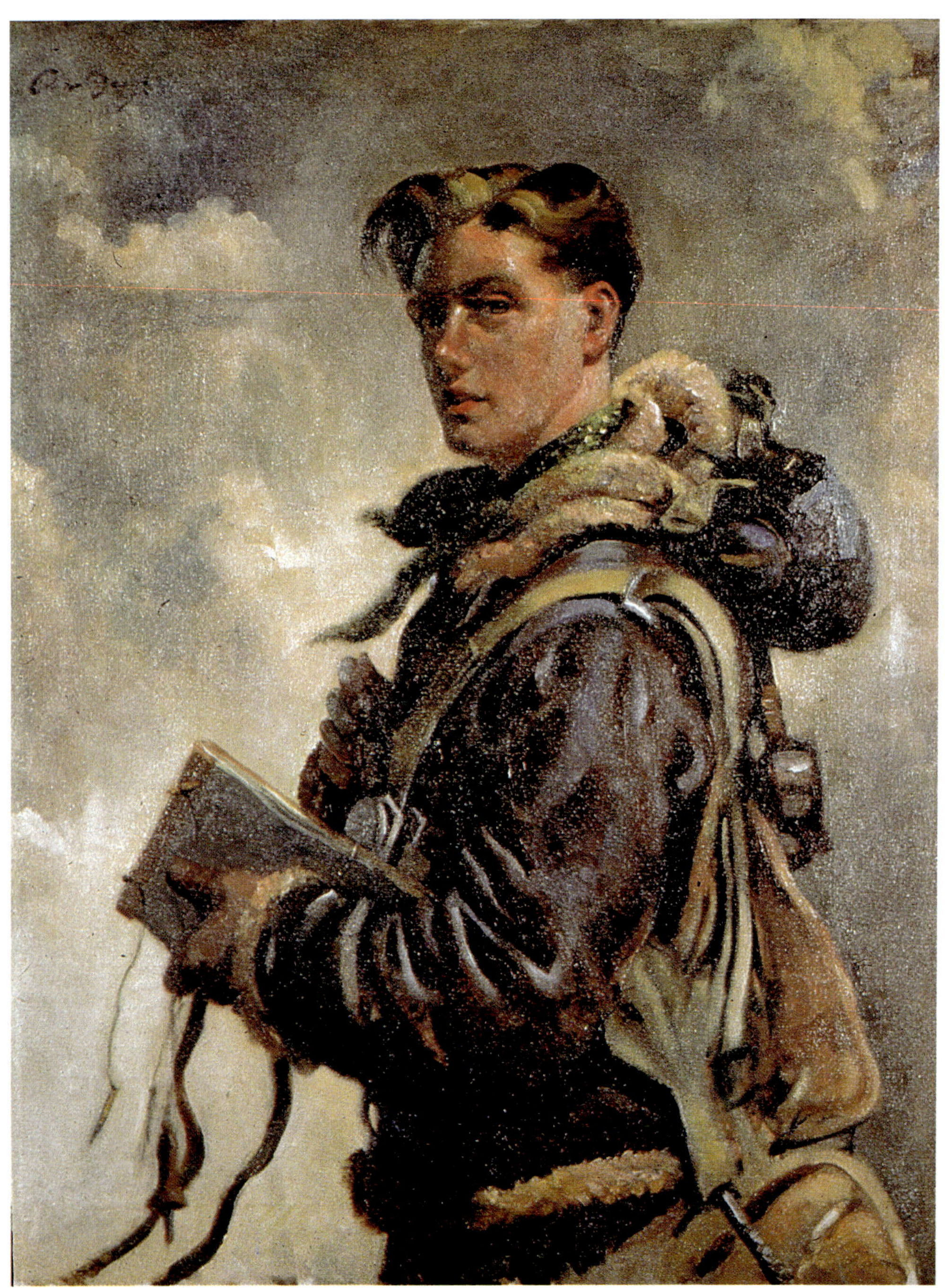

11. Bernard Clegg

The popular press seized on the story of the promising young painter who lived with circuses and who was smiled upon by the aristocracy. Again Munnings felt impelled to try and cut him down to size.

'Alas, are you getting in the thralls of such folk who turn anywhere for a guinea in these days?' he wrote. 'Don't be misled, my lad. The press only wants a cheap "sensation" for themselves. The photographers want pots of money – all parasites . . . You are already getting beyond the youthful years when the young brain absorbs easily and learns quickly. Begin to be a serious student and let all business of *young* Seago and young genius go and during years to come you'll possibly make a hit.

'When I was your age, if you imagine it,' he recalled, 'the *Daily Mail* had not come into being!!! *No pictures* in any papers. No *Daily Sketch*. No pictorials. No cheap rubbish and slosh. Don't be misled even by having this picture here in R.A. It was out and only got in by the smallest chance and then only allowed to go up there because I pleaded for it.'

He again urged Seago to talk to his father about art lessons and reminded him of the long studentships and years of learning of Velasquez, Rubens and Rembrandt and of the Italian artists.

'Why did the Academy start its schools 100 years ago if schools were not needed?' he asked. 'Why do grown up men go to night classes and draw from the nude, year in and year out? You have now to begin and learn something and from now until the end of this term you ought to go in to Norwich School and work there. Be yourself and do what you want to do. If the master there is *up to date* as they call it, regard him as you think fit but for God's sake go and do some real study and shake the dust of utter ignorance off your feet. Your health is not good. Make the best of it and if your father thinks you ought to be making a few pounds, show him my letter . . . Let him understand that he has to make a student of you for a while and not a young potboiler.'

The postscript carried an extra warning, no doubt to forestall any local adulation that might mitigate the advice of the wily letter-writer. It read: 'Don't regard what folk in Norfolk say at all. They know *nothing* of art. They think they do.'

Seago rarely disregarded the advice of his mentors and within a week, Munnings was writing again to express his satisfaction that he had taken his advice and enrolled at the art school where some twenty-six years before he himself had been a student. 'You will find much to interest you when you start to do *any kind of cast*,' he wrote, '– fruit – flowers – scrolls – such as I know there are at the School and start to really grasp the meaning of tone, light and shade, etc., etc.' He also urged him to get some good drawings from life and one good oil to submit for a scholarship to the Academy Schools and sent details of how to apply.

Whatever the shortcomings in Seago's ability as a painter, his personal self-confidence was developing rapidly. Priestman was uneasy when his pupil related some of his recent exploits, such as how he sought revenge on a Suffolk landowner who had turned some gypsies off his land. Seago and his friends drove over late one night and pasted brown paper over the windows of the gentleman's residence to give him all the privacy he needed. Always he tried to defend the underdog, quite literally in the case of the local farmer who kept his dogs chained up for an unreasonable length of time. As soon as Seago learned about them, he went and cut them loose.

Then there was the titled lady whom he regarded as a local snob. On his way over to visit Priestman in his little open baby Austin which was the pride of his life, he had seen the lady standing on the roadside, holding out her hand to ask for a lift. He had slowed down, leant over, cheerily shaken her outstretched hand and driven on. This was contrary to his usual habit of taking anyone he despised for a ride in his car and attempting to terrify them by driving at a furious rate.

Priestman was not amused. When Seago toyed with the idea of taking Munnings's advice and applying for a scholarship to the Academy Schools and asked Priestman to endorse his application, the form came back signed, but with a mild caution.

'I hope you will be careful not to go in for any of the practical jokes that would in any way be read as making you unsuitable as a student,' Priestman wrote, 'or you will let me down for my statement. I don't of course refer to harmless fun or reasonable jokes, but having signed this paper I feel obliged to refer to this, as you have certainly told us stories which lead to the supposition that you might join in some rag that would not be quite acceptable to the authorities . . . I hope you will be well enough to join the schools. I think it will be very good for you.'

In the end, Seago disregarded the advice of the two painters he most respected. The pull of the circus was too great. One term's evening classes at Norwich School of Art, studying drawing and working from a series of male models, convinced him that he was equipped with all the schooling he needed and immediately term was over he rejoined the Bakers.

Before he left Norfolk again there was a serious rift in his friendship with Tim Parker who, by that time, was recognized as a promising young amateur jockey. Seago painted him on his first winner at a local meeting. She was a chestnut mare called Sling Along and after the picture had been exhibited the painter gave it to Parker. A few weeks later a reproduction of it appeared in *The Field* over a caption describing the rider as 'a leading amateur'.

Parker was furious for he deeply resented the exaggerated description of his modest achievements. 'Ted just roared with laughter when I complained,' he said. 'He was such a practical joker and loved to pull people's legs. Although he said the Editor had written the caption I maintained he had and I told him that I never wanted to see him or his paintings again. I then took the picture into the woods and burnt it.'

Seago at that time was too involved with Tommy Baker to miss Parker's friendship. It seemed he could not have enough of the vagrant life of 'kicking sawdust' and travelling in a painted wagon through the by-roads of England. Only then did he feel it was really good to be alive. The Bakers, in circus tradition, had relations in most other travelling shows and after an introduction to members of the family in Duffy's, a smaller circus, Seago joined it for a time and travelled the West Country, retracing some of 'Pop' Baker's adventurous journeys.

Duffy's Circus moved to a new town each day and Seago, with all the company, was expected to lend a hand to pull down the Big Top, pack everything up and, after a four- or five-hour break for supper and a nap, drive off to build it all up again a few miles away by midday. It was a hard life with little sleep and no time to paint. Often Seago argued with himself about what he was really doing there and whether or not it was all a waste of time and he should go home and paint hunting and racing pictures. 'I could never make out which was my real self; and which ever was my real self, what was the other one . . . I was aware of a queer unrest and this, I supposed to be homesickness,' he recalled.

Was it Masefield who wrote a verse he remembered from his boyhood that kept jangling in his mind?

> My road calls me, lures me
> West, east, south and north;
> Most roads lead men homewards,
> My road leads me forth . . .

He remembered his own early attempts at writing and once again felt a desire to express himself in words. Perhaps the renewed urge to write arose because he half-sensed a somewhat repetitive tendency about the stream of circus pictures through which he tried to capture again and again the magic of his intoxicating existence and which, after all, was his justification for pursuing it.

Once again he was motivated by the unerring instinct which, at regular intervals, seemed to project him one step forward in terms of achievement. He recalled that Masefield, the recently-created Poet Laureate, lived near Oxford and he wrote to say he was a painter and a life-long admirer who happened to be travelling in the neighbourhood with a circus and would like to call. His letter was sympathetically received. Masefield loved young people and in his early years it had been touch and go whether he would become a painter or a writer. He was also fascinated by the circus and had once planned to tour Ireland with Hodginni's Italian Circus. He invited Mr Seago to lunch. His short, formal invitation represented the beginning of a deep friendship based on mutual admiration, that was to develop into a successful professional partnership and last until the poet died.

In the modest man over thirty years his senior, with whom he shared a passionate love of the sea and a ceaseless joy in nature, Seago might, originally, have subconsciously sought a father substitute which was a role to which Masefield could well have responded. Seago was exactly the same age as his only son Lewis, who also wanted to be a writer. After Lewis was killed in the Second World War Seago, contrary to the course of some of his friendships, however busy or whatever part of the world he found himself, never failed to keep in touch with the older man. There were always Christmas presents – either a painting or a copy of the latest Seago book and, in Masefield's later years when failing eyesight made it difficult for him to get about, Seago telephoned him frequently and was a regular visitor to the poet's home in Abingdon.

'What you want to do when you're beginning to write,' Masefield told Seago, 'is to write and write and write and then tear it up 'til you get it right,' and back in Brooke after the circus had disbanded for the winter the painter did just that. He also worked on the canvases he had started during the summer so that in two ways he kept his circus memories alive. This was probably to the advantage of his work in both media for the visual memory, so vital to his style of painting, could well have been stimulated by the exercise of writing, thus refuting Priestman's fears concerning his divided interests. Years later Masefield himself recognized the benefits of self-expression in dual media when he took up painting again and wrote to Seago: 'I would have tackled it many years since but for the time it would have taken from writing. Now I see that the two would have helped each other in many ways.'

That winter Seago finished eight circus pictures and in a letter to John said he was 'rather bucked with one' and thought it was the best thing he had done. However if, as seems likely, it was the large canvas he submitted to the Society of Animal Painters when he applied for membership the following year, he was over-optimistic. He was not elected to the Society for reasons explained in a personal letter from the President, Lucy Kemp-Welch, the animal painter. Her hard-hitting home truths carried more than an echo of Munnings's opinion. She wrote:

'Of course, it would be easy for me to make one of the usual excuses by which one gets out of explanations, but I am so sure that one day you will do big things – if you keep your face in the right direction – that I am going to tell you the truth about the large circus picture of yours, which was seen by myself and the Committee . . .

'My dear boy, that is not art! It might possibly be an advertisement – but it is vulgar because it tries to say too much and see too much and there is no restraint or reticence, or interest of tone or lighting or mass or any of the things which might make it tolerable and perhaps admirable.

'You have been so carried away by the passing show that you have overlooked what made you feel the impulse to paint it – not the facts – not the commonplaces of clowns and Red Indians, etc. They go for nothing. But a fine effect of light on a massive design with all the component parts and little masses lost or half seen in the group mass; everything secondary to some big idea or mass of colour or light – or all three with *one thing* – perhaps, such as the lady in feathers and such details lost in the mysterious blue haze, which is one of the strongest points in the circus as a painting ground.

'Well now I have had my say, and I hope you will take it as it is meant from a painter of long experience, who is very interested in your career.'

Lucy Kemp-Welch, of all painters, recognized the true magic of the circus. For months at a time she had attached herself to Lord John Sanger's Travelling Circus and lived in a motor-drawn caravan and painted.

Seago was grateful for her criticism. They kept in touch with one another and in 1937 he suggested a challenging subject for her to paint; the launching of the Isle of Wight's horse-drawn lifeboat, a painting she exhibited in the Royal Academy two years later. But he did not again apply for membership of her Society because rejection of any kind, since his parents' apparent rejection of his talent when he was a boy, was to be avoided at all costs. Meanwhile, in Brooke in the autumn of 1931, his writing and his painting were interrupted by an invitation which any ambitious young painter would have envied.

Once again Lady Evelyn Jones was instrumental in tempting Seago away from the circus, the second time through an invitation from Lord Harewood, a former ADC to her father, Lord Grey. Writing from Sandringham, the Earl invited Mr Seago to visit Egerton House, his Newmarket stud, to paint his Ascot winner Alcester. He suggested that after the painter had completed the preliminary sketches, he might like to stay the night.

'We dine in short jacket and black tie at Newmarket as we shall be no party, just Princess Mary and possibly my brother and sister-in-law,' Seago read as the pendulum of his life-style again started its upward swing away from fish-and-chip suppers in a horse-drawn circus wagon.

That evening at Newmarket proved a memorable one for the country as a whole as well as for Edward Seago enjoying his first sample of Royal hospitality. For he did enjoy himself once he had overcome his initial embarrassment during a dinner which lasted two hours and in which he recognized only a few of the dishes. It was the night of the 1931 General Election when the National Government, led by Ramsay MacDonald, gained a crushing victory with a majority of nearly five hundred. The party at Egerton House, so Seago wrote to his brother, sat up until after three o'clock in the morning eating chocolates and listening to the election results coming over the wireless. When the fire died out and no one answered the bell, Princess Mary, he said, took him along to the kitchen to find some coal. The following day he joined the Royal party for the Cambridgeshire and drove to the race course through cheering crowds, still demonstrating their election fever. Afterwards at lunch, he sat between Princess Mary and Lord Derby.

Princess Mary and Lord Harewood had also apparently enjoyed Seago's visit for it was followed by others and resulted in several commissions including a large painting of the Derby and an illustrated calendar for the Jockey Club. From then on, Seago never lacked commissions for equestrian portraits and his 'sitters' included the famous winners Hyperion and Blue Peter. He also painted a portrait of Princess Mary on horseback, as Munnings had done, and Lord Harewood publicly endorsed his opinion of his work when in 1933, at the Sporting Gallery in London, he opened his second one-man exhibition.

By then, Seago was writing a circus book and the Christmas after his meeting with Masefield, he told the Poet Laureate about it when he sent him a painting of the circus. 'I shall love to read it,' Masefield replied, 'whenever you care to send it, if you will be sure to send me a *copy*, not the only existing manuscript which would be too great a responsibility. With pictures by yourself it should be the book we have all longed for during all our lives.' But the first draft, when it arrived by return of post, hardly fulfilled such high expectations and before Masefield had finished reading it he was writing to Seago to point out its shortcomings.

'So far as I have read,' he wrote, 'the book's best passages are what I can only call word-pictures of what you have painted. I cannot help feeling that the world would like your letterpress to give more of the life not seen by the public and let your paintings shew the splendour.'

The letterpress, he said, was only half the length it should be and it omitted to tell enough of the writer's own life, such as how he came to join the circus and what his own feelings about it were at the time.

'Circus life is what the world wants from you,' Masefield wrote. 'So strong a dose of it that all readers will feel that they too have lived with the circus. Do not lose so splendid a chance. Turn to it again; fill in your story: and write a world-shattering book that will be read for centuries. Think what we would give for an account of Shakespeare's rough Globe Theatre as seen by an actor of the time and how eagerly every detail, even the stenches, would be followed.'

Seago, inspired to a second attempt, sent it to Masefield who again rated it as not good enough and returned it with the advice that the few lines describing how the writer came to join the circus should be extended into a whole chapter.

'. . . How did they take it when you joined? What did you think about? What sort of day was it? How deeply depressed were you?' were questions the master urged the pupil to answer and exhorted him to 'go at it again and squeeze the orange of your experience into this cup for our felicity'.

Seago tried again. The third draft included a new chapter and elicited an invitation from Masefield for Seago to go to Oxford so that they could work on the manuscript and 'try and pull it tighter'. Finally, after a couple of minor revisions, the poet recommended a publisher. The book was rejected. Masefield advised sending it to three more publishers and if they all turned it down he felt that Seago should print an album of the drawings at his own expense to have on sale at his next exhibition. Apparently the poet rated the painter's art work higher than his literary efforts.

However, despite his misgivings, Putnam accepted *Circus Company* for publication the following year, although the head of the firm, Constant Huntington, a tall, dignified American, considered the typescript needed further 'polishing' and allocated the author a table on the top floor of the firm's office in Bedford Street where, for several weeks, he worked on the book until Huntington was satisfied. Meanwhile a newcomer to the firm, Alan Delgado, was designated to look after the country boy who knew little about London life. Delgado was a year older than Seago and they became good friends.

Masefield, delighted that the book had been accepted, agreed to write an introduction. 'I'm afraid you were slow on your entry, but when you were really in the ring you did a very good act; much the best yet. Good Luck. I'll always gladly do the pencilling,' he wrote, couching his congratulatory letter in true showman's jargon. It was an appropriate choice of phrase for, at that time, Seago was more infatuated than ever with the circus. Neither literary encouragement nor intermittent tastes of English country living on the grand scale at great houses when he worked on portraits of well-known society people and their horses, could wean him away for long from the circus trail, either with Bertram Mills' tenting show or the smaller travelling shows.

Wherever he travelled he found the circus world, as he had painfully discovered in the early days, was one big family. He revelled in the privilege of belonging, knowing that within that family he had additional security in the unstinting admiration and affection of the hard-living, happy-go-lucky Bakers.

'In spite of the wind and cold, in spite of the long dreary miles, I could never remember when life had been so sweet,' he wrote in *Circus Company*. 'The sound of the iron tyres on the road was the gladdest music I had heard, the cheap, foul-smelling tobacco was more fragrant than any cigar and the narrow bunk which I shared in the shabby wagon was better than the softest feather bed. The brushwood from the roadside for a fire, and the springy heather roots for a carpet. All the countryside for a home, and above, all the blessed eternal covering of the stars.'

He might have been describing the setting for a love affair. The first threat to his idyllic existence was when Tommy Baker confided in him that he was seriously involved with one of the dancers in Bertram Mills' Circus and planned to marry. Seago recalled that when Tommy told him he felt a sudden strange emptiness inside.

'It was strange,' he said in his book, 'and I did not know what it was. I wondered if I should be jealous of this girl, and then felt rather ashamed of the thought. Our feelings towards each other were very different from those of a boy and a girl. This thing called "love" was the natural emotion between a man and woman which falls to the lot of almost every human at some period of their lives. The more uncommon friendship between two men, though more difficult to understand, could still exist and remain as steady as before.'

The friendship between the painter and the circus boy did survive. Founded on mutual admiration and respect for each other's very different qualities it developed through shared hardships and laughter and adventures on the long journeys, and Seago's gratitude to Tommy for giving him the security of his family. The strength of their mutual affection was proved at the end of the summer tenting season when Seago received a telegram telling him that Tommy was seriously ill in Liverpool Royal Infirmary where he had been operated on for appendicitis. Peritonitis set in and for weeks Seago hardly left his friend's bedside while it grew increasingly obvious that the sick boy would not recover.

Tommy's constant concern was what would happen to the family riding act which had been booked to appear in the Christmas Circus at Olympia. He brooded to such an extent about how his brothers would manage without him that Seago telephoned Bertram Mills. He asked if, for the sick boy's peace of mind, Mills would send a make-believe contract offering to engage the two younger brothers until Tommy was fit to ride again. He gave his word that Mills would not be held to the contract and promised to tear it up once Tommy had seen it.

Tommy Baker, believing his brothers' future assured, died on 7 December 1932, three months before his daughter was born. Seago, for a time, acted as guardian to the baby and for the rest of his life he wore Tommy's only piece of jewellery, his signet ring, which the baby's mother gave to him.

—— V ——

New Horizons

For months Seago kept in touch with the nurses who had become his friends during the long vigil at Tommy's bedside. Sister Doyle, on receiving a copy of *Circus Company* when it was published the following Christmas, wrote in a letter of thanks: 'I am sure it must be some consolation to you to know that you did everything he wanted and there was no one he liked better by his bedside.' By then Seago had assumed responsibility for young Pat Baker who had gone to live at Brooke for a year until he was considered old enough to join his brothers in the riding act.

Circus Company was dedicated to the memory of a circus rider who would be the first of three men its author would love and mourn before they reached the age of thirty. But although he did not realize it at the time, Tommy's death offered Seago a permanent release from the circus just as, more than two years before, his temporary break from it had been simplified by the fatal accident to Adolphe, the animal trainer. Tommy's death cut the main tie although for most of his life, whenever he found himself near a circus he would be drawn to it as if by a magnet, to recapture for a few hours or weeks, the memory of his first years of joyous freedom which were recorded in *Circus Company*.

The book was a significant milestone in Seago's career for two reasons: Although the extent of Masefield's assistance was not widely known it heralded a series of important collaborations between poet and painter. In addition *Circus Company* introduced the name of Edward Seago to a new public and gave him an authority it would otherwise have taken years to achieve. It is not surprising that the book was very well received for what would-be writer in compensation for a lack of formal education could have enlisted a more apposite tutor than a poet laureate? Initially Seago's approach to Masefield was for advice as to how to express himself in words and it is improbable that he foresaw the far-reaching potential implications. As with painting he had acted on a spontaneous instinct rather than on a contrived opportunity to further a long-term cause. His remarkable ability to respond unhesitatingly, immediately an opportunity presented itself, was perhaps because his lack of schooling and his country upbringing had left him uninhibited by a sense of formality or protocol. Despite his engagingly diffident manner there was little shyness in his make-up and if ever there had been it could well have resolved itself during the teenage years when he had forced himself to come to terms with the realistic business of living on borrowed time.

When *Circus Company* was published, the author was travelling round England and Ireland with a series of small circuses. He was existing mainly on a diet of bread and cheese, raw onions and boiled potatoes, living rough but undaunted as he described in a letter to Alan Delgado written from Proctor's Circus at Blackpool Fairground.

'Weather is simply foul and it's almost impossible to think of painting out of doors for it's either fog or raining hard,' he wrote. 'The grounds are deep in mud. We've been doing rotten business and some of the fellows have left. There are now 4 of us and two women (one of whom is over 80) and that completes the show!!! I might add that one of the men is under 10! He does a riding act. The other two do some acrobatic stunts and clowning. I am the Ring Master and the band!

'We are for ever trying to get on a hard ground for we are terrified of the wagons sticking in which case we should never get them out! As it is we have all our work cut out to get the tent up on our own. I am supposed to leave at the end of the week but now I shall find it a bit awkward and may have to stay on for a while.'

He stayed on to travel through County Clare and Galway and Connemara to act as Ring Master wearing old riding breeches, a pair of ancient riding boots and a lumber jacket instead of the traditional scarlet tail-coat, top hat and white tie. He cracked his whip at the horses, ad-libbed his chatter with the clowns and was soon presiding with convincing authority. Before each show he spread sawdust in the ring and, as an authentic artistic touch, traced in it a picture of a clown or a star or a horse's head. They were virtually the only pictures he had time to produce.

Sometimes the circus played to audiences of just seven or eight people or, if no one could be persuaded to pay their 2d admission, the show might be built up and taken down without giving a performance.

'There are six of us in the wagon I am living in, to say nothing of the parrot,' Seago wrote to Delgado. 'To cap it all we had *the* most marvellous fight the other night. We had a good 10 minutes before any cops got there. A fellow started it by smashing a lamp in a woman's face. Honestly, if the cops hadn't come I believe he'd have been killed . . .' As a postscript he added, 'I have solved a problem that has puzzled me for years. I *can* grow a beard!'

Inevitably there were moments of misgiving. 'I think this is the most severe test I have given the circus,' he wrote in the large red-leather exercise book in which he had formed the habit of recording the day to day impressions of his travels, adding, 'Some people have said to me "I suppose you have finished with the circus now, haven't you?" Why they should say this I can't think! I have grown to accept the circus as my lot and have never thought the time might come when I should no longer want to live with it.'

Meanwhile, the red-leather exercise book – and its successors – gradually replaced the long, detailed letters home, few of which exist after his first book was published. Undoubtedly the pages of flowing handwriting were intended as notes for a sequel to *Circus Company*.

There was little time for painting during the months he travelled with the small circus in Ireland but one or two of Seago's canvases, usually equestrian studies, could sometimes be seen at the Sporting Gallery in Grafton Street, London, where he planned to hold his next exhibition and which was as likely a place as any for his opportune meeting with the warm, sensitive patron who was to offer him an irresistible alternative to the compulsion of circus life.

Henry Melchett contributed to Seago's success in a special way. He transported him into a new world. Initially, his recognition that Seago was at a potential turning point in his life was perhaps due to the fact that at that time Melchett was also engaged in a heart-searching struggle to find his own identity, but in racial terms. He could therefore have been particularly sensitive to a young man's comparable search for self-identification. Uncharacteristically, Seago failed in the first instance to recognize a new opportunity to further his talent.

Henry Melchett, the man who offered him that opportunity, was the only son of the noted Jewish industrialist, the late Alfred Mond, the first Lord Melchett a founder of Imperial Chemical Industries.* Henry Melchett, like his mother, had been baptized and brought up as a Christian, but had come to share his father's passionate interest in Palestine and the Zionist movement. In particular the plight of the Jews in Nazi Germany had aroused his conscience until like his sister, Lady Reading, he eventually felt impelled to identify with them. In 1933 when he met Seago, Melchett and his sister, unbeknown to each other, were both on the point of being converted to Judaism.

Patronage of the arts was also a fundamental part of Melchett's background stemming from his German-born scientist grandfather Ludwig Mond who made a considerable fortune through his business enterprises. Ludwig was also a discriminating art collector as evidenced by the Mond Collection at the National Gallery in London.

Henry Melchett felt that it was his responsibility to continue the family tradition of patronage. With that in mind, he invited Seago to his home. But Seago, conditioned by the informality of the circus, was suspicious of any semblance of patronage and ungraciously declined the invitation.

---

* Also owner of *The English Review* in 1910 when it created a literary stir by publishing Masefield's 'The Everlasting Mercy'.

'You don't know me,' the painter is said to have replied to Melchett, 'so why do you want to ask me to dinner?'

'That's precisely the reason,' was the answer. 'I don't know you and I feel my wife and I might like to get to know you better.'

At last Seago grudgingly accepted the invitation to visit Melchett's home. He found himself in the flamboyant, exciting, sophisticated world of a wealthy man whose artistic wife, Gwen, was irresistibly good company, had a devastating wit and a figure to be envied. She was a friend of Augustus John and before her marriage had mixed in the Bohemian set associated with him.

The Melchetts' home, Woodfalls, had been built for them as a wedding present by Alfred Mond in the grounds of his own home Melchet Court, overlooking the New Forest. Many celebrities of the day visited the Melchetts; Mr and Mrs George Bernard Shaw, H. G. Wells and his friend Moura Budberg, the tempestuous exiled Princess Aspasia of Greece and her daughter Princess Alexandra who became the wife of King Peter of Yugoslavia. From the theatre came Gwen Farrer and her stage companion Norah Blaney. Others in the public eye included the aviators Jim Mollison and Amy Johnson, Brendan Bracken, Godfrey Winn and Randolph Churchill. Often Augustus John arrived with the beautiful Dorelia, his son Caspar and sometimes two of his and Dorelia's children.

There Seago found himself constantly exposed to the wit and wisdom, the conversational brilliance and the unexpected frailties of people whose interests extended to the corners of the earth and to almost every field of intellectual or artistic endeavour. At first he listened and said little, as he had in the drawing-rooms and at the dining tables of other great houses he had visited.

'As long as you kept silent at table you were in no danger whatsoever,' recalled Henry Maxwell, a writer and a contemporary of Seago's who was also a frequent visitor. 'You see, they all loved to hear themselves talk and as long as you didn't try and chip in, it was OK.'

For Seago there was ample time to talk when the other guests had gone, for before long he was living rent free in a little cottage in the grounds of Woodfalls, provided with all his meals and commissioned to paint. During the week Gwen and Henry Melchett lived at their London home, Mulberry House in Smith Square and with the children at school Seago had Woodfalls to himself, except for the army of grooms, gamekeepers, gardeners, chauffeurs and house staff. On Friday evenings when the place came alive again with house-guests, Henry Melchett's first stop on his way home from London was at Seago's cottage to unwind from the week's business tensions over a glass of sherry and bring himself up to date with the painter's work. After half an hour or so, completely relaxed, he and Seago would stroll up to the big house for dinner.

Before long, Seago was one of Melchett's closest confidants while to Gwen Melchett, who invariably liked to have a circle of intelligent male friends to amuse her without overstepping her own bounds of convention, he was an ideal companion – attractive, accomplished and entertaining. He painted her on her dappled grey, mounted sidesaddle, wearing a long skirt and casual open-necked shirt, hatless, with her fair, shoulder-length hair bright against a background of rhododendrons. Casually, hand on hip, young and poised, she confronts him out of the picture in one of the most totally revealing portraits of an attractive woman he ever painted.

Gwen and Henry also saw Seago as the stable, tutor-like influence their children needed in the volatile household. He adapted to all three roles, but at times his innate East Anglian pride and his independence nurtured in the circus, secretly resented the generous patronage. The world of Melchet Court, like an expensive college of further education, did a good deal to develop his personality while it gave him the much-needed security of being part of a stimulating and affectionate family.

The three children regarded Seago in a special way. He personified the romantic hero in their storybooks who, because of wicked parents, had been forced to leave home and live with the gypsies and the circus people. He was the writer who personally spun them tales of fishermen and poachers. He painted beautiful pictures for their delight while they made tea and toast in his studio. Moreover, he was always prepared to leave his work to join in their adventures.

He taught them to sail in their small cutter *Amy Gwen* and took them on riding picnics in the New Forest. He fixed their ponies up with special hand-grips in place of saddles and showed them how to ride bare-back and to vault on and off, like the circus artistes. Inevitably the youngsters were his staunchest champions, proud to be fellow-conspirators in all his practical jokes – like the time he chloroformed a pig and put it in the back of his car to take to a dance as revenge on a hostess who had once slighted him. Always as a hang-over from his boyhood, he tended to over-react to any semblance of rejection. In the case of the hostess and the pig, how-ever, the joke rather misfired.

At the dance he planted the unconscious animal behind a sofa in a sitting-room and, during the evening, went to see how it was getting on. He was bending down behind the sofa examining it when his hostess and a partner came into the room, switched off the light, settled themselves on the sofa, and were soon involved in passionate embraces. Eventually, the unwilling witness decided to attempt a surreptitious getaway but when he had crawled half-way across the floor the pig grunted. The startled couple switched on the light and were shocked to see a guest crouched on all fours in front of them.

'I'm just looking for my cigarette lighter,' was the best excuse he could muster on the spur of the moment.

For the rich it was an era of gay parties and practical jokes when anyone who could afford to indulge had no need to think of the con-sequences even if, at times, an element of cruelty was involved in the joke-making. Edward Seago, in fulfilment of Priestman's fears, behaved like a thoughtless undergraduate and sometimes antagon-ized the victims of his jokes. The cabaret artist, Gwen Farrer, got her revenge on the night he gave her a lift home after a party in London. When they arrived at her flat she found she had lost her door key and her resourceful escort offered to climb a convenient drain pipe and break in through a window. He had reached the upstairs window when a policeman passed by and asked what was going on. Gwen Farrer meanwhile had found her key and, characteristically deciding to teach her arrogant escort a lesson, told the constable that she had just arrived home to find a stranger trying to break into her flat. Seago was taken to Bow Street Police Station where he spent an uncomfortable night.

Such escapades were grist to the painter's image with the young Monds. They were always ready to come to his defence as when they punished a week-end guest, Adam de Hegedus, an impecunious Hungarian count, by floating his entire wardrobe in the swimming pool, because he had borrowed Seago's dinner jacket without permission and had stained the lapel.

The marble pool at Woodfalls was a focal point at week-ends. It is recalled how, after a dinner party, Winston Churchill was pushed into it fully clothed by his son Randolph. The future Prime Minister turned the incident to good account by removing his dinner jacket and trousers in the water to demonstrate his theory that people were often drowned unnecessarily by keeping their heavy clothes on after an accident in the water. Afterwards he slid down the chute with a glass of brandy in his hand.

In such company Seago realized that to be a painter in the 1930s was, in itself, no criterion for social acceptance. To be admitted into that circle, he realized one had to be an interesting personality as well as a promising artist and to that end his circus background gave him a good start. As an alibi for any intellectual shortcomings he exaggerated his lack of formal education, as he had done to the art critic at his first London exhibition. His new acquaintances were given the impression that he had never had a day's schooling in his life and had not even learned to read or write until he was well into his teens. He also elicited sympathy by implying that his parents, and his mother in particular, had done all they could to prevent him from painting, a myth he endlessly exploited, possibly in sub-conscious retaliation for the boyhood hurt at his parents' initial rejection of his talent. It was a belief he propounded until, in time, he probably convinced himself of the truth of his story which certainly impressed anyone who had not known the family in his boyhood days.

So Seago made new friends and lived surrounded by fine pictures and priceless sculpture and discussed his work with authorities like the painter Paul Maze and the sculptor Charles Sargeant Jagger, whose twin fountains surmounted by nymphs and fawns were the focal point of the matching Italian gardens at Woodfalls. Sometimes he must have found it a relief to escape to the children's world where the eldest son, although twelve years younger than Seago, from the time of their first meeting, claimed the painter as his closest friend.

There was no denying Derek Mond anything he set his heart on. He was a particularly gifted boy, strangely sophisticated, brilliantly clever and a fine sportsman who excelled at everything he chose to turn his hand to. From the nursery he had been made aware of the high expectations vested in him by his parents. Despite the disparity in age, in material affairs and emotional maturity, the precocious youngster was undoubtedly Seago's equal and although there was an element of hero-worship on Derek's part, the friendship was by no means one-sided. Through it Seago may have experienced again, not the infatuation, but something of the real affection he had felt for Tommy Baker. In his twenties for the first and only time, his emotional needs were focused on a boy who was undoubtedly his potential superior in intellect, poise and worldly matters.

There was a real satisfaction in knowing that he alone could help the difficult boy through the moods and problems of a traumatic adolescence, soothe him after the inevitable family argument arising from the perpetual battle of wills with anyone in authority and relax the tensions built up by the ceaseless cerebrations so characteristic of the dynamic men in the Melchetts' inventive family. Seago reciprocated Henry Melchett's confidence in him in two ways. He repaid it personally by helping Derek and professionally by many paintings including two large family portraits in the Royal Academy.*

Significantly, these paintings had succeeded chronologically a large circus picture 'The Wild Beast Show', hung in the 1933 Academy where its acclaim at last justified the time the painter had spent with the circus. It was hung 'on the line', a compelling study of a crowd of expectant spectators standing under the mysterious light of a striped awning outside the lion cage at Bostock's Menagerie. The picture was an ambitious composition, skilfully executed which earned Priestman's 'warm congratulations', and was bought by Bristol Corporation for the City Art Gallery.

Three weeks after the Summer Exhibition closed, Lord Harewood opened Seago's second London exhibition in the Sporting Gallery near Bond Street. The exhibition certainly proved the extent to which the circus had dominated the painter's life. Of the sixty pictures more than half were circus scenes, leaving six landscapes and twenty equestrian pictures to refute Priestman's misgivings about the direction his pupil's work was taking. The teacher could not know

---

* The first, hung in 1935, showed Lord Melchett as Master of the Tedworth Foxhounds and in 1937 Derek and Julian following the beagles.

that the circus pictures represented a tribute to the past rather than a commitment for the future. Among the guests at the Private View were three Bakers, Billy, Dick and young Pat, conspicuously self-conscious in unfamiliar dark suits, collars and ties. Seago would always remain loyal to them but with the death of Tommy there was only one more positive contribution for the Bakers to make in the life of the 'gajo' they had adopted as one of the family. The Bakers had brought to the exhibition an unobtrusive older man with a faint hare-lip partially concealed by a moustache, who had come especially to be introduced to their painter friend. He was Ronald Horton, agent for a firm of iron, steel and coal merchants, trainer of National Hunt horses, inveterate gambler and unofficial intelligence operator. Like an actor, this larger-than-life character entered Seago's life exactly 'on cue' to exert an influence.

Ronald Horton, then a bachelor aged thirty-one, was born in Gloucestershire, educated at Uppingham and had left school in 1920 when his father had sent him to France for a year with a few pounds in his pocket to make his own way in the world. In Paris he met a wealthy sixteen-year-old boy, Paul Charnaud, and the two worked up a dog-training act and toured with the Royal Italian Circus before taking a winter engagement in a Frankfurt music hall. By then, as with Seago, the circus was in Horton's blood. The following summer both youths again toured with their performing dogs in the Royal Italian Circus before Horton returned to England to embark on a business career. But he kept in touch with the circus and assumed the responsibility of supplying it with as many Welsh sheepdog puppies and white ponies as it required. When some ten years later the circus was in financial difficulties Horton and Charnaud saved it by jointly taking a quarter financial share, an investment which could have had ulterior motives in the light of the early trouble-warnings from Nazi Germany, for it possibly suited both the English and French patriot to have an inconspicuous cover enabling them to travel through Europe.

Horton by that time had other valid reasons for travelling extensively abroad. On his return to England in the autumn of 1921 from his year of travel, he joined the Birmingham firm of Charles Ryland & Son, iron and steel merchants and eventually became involved with allied concerns, including the Butterley Coal Company.

Such industries had one important common factor; in the event of war they could be switched over to help the rearmament programme.

Not until 1927 did Ronald Horton become aware of such implications. He was approached by a friend of his father's, Archibald Wall, an iron, steel and coal industrialist and asked if he was interested in the prospect of helping his country by combining his commercial interests with the gleaning of military intelligence. He was an ideal candidate for the work because he had legitimate business reasons for travelling in Germany, the Balkans and most countries where it was suspected trouble might be brewing and where some of his ready-made contacts might be relied upon to give unbiased reports on the current internal situations. However, Wall impressed on Horton that he should only agree to undertake such espionage work out of a genuine interest and a love of travel and adventure and on the understanding that if he ever got involved in any sort of trouble it would be no one's responsibility except his own.

'I was offered this work with no salary and even the actual expenses of such journeys would have to come out of my own pocket if they could not be debited to the business,' Horton recorded in his diary of the time. In the diary he reflected on the potential usefulness of his journeys to the mines of Poland and Czechoslovakia where the kind of equipment his engineering works could supply were needed 'even though we never obtain any orders on account of German competition!' he added ruefully. To the same end he foresaw as a convenient excuse for travelling further afield, his working agreement with Ceretti e Tanfin, the overhead rope makers of Milan, to try and influence the sale of their products in some Turkish coal pits under modernization. 'Never was I lacking for a perfectly good reason to be in any foreign country but, even so, I sometimes had a queer feeling inside me!' he wrote in his diary after his first secret missions, which were chiefly concerned with widening his circle of friends abroad to establish channels of information from many countries in the event of war.

Horton's association with the Baker Brothers and his subsequent meeting with Seago coincided with those early missions and his acquisition of a financial interest in the Royal Italian Circus. At the start of one circus season he learned that the trick riders in the show had been enticed away by a German circus and at short notice it was difficult to find a replacement. He remembered the Baker Brothers through earlier connections with the circus and recalled hearing that the eldest brother had died and the younger ones were trying to work up a new act with another Irish family, the Fossetts. He contacted them in Dublin, signed them on and one evening after the show was chatting to Billy and Dick in their van when they showed him the invitation from their friend Ted Seago to the Private View of his London exhibition. Horton said he would like to go along. It was no sudden whim on his part, although possibly he had recognized the name 'Seago' for Archibald Wall was a director of the parent company of Brian Seago's firm of coal merchants.

Wall, like Henry Melchett, was a great patron of the arts and was always willing to help any youngster he thought showed real talent; musicians and singers as well as painters and the tenor Heddle Nash was one protegé whose singing lessons he paid for. However, unlike Melchett, Wall had no inheritance and as the seventh of nine children, had gone out to work at an early age. By the time he was twenty-eight he reckoned his income was as high as it ever would be and he started investing it in the nucleus of a fine art collection. The likelihood was that Horton, influenced by Wall in so many respects, decided as soon as he had acquired a little money through horse racing and gambling as well as from his various business activities, to follow his example and also invest in paintings. 'During my travels in Europe, I had studied great works of art,' he explained in the diary, 'and although I knew I could never afford them I determined, one day, to make a collection of the work of one painter of recent times.'

That day came when he accompanied the Baker brothers to Seago's exhibition and found himself surrounded by paintings of a subject closest to his heart. That afternoon he bought two circus scenes which, in time, formed the nucleus of one of the largest private collections of Seago's paintings in the country – a representative group of more than fifty pictures, bought and exchanged over the next thirty years – always in the closest consultation with the painter so that it came to portray a unique record of personal experience and a vivid reminder of places, at home and abroad, which both men saw at different times and under different circumstances and which both, for respective reasons, chose to remember through a painting.

Moreover, Seago became one of the few people to know of Ronald Horton's intelligence activities and, according to the evidence of several close friends, felt impelled himself to join up with a Continental circus as a cover for a little unofficial and experimental espionage work. Using infra-red paint and with his artist's eye trained to observe and record every detail, in a matter of minutes it seems he made an exact portrayal of a strategically-placed bridge, an unusual fortification, an unfamiliar type of aeroplane or part of the lay-out of an aerodrome; anything that, in the event of war, might be of military significance. Then, within minutes of the paint drying, he over-painted the panel with an innocuous-looking landscape or a circus scene so that he could take it back to England without anyone suspecting that beneath the top layer of paint, ready to be revealed by photography, was a picture of quite a different subject. Such an ingenious exercise, conducted with a characteristic touch of bravado and a complete disregard for any personal risk involved, represented the beginning of Seago's interest in the use of anti-infra-red and cellulose type paints for wartime camouflage. He was to develop this in conjunction with ICI through Lord Melchett when war broke out in 1939.

Soon after Horton and Seago first met, the former was on his way from Dover to the Black Sea in his open 3-litre Bentley to obtain the reaction from other countries to the appointment of Hitler as Chancellor of Germany. Seago left for a holiday which would also, as it turned out, offer him an opportunity to go on an unorthodox patriotic mission. As soon as his exhibition closed he joined the Melchetts in Venice where he made a dozen or so paintings. Of this collection, four small water-colours were eventually bought by Horton, probably as reminders of his own diplomatic rendezvous at Harry's Bar in Venice.

Henry Melchett not only commissioned Seago to paint. At the same time he provided him with material security, treated him like a member of the family and also perceived the need for him to broaden his painting horizons. While he believed in his work he perceived the weaknesses, particularly an inability to draw and he was in a more subtle position than either Priestman or Munnings to do something about it.

In Venice that summer the family had rented a villa, Casa Leone, on the Giudecca and Melchett confronted Seago with the work of the great Italian masters and watched while he reacted to the wonders of the Titians and the Tintorettos, the Canalettos and the Bellinis and marvelled at the Italian skies over the lagoon and the sheer flamboyance of the Venetian sunset; skies such as Constable and the English school of painters had never attempted, where a painter might indulge in a riot of colour yet still paint well within the bounds of nature. But despite the exuberance around him, Seago was intrigued most by the subtle differences in light and atmosphere and, with the memory of Whistler's Nocturnes, he too expressed himself in a series of dark, emphatic waterscapes.

'Actually, I can't quite think how I came to be here,' he wrote to Alan Delgado. 'I like it – indeed I adore it. I think perhaps if my time were divided between here and the circus I should experience perfect bliss.' He added that he was hoping to return to the circus in about a month's time, but before he left Venice, as Melchett had foreseen, its centuries of history gave him a new perspective and his letters to Delgado reflected the first signs of real humility. 'Actually, I am trying to paint here,' he wrote. 'No very marked success so far! I have seen some pictures which clearly show me that (1) painting is *the* greatest of all; (2) I don't possess it? ! ! and what is more I see no way of attaining it!'

What he did attain on his first visit to Venice was a modest ability with a gondola, a healthy respect for scorpions and an impressive crop of mosquito bites which, for a whole day, convinced him he was suffering from measles. There is evidence of only one minor heart turn.

There is no written evidence, however, of a secret aeroplane flight Seago and Henry Melchett made at that time on a private mission to Austria where they met Chancellor Dollfüss. Seago, afterwards, told his brother that Dollfüss had sent his small private plane to meet them near Venice and, on the way to Austria, they had flown frighteningly low over the Dolomites. The pilot had told them that Dollfüss was a humble man who never forgot his peasant background and whenever the plane flew over his mother's cottage he had been instructed to make a circuit to greet her. Seago was just an observer on the trip, while Melchett's purpose in meeting Dollfüss, like that of similar meetings he is known to have had with Mussolini and General Pilsudski, would presumably have been to discuss ways of aiding Jewish refugees and obtaining information about the spread of Fascism and Nazism.

Apart from this incident, life at the Casa Leone was an idyllic extension of the Melchetts' week-end house-parties in England. Facing them across the canal was Princess Aspasia's villa, 'The Garden of Eden', its luxuriant gardens bounded by the canal on one side and the lagoon on the other. When the Melchetts were in Venice, it was their second home. It had a swimming pool and a gondolier waiting to bring mutual friends including Augustus John and Cecil Beaton to the steps, and there was an assortment of boats, including the Melchetts' yacht, the *Peau Bruin* for picnics and parties by sunlight and moonlight. A fancy dress ball was held and Seago and three others, including the regal owner of 'The Garden of Eden', decided their costumes should be based on the appropriate story. Seago wrote to Delgado that, regretfully, he had been the Serpent but that he had consoled himself by clinging pretty tightly to the beautiful damsel dressed as the Tree of Knowledge.

In the end, despite the grandeur of Venice with its wealth of treasures, it was a party given by Princess Aspasia that was ultimately to inspire Seago to make a permanent escape from the circus. One of the guests was the dancer Serge Lifar, then Maître de Ballet at the Paris Opera and at midnight, when the party broke up, he and Seago and two others took a gondola to the Lido. Lifar drove them to a remote beach and on the fringe of the water in the light of a full Venetian moon, he removed his clothes and danced for them, half in and half out of the sea. It seemed as if he was improvising a solo and not until later did Seago learn the dance had been the evocative *Spectre de la Rose*. But at the time, the painter was only aware of the breathtaking effect of the light on Lifar's body made silver by the moonlight. Always it was the male body rather than the female that he wanted to paint. The memory haunted him and germinated and he once said that it was the motivation for his entire series of ballet pictures.

A few days after the party Seago wrote to Delgado to say his paintings had been nailed up in a coffin to send to England. 'I have completed twelve pictures,' he wrote, 'one of which is a perfectly foul portrait of seven people.' It was probably the rather pleasant impression of a breakfast party in the vine-covered loggia at 'The Garden of Eden'. A week after he left Venice he was back with the circus but from then on his circus interludes grew shorter and further apart although, for the Bakers, Ted Seago would always remain one of the family and wherever he made his home, they often turned up on his doorstep wanting a bed for a few nights.

The Venetian paintings formed the nucleus of his next summer's exhibition but before then a new health trouble caused Seago even more concern than his heart condition. It affected his right eye and was so uncannily similar to an accident which Munnings, in his memoirs, referred to as 'the setback which happened just before my twenty-first birthday' that it would be as impossible to ignore the psychosomatic implications as it would be to exclude them as a reason for Seago's heart condition.

A psychologist might suggest that, painting apart, Seago had once subconsciously sought to identify with Munnings as a father figure. Certainly at twenty-three, in painting terms, he badly needed to resolve his own identity and finally defy comparison with the older man. This was an impossibility in the confusion of the exciting environments where he was coping with the conflicting demands of a steady flow of commissions for equestrian portraits, the repercussions of the successful *Circus Company* and producing pictures for a new exhibition. In an effort to shelve the fundamental problem of self-identification, the depth of his involvement with Munnings could have manifested itself by a strange coincidence of comparable accidents.

The 'setback' Munnings referred to occurred when he was lifting a heavy hound puppy over a hurdle and a spray of thorns rebounded, struck him in the right eye, pierced the lens and blinded him in that eye for life. Seago was hunting at Brooke, two days after Christmas, 1933, and after an unspecified 'accident' suffered acute pain in his eye, temporary blindness, and was ordered to bed for a complete rest. At the time he was convinced that, like Munnings, he had permanently lost the sight of his right eye. In a letter of 14 January

1934, Priestman tried his best to console him by citing 'at least five artists who only have the use of one eye – and one more artist, Munnings, who looks as though he had only one' and he rated all these artists, he said, as far above the average and believed that none of them was worried by his loss.

The letter was preceded by a single page printed in large block capitals and headed 'Notice' which read: 'Please get someone to read this letter to you as I fear it is rather small writing and, at best, I fear, not easy to read.' Then followed many heavily-underlined enjoinders appealing to the invalid to be very careful with the good eye and allow plenty of time for it to get used to its extra work. 'Your work will not suffer for six months rest,' Priestman told him – not for the first time. 'You will go on thinking about things and when you take up your brush again, I feel quite sure you will find you have got ahead. (At least that was my own experience, after a lapse at other work for nearly a year.)'

Seago had defied the doctors before and at the end of January while still in bed and forbidden to paint he wrote to tell Delgado that he had had three heart turns since Christmas.

'The Doctors tell me that my mode of life is stupid and likely to hasten my end somewhat, to which I replied "Let it – it's damn good while it lasts." They suggest that all my energy should be left for mental strain and that I should have a man servant in tow to do all else for me!!! Did you ever hear such bunk – and how the struggling painter in his garret with a herring can manage to indulge in this I can't imagine, not unless something like the "loaves and the fishes" happens. Am now plotting to do a bit of dirty work; in other words am going to make a bolt for it although I'm not even allowed to walk upstairs.'

He bolted, apparently to the cottage at Melchet and for a time wore an eye patch and complained sarcastically that people would say that even in that respect he had copied Munnings. But significantly, although the sight returned to his right eye he insisted that it was always slightly impaired and years later often assured new friends that he was quite blind in the eye because, he said, it had been pierced by a thorn when he was out hunting.

Four weeks after the accident, he wrote to Delgado from Melchet inviting him down to stay for the week-end. He said, with only three weeks to go before the Private View of his exhibition and with twenty pictures short, he was feeling pretty fed up. 'I do them by the hour almost!' he wrote. 'Actually I shall now only be about ten pictures short. Have almost worn the hairs of my brushes away.'

There were exactly ten pictures fewer than usual in the Alpine Gallery when the exhibition opened there on 25 May for a month. Five canvases had been lent by the Melchett family and of the rest, among some fine equestrian studies, was one of Foxhunter, latest winner of the Ascot Gold Cup and an impressive portrait of Michael Hornby in pink coat and silk hat riding his magnificent horse over the Oxfordshire countryside.

There were only half a dozen circus studies one of which, a painting of a wagon trail reaching the crest of a hill, was bought by Ronald Horton for £20. It was one of his favourite pictures and reminded him of a horse-drawn wagon he had toured with on the rough roads of the Balkans with the Royal Italian Circus. It later appeared along with another picture in the exhibition, a sensitive drawing of a sad-eyed clown, in Seago's second book *Sons of Sawdust* which he dedicated to his mother. Another drawing of the same clown illustrated the epilogue in the book. It was a poignant study of a middle-aged man in bedraggled ruffles and conical hat and with an anxious, puzzled expression discernible under the grease paint. The caption read:

> 'Smile at us, pay us, pass us.
> But do not quite forget!'

With Seago's time in the sawdust ring running out, it was a fitting epitaph to his own life with the circus people.

———— VI ————

A Poet and the Ballet

Sons of Sawdust, a fictionalized account of Seago's travels with the circus in Ireland intermingled with stories 'Pop' Baker had told him, did not have the commercial success of *Circus Company*. But it was nevertheless a more maturely written book and among the congratulatory letters was one from the Poet Laureate which began with scrupulous politeness and ended with an imaginative suggestion that changed Seago's life. Masefield wrote:

'Dear Seago,
(perhaps we might drop some of the formalities, if you don't object) . . .
'I have been enjoying your Irish book and feel (from the illustrations) that you have an extraordinary feeling for landscape. Why not give up a year to wonderful English country life, shepherding on the downs, horse-training at Newmarket, ploughing in Sussex and in Berkshire, hopping in Kent and in the West, a horse-fair and cattle market, a harvest home and a fruit picking; with views of some of our valleys, White Horse, the Golden Valley, the Wye, the Severn and the Avon?
'Our greetings to you
John Masefield.'

Seago's reply was suitably formal.

'Dear Mr Masefield,
    'Thank you so very much for your letter and thank you also for dropping some of the formalities, I do so wish you would go further and use my Christian name . . .
    'Your suggestion for a year of Country Life appeals to me enormously. If I can manage to tide myself over for a month or so financially there is nothing I should like better. For the moment I have had to abandon the idea of joining the Circus and start on a set of illustrations instead – the life story of a poacher – it's a frightfully interesting book written by himself.*
    'We had a grand hunt with the Staghounds yesterday – a 17-mile point.
'Yours very sincerely,
Ted Seago.'

Almost by chance, it seemed, Masefield had hit on a way to channel Seago's abilities in a more appropriate direction, away from the circus, towards subjects so close to his own poet's heart and doggedly he pursued the idea.
    In the next letter he put a match to the fire when he wrote:

'Dear Ted,
(Many thanks).
    'I can't help thinking that you would do a very precious thing recording the great scenes of the English country, while the country remains.
    'Could you not do a portfolio of drawings reproduced in colour, with two big drawings in colour for each month.'

There followed a list of seasonal occupations and happenings in the country during four months which, he suggested, might be included along with studies of local characters – not forgetting 'gypsies and showmen'.
    The letter went on: 'Think how grateful we are to those who recorded so clearly and well the England of 100 years ago (the great

---

* *I Walked by Night* by Lilias Rider Haggard.

days of the colour prints) and how grateful people will be 100 years hence to you if you record this.'

It was an echo of the exuberant encouragement the writer had used in connection with *Circus Company* and Seago responded enthusiastically, although neither then nor in the future did he address the older man by his Christian name. Seago wrote:

'. . . Your idea appeals to me more and more.

'I was wondering if it might be done in book form? A sort of Parlour table album with all the pictures reproduced in colour, with a note about each one and a thumb-nail drawing on the opposite page. The notes could deal, not so much with the pictures, but with the scenes and characters depicted and the whole thing bound under the title you first mentioned A Year of English Country Life.

'The subjects you put down give tremendous scope – I love the idea of bell ringers in the tower – and lambing on the downs, timber hauling, ploughing, etc., are all things I feel I could get to the heart of. And then there is Barnet Horse Fair and Derby Day on the Downs and Michaelmas Sales on the Norfolk farms – and even the travelling circus – and the wild fowler on the mud flats – Hundreds of things! It is most awfully good of you to take all this trouble. What do you think of the book idea? I ought to be able to do two a month in between commissions.'

'I had an album in mind,' Masefield replied. 'A good big one.' A poet, sensitive to moods and undertones, had succeeded where Priestman and to some extent Melchett, had failed by offering the painter an irresistible and logical progression from his over-long preoccupation with the circus. It would be presumptuous to suggest that it was a deliberate intrusion on Masefield's part to wean Seago away from the circus or that, initially, he saw himself in the role of collaborator in the album but by early August, judging from Seago's letters, the Poet Laureate had agreed to write a text to accompany the pictures.

They worked on the book for a year; Masefield suggested subjects and places in England where Seago might find inspiration such as Thame Fair and the Morris Dancers at Bampton.

'The Bampton dance is on Whit Monday,' he wrote. 'They dance all day and most of the night. If you go early, you will see the cake carried on the sword and the great demijohn of wine. It is wise to go fairly early, for later in the day the dance becomes a bit ragged owing to the demijohn.'

Seago's painting of six white-clad dancers, performing with precision before a well-mannered crowd in Bampton village square, showed that he had gone there very early.

'When I was a boy,' Masefield wrote, 'the last wagons from the corn-fields used to be crowded with men, women and children who sang as the last stooks came home. The women used to plait crowns of wheat, cornflowers, poppies, etc., and looked lovely. Men in those days still wore smocks. Could you get this?'

Apparently, Seago could not.

'Bread is an important matter,' the poet wrote, 'so I suggest we do Ploughing, Sowing, Harrowing, Rook scaring, Reaping, Carting, Threshing, Grinding, Baking and Eating. Ten out of bread alone.'

They settled for three.

Seago painted scenes he loved in Norfolk and pictures of gypsies and circus elephants and hounds in the snow and sent photographs of his pictures to Masefield who invariably produced verses to match – however short – while the longest poem 'A Midwife's Story', a whimsical tale of how a village lad was delivered of a swallowed frog, involved Seago meeting the elderly midwife who had inspired the poem and painting her portrait to illustrate it.

While working on the book Seago divided his time between Brooke and Melchet Court and fulfilled a steady flow of commissions, although his work was constantly interrupted by heart turns which confined him to bed for days and often weeks at a time.

'I have really had a most annoying winter,' he wrote to Masefield, early in '36, 'I'm still under the doctor and have to have treatment every day. But I've been able to work most of the time although only at home, of course. In December I had a wonderful piece of good fortune. A family of ten Rumanian gypsies passed through Norfolk. I have been able to get a meadow for them to camp on and I think they are the finest models I have had. They are the most marvellous people to look at and have such a grand sense of colour: dressing themselves in the most gaudy hues and yet they never seem to clash. Have done three large canvases of them and I now want to start one of the gypsy man and his hurdy-gurdy and monkey which they dress in scarlet trousers! I'm hoping you will pick one of the pictures for the book because a gypsy subject or two would be all very much a part of Country life, wouldn't it – or do you think they would not be English enough?'

Masefield obviously thought the Rumanians qualified, as evidenced by the painting 'Woodsmoke' in the book showing a group of gypsies huddled round a fire in front of their wagon in the corner of a snow-covered field – a picture matched by a five-line verse 'The Gypsies in the Snow'.

The Masefield–Seago working relationship was a joyous, unselfish one punctuated by social visits to each other's homes. Eventually, there was too much material and, during the process of elimination, they showed a scrupulous deference to each other's wishes. 'I would like to keep the wherry,' Masefield wrote, 'as water-carriage is a big feature of English life. However, if you would like the wherry away, why wherry well.'

The wherry stayed – a picture of a pair of black-sailed barges on a Norfolk waterway, matched by a vigorous eight-line poem. Masefield meanwhile submitted a list of possible titles for the book, including:

'The Things that Pass and Abide'
'Scenes and People'
'The Old Things With us'
'Studies of English Country Life'

In the end he preferred both of Seago's two suggestions, *The*

Country Scene or *The Changing Year*, and the former was the title chosen for the book which was published a year later and not only marked Seago's permanent break with the circus but brought him international recognition. It was published by Collins because by then Delgado had moved there from Putnam and Seago went with him.

In 1934 Seago's letters to Delgado indicate that he was also involved in trying to get a visa for Russia ostensibly to see a Russian circus but probably to embark on a little espionage work of his own, if only to the extent of applying his photographic memory for potentially useful military information. 'Secret business' was a phrase Delgado recalls him using in connection with his journeys abroad at that time. This action had probably been inspired by his thrilling unofficial flight to Austria with Melchett, and by Horton's undercover activities.

Moreover, it was in character for Seago to try and prove over and over again that whatever shortcomings he had, a lack of courage was not one of them. When he failed to get a visa and the Russian trip fell through, he wrote to tell Delgado that he was off to France for 'a *short* time' with a circus. He gave no motive for the trip and it was about then that his brother John recalls hearing him talk about experiments with infra-red paint, so it seems likely that was when he made diagrams of military objectives on the Continent and over-painted them with conventional circus pictures or landscapes. Moreover, subscribing to this supposition was the absence of any circus paintings to commemorate the French trip in his London exhibition the following year.

In 1937 at the time of the Coronation of King George VI, Seago rode a splendid sand-coloured Arab stallion and represented St George of England in a great commemorative carnival procession through the streets of Norwich. The mile and a half long parade of decorated floats and lorries and carts, some drawn by shire horses from Brian Seago's firm, had been organized by the coal merchant and represented every branch of local industry and social activity and included contingents from all the armed forces. At the head of it all, wearing a suit of chain mail with a crimson cross emblazoned on his white cloak rode the organizer's son, not on a docile horse from the local riding school, but thanks to the timely arrival in

Norwich of Bertram Mills' Circus, on a more worthy animal borrowed from his showmen friends, which tossed its head and foamed at the mouth and apparently required considerable ability to handle. As he controlled it with enviable nonchalance and rode to the music of the brass bands, Seago could have pictured himself in a circus procession sweeping into the ring at Olympia. This time the three Baker brothers were in the crowd, cheering him on as he made what amounted to his grand exit from their world.

His final tribute to the circus, his third book *Caravan*, was published the same year and was dedicated to Alan Delgado. It was a collection of pencil sketches and crayon drawings of gypsies and travelling showmen with a brief text in which Seago reiterated his admiration and sympathy with 'the wandering folk, educated not with books but by the hard experience of life . . . The moors and vales are their estate,' he wrote, 'and their wayside is their garden. Their independence is something to be envied; their courage and determination something to be admired.'

It was the first time he had written objectively about the world he had once belonged to and the drawings, fresh and spontaneous, reiterated his affection and understanding. Some were original sketches for early circus paintings but they showed a greater sincerity and assurance than many of the canvases subsequently derived from them in the after-thought of the studio and they gave the lie to critics who'd said that he could not draw. There were more immediate comparisons between pencil and brush in the sketches of the hurdy-gurdy man with his monkey, the dark-skinned children, the proud, flashing-eyed men and patient women which gave a more evocative impression of the Rumanian visitors to Norfolk than the oil paintings reproduced in *The Country Scene* or a similar portrait shown in the exhibition at the Alpine Galleries in London (an exhibition opened by Lord Melchett and which was memorable, according to the *Eastern Daily Press*, primarily for the number of Melchett portraits).

Caravan was greeted with universal approval. 'When he draws a horse you hear its hoofs stamp on the page,' commented the *Daily Telegraph*. 'His circus sketches are almost as authentic as the wind and the rain,' wrote the critic from the *Daily Herald*. The illustrations were also more impressive than those for *The Country Scene* shown in a London exhibition at the Sporting Gallery to coincide with the book's English publication and which also included Norfolk scenes, some fine equestrian studies and a clever portrait of Mr Ralph Lynn, the actor, in which the London *Evening Standard* noted a change in Mr Seago's technique by eliminating all except the essential characteristics of his subject. Once again there was the inevitable comparison with Munnings in connection with a portrait of a stallion owned by the Earl of Durham.

The modest press coverage of the exhibition was almost obliterated by the critical acclaim which greeted *The Country Scene*, the handsome quarto volume which represented, as a discerning critic from the *Spectator* noted, 'a surprisingly happy partnership of poet and painter'. The working relationship had been too happy a one to be impaired by occasional outspoken criticism of the forty-two pictures of which all but sixteen had been painted especially for the book. One critic referred to them as 'the perishable stuff of art' but outweighing such a remark was a plethora of congratulations spiced with attempts to pinpoint the influence of Constable and Claude in the landscapes (*The Field*), Henry Bright (*Times Literary Supplement*), De Wint and, for good measure, Whistler and the French Impressionists (the *Scotsman*). The *Eastern Daily Press*, local pride stirred, selected half a dozen seascapes and landscapes, of which their first choice was 'The Landmark' and prophesied these seemed to promise Seago a leading place among the modern artistic successors of the Norwich School. A discordant note was a scathing comment from the *New Statesman* whose critic wrote of 'the vulgar slickness of paintings in the much beloved Munningsy Royal Academic manner, painfully out of keeping with Mr Masefield's honest Muse'.

'The Landmark' was reproduced by most of the press. It was a vigorous marshland scene at Blakeney, full of a south-east gale, showing a man ploughing under a threatening sky with a windmill in the background. A flight of gulls wheeling behind the plough, gave recession to the whole picture which had been painted on three-ply wood from the top of a packing case. Although some years later the picture was rejected by the Academy it had by then become, through a miscalculation on the part of the lady who first bought it, probably the painter's best-known work. The purchaser had intended to fit the picture into the panelling over her drawing-room fireplace but it proved too large and was resold to the Medici Society who reproduced it commercially. Down the years, 'The Landmark' found its way into countless homes as the first of their many successful reproductions of Seago's work and eventually the original was acquired by Ronald Horton.

Despite the picture's immediate popularity, Seago was not ready to concentrate on landscape as an expression of his fundamental pre-occupation with the portrayal of light and atmosphere while, at the same time, he was desperately anxious to discard the label of 'horse painter'. His increasing dissatisfaction with the ever-growing list of money-spinning equestrian portraits was apparent in letters to Delgado. 'The picture I have been working on here I have now decided is B . . . . . . Y,' he wrote from one stately home. 'My first action on rising from my bed of sickness will be to destroy it. Actually, quite a normal turn of events for my portraits.' The boredom was again apparent in a letter written from the Midlands where, while engaged on a portrait of a horse and rider, he was asked by the local hunt committee for a drawing to auction at their Hunt Ball.

'My sense of humour so far misled me as to think it amusing to draw a funny picture of their very fat hunt secretary upside down in a bramble bush – a situation in which he had recently been,' he wrote to Delgado. 'I did the drawing and, to my mind it was very funny – the thorns were *very* large, the man *very* fat and it was like him. His name being West, my ardour so far carried me away as to write "Gone West" underneath. It went to the ball, so did I. I was lucky enough to escape with my life!'

It seemed that once again his penchant for exploiting the ridiculous in other people – possibly to contribute to his own sense of security – had gone too far because the auction was cancelled, the hunt secretary resigned, the hunt took sides and the picture ended up in a lawyer's office. Its creator left that particular area of hunt country, so he wrote, with considerable relief.

Before long, however, the barbed sense of humour was channelled into a more lucrative outlet, in the pages of *Punch* where his occasional cartoons of the hunting and shooting set invariably showed them in disadvantageous positions with the country folk. A typical example was a drawing of a young lady picnicking with her well-dressed friends near her chauffeur-driven Rolls-Royce. As a wagon-load of gypsies ambled past she explained, 'Of course, *that's* my idea of life.' There was also the picture of a liveried chauffeur holding open the door of a large limousine for his portly master in full hunting kit and reminding him, 'You've forgotten your trumpet, my Lord.' Many of the ideas for caricatures came from Lord Melchett, by then Master of the Tedworth Hounds. Always eager to encourage his protegé he frequently began a letter to Seago with the triumphant announcement: 'Another for *Punch*' and went on to relate an amusing incident.

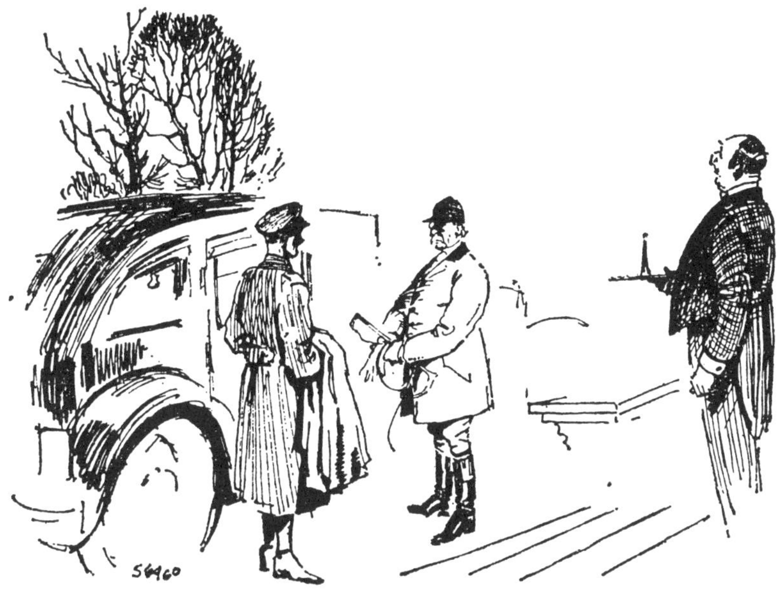

" You've forgotten your trumpet, my Lord."

Through such excursions into print, royalties from reproductions of his paintings, portraits and illustrations for magazines and books, Seago hoped to be able to manage without the commissions for equestrian paintings and was heard to vow that he would never paint another horse. At the same time, as his latest exhibition had shown, he no longer looked to the circus for inspiration but with the memory of a night in Venice and Lifar dancing on the sea-shore, he turned to Degas rather than to any of the painters to which the critics had compared him. He went to the ballet and discussed it with Masefield in terms of poems and pictures as a possible subject for a sequel to *The Country Scene*. Masefield, a staunch balletomane, was enthusiastic.

Aesthetically the ballet, for Seago, was merely a logical progression from the circus for it offered all the colour, light, movement and a world of make-believe. Off-stage it provided an antidote to loneliness in the opportunity of belonging to an unconventional élite – a substitute family to which it was by no means as difficult to gain admittance as it had been to his less sophisticated but closer-knit family of the circus.

He rented a room in Sidney Street, London, from a Mrs Moneypenny, a kindly landlady who was willing to provide beds for the Baker boys whenever they turned up. Nearly every night Seago went to the ballet at Sadler's Wells and Covent Garden. He saw the performances from the front of the house, well to the right, which afforded him a three-quarter view of the theatre taking in part of the wings and orchestra as well as the stage and giving the fullest dimension to the light and movement he longed to portray. During the day he watched rehearsals from the wings and sketched at the regular morning classes attended by even the leading dancers.

Within a few weeks many of the principal dancers were his friends and his brother recalls the evening when they both drove to an East End theatre with Anton Dolin who was dancing *David* there. Before the performance they dined in a Jewish restaurant where the waitresses apologized for being unable to serve them with bread because it was the week of the Passover when only unleaven cake could be eaten. They were delighted; there could have been no more appropriate introduction to the biblical ballet and Seago commemorated it by a movingly-simple study of Dolin caught in the moment of grandeur at his first entrance.

Dolin was impressed by Seago's work and introduced him to his friends. As well as ballet people Seago met the nightclub entertainer Marc Antony who kept open house for any impecunious young actor who needed a sympathetic ear and endless cups of tea. Antony had a fund of stories of the Edwardian music hall. Seago met the writer Beverley Nichols and the dancer Freddie Franklin, the son of a Liverpool butcher and a few years Seago's junior, who for a time became his close friend.

John Seago had by this time abandoned the idea of entering the Church in favour of film production and was in his element among his brother's new friends although he could not cope with the perpetual late nights in Dolin's Glebe Street studio. While the dancer was on tour abroad he lent the studio to Seago who thrived on a theatrical life such as he had already glimpsed in his Maddermarket days in Norwich. Parties began at midnight and lasted until dawn as the dancers and actors, fortified with tea and wine, entertained each other by re-enacting incidents from their working day, imitating, recounting stories and adding embellishments. It was a world Gwen Melchett had once loved and Seago took her to a party at Dolin's studio where she wore a grey floating gown, her long fingernails silvered to match, and executed an extempore dance with skilful grace and charm which drew applause from everyone.

Once again, through painting, Seago found himself in a new and exciting world. He painted a dramatic portrait of the Indian dancer, Uday Shankar, in a jewelled helmet, his bare skin gleaming through a shining breast plate, poised in a moment of the dance. It was the complete personification of the painter's new interest. 'It is strong in colouring, but I like it so,' the painter wrote in his diary. He admitted on the next page that an equestrian portrait he could hardly have declined because it had been commissioned by the West Norfolk hunt, was giving him as much enjoyment as any portrait he had ever done. 'I feel I have learnt something in painting it,' he wrote. 'I am pleased with the tone and composition. The portrait of horse and rider are certainly very like but the handling of the paint is still far from sure. In this my progress is much slower than I could wish.'

There could have been no greater contrast in two portraits; the impression of an Eastern dancer and the immaculate study of the pink-coated huntmaster, Colonel Oliver Birkbeck, riding to hounds on a winter's day in Norfolk. The two paintings represented a dual pull in Seago's life between the country scenes he had loved as a boy and – instead of the circus – the cosmopolitan glamour of the world of ballet.

Because of the demands of the ballet book he was planning with Masefield he postponed a visit to Scotland to paint a portrait of the

Duke and Duchess of Buccleuch. Meanwhile Freddie Franklin stayed at Brooke and Seago made studies of him and discussed the book. Later a friend, John Sayer, flew him to Masefield's home for further discussion. They flew from Norfolk intending to land at an aerodrome near Cirencester where the poet was living, but as the aerodrome had been turned into a poultry farm the previous year, they had to land on a golf course.

Both Masefield and Seago had arranged to visit Monte Carlo in the spring to study Massine's company. Meanwhile, Seago would make studies of the Vic Wells Company in London; Masefield had already started on the poems. 'Am more than delighted with the work that Masefield has already written,' Seago wrote in his diary in early February after a second visit to the poet's home. 'It has the whole essence of this subject, to my mind his poem to Fokine is particularly fine. He in turn was very pleased with my portrait of Uday Shankar which I took to show him. We had a long business chat that evening and then a game of bridge . . .'

During the following weeks Seago divided his time and energy between London and Norfolk. He sketched from the wings of Sadler's Wells but was in Norfolk after the February gales when the sea broke through at several places. He and John walked along the beach and he made a new study of Blakeney Mill where, he wrote, he had seldom been so cold and he could only just begin to feel his fingers when he arrived home for a late tea and a game of rummy.

He had an exciting aerial view of the floods from John Sayer's little plane in which they looped the loop twice over the house of Sayer's girl friend, 'to express our goodwill', Seago recorded in his diary and added:

'We flew all along the beach from Winterton to Horsey at 120 m.p.h. and only about 12 feet from the ground: A grand sensation, but rather bumpy owing to the undercurrents from the sandhills. We did the same thing over the floods and in so doing put up a flight of mallard. We circled and gave chase. They must fly the deuce of a rate because it was some time before we could overtake them. When we did, one old drake caught the current from the plane and for a moment went backwards. I have never seen such an expression of rank indignation which he gave us!'

A week later he and John visited the floods again and took a motor boat across Horsey Mere to the old water mill which was completely surrounded by the flood water. 'It really looked rather pitiful whirling its sails around in a vain effort to rid itself of the ocean encroaching it on all sides,' Seago wrote. He felt it deserved a picture and they purloined a rowing boat, punted across submerged marshes and moored to a gatepost from where Seago made his picture just as the sun was setting behind the old mill.

Between the two visits to the floods he had consolidated his position in London. Dolin was in Paris enjoying a tremendous success, and he wrote to suggest that Seago should stop there on his way to Monte Carlo to paint him in his *Giselle* costume as proposed for the book. Lifar and the much-loved Spanish dancer, Argentinita, were also there and willing to be painted. Before leaving England Seago moved out of Dolin's studio. It would be some time before he needed a base in London again but within days of the move he was offered a tiny corner house in his favourite part of London; an old pub just fifty yards from the river in Lawrence Street, Chelsea, which he found irresistible. 'It is a pity so many things come at once and that I have to go away just now,' he wrote in the diary where he also mentioned that as well as a studio, he had acquired a new secretary, John Gregory.

Gregory at twenty-four was trying to make his way on the stage and had worked at the Maddermarket Theatre as secretary to Nugent Monck for ten shillings a week, with the opportunity to act and learn everything he could about the theatre. At the Maddermarket he got to know John Seago who sometimes took him up to London in his Austin Seven. There he hoped to make some useful contacts in the film studios where John was working. Meanwhile John introduced Gregory to his brother.

At first Gregory resisted the suggestion that he should become secretary to the painter who in Norwich and particularly around the Maddermarket Theatre was already something of a legend. The younger man was puritanically unsophisticated and, despite his longing to make his way in the theatre, was suspicious of the motive behind Seago's offer of £2 a week for keeping accounts, taking a few letters and generally making himself useful. However, a visit to Brooke Lodge reassured him. He was charmed by Mrs Seago, impressed by the circus pictures and excited at the prospect of mixing in the entertainment world. Moreover, it was understood that he would not be expected to share a bedroom and his six months' contract stated 'acting in part time to be an agreed concession, to be fitted in as far as possible to the convenience of both parties'.

For the first few weeks in London he and Seago met decorators and electricians in the new studio, pickled furniture with caustic soda, arranged the trip to Paris and Monte Carlo, and most evenings went to a theatre. Seago was to be away in France for six weeks during which time Gregory would supervise the decoration of the studio and learn to drive his employer's long, low German sports car.

Masefield, who had spent a fortnight in Monte Carlo in February, had written to suggest three young ballerinas he felt should 'be joined to the book in some way' – Danilova, Maria Zarina and 'a charming danseuse' Nina Stroganova. 'I do especially long for you to do her for the book,' he wrote and advised Seago to delay his visit to France until the ballet season began in April so as to avoid the 'frightful strain of rehearsals' and see the perfected ballets as well as some of the rehearsals. Seago agreed to all suggestions.

It was April when he arrived in Paris en route for Monte Carlo. Dolin had found him a studio in his own apartment block where Seago painted him for the book wearing his famous *Espagnol* costume. He also did a portrait of Lifar as Alexander the Great. But he confessed in his diary that he was already depressed about his work with the ballet. 'There is so much to do and much of it has to be done from memory. It is all extremely difficult,' he wrote.

He also found there was much to do apart from painting, for the social life surrounding the ballet involved him in dinner and supper parties that lasted until dawn where 'Art' was an eternal topic of conversation. 'I maintained that one can no longer judge upon knowledge but only on one's own feelings upon the subject,' he commented in his diary. But he did not feel the same involvement with the ballet as he had with the circus and he never apparently considered that this might be the reason for his depression about the paintings he was doing. Then, on the sixth day in Paris he made one of the finest sketches for the book.

Dolin had gone to endless trouble to arrange for him to meet the

Russian prima ballerina, Olga Spessivtseva who, in private life, was already manifesting some of the symptoms she portrayed on stage in her supreme interpretation of the mad scene in *Giselle*. The great dancer was in bed when they arrived, but Dolin helped her to get up, dressed her in her *Giselle* costume and persuaded her to put on her ballet shoes and demonstrate her points. '. . . The most remarkable foot I have ever seen,' Seago wrote in his diary. 'She says she never dances now and that it hurts to stand on her points but the resin board stood in the corner of the studio and her feet seemed so supple that I think she must dance more than she says!'

He made a crayon study of the foot and a sad, haunting drawing of her head. 'A really beautiful face still,' he wrote, 'in fact I think it always will be. I have rarely seen such large eyes or more expressive ones. I was sorry they were so sad and to find her as she was. The laugh is odd and rather wild and she has to be humoured in a childish way which is sad to watch. Pat [Dolin] I thought was marvellous with her. He sat on the floor at her feet so that she was looking down at him which was a lovely pose. I was so very glad to meet her.'

Seago's emotional reaction to a real-life situation resulted in a drawing that fully justified his stay in Paris and its mood was echoed by Masefield in a romantic four-verse poem 'The Lovely Swan'. At the end of the week Mabel Seago and her sister arrived and they all three left for Monte Carlo where Freddie Franklin was at the station to meet them. That evening Markova joined Seago and Franklin for supper. 'We talked ourselves more or less silly and should have gone to bed before 1.00 a.m.,' the painter recorded in his diary. 'I want to paint Markova in "Sylphides" and she wants me to paint her in "Giselle" – I dare say she will win!' But he was the victor for he had already found his *Giselle* for the book.

He painted for most of the day. His studio, over a pastry shop, had a large window with a balcony and a view of an old wall covered with wisteria in full bloom and a distant glimpse of the sea. His mother and aunt, established nearby in a small hotel, were having the holiday of their lives. The Melchetts were living aboard their yacht anchored at Cap Martin and invariably included him in their social arrangements. In the evening he was at the theatre to see the ballet, and afterwards joined some of the dancers for supper. Once again his talent had precipitated him into an intoxicating social life which, nevertheless, was not necessarily conducive to painting and he was increasingly dissatisfied about his work.

'It depresses me frightfully,' he wrote in the diary, 'and yet there seems so little I can do about it. The difficulties are almost insurmountable with this subject, apart from the ordinary problem which a painter has to contend with. I console myself by the assurance that this work is an artist's impression of another art and should not be regarded in any other way, but I don't find it very comforting. I am very well aware of the shortcomings and can see so few virtues to counteract them. The more I see of the ballet the more I long to paint it and the more futile my efforts appear. Today, I felt more than half inclined to put my foot through the lot. Even now I think I should have been wiser to have done so ... It all seems so pointless and my own pleasure in painting is almost entirely drowned by the despair which accompanies it and the gnawing worry of the practical sides of life which I sometimes feel I just cannot cope with.'

To add to his depression he learned that his painting of horses in the flood at Horsey Mere had been rejected by the Academy. 'I am conceited enough to feel it rather a lot and am very disappointed,' he confessed.

Even at the ballet he could not escape his depression. 'As always when I see "Petrouchka", I was deeply depressed,' he wrote. 'I think it is the finest of all ballets and Massine was absolutely masterly. I ached for the soul of the doll and it was really amazing how he can dance that part with all the agony of the human and yet never break the illusion of the puppet ...'

Perhaps because as he admitted, he had been moved to depression until he 'ached for the soul of the doll', Seago's painting of a scene from *Petrouchka* was the only ballet picture he accepted gave him real satisfaction. It merited a prominent place in the book and was bought there and then by Melchett who paid for it after a profound lunch-time discussion about poetry and their own lives and ambitions. According to a third party at the lunch, Melchett took the opportunity to express the view that matrimony was a more serious business for the artist than for the ordinary man because domestic cares and the responsibilities of providing for a family might constrain his talent by tempting him to work for financial return. Afterwards, in his diary, Seago interpreted the generalization more categorically, in line with a tendency he showed at times as a truly creative writer, to use poetic licence to formulate his own biography.

'Henry maintained that no artist should marry,' he wrote. 'I hesitated to agree. It was a sweeping statement which seemed too drastic, cutting off all the joys of married life from the artist; mainly children. Henry replied that one cannot have one's cake and eat it and that an artist must not expect to get off easily for the blessings of his life.' It was a more acceptable interpretation of Mabel Seago's prophecy that her son would never marry because he was irrevocably wedded to his painting.

Consistently Seago was his own sternest critic and, three days before he packed his canvases, he wrote in the diary, 'I feel that I am only now starting and all the work in the future may be better. However, I think, actually, I have made the most of my time and I'm lucky to have been able to work here at all.' On his last day in Monte Carlo he called on Markova to say goodbye and found her resting in her room. 'I thought she looked small and attractive, lying on the bed,' he wrote, 'the yellow cover thrown back and the room a mass of flowers. All along the top of one of the travelling trunks was a row of ballet shoes, their pale ribbons hanging down . . .'

It was the stuff of ballet, a Degas pose, which Seago captured in a sentence but which so often eluded him on canvas in his brave attempts at literal transcriptions of the ballet in action. Nevertheless, in 1938 *Tribute to Ballet* made its impact and was recognized by the public and the critics as a handsome recognition by two arts of a third one, rather than as an example of poetry and painting. At the same time it represented the beginning and the end of Seago's short-lived ballet period.

There had been one minor difference of opinion between its collaborators and this had concerned the Ballet Joos's famous ballet *The Green Table* which Masefield disliked on the grounds that propaganda should not be brought into the sphere of ballet. Seago disagreed because he felt that art in any form, properly used in all sincerity, should be added to any cause if it helped to restore the balance of a tottering civilization. A scene from *The Green Table* was included in the book but unlike most of the illustrations, beginning with the frontispiece portrait of Fokine (to whom the book was dedicated) it was without a complementary poem by Masefield to match it. On the other hand the last verse of the dedicatory poem spoke for both poet and painter:

'We are not dancers, and we know no more
Of Ballet and the Dance than watchers know
Of horses that at gallop scatter by
Tossing the cutted hoof-casts at the sky,
Ears pointed and eyes burning as they go;
Or the ships that at an anchor lie,
Or pass into dim distance from the shore.
But as those watchers may, we, too, perceive
Something of this third beauty, and are glad
To thank some of its makers as we may . . .'

But Seago had watched and painted the worlds of make-believe for long enough and in the year *Tribute to Ballet* was published, he made two journeys abroad which at last persuaded him to concentrate his talent on portraying life's realities.

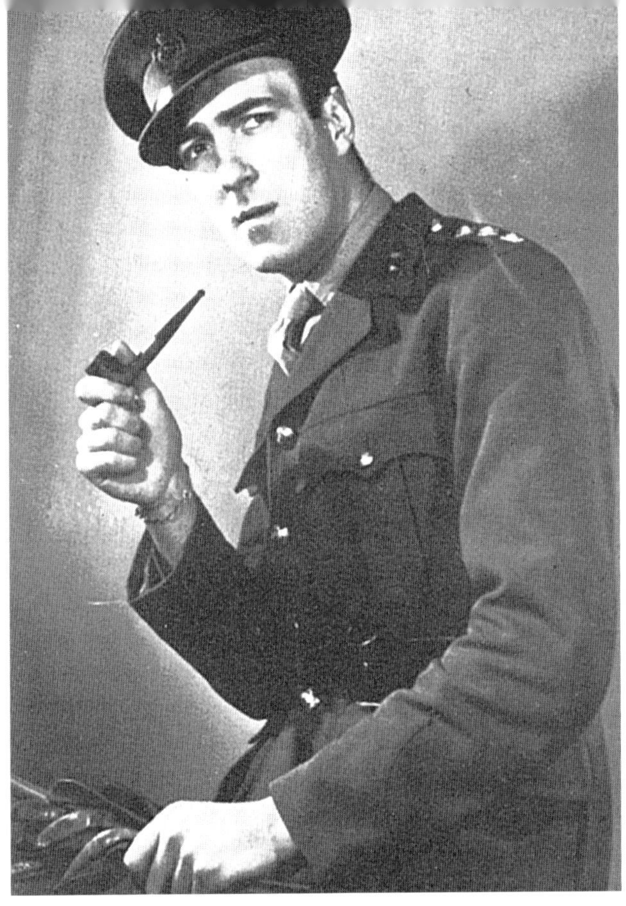

1. Edward Seago

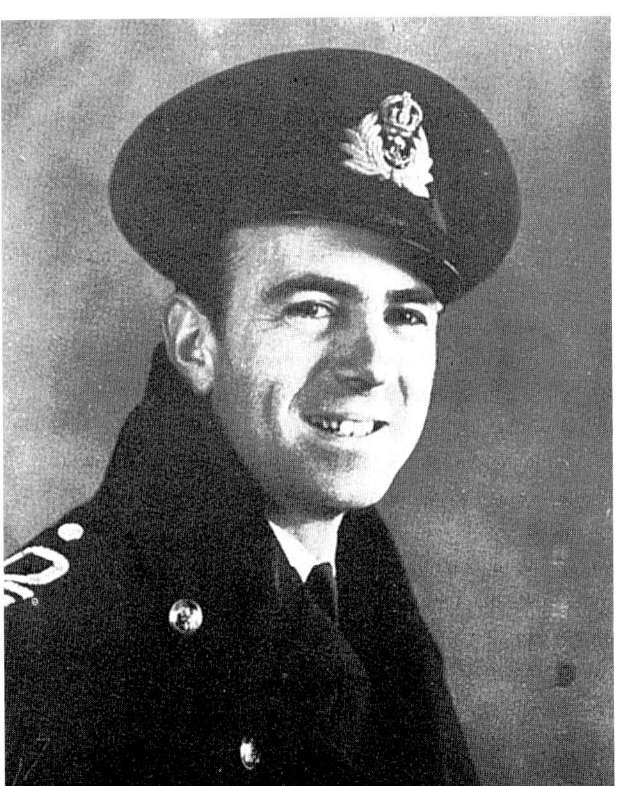

2. John Seago

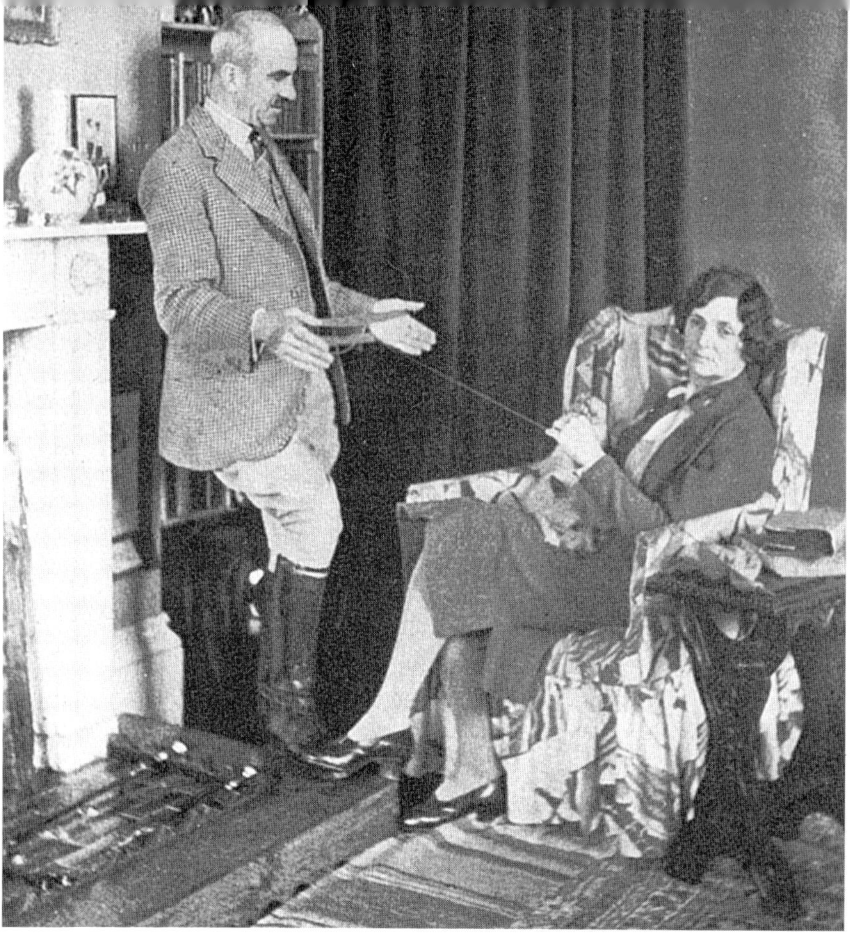

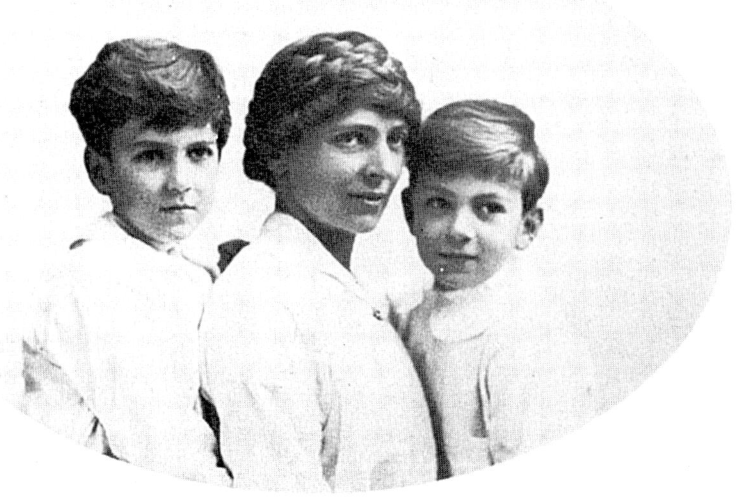

3. Brian and Mabel Seago

4. Mabel with Edward (left) and John

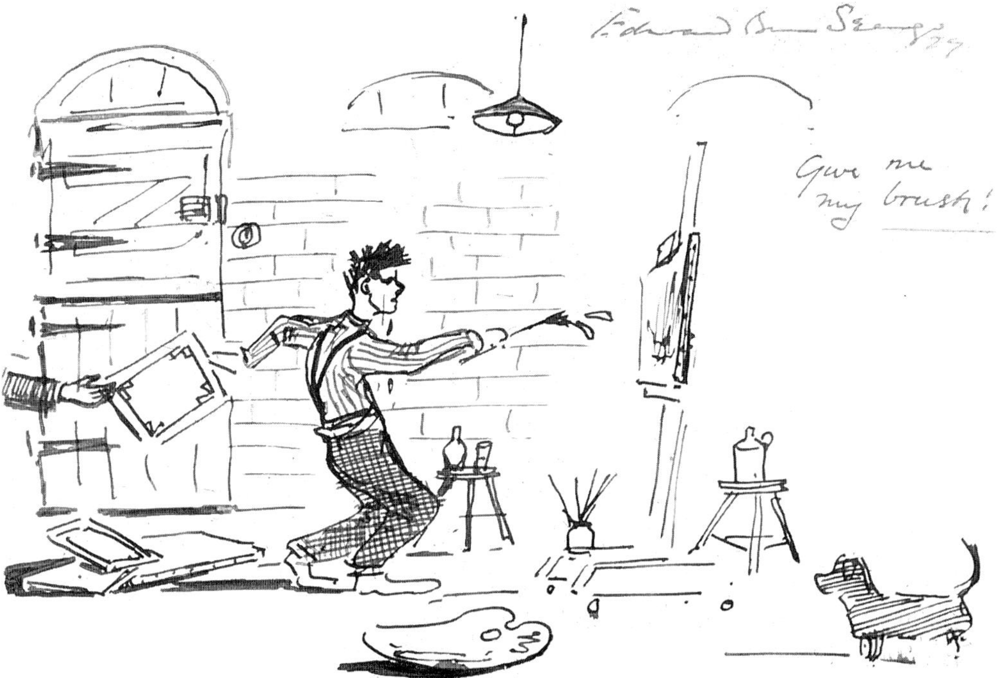

5. After a very successful (and profitable) exhibition:
A cartoon sent to brother John showing Edward painting with one hand
whilst passing finished canvasses out the door with the other.

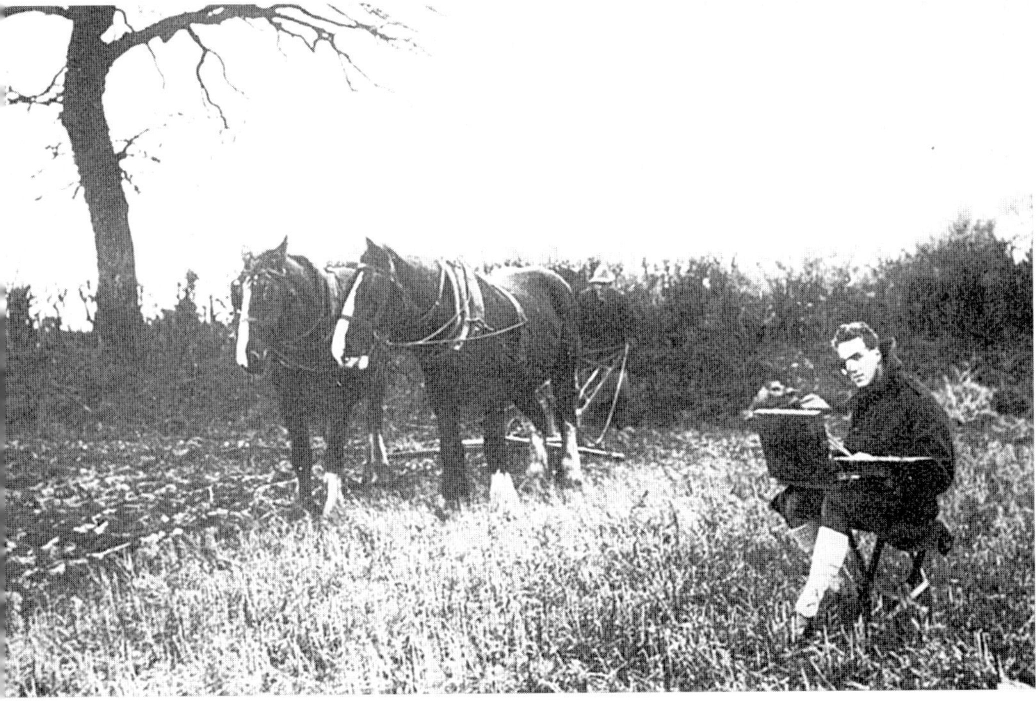

6. The artist photographed (with black eye patch) painting horses

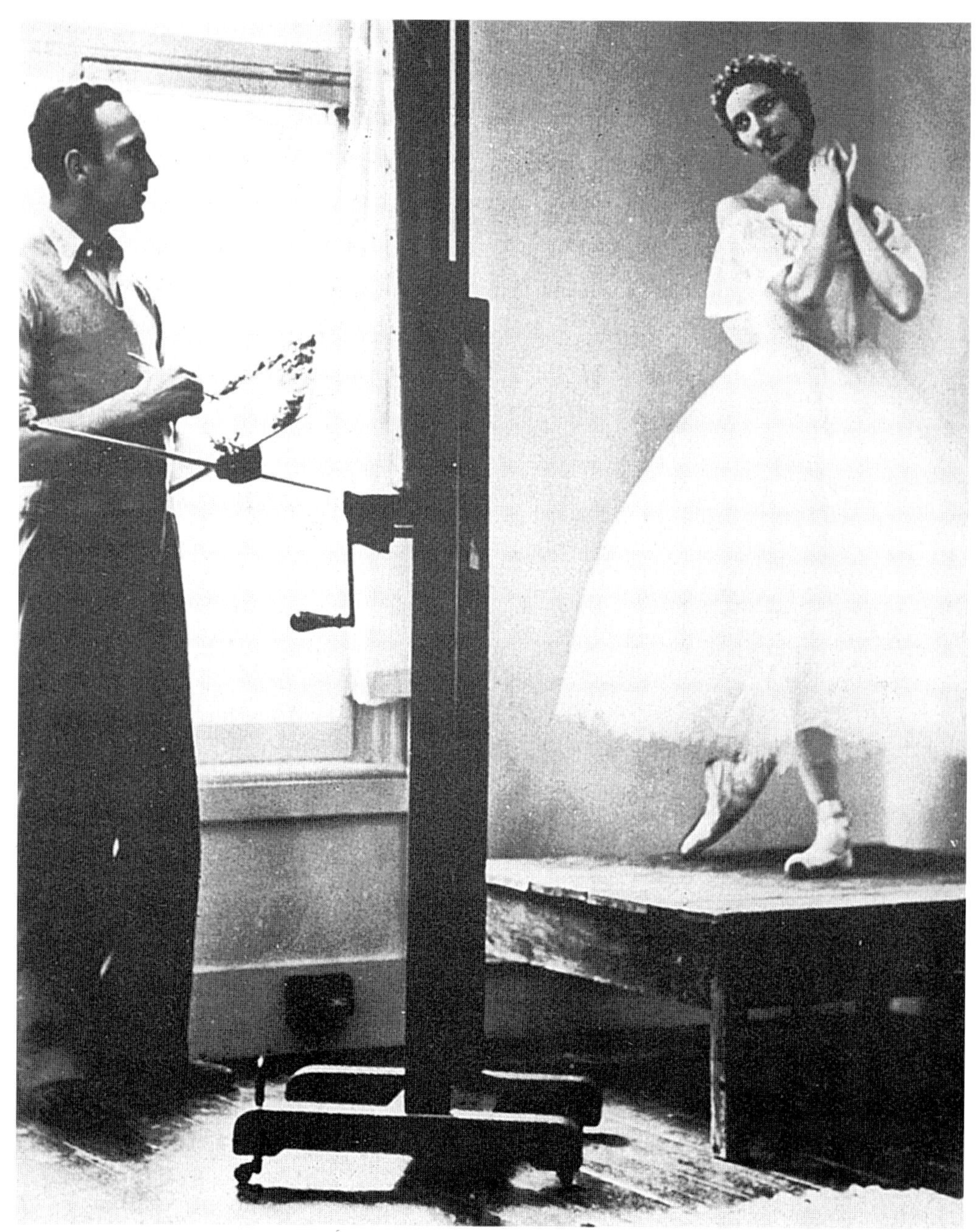

7. Seago painting Alicia Markova

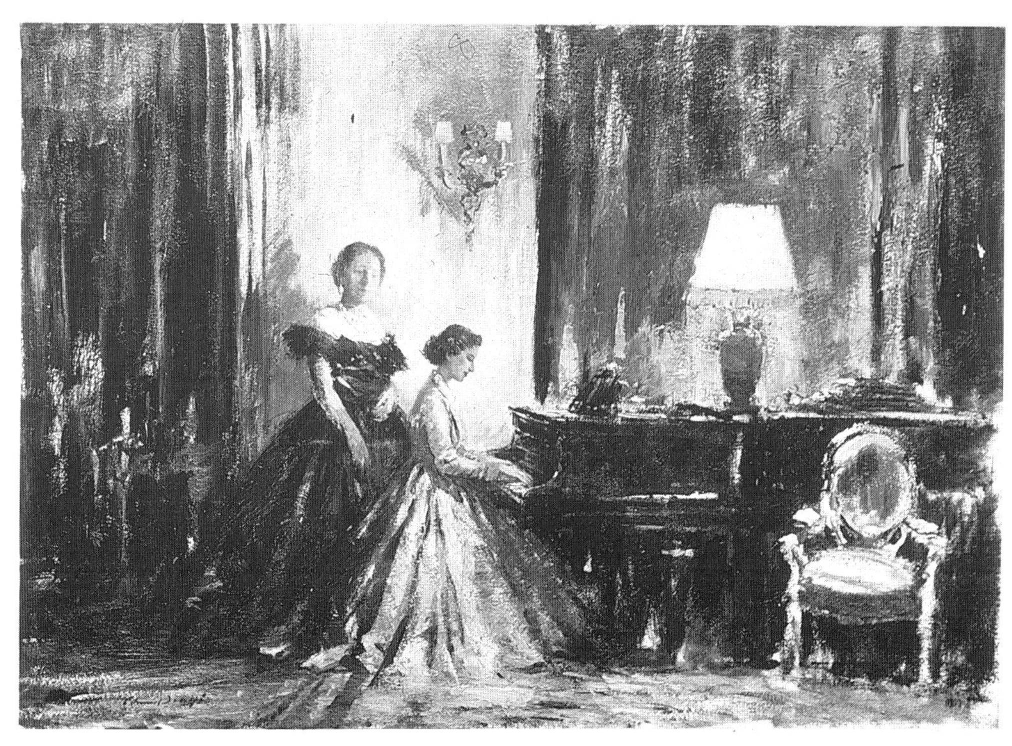

8. Conversation Piece, Sandringham

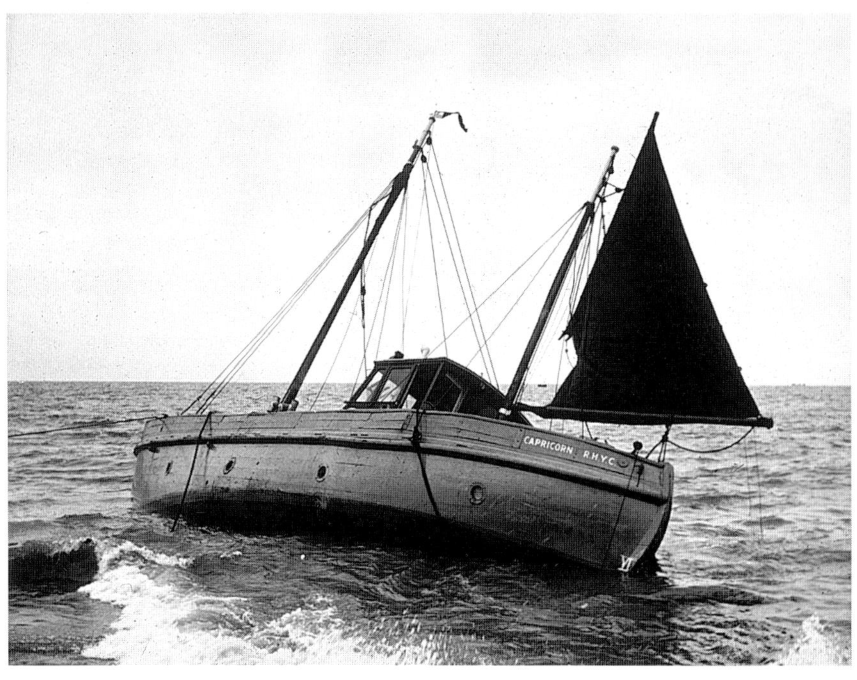

9. His boat, *Capricorn*, capsized after hitting a buoy out of Great Yarmouth. His quote in the next day's paper was 'Little buoys should be seen and not hit'.

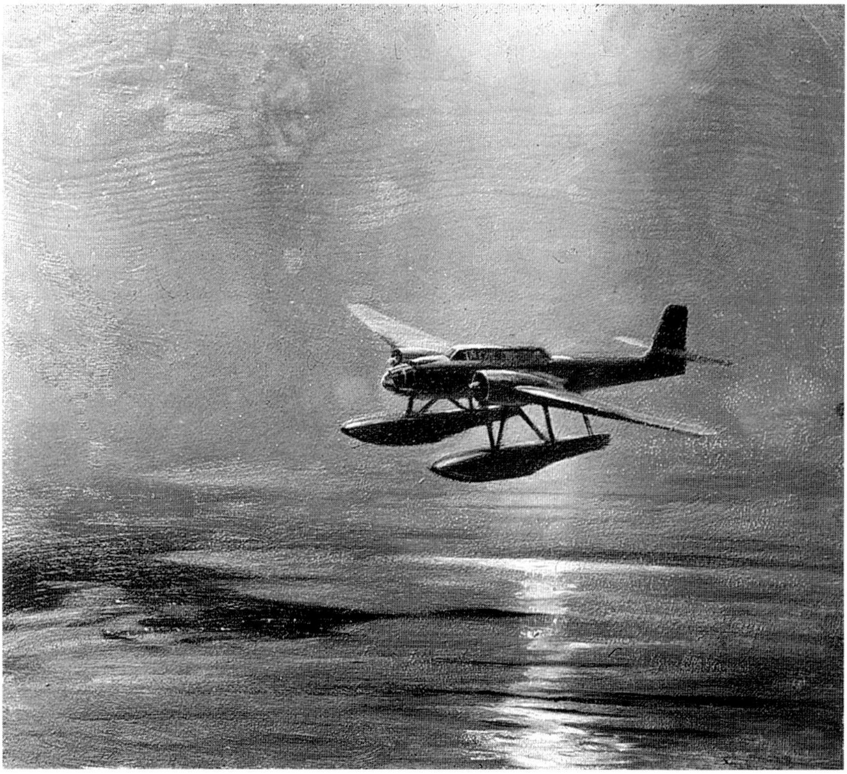

10. A war-time sketch of a German Heinkel '… no time for oils.'

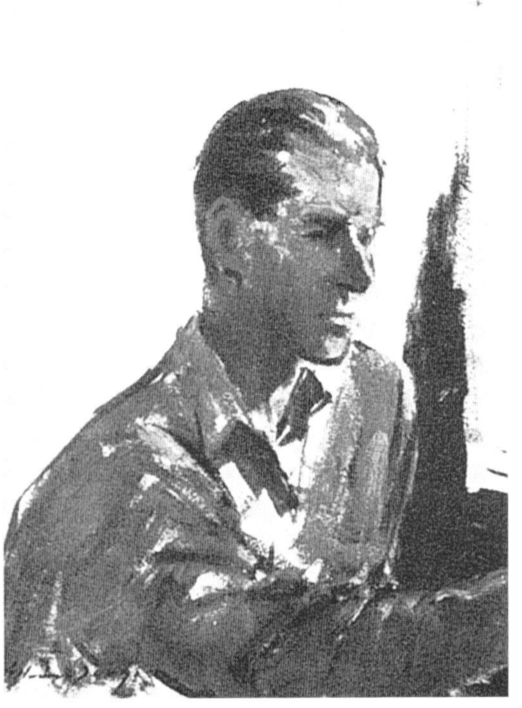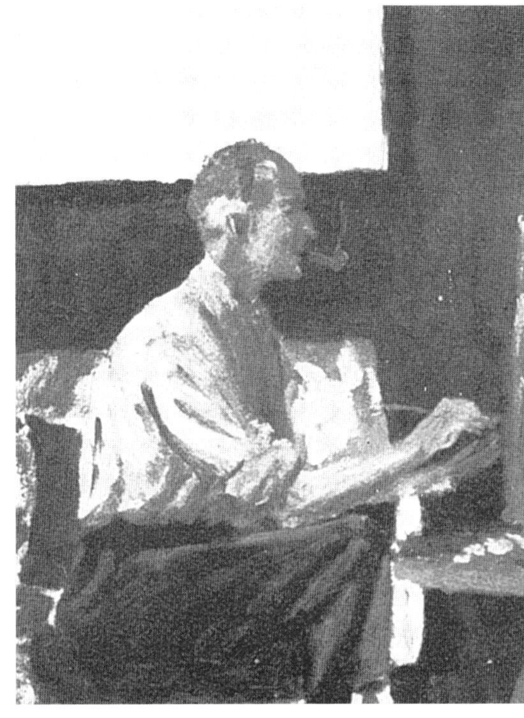

11. H.R.H. Prince Philip's and Seago's painting of each other

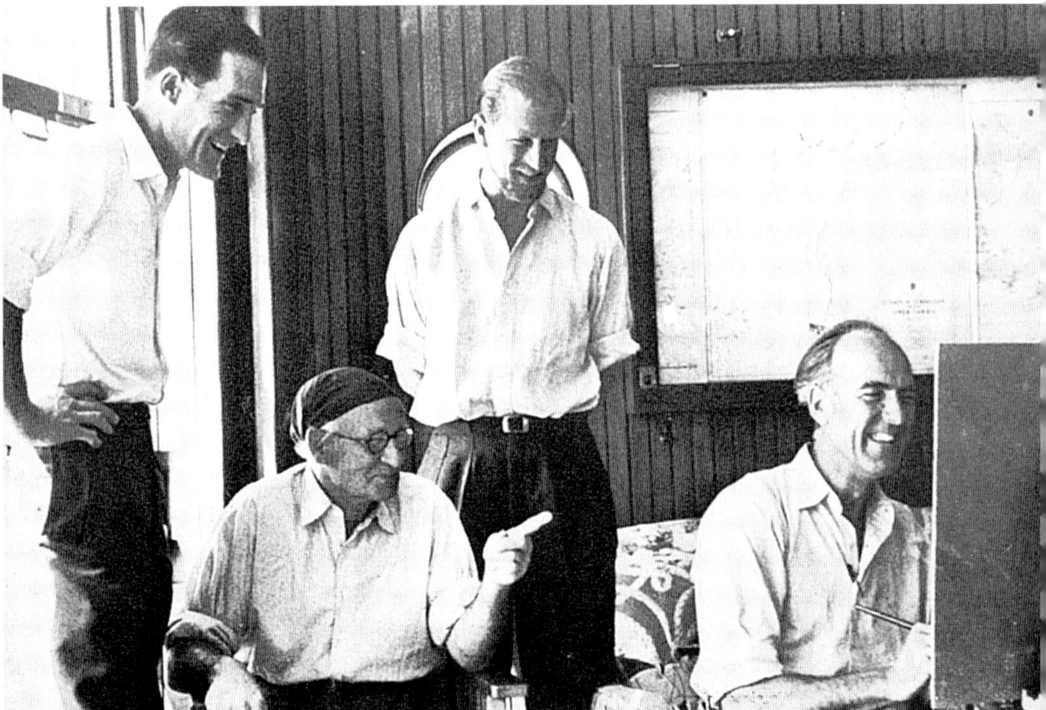

12. Seago painting on the *Britannia*

2.

COURTEENHALL.
NORTHAMPTON
TEL. & TELEGRAMS, ROADE 4.

On the way we called and had lunch with Sir Thomas ——. One of England's real gentleman. Sir Thomas is of blue blood, (a little has settled in the end of his nose!) There I met Simon E— the portrait painter — rather arty "and" therefore amusing. His wife is quite charming.

13. A letter sent to Sir Hereward Wake after his first visit. The large head is a 'blue blood' who came to lunch. The bottom head is the portrait painter Simon Elwes.

——— VII ———

American Interlude

In 1938 Henry Melchett again took Seago to Italy, this time to Florence, and his perception of the painter's need was justified from the moment Seago looked out of the window of the train. Afterwards Seago wrote in his diary:

'The landscape and country through which we passed was so lovely it made me long to settle in a little village here and paint. On the whole it is flat, but there is always the skyline of mountains getting every blue in successive stages until the far distant range merges with the sky . . . In some of the fields the young wheat – green-eared just about to turn gold – and in others they were cutting hay, which, even from the train, I could smell. Wagons drawn by oxen, mostly white, were being loaded by men and women clad in blue smocks and wide straw hats on their heads. Mostly these meadows were fringed with willow trees or tall poplars, and in the background nestled the farmsteads, with their washed walls and red roofs and the bright green shutters of their windows . . .'

It was dark when he arrived at the hotel where Melchett took him on to his balcony for a first sight of Florence under the stars. Again the painter's diary revealed his reaction:

'The scene before us was beyond description. Beneath us flowed the river, grey and mysterious reflecting a chain of silver lights as it dreamed its way through the city. Rising on either side were the groups of irregular houses, climbing in haphazard fashion up the hill, their lamplit windows winking far up into the mountains. Where earth met sky a monastery tower stood sentinel surrounded by a shadow guard of cypress trees. About the scene was a spirit of contentment which alone would calm the most troubled spirit. In the distance a bell tolled, while near at hand was the placid sound of the water falling over the dam further down the river, singing its never-ending hymn of praise to the creation of the land through which it flows. Along the narrow stone paved streets passed horse-drawn carriages, their wheels turning to a jingle of the horses' bells as they jogged and trotted out of sight. The candle lamps flickering, and the huddled figure of the coachman swaying to the motion of the vehicle.'

In the morning Seago awoke to the sound of the river mingled with shouting and laughter and, going to the window, he saw a crowd of lads splashing in the water, their naked bodies the colour of copper. He and Melchett ate a leisurely breakfast of coffee and rolls and then took a horse and carriage to a hillside monastery to see the della Robbia medallions, the first of the sights which, during the next seven days, caused the painter to experience emotions ranging from depression to a great sense of peace.

The depression, he wrote, was a reaction to the preponderance of scenes of indescribable horror depicted with immense gusto in the early frescoes, an inclination on the part of their creators he found hard to understand. He wearied too of the Renaissance painters' use of landscape only as a background to figure composition, for he longed to escape from the overpowering designs of figures, robed and unrobed, to the unruffled quiet of pure landscape. 'Were I living in Florence for longer I should, of course, take these masters in smaller doses which, of course, would be a wise plan,' he wrote.

But he found his peace at San Gimignano, the little hill-town fifty miles from Florence, when he and Melchett drove between medieval houses, palaces and towers to the thirteenth-century Church of Sant 'Agostino. They declined the offer of a guide but while they were admiring the famous Benozzo Gozzoli frescoes behind an altar, an old friar appeared, greeted them with great courtesy and in reply to their questions produced a long cane. With great simplicity and charm, like a schoolmaster, he pointed out to them in the frescoes episodes in the life of St Augustine.

'So beautifully did he tell the story,' Seago recalled, 'that I forgot completely the time and place. He was a small man, tanned and rather weather-beaten. His monk's robes were old and dirty and the tuft of iron-grey hair which sprouted in a wire fringe across his forehead had not seen a comb for months. And yet there was something so saintly about him that he gave one the impression of maturity . . .'

They thanked the friar and were about to leave when he called them back and asked if they would like to go into the monastery garden. There, in the warm afternoon sunshine they experienced a cloistered quiet such as Seago had never known. Between the flower beds paved pathways led to an old stone well-head, and the scent from beds of red roses and lavender pervaded the whole place. For a while they sat in silence, the old friar between them. The only sound was the drone of bees in the lavender and the distant song of the birds.

Eventually, the old man rose and beckoning them to follow, vanished through a doorway at the far end of the cloisters into a disused dairy. He turned the key in a door leading to a small, carefully-tended walled vegetable garden and pointing to the furthest wall invited them to go alone and look over. They walked across a bed of lettuce and climbed on to the wall.

'I cannot describe what met our eyes,' Seago wrote. 'It seemed that the whole of Italy lay spread before us. Mile upon mile of vine fields and green corn stretched almost to eternity, interlaced with ribbons of white roads linking villages and monasteries into a network of such superb design that it seemed too beautiful to be of this earth. Cypress trees and olive trees grew together on the slopes and lined the roads. The colour was soft and clear and yet it abounded in every inch of landscape. A more joyous land it would be hard to imagine.

'We sat for a long time on that wall and when I left it I felt that

I could begin to understand the reason for that calm maturity of the old friar and I was almost frightened.'

The old man was waiting at the door. He smiled and led them back to the cloisters and when he spoke it was about the frescoes and the old Italian masters. He told them that many of the figures in the frescoes were portraits of types still to be found in the neighbourhood and, as evidence, he pointed to one of the figures and then to himself and, to their amazement, they saw that the figure on the wall was a perfect portrait of the old friar. They shook hands, he led them to a door, let them out into the street and lifted his hand in blessing. 'With the closing of the door I felt that a moment almost sacred had passed,' Seago wrote. 'A moment of clarity had gone and I was left with the feeling that it could never be recaptured. I don't think it was due to the sanctity of the scene or to the impression the great masterpieces had upon me. But I believe there was a faith, so simple and secure which alone accounted for the sense of divine peace which surrounded one – a sense which can only be described as the love of God.'

He made enquiries at a hotel in the town and tentatively arranged to be back in September for the harvest when the grapes were honey-coloured and the blue-frocked peasants collected them in the carts drawn by white oxen. That was the Italy he dreamed of painting. But it would be six years before he returned and then it would be to portray a very different Italy.

Back in England he found life for a painter of ballet pictures was eminently satisfying. John Gregory introduced a routine into his life so that painting became the focal point of an exciting but orderly pattern. He worked on the pictures for *Tribute to Ballet* in a setting that, for the first time in his life, he himself had created. He and Gregory transformed the dingy two-roomed house in Lawrence Street which he rented at £125 a year. They had the walls painted white, made imaginative curtains from inexpensive fabrics, pickled and painted old furniture and hung some of Seago's best paintings on the walls. In the studio, in pride of place, a huge plaster cast of a Jagger sculpture mounted over the mantelpiece showed Pan bribing a nymph with a string of beads from behind a tree. It put the finishing touch to the unique atmosphere the painter always seemed able to create in his home, from organized chaos.

There was no shortage of admiring visitors. Alicia Markova and Michael Fokine sat for their portraits for the book which John Masefield and Alan Delgado came along to discuss. Patrons including Violet, Lady Melchett, Lady Evelyn Jones and Archie Jamieson took friends along to view his work and the actors Raymond Massey and Owen Nares had their portraits painted.

Seago and Gregory regularly lunched at the Candy Shop in Old Church Street run by two spinsters known as 'The Candy Ladies' who laced their cooking with kindness and established a warm friendship with the two patrons who every evening deserted them. Resplendent in white tie and tails the pair of good-looking bachelors could usually be seen careering down the King's Road to dine at their favourite Italian restaurant. They then took a bus to Drury Lane to see the Ballet Russe de Monte Carlo and after the performance went backstage to join the dancers for supper or a late-night snack at Quaglino's. It seemed that Seago could never have enough of the ballet. He still went to practice classes to work on his sketches of the dancers holding their correct positions and soon he accumulated a huge portfolio of ballet drawings. One evening, in his haste to get to the theatre, he left it on a bus. It was never recovered but Seago was in too buoyant a mood to let the loss upset him.

At this period he also practised regularly an exercise in memory-training. He would stand in a street in Chelsea and memorize the scene, and back in his studio reproduce it with as much detail as he could recall. He then returned to the street and compared his drawing with the scene and noted his omissions.

He and Gregory usually spent the week-ends at Brooke where, in the countryside, Seago practised a self-taught painting technique. He went out with small boards and, working quickly, splashed on the tone and colour of the scene without attempting to draw in any shapes. He then made a careful pencil drawing of the same scene and, finally, combined the two.

At the end of the summer the Ballet Company was booked to dance in New York and it was suggested to Seago that he should go there too and show his ballet pictures. After some negotiation, an exhibition was arranged at the Carroll Carstairs Gallery in New York to coincide with the publication of *Tribute to Ballet* and also with the opening of the ballet season at the Metropolitan Opera. But in the autumn of 1938 Seago's plans were jeopardized until literally the eleventh hour, by the threat of war. On the eve of the Munich crisis it was with grave misgivings that he allowed his pictures, some forty-five oils and twelve drawings, to go ahead of him in the *Queen Mary*. He and Gregory were due to follow a week later, in the *Ile de France* but, as he recorded in his diary, at the time the paintings went he rather doubted whether he would ever see them again.

As a diarist, incidentally, Seago was far from consistent, unlike Gregory who, with true Boswellian enthusiasm, recorded full details of his first trip abroad. It is interesting to compare the painter's comparatively prosaic account of their American travels with his companion's fuller, more thoughtful impression. For instance, while their plans hung in the balance, Seago merely noted in his expensive-looking red-leather, gold-edged book: 'It is pointless for me to record the details of that crisis [Munich] in this journal. They are already recorded accurately and in detail, time and again, elsewhere . . .' Gregory, however, in a plain exercise book noted that on the way to collect their visas they passed long queues of people outside the Town Hall in the King's Road, Chelsea, waiting to collect their gas masks and found even larger queues at the American Consulate where others were trying to obtain visas to leave the country. In Hyde Park, with a sickening feeling he watched fellow Londoners packing earth into hessian sacks for protection against enemy air attacks.

Seago, doing his last-minute shopping in Norwich on 29 September was worried and morose, but his mood lightened temporarily when in the afternoon Neville Chamberlain flew back from Munich after his meeting with Hitler with his slip of paper offering a reprieve from war. Edward and John Seago and their parents heard the news over the wireless at Brooke. 'We fetched wine and drank a toast and I said a little prayer of thanksgiving that the nightmare of war had been averted,' the painter wrote but, mindful of all he had learned from Melchett and Jamieson, his relief was tempered with the certainty that sooner or later Britain must either fight or lose her prestige. So the farewell family lunch the following day in London at the Candy Shop was a gloomy meal in which gratitude for the aversion of war was tinged with fears for the future and, more immediately, apprehension on all sides about the trip to America. 'Don't part with the money boy, till you see everything is safe,' was Brian Seago's parting advice at Waterloo Station when the inexperienced Gregory nervously tipped a porter £1 in advance for taking their luggage to the boat train.

The crossing on the *Ile de France* did little to raise either man's spirits. The ship was full, the weather was dreadful and their cabin steward assured them that it was the worst Atlantic crossing since March and the sea could never be rougher. Seago, quite unperturbed by the weather and determined not to miss a meal, walked the decks to work up an appetite and ate in the huge dining-room in almost solitary splendour. He ploughed his way through sophisticated menus and practised his schoolboy French learned during his trips with the circus, on the few waiters who had not retired to their cabins. In a letter to Delgado he boasted:

'I should have been a sailor. There is only one snag – boredom. Never have I been so bored! The atmosphere of sickness, which has been unpleasantly obvious whenever and wherever the spirit moves, has caused even the lounges to be danger zones so there is really nothing to do but just sit.'

However, on the fourth day, the weather improved so that between meals Seago worked off his surplus energy by beating Gregory relentlessly and alternately at table-tennis and deck quoits. Intermittently throughout the day, a fellow passenger, Fats Waller, the jazz musician, played the piano and rolled his great eyes and crooned to all and sundry 'I'm Gonna Sit Right Down and Write Myself a Letter'.

Seago and Gregory made no acquaintances on the trip, possibly because each in his own way was too preoccupied about what awaited them at the end of the voyage, to indulge in small-talk. On arrival in New York their taxi driver recommended them to a thousand-room hotel on 42nd Street which, on closer inspection, turned out to be a glorious chromium-plated type of commercial brothel. Without bothering to unpack, Seago by-passed the bewildering array of gadgets and notices on their bedroom wall to telephone the Carroll Carstairs Gallery and by noon on the crisp October morning they were on their way to East 57th Street to discuss the exhibition with the plump, amiable manager, Mr Grady. He advised them to move out of their undesirable accommodation and take temporary rooms at a Park Avenue hotel. While the move was being arranged there was a telephone call for Seago from Mimi Cushing, an American he had met through the Melchetts and who had sent him a welcoming message to the ship. 'Will call the Gallery some time on Saturday,' the eldest of the three popular Cushing sisters had written. 'Please save dinner Tuesday night and we might meet on Monday afternoon for tea, if it's convenient for you.' But within half an hour of her telephone call, two rather bemused Norfolk travellers, still tending to stagger on their sea legs and somewhat dazed by the heady opulence of Fifth Avenue, found themselves lunching at three o'clock in the afternoon in a near-deserted dining-room at the Ritz-Carlton with the frail-looking elegant young woman who was a target for every New York gossip columnist.

They talked through teatime with the thirty-two-year-old daughter of Dr Harvey Cushing, the distinguished Boston brain surgeon, about the happenings in England, the forthcoming ballet season in New York and the young English conductor John Barbirolli who was making a tremendous name with the New York Symphony Orchestra. Mimi Cushing invariably made a point of choosing her friends from among those who did interesting or creative work. Before she finally settled down with her staid millionaire, Vincent Astor, Edward Seago was just the unconventional companion she needed and the promotion of his work became her prime concern. Once again, with uncanny timing another character had entered his life at an opportune moment to further his career.

On their first evening in New York, a second friend Seago had met through Melchett was also waiting to welcome him. She was the fashion-writer Jean Pendar, and Seago and Gregory dined with her and some of her friends and afterwards went on to a penthouse party where they were shown a magnificent view of the city at midnight which Gregory confessed he was too worn out to appreciate. Seago, he complained, was inexhaustible.

The next morning they moved into an expensive room in a Park Avenue hotel, walked in Central Park and read the art and theatre section in the 150-page *New York Times*. This, Gregory noted, suddenly brought home to Seago the practical difficulties of ensuring that his own exhibition made the slightest impact on the slick, sensation-loving cosmopolitan art scene of the New World.

Gregory felt lonely and inadequate and had a bad sore throat which heralded the onset of a feverish cold. He wrote in his diary: 'Ted is angry. He is afraid of catching my cold. We are really rather knocked out by the pace of things. Ted has become strangely remote, almost shut in. His brain is deeply engrossed in devising the master plan. He knows what he is about and I can only follow blindly.'

The master plan, it turned out, involved the closest association with the Ballet Russe, due in New York the following morning. Two nights later at the Metropolitan Opera, at the opening performance Seago had arranged for flowers to be delivered to Markova and to Freddie Franklin. He and Gregory, by then both with feverish colds, were in white ties and tails and the noise and hubbub, so Gregory wrote, was far removed from a first night at London's Covent Garden. In the foyer the ushers declaimed the price and contents of the programme at the top of their voices, lights flashed as pressmen spotted the celebrities and, in vain, Seago urged Gregory to try and persuade the cameramen to look his way. 'I need the publicity,' he said despondently. 'After the opening of my show it will be too late.'

Nor did his depression diminish when, at the end of the final ballet *Gaieté Parisienne*, he watched the expensive floral sheaf he had ordered for Franklin presented by mistake to Massine who, after reading the inscription, flung the flowers down on the stage. However, afterwards backstage, Massine was at his most charming, shook hands and wished Seago 'good luck' with his exhibition, although he turned down the painter's invitation to open the exhibition because, he said, the ballet book had been dedicated to Fokine. Fortunately Fokine then agreed to open the exhibition.

For the rest of the week Seago divided his time between nursing his heavy cold and supervising the hanging of his pictures in the Gallery where he was persuaded by the manager to hire a publicity agent. At the week-end however, any eve of exhibition nerves were forgotten during a visit to Jean Pendar's little wooden cottage in Bedford Village, Connecticut.

The trees, in the New England fall, were dazzling colours and after a two-hour drive, when they arrived at the Pendars' tiny red-painted white-shuttered cottage perched on the top of a hill, a house boy served a lunch of black bean soup, cheese soufflé, raisin bread and fruit salad. Afterwards, they walked through the long grass along an avenue of trees and followed a narrow path through the wood down into a gorge where they sat on a rock by the stream and Seago took out his sketch pad for the first time since he had left England. Later he wrote in his diary: 'It has been a grand week-end; one to remember.'

Back in New York, on the eve of the exhibition, according to his diary he hardly slept a wink and dreamt that no one was at the Private View. 'I woke up in a cold sweat,' he wrote. 'I had tooth-ache and in the middle of the night I got up and applied oil of cloves.' But in the morning Mimi Cushing arrived to sweep them off to lunch at the St Regis and to fill in time before four o'clock took them to Radio City and to the top of the Rockefeller Building to admire the view from the fifty-ninth floor.

Promptly at four o'clock Fokine arrived at the Carstairs Gallery, true to his promise and he was almost immediately followed by Markova, limping heavily on a strapped ankle because she had torn a ligament on the second night of the ballet when Lifar dropped her while executing a lift. The press photographers were also waiting but there were no other visitors and, after half an hour, Fokine left without making his opening speech. Seago, for once, seemed in real danger of losing his composure, despite Carstairs's insistence that everything would be all right and the delay in starting was merely because New York society considered it was unfashionable to be punctual. The painter was convinced that his worst fears about the exhibition were in the process of being realized and afterwards he admitted in his diary: 'I was in a cold sweat and would have given anything to go home.'

Then, at four forty-five precisely, as if at a given signal, the crowd swarmed in; a seemingly never-ending stream of smart women in elegant clothes with escorts to match who all vied with each other to catch the eye of the press photographers. They greeted one another effusively, chatted like old friends, more or less ignored the artist, scarcely noticed his pictures, and left. Not a picture was sold. To Seago, the whole procedure, unprecedented at his London exhibitions, was as unreal as it was nerve-racking. However, Carstairs looked relaxed and happy and the hired publicity agent assured him that Society had now definitely noticed the exhibition so there was nothing to worry about.

Such sublime confidence seemed fully justified by the reports in the social columns of many newspapers the next day. 'Talk of the Ballet Russe punctuates every drawing-room conversation or supper club chat,' wrote Patricia Coffin in the *World Telegram* where it seemed that anyone who was anybody had been to the opening of Edward Seago's brilliant exhibition of Monte Carlo ballet scenes which Michael Fokine had opened 'with appropriate remarks'. The report described how 'Prince Serge Obolensky dashed in for a moment and Lucius Beebé put in an appearance but preferred chatting with friends to looking at the pictures.' Apparently his was a fairly representative attitude because the one and only mention of the pictures described them as 'a background of brilliantly-coloured Degas-like canvases'.

Hardly a newspaper failed to notice the exhibition and the glossy *New York Art Review* chose to introduce the arrival of the Ballet Russe de Monte Carlo at the Metropolitan Opera, with a reproduction of a Seago painting, 'Before the Curtain Rises' and a story about his exhibition. ' "The master plan" it seemed had worked well! Ted reads aloud every line and we laugh till our sides ache,' Gregory wrote in his diary. 'What a great big joke. We feel a little bit sick.'

Ironically, there was real cause for unease in one or two of the shorter, more considered reports written by serious art critics who visited the exhibition several days after the social columnists had had their say. '. . . Not very deep stuff. Done lightly, with an impressionistic brush dipped into bright, luminous colour. They do have charm but it derives for the most part from the subject itself . . . pleasantly but not provocatively displayed' (*World Telegram*). '. . . There is a lot of cleverness but very little design or substance in his work' (*Herald Tribune*). It had been a long time since Seago had been publicly taken to task so frankly.

There was little opportunity to brood because, by the time the later criticisms appeared, the painter was fulfilling the prophecy of one far-sighted reporter who, anticipating the outcome of the show, wrote: 'Mr Seago acknowledged introductions and accepted invitations all afternoon.' By the next week-end Mr Seago had embarked on a social round among people who proved to be far more interested in being painted on their fine blood-stock by an English artist than in buying his ballet pictures. As a result during the next few weeks he once and for all moved away from the ballet and, out of necessity reverted to an earlier stage of his painting which he thought he had already discarded. But he learned otherwise when, with not one picture sold, he and Gregory went with Mimi Cushing to stay at an attractive stone house at Bernardsville, New Jersey, home of her friend, the horse-loving Mrs Mary Stevens Baird.

His hostess recalled the name Seago from a reproduction on a Christmas card of a painting showing two of her riding friends going to the post at a Cheltenham meeting and she was disappointed to find that the painter had only one equestrian picture to show in America. She rode with him in the early morning over miles of rambling countryside to Auble Hill – she on her young chestnut mare Shortcomings and he on a black hunter called Anchors Aweigh by the legendary winner Man of War out of Good Bye which he reckoned was the best-named horse he had ever known. They galloped through the woods, splashed through streams and jumped fallen tree trunks until they found themselves high on the hill where, two centuries before, George Washington had established tin mines. Below them, the valley studded with wild cedar trees was flushed to a pearly pink with 'poverty grass', knee high at that time of year. Seago decided that, after all, there might be compensations attached to painting equestrian portraits.

In the afternoon, accompanied by a Great Dane and two Dalmatians, they all went for a ten-mile walk, the two girls taking it in turns to ride in a little wicker governess cart drawn by Tiny Tot, a piebald Shetland, the Englishmen walking. Before he left America, Seago sent his hostess a sketch as a 'thank you' for her hospitality. It showed the end of the walk with everyone exhausted, the dogs with their tails down and tongues hanging out, the two girls helping the pony by pushing the cart up the hill, and Gregory and Seago lagging a long way behind.

Mary Stevens Baird treasured the sketch and hung it beside her portrait by Seago which, on her suggestion, had been painted at 'cut price' in return for her getting the painter other commissions. He had agreed to the terms. She certainly looked her best on a horse, or behind the wheel of a fast car, and true to her promise to introduce him to her friends, on their first night in Bernardsville she drove them smothered in rugs in her open Packard to dine with a neighbour, Percy R. Pyne, Jnr, known as 'Toughy', a handsome millionaire who had developed multiple sclerosis when he left Oxford after war service with the Lafayette Escadrille. At dinner, he was wheeled to the head of the table in an invalid chair to sit between two chocolate-box blondes. During the meal he suggested to Seago that he might arrange an informal exhibition of his work at his parents' house in Park Avenue, New York.

The food at the candlelit table, according to Gregory, was exquisite and the champagne flowed freely. By the end of the evening conversation dulled. The talk turned to the ballet and a Polish doctor who had seen *Les Sylphides* said he thought he had turned up at a practice class by mistake because all the dancers wore white dresses and danced under a dull, blue light. Seago forced himself to explain that this was because it was an old, classical ballet, whereupon the doctor retorted that if they couldn't liven it up a bit by introducing a few pinks and ambers then they shouldn't keep on doing it. Seago withdrew from the conversation and was contemplating whether the time had come to leave when a dowdy woman of uncertain age told him she wrote poetry and demonstrated her ability by staring into his eyes and reciting rather emotionally: 'When the day is hot and sultry, one can't be bothered to commit adultery.' Like a conscientious salesman who could not risk absenting himself from the scene of a potential deal, Seago stayed until the host's head lolled during a conversation about horses and his watchful mother, with quiet dignity, signalled a manservant and together they gently wheeled him away.

At that stage the prospect of the evening yielding Seago anything worthwhile looked distinctly remote; but it proved otherwise. 'Toughy' Pyne's good-looking sister, Mary Filley, had visited England and been painted on horseback by Munnings and she offered Seago a fee of a thousand dollars to do a companion portrait of her husband Oliver. It proved the first of a series of similar commissions from hunt country people eager to be portrayed on their favourite horses. It indicated the time had come for Seago to take a furnished studio in New York and after a frustrating search, he and Gregory found one in Greenwich Village at 4 East Ninth Street, in a house belonging to an institution for retired mariners called 'Sailors' Snug Harbour'. It was an appropriate address for a traveller called Seago and he rented the studio for eighty dollars a month.

Once installed there, the second week passed quickly. He worked on a portrait of Mimi Cushing, went to the theatre and to parties and dined with his new friends in an assortment of small, interesting restaurants. During the day Gregory explored the possibility of getting an acting job, but with no success. He was bored and Seago was busy but both men were ill at ease, overwhelmed by the strangeness and apparent superficiality of the city. They felt able to relax for a few hours only when they went to a performance at the ballet. Then in an illusion of familiar security they could accept that there was a valid justification for punishing themselves by trying to make a success so far from home.

Still no ballet paintings had been sold and on their return from New Jersey, Seago, with a touch of bravado and in an attempt, he said, to make the exhibition look a little less neglected, had stuck red dots on a few of the pictures. The gesture brought a touch of success for on the tenth day of the exhibition, which coincided with Mimi Cushing's first of three sittings for her portrait, one picture was sold.

So with his confidence somewhat restored Seago set off with Gregory for his third week-end in the American countryside. They went to Greenwich, Connecticut, to stay with a friend of Archie Jamieson, George Ohrstrom, the Wall Street financier and industrialist who as a pilot in World War I was credited with bringing down the last German plane before the Armistice was signed. As an anglophile his country home was a perfect replica of a handsome Elizabethan mansion with huge chimney stacks, stained-glass mullioned windows, a great hall with a minstrels' gallery and a high raftered roof, which was a replica of one he had seen in an old house in Kent. A log fire blazed in the open hearth and the house was filled with fine English and Italian antiques, but there were few pictures.

Painting was not one of the interests of the Master of the local Hunt kennels whose week-end image was exemplified by several large Irish wolfhounds strolling decoratively about his home.

In this comparatively English setting however, Seago's newly-restored confidence was to be short-lived. He and Gregory were immediately immersed in a race meeting followed by a dinner party and on the Sunday, as the highlight of the week-end, they attended the neighbouring Silver Valley Hunter Trials. There Seago was shocked to see the trophy of the day awarded to the local team led by an aggressive lady who was Master of the Silver Valley Hunt, rather than to Ohrstrom's team which seemed the obvious winner. He was exhausted rather than relaxed by his country week-end and so were his host and hostess and after two final cocktail parties it was decided that everyone would have an early night. At one o'clock in the morning Seago was awakened by the familiar symptoms of heart trouble.

He woke Gregory who found his way to Ohrstrom's bedroom to telephone for a doctor and very soon Seago was given an injection of morphia and atropine which he knew were the drugs that curtailed an attack. Gregory had been warned about the painter's heart turns but it was the first one he had seen, and after the doctor had left he watched in growing fear as Seago got more and more distressed and threw himself about the bed, groaning and chattering incoherently, eventually becoming wild and frenzied. Then suddenly he seemed to tire, complained of being parched with thirst and after a drink of water, gradually relaxed into a state of calm until he lay pale and still and sleep took over. The next morning he awoke perfectly well to the relief and astonishment of the exhausted Gregory who fortunately did not realize that the attack he had just seen had been only a very mild one. Seago certainly did not bother to enlighten him.

Both men were glad to be back in New York again where they found a mounting list of commissions, invitations from Mimi Cushing to join her on an endless round of social activities and two more ballet paintings sold so that Carroll Carstairs was prompted to extend the exhibition for another week. Seago was no longer unhappy in America despite the heart attack which might well have been attributable to his growing realization that he was still not free

to express himself in his work in exactly the way that he wanted to
do.

> 'New York I am beginning to like a lot,' he wrote to Delgado.
> 'The beginning was definitely tough but I have no cause for
> regret and am very glad I came . . . The show I think will pay for
> itself and there are now one or two commissions to paint which
> should bring me home. This, in some ways, is a bore because it
> means I have got to remain here to paint them and I expect,
> by the time they are finished, I shall have spent all the money I
> make . . . I am sure you will realize I am appreciated in America
> when I tell you that one of my drawings was stolen; and when I
> say stolen I mean taken out of the exhibition between two and
> three in the afternoon.'

Was the 'theft' another instance of the showman's inventive
attempt at self-advertisement meant to confirm, even to himself,
that he was appreciated across the Atlantic? For there is no evidence
of any theft and curiously enough Gregory, in his meticulously kept
diary, never referred to such an incident.

Although most of the exhibition pictures remained unsold, the
one or two commissions proved to be only the start of a steady
stream of requests for portraits. It reached a crescendo when a chance
remark to a reporter from a newspaper syndicate was blown up into
a story that made full-page spreads in many of the national Sunday
newspapers and far exceeded the modest success of Seago's original
conception of 'the master plan'.

'Ballet Dancers are Same Animals as Race-Horses, says Noted
Artist,' was a typical headline that swept America from coast to
coast. Nearly all the newspapers showed a large photograph of
Maria Gambarelli, the new première danseuse at the Metropolitan
Opera, opposite a picture of the race-horse War Admiral, rearing up
on his hind legs 'as if attempting to dance' and many carried close-ups
comparing the under-pinnings of three members of the corps de
ballet with the hoofs of a pair of race-horses.

'There is nothing really extraordinary about it,' Seago was quoted
as saying by the *Detroit Sunday Times* and the *Boston Sunday
Advertiser*, just two of a spate of papers that repeated in full the

observations of 'the noted British artist whose ballet and equestrian pictures, seven of which hang in the castle of the Earl of Harewood, a connection of the British Royal Family, are on show in the Carroll Carstairs Gallery'.

'A fine dancer and a great horse are, literally, the same in their bodies and in their temperament,' the painter explained. 'A dancer's feet and legs must develop the same terrific suppleness that a horse's delicate little legs have. If you watch slow motion pictures of a horse taking a jump and a dancer leaping into the air, you realize that the movement of the two bodies is identical and, watching a group of horses in action – a race, a hunt or training gallops in the early morning mist, is like seeing a perfectly directed ballet.

'The better a dancer is, the more nearly his feet grow to resemble an animal rather than a human foot. Nijinsky's feet were so far developed in this way that X-rays of his strange bone formation were recorded by the medical profession.

'Most famous dancers and all famous race horses have tiny feet,' he continued, comparing the minute under-pinnings of Alicia Markova, prima ballerina of the Ballet Russe, of whom he had painted numerous portraits, to the miniature hoofs of Hyperion, Lord Derby's record-time Derby winner.

Most reports included a neat little pen-portrait of the painter who had expounded the entertaining theory. '. . . Tall, slender brunette and given to pipe smoking,' one read, 'Mr Seago has only two hobbies in life; sitting on a fence watching horses and sitting in the gallery watching the ballet. (Orchestra seats give you no perspective.) He is not married to a ballet dancer, he isn't married at all. During the summer, Mr Seago has been catching up on commissions for horse pictures.' Mr Seago then proffered the press some sound advice. 'Go to a ballet,' he said. 'You'll see the same type of leg action without dropping anything to the bookies.'

There was no further need for the publicity agent. From then on, the painter had more commissions than he could cope with and probably regretted that he had also agreed to paint Mrs Rhoda Cameron Clarke on the same 'half-price-in-return-for-introductions' terms as her friend and neighbour Mary Stevens Baird. As it turned out he had real cause for regret about Rhoda Cameron Clarke's portrait because, for the first time in America, he had difficulty in getting a likeness. For three days he and Gregory stayed at her home in Far Hills, New Jersey where he struggled with his painting of the woman in her mid-thirties just past her prime in looks, who had been married but who never spoke of her husband. 'There is a harmony about her, and yet a loneliness . . . something missing,' Gregory noted in his diary, while Seago shelved the problem of trying to portray it all and concentrated on the comparatively straight-forward study of Mary Stevens Baird who was delighted with her picture. 'The horses he did could not be mistaken for any other thoroughbred hunters,' she said. 'He portrayed your seat on a horse perfectly and his backgrounds were pure Virginia or New Jersey and his colours were vivid and true.' 'Toughy' Pyne, when he was driven over to see the pictures, was equally impressed and invited Seago to paint two of his horses in Virginia where he thought his friend, Mrs Johnson Redmond, might also like to have her portrait painted.

So Seago and Gregory found themselves in Middleburgh as guests of Kate Redmond where they were visited again by 'Toughy' Pyne and mutual friends from New Jersey. They included Rhoda Cameron Clarke still complaining that she was dissatisfied with her portrait and wanting more sittings to try and get it right. Seago was too busy working on his new commissions to find time and one way and another, the harmonious atmosphere of the house was marred. That evening, after dinner, Seago's heart started its familiar distressing symptoms.

'I cannot believe it,' Gregory wrote in the diary. 'It is as though he willed it to help us out of a situation . . . At times it seems as if he can switch on his malady at will. But, even if he can, he had not the power to switch it off.' The latter part of the observation was borne out when, two days later, Seago had not responded to the morphia injections from the local doctor and light-headed from lack of food lay struggling for breath, glassy-eyed and with his lips white and coated. Kate Redmond then insisted that it was time to get him to hospital in Washington, fifty miles away.

The arrival of the ambulance appeared to cause a slight improvement in his condition for, as he was wheeled out on a stretcher into the bright winter sunshine, showman that he was, he called out for a photograph to be taken, and although the motion over the rough roads distressed him he revived a little when they neared the capital. On admittance to hospital he was given a hyercine injection and fell fast asleep. Gregory, returning a few hours later found him sitting up in bed wearing a trilby hat, talking gibberish and delighting an audience of nurses with his antics. To the amazement of the doctors his pulse was normal and despite their appeals to him to stay long enough for them to investigate his case thoroughly and their pro-testations that he was not fit to leave hospital, the next morning he insisted on signing himself out.

Seago rarely talked to people about his heart condition and, as the years passed, he grew increasingly determined to conceal it because he considered any such sign of physical weakness was something to be despised. Nevertheless, the attack in Virginia and the fifty-mile journey across the rough country had an element of adventure about it so that years later he could not resist exaggerating the episode into a good story when he was the guest speaker at a medical dinner in Norwich. He transposed it into a hair-raising journey which took them within view of 'the blue hills of Arizona' and re-lated how he called out to the negro who was driving them to stop and let him see the hills which he had always planned to do before he died. He was, he said, afraid he was not going to survive the journey. 'Don't you worry the least bit about that, Mas'r,' the driver consoled him. 'You'll be OK if you do die. This ambulance is really a fine hearse.'

Two days after he left hospital he was back in Virginia staying at a country lodge belonging to the Oliver Filleys, to finish the por-trait of Kate Redmond and work on the pictures of 'Toughy' Pyne's horses and other commissions. He was limp and irritable and far from fit, and for almost the only time on record refused to allow anyone to watch him paint; not even the crippled 'Toughy' Pyne who had been so helpful and generous. His excuse was that his nerves were at breaking point and he could not concentrate while anyone was hovering around behind him. Everyone except Gregory was banned from the makeshift studio. Nevertheless, despite the un-familiar display of temperament, Gregory thought the equestrian pictures were the best Seago had done.

It was early December and there were the first heavy falls of snow. For two days the lodge was completely cut off, but Seago hardly noticed. He and Gregory had the house to themselves, apart from the servants who attended to the huge log fires and at regular intervals produced trays of delicious food. As the days passed Seago felt a little better and, after a fortnight when he had completed six portraits, he decided to cancel their homeward passage on the *Aquitania* to tackle two more commissions and then have a week's holiday before sailing on the *Queen Mary* to be home in time for Christmas.

The holiday started in Washington with a luncheon party given by a grateful sitter, Countess Roberti. The guests, chiefly members of the Diplomatic Corps, admired her portrait and Seago was offered several immediate commissions which he wearily declined. In two hours he and Gregory were to fly to Buffalo to spend the last days of their American trip with Sargeant Jagger's widow, Evelyn, who had married John Quinton Clarke, a wealthy coal merchant. Seago made little secret of the fact that he would far rather have been going straight back to England and, before the lunch was over, the onset of a heart attack ensured that he got his wish and confirmed Gregory in his belief that the disability could be switched on at will.

Just one hour before they were due to leave for the plane for Buffalo the painter retired to his hostess's bedroom where he lay for three days until eventually he responded to an injection given by a second doctor who had to be called in after the first doctor had refused to give him hyercine. On the fourth day his heart steadied. He was able to shave and he caught the train to New York for an eve-of-departure reception arranged by Mary and Oliver Filley in their family home on Park Avenue.

The display of paintings was very different from Seago's Private View in New York ten weeks previously for most of the ballet pictures were on their way back to England. As he entered the hall he saw every equestrian portrait he had painted in America varnished and in a fine frame displayed to its best advantage under an individual light.

'I have never seen my pictures so beautifully hung,' Seago wrote in his diary. It was left to Gregory to describe the liveried footmen who ushered the hundred or so guests up the grand stairway and record that all Seago's sitters were there, eager to display their portraits to their friends. He noted that 'Toughy' Pyne, in his wheel-chair looked proud and excited as, once again, for an hour or two, he found himself the centre of the hunting set and received their congratulations for his part in discovering such a magnificent painter of horseflesh. 'What a fine collection it is,' Gregory wrote of the paintings. 'Ted has made a success out of failure and almost wrecked himself in the doing.'

Seago would have scoffed at the reference to his health and the following day when they sailed for home on the *Queen Mary* he was full of plans for a second exhibition in New York in the autumn, and had already accepted four commissions for his return visit to America.

—— VIII ——

'O Youth Whose Hope is High'

More commissions to paint equestrian portraits awaited Seago on his return to England and he painted every one of Lord Derby's winners, including a fine portrait of Hyperion which the owner gave to the naval destroyer of that name. There was also a magnificent composite picture of six of Lord Derby's unbeaten stallions on one canvas in justification of Mary Stevens Baird's comment that 'when he painted a horse it could not be mistaken for any other thoroughbred'.

'If I had some more winners I would be able to give the artist some more commissions,' the Earl said on the eve of Derby Day when he opened an exhibition of the painter's work at the Medici Galleries in 1939. He added that if he were lucky enough to have a winner the next day, Mr Seago could prepare his canvas the day after – but not before!

Dominating the exhibition was an impressive portrait of the Duke and Duchess of Buccleuch and their three children riding in the grounds of Drumlanrig Castle which Seago had painted on his return from Florence. Other pictures on show were the portrait of the actor Raymond Massey, paintings from *The Country Scene* including 'The Landmark' and a second picture rejected by the Academy. This was the study of colts being led through the flood water at Horsey Mere. There was also the first of several studies of the talented ailing actor John Carol in costume for his part of Oswald the tragic syphilitic son in Ibsen's *Ghosts*. The wide range of pictures on view also included ballet pictures and showed once and for all that despite Lord Derby's loyal patronage, the label 'horse painter' was no longer applicable.

'In his refusal to specialize lies the proof of his artistic integrity,' wrote the critic from *Country Life*, and added that the artist gave the impression of being set on a pilgrimage to find and express the spark that flies through the world. 'He is a true artist with a healthy delight in the good moments of life,' he wrote. 'Man is only one of the manifestations of some power infinitely greater than himself; the sun, the wind and the rain are his brothers. One perceives this in almost all Seago's pictures, from landscapes to circus, horses and ballet. What he sees and interprets with such honest brilliance is, in his own mind, I believe only part of a great and beautiful activity in which we human beings are concerned.' The critic's considered comment indicated the path which for a time during the ballet period and in America, Seago had seemed in danger of losing.

The return trip to America never materialized. It was forestalled by a war that offered Edward Seago an even greater challenge. In health terms he had proved that he could manage to lead a comparatively normal life surrounded by the unconventional rigours of the circus or the ballet or the cushioned comfort of high society but early in 1939, patriotism apart, it was vital to him to prove himself just as good as the next man whatever physical indications there were to the contrary.

He had successfully cheated medical opinion since boyhood and as a result he saw no reason why any bunch of army doctors had the power to dictate his future. Again, the familiar singlemindedness took over but perhaps for the first time it was focused firmly on his own ends rather than on furthering the cause of his art. In any event he discovered that painting, like many a mistress in the face of a major national disaster, could no longer claim his full attention. For the time being the satisfaction in his great love had gone despite the fact that as an artist in the spring of 1939, when the threat of destruction hung over the peaceful Norfolk landscape, he might have found it doubly precious to paint.

Soon after a prolonged heart turn which left him, as he wrote to Gregory, feeling 'lousy and far from well again and with the usual acute depression . . .' he volunteered for the Officers' Emergency Reserve and attended a short initiation course in Army Intelligence at the Royal United Service Institute in London. It was followed by the offer of a 'mobilization commission' in the Intelligence Corps providing he was declared fit by 'the nearest convenient medical officer in charge of troops'. It was hardly likely that such a doctor would be a match for a healthy-looking determined volunteer whose heart, in between attacks, showed no sign of abnormality. Seago, on his part, had not the slightest hesitation in signing the form stating that he was 'medically fit to take up the appointment'.

On his terms it was true and in due course, with relieved satisfaction, he fingered a Railway Warrant to be used according to secret instructions from the War Office on receipt of a coded telegram calling him up for duty. As the last weeks of peace slipped away he waited impatiently at Brooke for the telegram to arrive, although he had been warned there might be quite a delay.

When war was declared his impatience to take up the threads of his pre-war undercover excursions into Europe turned to intolerable frustration. It was inconceivable that there had been any hitch with his call-up on medical grounds. Nevertheless, there was a sense of panic in which, in near-desperation, he wrote off during September and October to anyone and everyone he thought might be able to help him to get involved in the war effort. He applied to become a camoufleur in Air Raid Precaution, volunteered for the air force, pestered Lord Melchett (then a Trustee of the War Museum) and other influential friends to write to even more influential people on his behalf. Eventually he managed to become enrolled on the Ministry of Information's Register of would-be official war artists.

While he waited despairingly he fulfilled two particularly satisfying commissions and painted the Earl of Rosebery's unbeaten colt Blue Peter and a portrait of the writer Robert Flaherty. In late November the longed-for call-up notice arrived and he was told to report as a Camouflage Officer to the Headquarters of the School of Military Engineers at Chatham in four days' time. His relief was mixed with deep gratitude as he systematically cleaned his paint brushes, stacked his canvases carefully away and, with a nice sense of the dramatic, closed up the studio. God knew when he would use it again! But somehow he never doubted that he would and deep inside his soldier's valise went the inevitable paint-box. He could not have seen it as a key to friendships and wartime adventures beyond the dreams of the most ambitious peacetime soldier which would fully justify his impatience to face his new challenge. There was a subtle irony in the fact that in meeting the challenge of war, an artist who loved to paint in the quiet of his native Norfolk would find himself at last.

He had no time to think of painting during the first confused weeks of army life. After a brief course on 'camouflage', he went to France as a Second Lieutenant with the British Expeditionary Force. From there, in a bout of acute depression after a heart attack which he camouflaged as ''flu', he sent a gloomy letter to Delgado. 'The one thing I cling to and which makes the present bearable, is the certainty that we shall carry on the same when the blight has passed. We always have done and we always will . . .' he wrote.

During the first bitterly cold weeks in France there was little else but that belief to cling to and surrounded by a bleak, alien landscape which he had no desire to paint he was often irritated by the in-nocent question proffered as a tentative overture of friendship: 'You were an artist, weren't you, before the war?'

'I am an artist,' he protested with a superciliousness that defied conversation and concealed the agony, lest he acknowledge even to himself that his new life-style might be considered more than superficial. Once having proved that he was capable of getting into the army he needed to reassert himself, preferably with official recognition as a war artist. But the nearest he got to this goal was an invitation through Lady Melchett from Sir Muirhead Bone of the Ministry of Information's Artists Advisory Committee to make some sketches of war activities to submit to the Committee who might be prepared to purchase anything particularly striking or exceptional.

Henry Melchett, as usual sensitive to his need and anxiety, wrote to reassure him:

'I should not worry if I were you . . . The only great artist that emerged to express the last war was Peter Jagger. He was not an official artist and, had anybody proposed to make him one, there would have been roars of laughter. His greatest piece of work he did with some odd bits of clay and board, sitting in the trenches.

'I feel sure that you will do great work in this war and the chief thing is that you have got to France where you will see the war, not as an official artist from the outside but as an officer and, therefore, from the inside. Paint and draw all you know and don't take too many chances with your health.'

His 'sketches of war activities' took the form of portraits of war leaders including a fine study of General Lord Gort, VC, painted at the headquarters of the British Expeditionary Force. It now hangs in the Imperial War Museum and for it the authorities paid a special wartime price of £25. Soon afterwards Seago found himself posted back to England with the rank of Major in the newly-formed Camouflage Corps at Farnham Castle, near Salisbury and eventually he was appointed Camouflage Officer, 5th Corps, Southern Command. Nearly every day he drove across the calm Wiltshire countryside to Command Headquarters at Wilton House.

It was spring. '. . . The time of year I long to paint more than any other . . .' he once told Gregory and there could be no better time to see Wilton than with the daffodils gilding the lawns under the great cedars and warming, in their reflection, the austerity of the pale stone of the one-time abbey which since the sixteenth century had been the magnificent home of the Herberts, Earls of Pembroke.

Constable must have admired Wilton on his frequent painting trips to a part of England so reminiscent of his beloved East Anglia. In the house's fine parkland, sweeping down to the river, Shakespeare had acted and Philip Sidney had written his *Arcadia*. During the seventeenth century much of the original Tudor house had been replaced by a set of elegant rooms designed by Inigo Jones. Of these, the most glorious was the Double Cube Room, measuring sixty feet long, thirty feet high and thirty feet wide. As the wartime operations centre of an army command headquarters it was shrouded in plywood to protect the famous Van Dyke portraits inset in its panels, but the magnificent painted ceiling, representing the story of Perseus, remained exposed as if to inspire the modern gladiators.

The General Officer Commander-in-Chief Southern Command

was Claude Auchinleck, a proud, lonely soldier, disillusioned after the recent frustrations of the unsuccessful Norwegian campaign. Ostensibly, there was little likelihood of anything but a formal acquaintanceship developing between the professional soldier and Edward Seago, probably the least disciplined of all his officers, and 26 years his junior. But underlying their apparent differences were two common fundamentals – a love of painting and a mistrust of women.

Auchinleck, a keen amateur painter, liked Seago from the beginning. Confronted by the heavy new responsibilities of repelling an apparently imminent invasion, he was relieved to find an officer who could be relied on not to talk 'shop' all the time. As a companion his Camouflage Officer was shrewd, amusing and a good listener, but he refrained from showing his Commanding Officer the usual exaggerated degree of respect which was a barrier to real friendship. Instead he had the rare gift of making the serious soldier laugh so that Auchinleck remembered him as 'a refreshing relief from the usual died-in-the-wool staff officers who invariably surrounded me and I was delighted to have him around'.

'We had some fun together, camouflaging Chesil Beach,' Auchinleck recalled in his biography. 'He invented a wonderful camouflage material out of horse-hair which was the best I have ever seen; but the War Office said there were not enough horses to provide the necessary hair.' Seago's long and detailed accounts of his experiments with his 'wig-netting', as he named it, showed that because it was non-inflammable it could be shot at without disintegrating, as well as affording a versatile form of cover.

Regularly, during the short time he was at Wilton, Auchinleck invited his Camouflage Officer to join him on tours along the hundred-mile coast-line under his command, to assess the terrain from Bognor to Bristol in terms of defence in the light of the threatened German invasion.

'Seago had a way with Generals,' a fellow officer of his of that time complained grudgingly. But the jealous statement made no allowance for the ready admiration a military man often felt for artists. The admiration might be tinged with envy if the soldier had the urge, during leisure moments, to record on canvas the events he had been trained to observe so sharply but felt inadequate to portray.

In addition a soldier, his life a disciplined routine, might envy the artist his freedom to be answerable only to himself.

'Generals hero-worship people who can paint and because of Seago's powerful artistic personality, they were clay in his hands,' was the summing up of Sir John Anderson, an impartial observer. Auchinleck typified this. As a leader accustomed to ordering other people about he found it a relief to be able to defer, for a change, to an unquestionable expert in a subject like painting in which he was anxious to excel and where, for once, he could be the subordinate, without loss of dignity. At that time he and Seago only discussed their mutual love of painting for Auchinleck had no ability to 'cut off' from the exigencies of war long enough to indulge his hobby. So in the lengthening evenings, Seago strolled alone along the bank of the River Avon, where primroses clustered under the tall chestnuts. It was hard to visualize the place as his country's first line of defence should the invaders get a foothold, and his main emotion was joy at being back in England in time to see the spring. At last the old familiar longing to capture the moment in paint returned.

When he prised his paint-box open, it was a struggle to lever the palette apart from the panel rack. The brushes felt soft, but unfamiliar to his touch and the caps on the paint tubes were stiff to unscrew. But the paint squeezed out, pure and moist, and for the time being it was enough to daub it on to the palette, to touch with the tip of a finger, feeling and smelling, savouring the moment to come when he would lose himself in its use.

A few evenings later as the army prepared to evacuate Dunkirk, Seago sat by the river sketching the trees and the superb little Palladian Bridge with its arches and columns mirrored in the water. There was a feeling of both excitement and repose there, so that when the light failed and he packed away his paints he stayed for a while, puffing at his pipe with the old but familiar sense of contentment. Henry Melchett had been right. He visualized another evening when he would return to paint the chestnut trees in full flower.

But the chestnuts flowered late that summer of invasion rumours. He grew afraid to wait, and compromised by painting the trees just as they broke into leaf. A young subaltern admired the picture while it was drying in the mess. 'I don't know if you ever sell any of your things,' he asked, 'but I wouldn't mind giving you a quid for that one.' That wartime sale was one of the most satisfying he ever made.

Gradually he slipped into an eminently satisfying routine. His job – involving close co-operation with the air force – was broadly speaking to conceal identifiable places and military objectives from the air and although the 'wig-netting' invention had been rejected as impractical, his knowledge translated to meet wartime requirements proved of real value.

His approach to the problem of camouflage was refreshingly new. He made no attempt to paint out buildings and identifiable objects individually so that, from the air, it appeared that they did not exist, but he set out to make them converge with their background or look like completely different objects. For instance a battleship could be painted so that, from the air, it looked like a string of barges. His method was that of the picture restorer who must first of all consider the general tone, shape and pattern of the canvas to be restored or, in military terms, the object to be camouflaged. Texture was of prime importance. On canvas it could vary between a thin covering of paint, broad sweeping brush strokes or daubs of colour applied with a trowel by a mad impressionist which, in landscape terms, he saw as the equivalent of arable, pasture or scrub.

He wrote a thesis on dummy shadows advocating that they should not, as in the past, be applied as flat, dark green or brown areas, but with the addition of half-tones and dark tones to reproduce the luminosity of real shadows and provide a complete camouflage even in sunlight, against both the human eye and the camera.

The camera's newest weapon against camouflage, infra-red film, necessitated a new appraisal of colour values and through Melchett, Seago was in close touch with ICI's newest developments in anti-infra-red camouflage paint and material. He advocated camouflaging a large area, like an aerodrome, with groups of painted trees and four or more sets of dummy shadows to each group so that some shadows were in the right direction at any time of day. If the central target were similarly shadowed the enemy would be confused as to its whereabouts.

Moreover, alongside the technique of the artist he brought the imagination of the showman to the business of camouflage as when he requisitioned a London film studio to produce hundreds of life-size models of Neville Chamberlain wearing battle-dress and a tin hat. Every model had a rifle fixed at a different angle and was mounted on an individual turntable and used to man dummy anti-aircraft sites, strategically placed around the south coast to deter the invaders. The guns and the soldiers were remotely controlled from several central points so that they rotated and changed positions to give a most realistic effect when photographed from the air. Nothing delighted Seago's sense of humour more than to think of the model Neville Chamberlains he had created defending their country!

He also realized the necessity of working simply and quickly with the minimum of labour and materials; a far more practical approach than some of his fellow camouflage artists, including the theatrical designer Oliver Messel, who devoted much loving care and many valuable man hours to create an ornate and beautifully meticulous reproduction of a little gazebo to mask a concrete pillbox.

In the new-found camaraderie of a predominantly male society, freed at last from the tensions of maternal over-protection and faced with the unfamiliar challenge of meeting up to daily responsibilities, Seago became, to quote one of his senior messing officers, 'the life and soul of the outfit' and enjoyed a popularity he had not believed possible.

Fortunately, as a soldier who was a complete individualist, his job involving close co-operation between the army and the air force was unprecedented enough to permit the minimum of regimentation. At first he lived at the School of Army Co-operation at Old Sarum RAF Station on the opposite side of Salisbury from Wilton House, a cheerful little station which boasted a comfortable, old-fashioned type of mess shared by both army and RAF officers and retained its peacetime practice of being staffed by civilian batmen. Here, among the pilots and young army officers, he was 'that erudite, artist fellow, with a fund of marvellous stories', and his popularity soared. His reputation as a showman and raconteur also grew as his well-attended lectures on 'Camouflage Principles and Procedures' took on the nature of one-man entertainments.

'We have it on the highest authority,' one lecture began, 'and the highest authority is God's authority, that one house on one hill cannot be hidden. Nevertheless, God cannot have seen our camouflage netting.' But it was the manner of the delivery as much as the content that captured his audience. The drawled understatement, a disarming trace of shyness, the cool, sophisticated appraisal of his audience as if he were memorizing the scene for a painting, and the throw-away line. For the first time since his circus days, when he had found himself acting as ring-master, he held the centre of the stage – and revelled in it.

He contrived amusing aids to illustrate his lectures. There was the bedroom scene where a nude lady was revealed stepping into her bath believing herself to be completely concealed behind what he demonstrated, as the light changed, were quite inadequate curtains. The applause from his young audience was loud and approving. It was music to his ears.

Here, at last, he felt completely at home amongst young airmen whose daily journeys took them close to the skies he had studied for so long, whose conversation was punctuated by the magic words 'Cirrus, Nimbus, Cumulus . . .' and who studied air currents and learned the contrary ways of the wind much as the artist Leonardo da Vinci had done some six centuries before. Gradually, the conviction grew that he must join them. He too must learn to fly.

Like many of the best wartime operations, it was highly irregular. His friend, Squadron-Leader Peter Hurndall, DFC, who often piloted him on camouflage reconnaissance, was not a qualified flying instructor, but no one could have sympathized more than he with a man's frustration at not being allowed to go alone into the sky. He had left school intending to make flying his career but had failed the entrance exam to the RAF Cranwell and, as a second choice, had joined his father's army regiment, the 13th-18th Hussars. However, he never abandoned his flying dream and on the outbreak of war succeeded in getting secondment from his regiment to the RAF. In May 1940, he was shot down flying a Lysander with No. 13 Squadron over France and badly injured, but not before he had shot down three German ME 109s. For this he was awarded the DFC. He, of all people, was willing to help another army officer to become airborne.

He taught Seago in the station's little dual-control Miles Magister and, after twelve hours instruction in the forward cockpit, there was the autumn afternoon when his pupil went solo. 'I remember how everything I had been taught went completely out of my mind,' Seago wrote afterwards, 'and I remember that it didn't seem to matter. There was only one thing that mattered: I was alone in the sky. A new life had begun. The blue sky had become an ocean to voyage upon. The clouds, countries to explore. I could not possibly have grown so much older . . .'

From then on, at least two or three times a week, Major Seago's name appeared in the station's flight book recording his use of the little low-level training plane. The precise purpose of the flights as entered in the authorization book was 'hither and thither'. Their true purpose, as he admitted to his close friends, was 'to see the other side of the clouds'.

In the meantime, in the second winter of the war Auchinleck was appointed C-in-C India. When Seago asked who was to succeed him all 'the Auk' would say was: 'Oh, you'll like him. I'm not telling you who he is, but you'll like him.' He had no idea how prophetic his words were to prove.

A few days later, just before Christmas, the new General Officer C-in-C, Southern Command, Lieutenant-General Harold Alexander, arrived at Wilton and, without delay, invited his Camouflage Officer to his study; a small, corner room, its walls lined with crimson damask, its windows looking to the Palladian Bridge beyond wide lawns by then studded with machine-gun emplacements.

'You're the painter, aren't you?' Alexander opened the conversation. 'I've always admired your work.'

'What particular pictures had you in mind?' Seago enquired bluntly. Alexander mentioned a painting he had seen, but the artist pursued the question.

'What other pictures?'

The General with a reputation for being in complete control of every situation was, for a moment, off balance.

'I can't remember anything else, specifically,' he confessed and both men, simultaneously, roared with laughter. The General was the second to recover. His amusement was heightened by delight at meeting a soldier who, like himself, could not be intimidated. Here, at last, was someone he could really talk to and, for the next hour, the conversation in that small, pleasant room was of painting and Alexander's regret that he had hardly done any serious painting since leaving school. Seago was relieved and delighted. Were all Generals at heart frustrated artists?

Alexander was impatient to explore the friendship. The next week-end he invited Seago to join him and his wife and their young children at The Vale, their small Regency house on the edge of Windsor Great Park. It was the beginning of a life-long friendship that was equally opportune for both men. Alexander had made few intimate friends since the death of Eric Greer, who had joined the Irish Guards with him as a fellow Second Lieutenant and had been killed at Passchendaele and, with the strain of increased responsibility, he welcomed the arrival of a close companion to help at times to take his mind off the war.

Seago was the first to benefit from the friendship because until then there had been no proper studio for camouflage work. Alexander arranged for a hut to be put at his disposal, half for the official workshop and the other half for a private studio which the General often frequented, and where he needed little persuasion in the few free hours at his disposal to take up painting again. There he rediscovered a talent first displayed in a picture of an officer's plumed hat and sword with which he had won the drawing prize at Harrow and, subsequently, in three full sketch-books from the Western Front when he was a young officer in the First World War.

About that time Seago resumed his boyhood practice of painting in water-colour which, since his early teens, he had hardly used. He had then realized that it was a medium for experienced and practised hands because much of its beauty lay in direct and rapid painting done without hesitation so that it retained the liquid luminosity that was one of its greatest qualities. With oil colour, mistakes or a whole picture could be blotted out, and the same canvas could be used again. However, in wartime, canvases and oil panels were bulky to carry about and, unlike water-colours, oils required time for drying.

At first, when he used water-colour again, Seago worked in phases, using water-colour for several weeks and then changing to oils because he found it difficult to alternate quickly between two such different processes. With oils he worked from dark to light and the opposite applied with water-colour and not until long after the war did he feel able to use either medium as the mood took him.

Meanwhile, at Wilton in the lengthening evenings, Seago and

Alexander went on painting excursions by the river. Walking along the bank the General, a conspicuous figure in his uniform covered with medal ribbons, caused considerable embarrassment to his soldiers and their girls enjoying their off-duty. Seago invariably changed into a sweater and pair of old slacks to paint and eventually he protested: 'You can't come down here in full uniform. If I were you I'd get into civilian clothes to paint.'

The next morning he found Alexander had taken his advice and was sitting in his office at army headquarters, a relaxed figure in his oldest civilian clothes. 'Well, we're going painting, aren't we?' he reasoned logically, in reply to Seago's shocked query.

'Yes, but not 'til this afternoon,' Seago countered, as if to a child.

Alexander, as an artist, surprised Seago. The first time they painted together he recognized that the great soldier could have been a very good artist had he chosen to devote his whole life to painting. 'He had all the instinct and the attitude of a painter,' Seago maintained. 'What he lacked was time. You need years of practice before you can control your brush. You can't give it up for six months. You've got to go on and on.'

The friendship was strengthened when he realized that Alexander had the attitude of a professional painter in terms in which he, Seago, distinguished between the amateur and the professional. 'In my own mind,' he said, 'I see the amateur as somebody who is very often pleased with something they've done and I see the professional as someone who is always disappointed with something they've done. If you take that sort of yardstick, then Alex comes down slightly on the side of the professional. And this is what I found interesting about him.'

So, as he would have done with another professional, Seago never hesitated to criticize Alexander's work in painters' language which he knew his companion would understand. This was contrary to his habit with those who painted purely as a hobby and as a means of relaxing.

'I wouldn't dream of criticizing their pictures,' he said, 'because I'd only spoil their fun and what I said wouldn't make any sense to them. If I said: "this is out of tone," they wouldn't know what I was talking about. But Alex would. So I would criticize him up to the point of saying: "look Alex, you're not getting anywhere. Scrub it and do it again." I wouldn't go as far as actually saying that, because it would be merely spoiling his fun. If he asked, I would just tell him where he'd gone wrong.'

Over supper they discussed their work and the English painters they both admired such as William Nicholson, Wilson Steer, Sickert and Augustus John at his best – who had all succeeded in capturing the quality of light and atmosphere they both aimed to convey.

Seago's friendship with Alexander allied to other successful relationships and the immediate challenge of his camouflage work was reflected in a new authority in his painting which he, however, attributed to a different cause. He recognized that as a painter his perception was growing stronger and his feelings asserting themselves with greater definition, but he assumed that this was the result of frustrating periods of artistic inactivity when war deprived him of the chance to express himself on canvas. In support of this theory he recalled the experiences of artists like Jagger, whose finest work had been achieved in times of greatest trial.

He considered that, contrary to the popular view that sensitive artistic people were unsuited to army life, a painter was particularly fortunate because his keenly-developed perception of beauty helped him to find a strange consolation in apparently uncongenial conditions.

'This inward happiness is a continual source of joy which cannot be taken away,' he wrote, 'but with it there is the pain of being deprived of the means to express it.'

Nevertheless, as a wealth of paintings from that period testifies, he did manage to express it, that new happiness, born not only from the real challenges and the warm comradeship that surrounded him, but from a friendship that meant more than any he had ever known.

Seago's greatest friendship was with a young airman. In 1941, Ronald Horton introduced him to twenty-one-year-old Flight-Lieutenant Bernard Clegg. Horton was then a King's Messenger and met Clegg at the RAF School of Army Co-operation at Old Sarum to where the airman had been posted for a period of rest and recuperation after a hard bout of operational flying at Dunkirk. One of his less arduous flying duties was to accompany Horton on his secret missions.

One evening in July 1941, Horton and Clegg had met in the bar of a Bournemouth hotel at six o'clock. Clegg was to be the observer in a crew of three chosen to take Horton on a mission to Yugoslavia. The party flew out to Gibraltar in a Sunderland and from there to Malta where they transferred to a Heinkel Float Plane, moored in a small bay. It was one of six Heinkels captured from the Germans during the Norwegian campaign.

Until then, no use had been made of these enemy planes, five of which had been shot up at their moorings by German fighters. The remaining one was nicknamed 'The Winkle'. It was planned to land it at night on a lonely lake in Yugoslavia to rendezvous with partisans in a small motor boat and transfer a light cargo of radio transmission sets. Admittedly, the noise of the plane would be picked up by enemy radio-location stations, but it would be identified as one of their own and allow time to get away before the enemy realized that no Heinkel 115 should have been in the area.

'Everything went according to plan,' Horton recorded in his diary. 'It was bright moonlight when Bernard brought us to the long narrow lake, its water standing out clearly from the dark mountains surrounding it, whose steep sides came down sheer to the very edge. By the light of the moon I was soon able to recognize the spot where a steep, winding track led down to the water, and here I knew our friends would be awaiting me.' The outcome of this adventure was successful, as were many that were to follow.

The last mission on which Bernard Clegg was the navigator in 'The Winkle' brought Horton's overseas adventures round full circle to his visit to France twenty-one years before and his meeting with Paul Charnaud. On Horton's instigation the Frenchman had become a wartime organizer in his country's underground movement and had sent a message requesting direct communication with England in connection with a new scheme for returning allied airmen shot down over occupied territory. In the summer of '42 'The Winkle' was operating from Poole Harbour and it flew on the mission to rendezvous with Charnaud as Horton described:

'Under cover of clouds on a dark, moonless night, we landed the plane in a small, sheltered bay of the N-W coast of France where there was supposed to be the least risk of detection as the nearest inhabitants, fishing folk, lived about two miles away. No troops were supposed to be in the district and the cliffs were so steep as to make any attempt at invasion landings unlikely so that the sector had virtually been left unguarded, apart from an occasional routine patrol. With the engines switched off, we bobbed gently up and down on the swell, the water lapping against the floats. We could see absolutely nothing for it was as black as pitch.

'We must have waited nearly half an hour before a dinghy slid silently out of the night and drew alongside and we saw two hefty fishermen grinning at us. The pilot and I climbed out of the cockpit and dropped ourselves into their boat, leaving Bernard in charge of the Heinkel. We pushed off and rowed, not to the shore, but right round one arm of the bay and in forty minutes felt the boat run aground on the sand of a secluded little cove. One of the fisherlads whispered instructions and pointed out a narrow, winding path up to a little black hut on the cliff top, where Paul would be waiting.

'The pilot remained by the boat with one of the lads while the other Frenchman guided me through the darkness. I actually saw the outline of Paul's figure as he came out of the hut and down the path to meet me, but before either of us had time to speak there was a blaze of fire and I remembered no more until I regained consciousness, fifteen hours later, back in England.'

Later he learned that his pilot and the Frenchman had collected him from the bottom of the cliff where Paul Charnaud lay dead by his side. How the plan had gone wrong he never knew but perhaps by sheer bad luck a sleepy, trigger-happy patrol chanced to pass close to the hut, thought they saw something suspicious and, probably believing the shadowy target was a sheep or a cow, fired their rifles and passed on without further investigation.

After Horton and his companions had made several missions in 'The Winkle', the pilot commissioned Seago to paint an impression of the plane to give to Horton as a token of his admiration. The painting could only be based on the RAF's official identification photographs of a Heinkel but it succeeded in conveying a feeling of suspense and loneliness which perhaps Seago recalled from another unofficial flight he had made in a small plane, before the war, with

Henry Melchett when they went to visit Dollfüss. For some reason, perhaps in an ironic or over-zealous attempt to preserve official secrecy in the cause of undercover activities, the painting, which was called 'Unidentified Aircraft' and merited a prominent place in Horton's collection, was never signed.

Bernard Clegg was the only member of 'The Winkle' crew to be stationed at Old Sarum and Horton asked Seago to paint his portrait as a companion picture to 'Unidentified Aircraft'. In the painting the cheerful fresh-faced young man with boyish good looks and the build of a rather stocky athlete had something very reminiscent of Tommy Baker about him. But the resemblance was purely physical. Clegg was a brilliant scholar and a perfectionist in everything he attempted. It had been his boyhood ambition to fly but before the war his family's social position made it unlikely he would achieve his aim. However he won a scholarship to the local grammar school and from there, at fifteen years of age, was accepted on competitive entry as an aircraft apprentice at the RAF electrical and wireless school and trained as an instrument maker. From there he won a cadetship to Cranwell and was awarded the Hyde-Thompson Memorial Prize for the apprentice-applicant with the highest number of marks. He was also a fine athlete and had fenced for the RAF since his first year at Cranwell.

Clegg passed out from Cranwell just as war started and joined Number 26 Squadron, Army Co-operation in France where, during the army's evacuation from Dunkirk, he made twelve cross-Channel trips in two days in a slow old Lysander dropping food to the troops on the beaches. He had no sleep for forty-eight hours and his plane was badly holed in one wing but he was one of the lucky ones who miraculously survived that and many crashes during his flying career. However, as a result of seeing the in-describable horror of German planes bombing lines of refugees and open towns, he decided that although he loved flying, under no circumstances was he prepared to take human life. He was neverthe-less willing to run any risk to save it, and to that end his plane never again carried armament. It was at this point that he and Seago met.

Seago was immediately impressed by his courage, his warm, sensitive personality and many accomplishments. He loved classical music, was an avid reader and, moreover, hearing him talk about his boyhood in his surprisingly soft, flat-vowelled Yorkshire accent, Seago could have been struck by some marked coincidences in their formative years.

Bernard Clegg too had been afflicted by a mysterious illness when he was about six years old and it was feared he would not survive. The doctor could only describe it as 'near-typhoid' attributable to eating shellfish on holiday. Whatever the illness really was the boy was fed on nothing but milk for six months and was nursed devotedly by his distraught mother who hardly left his bedside. By the time he recovered, he had acquired a deep resentment for his father and the label of 'delicate' which, despite early signs of athletic prowess, was with him throughout his schooldays.

Before the portrait of Bernard Clegg was finished he and Seago were spending all their free time together. Seago had by now acquired an empty gardener's cottage in the grounds of 5th Corps Officers' Mess at Britford called the Moat Cottage, a tiny two up and two down with a walled garden, bounded on three sides by the moat which gave it its name and rendered it picturesque, very cold and extremely damp. There was no electricity and all water had to be pumped by hand into an egg-shaped marble sink in the corner of a tiny kitchen extension off the small sitting-room. The used water went down into an open drain through the wall and out into the back garden from which, on summer evenings, a procession of forty or fifty snails could be relied on to crawl in under the back door across the stone floor and up the wall to the sink.

'They're only here for the water,' the conservation-minded host announced proudly to any squeamish guests.

The Moat Cottage boasted a sitting-room, twelve feet by ten and a small bedroom downstairs, and two upstairs rooms which Seago used as his bedroom and studio; the rent was £20 a year. Outweighing any minor disadvantages, old-fashioned roses rioted over the stone walls and the tiny windows overlooked water meadows studded with great elms. In the distance, the spire of Salisbury Cathedral rose like a finger from a flat landscape reminiscent of his beloved East Anglia. This, too, was painter's country and in the centuries-old stone cottage he felt secure enough to ignore the war for precious hours at a time and paint some of the best pictures he had ever done; timeless oils, to endure long after the memories of war had faded.

There was one week-end when he and Bernard, after a glorious afternoon's flying in which they had indulged in the heady exercise of 'practising landings on the clouds', decided to tackle the job of redecorating their much-prized home. The electricity had just been installed and they distempered the dirty cream walls pale green and painted the woodwork ivory. They worked with hardly a break until by Sunday afternoon the job was complete and after a celebration tea of rather stale cream cakes, Bernard relaxed with a book in the newly decorated sitting-room. Seago puffed contentedly at his pipe, took out his paints and made a picture of Bernard reading, with the late sun streaming in through the window on to his book. Swiftly he caught the mood of the moment, a memory he instinctively knew he should hold on canvas.*

He had never been so content. His relationship with Bernard was deep and satisfying. At last he had a friend with an intellect as sharp as his own; who mirrored his own sensitivity and fun, yet who did not suffer fools gladly; who admired and who justified admiration and who, above all, did not compete. Bernard had a great zest for living and lived (as Seago aimed to do) every moment of every day to the full and accepted gratefully and unquestioningly whatever life offered. Never again, the painter felt, need he lie alone to struggle with a pounding heart through the long night or feel beholden to some paid attendant to conceal, as gracefully as he could, in the name of friendship, an instinctive aversion to the abject sight he presented in one of his attacks. With Bernard there could be no degradation.

Despite his new-found contentment he was still having heart attacks about which he knew the army should remain in complete ignorance. Here fate played into his hands with the timely reappearance of his boyhood friend Parker. He was Sapper Parker when the two men met again after the abrupt termination of their friendship ten years previously over the episode of the horse Sling Along. In the army he had suffered a series of slight wartime misadventures culminating in the loss of rank as a result of a brush with authority. It happened because the amateur jockey had gone absent without leave to ride at a race meeting and when Seago came across

* 'The Moat Cottage'.

him in a transit camp he found him completely disillusioned with army life. Seago saw at once how a reconciliation could be used to his advantage for Parker was the one soldier who knew all about his heart turns and would be quite willing to join in any conspiracy to conceal them. He had no difficulty in getting permission for his old friend to be his driver-cum-batman whose most important (unofficial) duty, in the event of his officer going sick, would be to call in a civilian doctor rather than an army one who would have taken drastic action in respect of the cardiac disability. To this end Parker carried a sealed envelope containing written instructions to give to a new doctor unfamiliar with Seago's condition, in the event of a heart turn.

Having taken reasonable steps to protect a way of life that was near-idyllic – apart from the existence of a war – Edward Seago and Bernard Clegg fell into a routine as enviable as it was unusual. Bernard often brought a girl friend to stay at the cottage but two or three evenings a week he and Seago were on their own and went to the Haunch of Venison in Salisbury for hot baths followed by a good dinner, willingly provided by the landlord's daughter, Dolly Bradbeer. The splendid fourteenth-century inn was a regular haunt of Augustus John when he was living at his old manor, Fryern Court at Fordingbridge. There the elderly artist, a solitary figure in a muffler and shabby corduroys, tried to obliterate for an hour or two his awareness of his diminishing capabilities in the seclusion of the Captain's Cabin, a little room up a short flight of steps with a window looking down on to the saloon bar.

Peering down on a company where at one time, before his tolerance to alcohol diminished he would have been able to keep up with the best, Augustus John might have noticed with momentary amusement the young artist he had met at Melchet Court, seated in front of the huge fireplace demonstrating his latest party piece. Taking a penny with a postage stamp adhering to it sticky side uppermost, Seago would nonchalantly flick the coin up over his head so that the stamp stuck to the ceiling and the coin fell back into his hand. By the end of the war the stamp-starred area of the ceiling round the fireplace commemorated his skill. Few of the endless stream of customers who tried to copy him managed to acquire the knack. He had come a long way from his corner seat at Ada Cannell's bar at the Beaufort Hotel in Norwich.

This landlord's daughter, Dolly Bradbeer, was one of the staunchest women friends he ever made. A pleasant, forthright young woman, she had intended to be an artist and studied for admission to the Slade School before a drop in the family's finances turned her to journalism and newspaper reporting. The war brought her and her sister home to help their father run the pub. But Dolly and her favourite customer had more in common than her mild interest in art. Both had a determination of character born of a decision to lead a normal life despite their respective physical handicaps.

At first glance Dolly's handicap was only too apparent for the left side of her face was cruelly puckered and scarred by an ill-managed operation for a malignant birthmark when she was three months old. However before her schooldays were over she had coolly and completely managed to come to terms with her disfigurement and had decided that if she would not concede that it made the slightest difference to her life, no one else's opinion mattered. In this she mirrored the philosophy of Edward Seago's attitude towards his heart condition.

Ironically he failed to appreciate that there was a possibility of a deep relationship developing between them. He apparently never considered that Dolly who was two or three years older than he was, did not accept her facial disfigurement as a barrier to anything more than a purely platonic friendship. Dolly, with innate pride, came to accept this, made no emotional demands on him and therefore was a welcome visitor at the Moat Cottage. There he played the spinnet and she saw his first excursion into sculpture and to her must go some credit for his model of Pegasus, the flying horse of Greek mythology, ridden by the winged hero Bellerophon. While she watched Seago at work on the plaster model for an officers' mess of the Airborne Forces, he suddenly appealed to her: 'Should we make it a mare or a stallion?'

'A stallion,' she replied instinctively and, thereafter, searched the local markets and secondhand shops for bits of old bronze to ensure the main casting did the splendid figure full justice, even in wartime.

No commission ever gave Seago more pleasure. His design for the sculpture in pale blue on a maroon ground, after consultation with

General ('Boy') Browning, Formation Commander, was adopted as the insignia of the Airborne Forces and all his life Seago carried the fabric shoulder flash, as worn by 'The Red Devils', in a small wallet along with two snapshots, one of Bernard and one of his father. Eventually the original casting of Pegasus and Bellerophon was sent to the Headquarters of the Airborne Forces.

Seago and Bernard never lacked visitors at the Moat Cottage for friends or mere acquaintances who found themselves with a few hours to spare and within travelling distance, would contrive an invitation to their home where their happiness was infectious. John Hill, subsequently MP for South Norfolk, recalled in his diary a particularly pleasant evening he spent with them when he visited Old Sarum as an Army Liaison Officer. After dinner in mess, he and Clegg, sprawled in armchairs, sipped Pimms from silver tankards and listened to records of the Grieg Piano Concerto and Bach organ music while Seago made a quick pencil sketch. Afterwards, Seago constructed amusing caricatures of little men around their respective signatures.

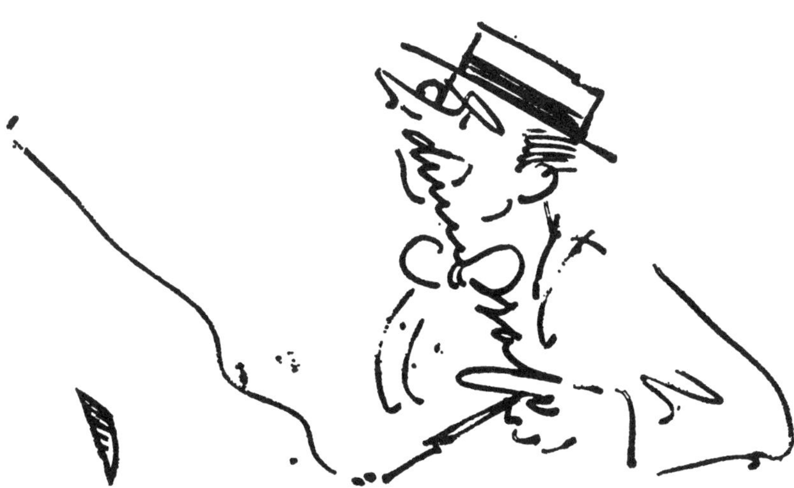

He followed this up by demonstrating a professional way of forging a signature by getting his visitors to sign their names and then turning the paper upside down and copying the writing backwards.

'What a grand evening it was,' Hill wrote. 'One to remember with pleasure all my life. Seago has a cheerful way with him. I had never been drawn before or afterwards by so good an artist. It was exciting and wonderful to see the thing grow. I would have loved to have the drawing, but was too shy to ask.'

The next time Hill saw the drawing it was reproduced in *A Generation Risen,** the third book in which a selection of Seago's pictures were matched to poems by John Masefield. Its inclusion proved that he was not the only one who had treasured the evening. The poem accompanying it was written after close discussion between poet and artist.

> 'What do these unknown warriors talk about?
> The war, the latest bomb, a cunning gun,
> The methods by which battles may be won
> And Europe's ugly scarecrows put to rout?
>
> 'Not altogether; for the ALO
> Talks of strange hands of bridge, and subtle play
> Seen at the Oval, seven years ago
> And seeming still a miracle today.
>
> 'The Pilot talks of what he hopes to see,
> The Opera and the Ballets still unplanned,
> In theatres which England will demand
> In the more splendid England still to be.'

Masefield had been hard put to find time to write all the poems needed for the book because he had committed himself to do war work. 'The composition may take longer than I supposed,' he wrote. 'As to the title *A Generation Risen* comes near to what is wanted, but

---

* In the London blitz the offices of Collins, the publishers, were damaged. Afterwards a demolition worker found a bundle of papers in a cupboard. They were slightly damaged by water and proved to be the original drawings for *A Generation Risen*. Eventually they were returned to Seago and some were restored.

I believe we can get it just a shade nearer presently. There ought to be some hint, that this generation does a harder thing than the 1914 lot.'

It was a comparison the readers were left to decide for themselves because *A Generation Risen* was the title of the tribute in pictures and poetry to the anonymous heroes of war. The book was the only instance of Seago's collaboration with Masefield in which the illustrations were rated higher than the poems.

'. . . Seago has gone to the source for his material while Masefield has gone to Seago,' wrote the critics of the *New York Times*, unfairly discounting the older man's experience of an earlier war. Undoubtedly there was a new strength of draughtsmanship and a stark realism in the lightning pencil drawings of groups of young soldiers and airmen preparing for battle, planes wheeling into the sky, lorries lumbering along rain-lashed roads; the relentless war march, halted for a series of brief moments by a painter who was acutely aware, because he was part of it all, and had trained and exercised his talent in the make-believe worlds of the circus and the ballet until he was completely equipped to portray the dramas of real life.

Melchett had been right when he had told Seago that, like Jagger, he would do great work in the war because he was seeing it from the inside and not as an official artist. One drawing in the book, 'The Bronze Soldier', was a personal tribute to Jagger who had died in 1934 and whose greatest work resulted from the First World War. Seago's picture showed a group of soldiers standing in front of Jagger's colossal bronze memorial at Paddington Station, perhaps his friend's own most impressive memorial.

Anonymous though the people were in the drawings many can be identified: 'The Reconnaissance Pilot' in the book was his closest friend Bernard Clegg and Peter Hurndall, the man who taught him to fly, had sat for the 'Portrait Study of a Pilot'.

Clegg and Seago spent all their leaves at Brooke and, one bleak day in March, they decided that, good or bad weather, they would use some of their precious petrol ration to picnic at a favourite painting spot in the estuary of the River Blyth in Suffolk. The wind was firmly in the north-east but Mabel Seago and the indomitable Lilias Rider Haggard, who lived nearby, were equally undeterred and appeared swathed in warm clothing carrying a splendid picnic basket. Bernard turned up for the outing incongruously dressed in cotton shorts and open-necked shirt with his knees turning faintly blue and insisted, with an optimism that seemed sadly misplaced as the rain lashed the windscreen, that his dress was entirely appropriate for a spring leave. Indeed, when they arrived at the estuary, the clouds suddenly broke and the sun gleamed across the water, but the wind remained bitterly cold.

They picnicked out of the wind in a dip in the dunes, and afterwards while the others went for a walk, Seago set up his painting stool in an exposed spot and, muffled in rugs scarves and a sheepskin coat, his fingers numb with cold, he painted 'The Rain Cloud', a moment of peace in war, destined for a book he had already discussed with his old friend and neighbour, the writer Henry Williamson.

They had talked about it during an earlier leave on the day when Williamson saw Seago on the uplands of his farm, huddled on a stool, wrapped in a rug against the east wind, painting for hour after hour. Williamson met him going home in the twilight, lamenting in his quiet voice that the sky tints changed so rapidly and each so marvellously that he could hardly bring himself to leave them. Williamson invited Seago to join him for a cup of tea in the old smallholder's barn where he wrote his books. There they smoked their pipes before the open fire, surrounded by books, farm paraphernalia and hanging bunches of dried tobacco leaves, and discussed the better England they both believed would emerge from the war. Seago told the older man about his next book which he saw as a combination of pictures and essays describing how each illustration came to be painted. It was to be called *Peace in War*.

'It was to be a record,' Williamson recalled, 'of his escapes into the world of colour and form and line. Which is not to say that the good artist cannot also be the good soldier.'

Regardless of the artistic merit of *Peace in War* it was enthusiastically received as a sincere attempt at complete self-expression by a soldier-artist through the dual media of prose and painting. The writing was as refreshingly revealing as the pictures as, for instance, when Seago recalled the day on that spring leave when he had painted 'The Rain Cloud':

'To my mind there are few places to equal the bleak stretches of the East Anglian coast,' he wrote. 'Perhaps one has to be born and bred there for it really to get in one's blood. But it has a powerful hold on me and, wherever I go, I feel a longing to return there.'

Time and again he put into words his feeling for East Anglia as when he wrote:

'There is a strange grandeur . . . and a strange subtlety of constant change, which has inspired some of the greatest English landscapes. Each mood has a beauty of its own, whether in repose, or raked by a sharp east wind. In the happy painting ground of Cotman, Crome and Constable, I am making no more than a modest attempt to follow in the traditions of the English school, which they endowed with such brilliance and harmony . . . I have only a simple perception, but the country is full of simple things of real beauty, and many of them pass unnoticed by those more out of touch with a simple life.'

Edward Seago had travelled a long way to discover that philosophy and it took a war for him to recognize it so that at first only in rare moments did he express it through painting. Meanwhile, the book in which he stated it, categorically and for the first time, was dedicated to Bernard.

'The Rain Cloud', the painting that represented a small but perfect example of Seago's complete awareness of a moment of visual ecstasy, was bought by John Hill for twelve and a half guineas. He saw it on a visit to the Moat Cottage, paid £6 on account and took it back unframed in a large Government envelope to his room at the War Office. For him it proved a prophetic purchase for, after the war, quite unexpectedly, he bought an old water mill to convert into a home and afterwards discovered he was living not two miles from the scene in the picture.

Soon after the leave when the picture was painted, Bernard grew restless at Old Sarum. He had recovered from the strain of his Dunkirk experiences and was anxious to make a more positive contribution to the war effort and he was also tremendously keen to fly Spitfires. They were his ultimate ideal and with Seago's help he achieved this ambition when he was posted to the Photographic Reconnaissance Unit at RAF Benson and flew a Spitfire, stripped of all armament so that it could carry as much fuel as possible. Relying purely on his plane's speed to make an escape if attacked, he made regular reconnaissance flights over Germany and in due course was the first pilot to photograph the Mohne Dam in preparation for Guy Gibson's daring attack on it.

Benson was too far from Old Sarum for Bernard to commute and at first Seago knew no one else at the station with whom he wanted to share the Moat Cottage. But once again it seemed as if fate intervened for a letter arrived from John Carol saying that his asthma was too bad for him to continue working and the doctor had advised him to leave London.

Early in the war Seago had already arranged for the sick actor to spend some months in Norfolk and now it seemed obvious to invite him to the Moat Cottage to convalesce; when he was fit again he could stay on and take over the running of the place. The idea presented itself as a timely compensation for Bernard's departure and Seago welcomed the challenge of looking after someone else for a change. He visualized nursing Carol back to health and in the process consolidating a friendship associated with all the glamour of the stage – a world which he had almost forgotten but to which one day he hoped to return.

For once, his seemingly infallible instinct had played him false. Beneath his sophisticated veneer the youthful-looking actor was a down-to-earth Cockney born in the East End of London, whose character was very different from the elegant intellectual in Ibsen's *Ghosts* which was how Seago had painted his portrait. Moreover, confined to the Moat Cottage, Carol found it impossible to reconcile the solicitous, over-considerate officer, eager to take care of him, with the unconventional painter he had known in London. He was as embarrassed and sickened by the new Seago as he was by his asthma and bored to distraction by the loneliness. Clean air or no, after a few months he had had enough of country living and returned to London.

For Seago it was a humiliating rejection. He was deeply hurt by the complete renunciation of his first attempt to adopt an unselfish role and although the friendship was ostensibly patched up when

Carol telephoned him towards the end of the long illness which terminated his brilliant career, as far as Seago was concerned the association ended on the day when the actor walked out of the Moat Cottage and went back to London.

Meanwhile whenever Bernard could spend twenty-four hours at the Moat Cottage he flew down from Benson to Old Sarum. They made plans for after the war when Bernard would leave the air force and they would set up house. Seago was all for settling in Wiltshire; Bernard, after his visit to Brooke, preferred Norfolk. But wherever they lived, so Bernard confided to his elder brother, Jack, he would have a flat of his own in London so that he could entertain his girl friends for, like Tommy Baker, he also enjoyed women's company. The deeper implications of a lifetime friendship with the man he loved and admired may never have occurred to a twenty-two-year-old pilot, eager for new experiences. By the very nature of his training he lived for the moment even more than Seago. Again, like Seago he found, in wartime, a greater happiness than he had ever known.

The tenuous quality of this happiness had been reflected in *Peace in War* which had been written and illustrated with consummate ease in periods off duty. Within one week of its publication, on a midsummer day with just a few cumulus clouds about, Bernard, flying his Spitfire over Benson at six thousand feet, collided in a cloud with a plane flown by his Commanding Officer and both men were killed instantly.

Peace in War, Seago always said, was Bernard's book and Bernard, nicknamed 'Crasher' by his Commanding Officer after he had seen him miraculously survive several flying accidents, saw the first copy of the book a week before he died on 6 June 1943. On the fly-leaf was written 'Crasher – Here is the first copy of the first book – Ted.' Beneath, in printed text, a quotation from a poem by Robert Bridges proved an apt memorial:

> 'O youth whose hope is high
> Who doth to Truth aspire,
> Whether thou live or die,
> O look not back or tire.'

A Painter at War

Bernard Clegg left all his possessions 'to Ted'. That was the extent of his will. His portrait 'Reconnaissance Pilot' which had been commissioned by Ronald Horton and reproduced in *A Generation Risen* was given back to Seago and held pride of place in his studio for twenty-three years. Then he gave it to the RAF College at Cranwell. There new generations of airmen can speculate about the quizzical expression on the young, stubby features of a pilot who once studied there.

For the second time death had deprived Seago of his closest friend. It was a bitter irony for the painter who, if the doctors were to be believed, always lived with the threat of his own death inherent in his extraordinary heart condition. Although in wartime it was unrealistic to be surprised by it, death was something that Seago had never applied to Bernard and for weeks he found it impossible to comprehend. Bernard – the young, energetic, sensitive personality – had so much to learn despite his wisdom. It was difficult to believe that in the long years after the war there would not be time to teach him. For months Seago had tortured dreams in which he heard Bernard telling him that he was quite conscious when his plane had blown up and that 'it had hurt a lot'.

Friends rallied round. Henry Melchett went to his cottage within hours of the accident and Dolly Bradbeer was constantly there

because she had learnt early in the war what it was like to lose someone you loved. But for months Seago was inconsolable and it was
six months before he was able to write about the friendship to Alan
Delgado:

> 'It was something which I imagine only happens once in a life-
> time – if that – that two people who think completely on the same
> lines with similar ideas and the same tastes. One day I shall like to
> tell you a lot about him . . . I have found it very hard to sort my-
> self out and have not yet succeeded in doing so.
>
> 'I did not paint at all for about four months – which surprised
> me because I have always imagined that the painter has a great
> standby in his work when he mosts needs it. It's not true. Now I'm
> working pretty hard again – but seem to have lost interest in most
> other things, which worries me.'

In 1943 Seago's work concerned 'Operation Overlord' which
involved him sitting in on high-level conferences about the forthcoming invasion of Normandy. With a staff of two he organized a
series of training courses at Old Sarum and demonstrated, by means
of large-scale models, his plans for air-to-ground concealment of
troops waiting to embark.

At that time, in order to make the enemy believe the invasion
would be launched from the east coast, wagon-loads of dummy
supplies were regularly dispatched to the coast of Norfolk and
Suffolk and at night the wagons returned, apparently empty, with
their mock collapsible cargo stowed neatly away under the tar-
paulins. So meticulously aware was Seago about the need to conceal
the build-up of troops in Southern Command that he vetoed the
playing of football in case a path to a new football pitch might
indicate to the enemy the presence of more troops than usual.

Harry Colmer, a Lieutenant in the Artillery, was on the 'Overlord' training course and Seago invited him to stay at the Moat
Cottage. Colmer recalls the painter's emphatic dislike of the word
'camouflage' in favour of the term 'concealment'. To impress his
theories about concealment on his audiences Seago enlisted the help
of Sergeant Edwards, an amateur ventriloquist, and wrote an
amusing script recapitulating the points of his lecture for the

Sergeant and his soldier-doll to enact.

When the plans for 'Overlord' were complete, Seago became involved in the air-to-ground concealment of the huge storage tanks to be assembled overnight on the Isle of Wight for 'Operation Pluto', designed to carry the piped oil from England to France after the invasion.

At the time of Bernard's death, Seago had also been writing another book, *High Endeavour*, the true story of Jimmy Chipperfield, the circus man and animal trainer who, on the outbreak of war, with little education and against heavy odds, was determined to become an air force pilot. It was Seago's second book within a year, written and illustrated in periods of off-duty, and in content it aptly united the two worlds of the men Seago had loved – the circus and the air force. Two months after Bernard died, the author added an epilogue which had required much more effort to write than any other part of the book:

> 'In my mind I am convinced that we have a greater purpose; but I have no conception of something so un-understandable. I envy those who have been able to form definite beliefs upon which their faith is founded; I even envy those who can accept a belief they cannot comprehend, for both, I think, find comfort.
>
> 'I can do neither. In my heart I have profound faith in something I would call Divine; something far beyond the vision of men to conceive, beyond the expression of human speech. I cling to this blind faith, and the unanswerable questions will not shake it . . . I no longer seek an explanation. I go no further than myself, and if I can only justify myself it will be as much as I can do. In the end it comes down to individual man, and he must seek his own fulfilment according to his faith, which shall, indeed, constitute his duty . . .'

It had required much agonized soul-searching to work through his grief and come to his conclusions, and having formulated his feelings on paper he was able to try and pick up the torn threads of his life again. His involvement with Bernard, however, had not ended with writing an obituary notice for the local newspaper. He assumed obligations to his friend's family as if it were his own. He paid for the text books Jack Clegg needed at the start of his musical career, helped the younger sister Jean to pursue her career as a textile designer, and every year for the rest of his life sent Mrs Clegg a present on the anniversary of her son's death.

As frequently happens, once a hard-fought crisis has been resolved and a course of action decided upon, help in implementing it arrived from an unexpected source. In Seago's case it was in the form of a letter from an old friend, Miss Gladys Barnard, Curator of the Castle Museum, Norwich, inviting him to hold his first one-man exhibition in the city. Such recognition could not have come at a more opportune moment. It was impossible not to feel excited at the prospect of a hundred of his paintings hanging in the Castle. It seemed only a short time ago that his mother had taken him there to admire the work of Munnings and Crome, Constable and Cotman.

Doubtless the critics would look for comparisons. Well, they should have every opportunity of finding them for he would make sure that, despite wartime difficulties, it would be the most comprehensive display of his work that could be assembled and he advertised in *The Times* for an assistant to help him prepare it.

The successful applicant was nineteen-year-old Vernon Russell Smith, recently invalided out of the RAF and waiting to go up to Oxford to study architecture. On Seago's instructions he assembled oils and water-colours, portraits and landscapes, ballet and circus scenes, and wartime studies including a fine portrait of General Montgomery in uniform and, characteristically, in juxtaposition, an informal picture of General Alexander on a week-end painting expedition at his home.

'What fun it was painting that Sunday afternoon,' Alexander who had left Wilton in 1942, recalled, writing from his Army Headquarters during the battles around Cassino to wish Seago good luck with the exhibition. 'Now *that* is what I call enjoyment. When the war is over, we will be able to have some lovely days painting. We are in the middle of a battle here, so I haven't much news I can give you.'

Alexander lent three paintings for the exhibition. They justified his comments at their first meeting when he had said he always admired Seago's work. Masefield lent two pictures and agreed to write a foreword to the catalogue; Ronald Horton's sustained enthusiam could be judged by the fact that nine pictures, including the finest, came from his collection.

In the six weeks before the exhibition Seago had struggled unsuccessfully with a new painting – a large canvas of cattle in the snow in Norfolk, a composite picture painted in retrospect at the Moat Cottage – but, for once, he could not get it right.

'It's the most extraordinary thing. It's almost right but not quite,' he complained to Vernon over and over again, but his new assistant was unable to make any suggestions. He felt equally helpless when, as the exhibition approached, Seago retired to bed with a heart turn and for twenty-four hours the terrifying sound of his pounding heart and his laboured breathing could be heard all over the tiny cottage. Vernon had been warned that this could happen, but he was completely unprepared for the frightening sight and at times had real doubts as to whether the exhibition would be anything but a posthumous one.

When the attack was over Seago lay propped up in bed, relaxing, while the late afternoon sunlight traced shadows of the small square panes of glass on the flimsy curtains. He was fascinated by the play of light and his fingers itched for a paint brush; often, in the hours of well-being after struggling through the whirlpool of an attack he longed to paint, almost as if his creative energy had been recharged by adversity.

When he was up and about again he was haunted by the memory of the sunlight flushing the bedroom curtains to a warm pink and he toyed with the idea of making a picture but could think of no context in which to use the effect of the light playing on the curtains. Then, one afternoon, he noticed Vernon shaving at the kitchen sink, with the light from the kitchen window falling across his face. He saw his picture. At four o'clock in the afternoon he persuaded Vernon to change into pyjamas and transfer his shaving operation to the upstairs bedroom. By the end of the day, in contrast to the struggle he had had with the canvas of cattle in the snow, he had completed what he considered to be one of the best pictures he ever painted.

The small oil of a young man shaving in front of a bedroom window was listed No. 1 in the exhibition and afterwards Seago gave it to the City of Norwich to commemorate the exhibition. It was called 'The East Window', implying that morning was normally the time for shaving. A keen observer, however, might detect a soft mellow quality about the sunlight, more evocative of afternoon than morning and a visit to the Moat Cottage would prove that not one of the tiny windows there faced the east.

Seago's war had consolidated into a satisfying way of life. Whatever time he got back to the Moat Cottage after the day's work he would usually settle down after supper and paint his own kind of pictures, often working until the small hours of the morning or right through the night. He also found a new interest in working in the garden which Vernon had tamed and cultivated and which represented the beginning of the young man's eventual career as one of the country's foremost landscape architects.

Moreover Seago was never short of stimulating companions. Siegfried Sassoon lived nearby and they had long discussions and when Alexander was on leave from Burma or North Africa, or came back to England for thirty-six hours for a high-level conference, he and Seago met in London for an hour or two and usually managed to visit an art exhibition and occasionally a theatre. Derek Mond, now a Lieutenant in the RNVR, spent many leaves at the Moat Cottage. In 1942 when he was up at Oxford, he had married an undergraduate but he felt so drawn to Seago and eager to be with him that he had taken his bride Yvonne to Brooke for their honeymoon. Summing up the relationship Derek's young sister Karis said, 'Derek loved Ted, showed off to me, and Yvonne was his possession.'

Derek and Yvonne spent many leaves with Seago and in 1944 at the Moat Cottage the painter made a new portrait of the friend he had so often painted. It showed a bearded, confident young officer wearing a duffel coat over his uniform, nonchalantly smoking a pipe. Seago had objected to the duffel coat; he remembered that Bernard Clegg had worn one for his last portrait but, as usual, Derek had his own way.

Soon afterwards Seago was taken ill with a prolonged heart turn and, as usual, was in the care of a civilian doctor. After he had been absent for a couple of weeks, a conscientious army medical officer decided to pay a courtesy call on the Major whom he thought was suffering from influenza. He was shocked and startled to discover the real nature of his illness. On his report, Seago was summoned before a medical board and told to consider himself out of the army from the moment he left their presence.

'This annoyed me very much,' Seago recalled. 'I said "I shall do no such thing. You're a medical board and you can't turn me out of the army; you can only recommend that I shall be turned out." I was very incensed by this but, of course, it went through.' It went through in record time, and as far as Seago was concerned it was the ultimate rejection.

The pain and humiliation were clearly apparent in a letter which Seago wrote to Alexander, by then Commander-in-Chief of the 15th Army Group in Italy. The General's reply, written from his headquarters on 1 October 1944, was characteristic of his firmness and readiness to turn his power to patrician use. He wrote in long-hand:

'My Dear Ted –
'My aeroplane (DC3) is taking home the Commander of the 8th Army and returning empty except for Rupert Clarke and one of my drivers whom I am sending on a few days leave.

'This will be a grand opportunity for you to come out and pay me a limitless visit. You will stay at my HQ as my guest and I can probably find some work for you to do if you get bored – but bring all your painting materials and you will be able to paint to your heart's content.

'Come in uniform (it will be easier) – I am also giving you a pass which you can show if anyone is too much of a busybody.

'Looking forward very much to seeing you,
                              Yours ever,
                                    Alex.

'PS. I can send you home whenever you want to go back – I have my own machine and crew – and the journey is only 7–8 hours.'

A few days later Seago had a telephone call from Alexander's ADC, Rupert Clarke, asking if he could come to London immediately and leave from Northolt the following morning. Ralph Snagge, the Military Assistant to General Sir John Harding, recalls meeting Seago for the first time when he and Clarke collected him from a house in Grosvenor Square at six o'clock on a misty autumn morning.

'He was just stepping into the car,' Snagge said, 'when he said "Oh, my goodness, I ought to bring my paints".'

'Do you paint?' Snagge recalled he enquired conversationally.

'I am going to try,' Seago said and rushed back into the house and after a few minutes emerged with an armful of painting gear. When he heard they were flying across France he was very surprised. 'Isn't there a battle going on?' he asked, and when Snagge said he hoped they would be flying far above it Seago fervently agreed.

The weather was so appalling that they were forced down by an electric storm and compelled to make a landing in Corsica which was occupied by the Americans. They spent the night there and were rather concerned because Seago had no official papers, but at five o'clock a.m. they took off and landed in Rome and from there drove to Alexander's advance headquarters which was a little group of caravans and tents in the middle of a wood about five miles from Siena. Seago takes up the story.*

'I went there, and said "What's the idea?" Alexander told me: "I thought you might like to come and paint here. If the army don't want you, you might as well paint and what better place to paint, than Italy? You can paint the campaign."

'I said that I would be out of the army and wouldn't be allowed to wear uniform.

'He said, "Who says you can't?"

'I said, "Well, I suppose the War Office."

'He said "You don't suppose I pay much attention to what they say. I appoint you now to my staff."

'I never knew what position I was appointed to. I had a driver, Driver Fleming, and a jeep and a pass from Alex which enabled me to go anywhere from the 5th Army to the 8th Army and attach myself to any Battalion on either front. I wasn't an official war artist, I was Alex's official artist and I remained a Major.'

* The author is indebted to Mr Nigel Nicolson for this and other extracts from Seago's con-
versations with General Alexander.

Whenever he was at headquarters Seago dined with Alexander and about half a dozen of his senior officers and their aides who took it in turns to join their Commander-in-Chief. They included John Harding, his Chief of Staff, Lyman L. Lemnitzer, his American Deputy Chief of Staff, Bill Cunningham, his Military Assistant, Ralph Snagge, Harding's Military Assistant and Brian Robertson, Chief Administrative Officer. They dined in a tent which they used as a simple mess and where, once they had related the experiences of the day, shop-talk was discouraged.

'Alex asked Bill Cunningham and me, between us, to look after Ted,' Ralph Snagge recalled. 'The atmosphere in that mess was that of a family; we were senior and junior men who'd been thrown together for a long time by the accident of war and there was an easy camaraderie, some ragging as a relief from tension and, added to it all, the excitement of being in the thick of war, which must have made a profound impression on Seago. "We are each of us so lucky to be in the front row of the stalls at the drama of war – noise effects and all," Alexander used to tell his officers.

'From the moment of his arrival when he sat down and lit up his pipe, Ted came in for his share of ragging for someone immediately shouted: "Put out that pipe. The Germans will see the smoke."'

Seago as usual thrived in the atmosphere of a family although day after day when his companions went off to battle he was left behind to paint. At first he was completely bewildered and did not paint at all, but just absorbed the chaotic maze of colour and incident in the countryside around him. He saw again the Bellini skylines and, near at hand, cart-loads of grapes drawn by white oxen wending their way down the roads he had already glimpsed from a hill-top monastery in peacetime. But although the blue hills and the rich, terracotta earth were the colours he remembered, the earth was churned up with the tracks of vehicles and tanks and the workers in the fields wore black shawls and drab skirts instead of the bright blue smocks and white hats he had longed to paint.

Again, he knew an overwhelming desire to paint, but for once he felt quite unable to express his feelings by selecting a focal point and then seeing the whole of the picture in relation to it. 'The battered towers of ruined churches signified so much more than an "upright" of value to the composition,' he wrote. 'Groups of rain-sodden men and canting vehicles, deep in mud, ceased to be mere combinations of shape and tone. Shattered houses, spilling their structure in a pile of rubble could not be dismissed as a pattern arrangement of coloured walls, and weary refugees on their journey without purpose could hardly be sketched as "incidentals" in a landscape.'

The war scenes were extensions of those he had recorded in *A Generation Risen* but, with a memory of his first visit to Florence and his vision of the pattern as a whole, he recognized, as Alexander had foreseen he would, the challenge of expressing the spirit of the moving front in which he was submerged while it ravaged the very spot immortalized down the centuries by poets and painters. He drove to the front lines and attached himself to a battalion or a company for two or three days at a time, accepting a bedouin-type hospitality and recording the scenes around him in pen and ink washes because oil paint became smudged before it had time to dry.

He sketched his impressions of men, mud and movement, often in driving rain or a thick fog of dust and he drew the backwaters of war where old men and crying children returned from the hills to their ruined homes. He flew over the mountains and saw the blue-green of the Adriatic and, always, he wanted to paint at St Gimignano. He went there one day. The church of Sant 'Agostino was undamaged by the German artillery which had shelled the town for twenty-four hours but it was a sad pilgrimage and he did not paint for the old monk had died, the cloistered garden was overgrown and rain dimmed the view from the wall.

Suddenly, it was winter and often Seago went alone up to Alexander's little guest house, high in the hills, where one night he was joined by Anthony Eden, visiting the front on his way back to England from Moscow. That night seven inches of rain fell in a torrential downpour and the terrain was flooded so that for thirty-six hours the Foreign Secretary and Seago, who had not previously met, were marooned alone in the small farmhouse.

They found they had much in common. Eden, the son of an accomplished painter who often entertained artists including Whistler, Sickert and Augustus John, was not only a discriminating collector but had also inherited a talent which might well have led him to the same career as Seago, had politics not taken over. 'Certainly, I enjoyed myself,' Eden recalled. 'I found Mr Seago a very sympathetic character' – sentiments which evidently the painter reciprocated because in the following year he sent Eden a copy of his book of war paintings.

There were many distinguished visitors to the camp in the woods, including Churchill, Harold Macmillan and King George VI. The King's visit was surrounded by great secrecy but Alexander made a point of sending a message to Seago to join them for a glass of sherry. 'Afterwards, sitting in the sun with me, he did this sketch of the King on my message pad from memory,' Snagge said when, as Under-Sheriff of London's Old Bailey, he looked at the striking likeness framed on his office wall.

During these last months of war Seago recognized his privileged position but was not overawed. In the mess he was the only person not on the immediate staff but invariably, Snagge recalled, he contributed a good anecdote or two to the conversation – usually against himself. Like the time on the eve of a battle when his batman had driven him up almost to the front line. It was a bitterly cold day with a dark, lowering sky such as he loved to paint; with the gun positions in the foreground and an occasional shell whining across the river, it represented the very essence of war. For hours Seago lost himself in an attempt to capture the scene while his batman crouched under a rock cold, hungry and slightly scared, until with a sigh of relief he saw signs that Seago too had had enough. Stiff with cold he asked if he could see the picture and was disappointed to find it was just the sky with lots of pencilled notes in the margin. But for Fleming it was more than enough. 'Hm!' was his only comment. 'Now you've done the easy bit, sir, you'll have to do the rest tomorrow.' Relating the incident in the mess that night Seago added his punchline: 'I heard the rustle of Turner's body as he turned in his grave.'

Then there was the time he set up his easel on a roadside near Siena and spent hours struggling to capture the strange, sombre quality of the light. He had just decided to abandon the attempt and pack up when a convoy of trucks arrived carrying advance forces for the front and Seago became aware of a bucolic-looking Colonel peering through a monocle at the painting. 'I say old boy,' the Colonel muttered sympathetically, 'if you're really interested in this sort of thing why don't you come to lunch and see what my blasted batman's done at the end of our portable bar?'

The measure of Seago's personal success in the extraordinary situation in which he found himself can be assessed by the fact that, of the distinguished military company, many officers who had known him and returned home after the war made an effort to keep in touch and become his life-long friends. Usually Seago left it to them to take the initiative because over the years he grew less inclined to leave Norfolk although he was always eager to entertain and at one time or another all his wartime friends and their wives stayed at his home.

Occasionally, Alexander and Seago took a picnic lunch and escaped for a few hours into the wooded hills, the Field-Marshal wearing a khaki shirt, and the stars on the number plate of his jeep covered, so that he could wander unrecognized about the country-side. Sometimes the two men set up their easels and painted. They were together whenever it was possible and when Alexander flew to Rome in his private plane on official business, Seago accompanied him to spend two or three days exploring the captured city; in December when Alexander flew to London to be briefed for new responsibilities Seago went with him to collect some clothes.

Both men returned to Italy, Seago to paint, Alexander to prepare for the final offensive. Seago recalled the morning of 9 April 1945 when he knew the great attack was going to start. To his surprise, Alexander said to him at breakfast, 'What a lovely day. Shall we go into the hills?'

'He went and changed,' Seago recalled, 'and we went off into the hills and found a lovely place by a stream and a little boy came by with some goats and we gave him some of our lunch and he gave us some grapes. I couldn't keep quiet any longer. I said "Alex, I must know. You know what's going on at this moment and here we are sitting by the stream, talking to a little boy and eating grapes. How can we be doing this?" He said, "Of course I know what's going on; I've worked for days on this. I've planned every bit of it. I've now got to hand it to my generals and they've got to put it into action. I can't know anything more until the reports come in. And you know, 'til that time, they'd much rather I was out of the way." After lunch he stretched out on the grass and went sound asleep 'til four-thirty, when he returned to the operations room and was awake the whole night. I thought, my God, you've got to be a big man to do that!'

Seago respected Alexander more than any man he had ever met. He responded to the soldier's simplicity, humility and utter integrity. He recognized that Alexander, like he himself, did not consider he was a philosopher or an intellectual although he had a very agile brain which enabled him to assimilate information and dip into it for a few names at the appropriate moment. Seago told the story of the time Alexander was asked if he was fond of music. He said he was and as an example of something he particularly liked, cited 'Lily Marlene'.

'That was about the mark,' Seago said, '– which is more or less my mark too. He liked a good tune and "Lily Marlene" was a good tune.'

Alexander and Seago had other characteristics in common, apart from painting. Both had tremendous charm, loved to laugh and had a great sense of fun and an eye for the ludicrous. In each was a streak of childish vanity manifested by a tendency to dress up – Seago in flamboyant painting outfits, Alexander in uniforms he designed himself and had especially made by a Rome tailor. Yet in private life, they both lived simply. Always they enjoyed each other's company, and Alexander confided in Seago about his family, his money and his occasional worries. He was never happier than when they went painting together, with their easels set up some twenty feet apart and afterwards discussed their pictures, or when going to picture galleries with Seago to explore paintings with a knowledgeable companion who pointed out significant details in other painters' work which he, Alexander, might have failed to notice.

When the Italian campaign neared its close, there was a question of getting Seago back to England without official papers. Eventually a spare seat was found for him on the plane taking Anthony Eden home from a Mediterranean conference. Within days of arriving home the painter learned that Derek Mond, whose brilliance had foreshadowed greatness, had been killed, like Bernard Clegg, in a seemingly improvident accident when the plane carrying him back to his naval training ship dived into a Scottish loch. He was the third young man Seago had deeply cared about to be killed in his prime.

Seago learned of Derek's death from his young widow, Yvonne. Just as she had accepted Derek's affinity with the painter on her honeymoon, she now accepted Seago's spontaneous invitation to go to Brooke in her grief. Once again Seago's role was to comfort the mourners, for unfailingly he had an immense capacity to sympathize with those in trouble.

—————— X ——————

Peace and Friendship

On 25 May 1945, a month after Derek's death, Alexander wrote to Seago: 'When I get back, which I hope won't be too long now, I am really going to do a lot of painting and am looking forward to it most awfully.' He suggested that as soon as he returned they should take a car and load themselves up with material and go to his native Ireland and paint. They never did for Alexander was appointed Governor-General of Canada and before he left there was only time for him and Lady Alexander to spend a wintry week sailing on the Norfolk Broads with Seago.

One of Alexander's first engagements on his return to England after the war had been to attend the opening of the exhibition of Seago's Italian war paintings at the Colnaghi galleries in London. Seago had chosen to exhibit there after the day when he had walked down Bond Street with £5 in the pocket of his army uniform, intent on buying a drawing. Colnaghi's window attracted his attention; he went in and was soon involved in a discussion about pictures with the director, Tom Baskett who, on learning that his knowledgeable customer was a painter, asked to see some of his work. Seago showed him the pen and wash impressions of the war-torn stretch of Italy where, at the church of St Gimignano he had experienced a peace-time vision. They were some of the most emotionally-moving pictures he had ever made.

Displayed on the walls of a gallery usually hung with Old Masters the pictures of a modern army were startling in their impact. The unusual medium was ideal for conveying the immediacy of military operations and Seago had handled it with all the freedom and vigour of his later gypsy drawings. combined with a new authority and solidity of effect. The exhibition was called *With the Allied Armies in Italy* and, simultaneously, the book of that name of reproductions of the pictures headed the recommended list of Christmas books in several newspapers. In an effusive foreword Alexander, then at the height of his popularity, perhaps rendered the painter a disservice when he wrote that in his opinion, Seago was the most promising English landscape painter of his generation. Such praise provoked some sceptical critics to a more moderate assessment and in years to come when they failed to acknowledge the painter had fulfilled that early promise, it gave him a cause for some bitterness.

If, as was said of Turner, to paint prolifically is a mark of talent, Seago seemed to be well on his way to achieve the potential visualized by Alexander when, immediately after the exhibition of war pictures, the Colnaghi gallery mounted a second one of forty oil paintings – mostly landscapes of Norfolk and Italy all painted since the German surrender. It caused at least one newspaper to query how the painter had succeeded in doing so much in such a short time; a question that would be asked repeatedly down the years when his annual exhibitions, alternatively of oils and water-colours, attracted queues of would-be purchasers outside Colnaghi's in Bond Street waiting for the door to open.

Meanwhile, throughout his six-year term of office as Governor-General of Canada, Alexander consistently tried to persuade Seago to visit him, as a typical letter from Government House, Ottawa, shows:

'. . . I have done quite a number of pictures of sorts, but whether I am improving is another matter,' he wrote. 'I wish you were here to spur me on and tell me where I am wrong. If I could persuade you to come out here I know you would love it and I think you would find some excellent subjects. In fact, some days in Winter, Spring and Fall, the light and colouring is really enchanting and very much your cup of tea. I don't know what sort of time would suit you best but to help you choose this is my programme for the year . . . You must come.'

Seago played a delaying action although he was fully aware of the debt he owed Alexander but in the years after the war he chose not to respond to the older man's obvious desire for his advice and company. Eventually, Alexander resorted to sending photographs of his paintings to Seago, 'to act as a stop gap until you can come out here – I badly need your advice and instruction – and I take it that you are coming . . .' he wrote. It is doubtful whether Seago ever had any intention of going.

They met occasionally whenever Alexander was in England for a few days and more regularly after he returned for good. As soon as he retired from politics he wrote to Seago from the House of Lords: 'I am now, at last, a free man and can do exactly what I want to do and, of that, painting comes first so your pupil is at the service of the maestro. I think we can have some tremendous fun . . . Let me know when you'll be up in London and we can start laying plans for the future.'

Despite the letters, it seems unlikely it occurred to Seago that Alexander almost certainly regarded him as his most intimate friend and when, years later, this was suggested to him by Nigel Nicolson, he refuted the idea either from modesty or a wish to abdicate from a responsibility that had conflicted with his own plans when, immediately after the war, he deliberately sought to withdraw from any social life that took him away from Norfolk.

'Why don't you come out to India for a spell this winter and get the local atmosphere?' Auchinleck wrote. 'I am sure you would enjoy yourself here and find lots to draw and paint.' But, at that time it seemed that Seago had had his fill of travel and adventure. He recognized that it was his talent that had been his justification for mixing with the rich and famous and had enabled him to 'sit in' on the making of history. In the excitement of it all there had been a danger of subordinating that talent to the business of living. He had been given abundant opportunity to equip his talent and measure it against exacting standards while at the same time broadening his own horizons to an undreamt-of extent. Thus armed he saw his first peacetime responsibility was to harbour his talent and allow it to develop spontaneously at its own pace and in its own setting.

He returned to Norfolk where, as a boy, painting had been his very reason for living. He went home to Brooke where, sixteen years before, he had escaped from Mabel Seago's possessive domination to make his own life, but his boyhood scar was his fear that his mother or anyone else might undermine his hard-won independence. As a result of his early memories he apparently chose to avoid involving himself in anything more than superficial or platonic friendships with the many attractive women who sought his company, perhaps because he saw any eligible woman as a potential threat to his way of life, liable to curb his freedom of spirit, disrupt his thought processes and cause him to deviate from his tenuously-held sense of direction.

At the same time, affectionate, sensitive and fundamentally insecure, he must have longed for a permanent, emotional attachment such as he had known, first with Tommy Baker and then with Bernard Clegg. Time and again, he sought in vain to establish similar relationships with a succession of young assistants whose terms of employment perhaps indicated Seago's underlying desire for something more than the normal bond between employer and employee. For instance, there was no mention of salary with twenty-four-year-old Peter Vanzeller, a one-armed ex-serviceman whom Seago engaged immediately after the war and whom he precipitated, straight from hospital, into the responsibilities of driving the car using his left hand and the stick with a rubber knob on the end that replaced his amputated right one. Other duties were making stretchers for canvases and a wooden rack to hold painting panels (fortunately carpentry was standard hospital procedure for patients with artificial hands), typing the first draft of Seago's *A Canvas to Cover* with his left hand and because of the post-war shortage of painting materials, combing Norwich for old oil paintings where the canvas could be cleaned off and used again. Tea-chests were broken up into sheets of plywood and lengths of hessian stretched over hand-made wooden frames as a substitute for canvas.

Vanzeller responded to the challenge of his new job. He had been discharged from hospital severely demoralized after his wartime experiences, mentally and physically in need of rehabilitation and trained only in flying, carpentry and fighting. As he gained confidence, he was overjoyed that someone was prepared to throw real responsibility at him, even if no official salary went with it. For instance when he wanted to buy a new suit, Seago sent him to his own tailor and told him to have it put on his account.

'Money was short,' Vanzeller recalled, 'so Ted made himself paint commissioned portraits and he often groaned when I reminded him of an appointment for a sitting with some fat woman he was painting. But he never refused a commission because he was really worried about making a living from painting, anxious that his landscapes weren't good enough and very concerned about the future and I felt he needed a lot of encouragement. I was raw and unsophisticated and pretty immature but, all the same, he kept asking for my criticism. All I said was: "That picture is what I see and what we both see, so I think if people don't like your painting they're wrong in the head".'

So in his late thirties the painter who, as a boy had shown remarkable promise, had to make do with that well-meaning encouragement. He and Vanzeller were living at Brooke Lodge under claustrophobic conditions, committed to regular mealtimes and sharing the family sitting-room with the Seago parents. Only in the studio could they both be on their own, away from the unendurable tensions created by Mabel. 'Poor dear baby! He's ill you know,' was the justification of the mother who had raised her son against all odds and who could not bring herself to let him go. Time and time again, she tried to persuade Vanzeller to influence him to her point of view.

It seemed that the son had inherited his mother's tendency to depressions for there were days at a time, Vanzeller recalls, when Seago would neither talk nor eat, but would go off into the countryside looking white and strained to sketch on his hardboard panels. Only when the light failed did he return to work on them all through the night.

As a landscape painter he knew that his boyhood experiences on the farm and in the country had been essential. To paint the skies he had studied them like a scientist; for equestrian portraits he had learned anatomy like a veterinary student. Similarly, to paint the fields and the woods it was important to know the structure of the earth and the soil and what went on below the expanse of land and to understand the cycle of crops and the structure of the hedgerows.

'Truthful painting must be based on total understanding and an ability to draw in great detail if you have to,' he said when in a seascape he sublimated his nautical knowledge of boats into a couple of authoritative strokes to indicate the rigging of a Thames barge or other craft.

One week-end Seago took Vanzeller to stay at the Moat Cottage at Britford where the view from the sitting-room window of the water-meadows and beyond, a glimpse of a cathedral spire he considered 'the most beautiful in all England' were just as he remembered. He recalled his joy when he had lived there, surrounded by subjects he had been inspired to paint and which were available to him from dawn to sunset, in all weathers and at all seasons of the year. In contrast his present existence meant a car journey to reach his painting grounds. To add to his dissatisfaction he learned, in the tiny cottage where he had been happier than anywhere in his life, that Vanzeller had no intention of remaining his life-long companion.

'I said I would be eternally grateful to him,' Vanzeller recalls, 'for lifting me out of despair and giving me back my independence, but that week-end in Wiltshire I realized that I wanted to go on and try out the independence he had given me and not be mentally married to Seago for the rest of my life.'

Once again Seago faced loneliness and rejection but back in Norfolk both men found a temporary antidote to their respective restlessness in an old sailing wherry which Seago hired for them to live on during the last few weeks of the summer. One day, in a Broadland dyke they came across a more permanent solution in the shape of an old naval pinnace which had been converted into an auxiliary ketch and sported a 'For Sale' notice across her bows. She was fifty-two feet long, sturdily built and suitable for cruising on the Broadland rivers and at sea. Seago visualized sailing her up the Norfolk coast to familiar painting spots or going south to explore the Suffolk and Essex estuaries and then cruising up the Thames, lingering in the Pool of London to paint before working his way up river to Oxford and the Berkshire meadows in *Endeavour*.

Rarely were his castles in the air without foundation and all these dreams were destined to materialize. But when, with Vanzeller and his brother and another naval friend, Reg Bloom, Seago took *Endeavour* on her initial cruise down river from the local boatyard, his long-term plans were forgotten. As a new skipper his pride in ownership was tempered by his preoccupation with tantalizing views from the wheelhouse of subjects he could hardly wait to paint. He visualized himself, during the coming years, mooring his floating studio to every yard of bank along some two hundred miles of local rivers. So he finally embarked on his life-long mission which was to discover and portray the meaning behind the beauties of nature he recognized all round.

From then on, like Constable, he took nature as his subject and was the constant student. 'My attitude to nature is one of enquiry – an endless search for explanations and discovery,' he noted in pencil on blank pages of his sketch-book. 'I believe that the more searching one does the more one's appreciation grows. Subjects present themselves which had not been apparent before, and fresh lines of thought invite enquiry.'

It was the first time since his lonely boyhood that he had long periods of quiet to indulge his thoughts uninterrupted by the succession of events that had crowded his life since the day, sixteen years ago, when he had left home to join the circus. The flexibility of his mind was evident at this time in his admission that his conclusions about art and nature were liable to revision and only served their purpose until superseded by other beliefs based on wider experience. Yet he discounted the possibility of original thought because, he said, when outlook was dependent on existing knowledge the best one could hope to achieve was to carry a line further, in a certain direction or to provide a different pair of spectacles.

He cherished his talent and there were invariably signs he feared it might desert him as when he suggested it might be dangerous to start upon a thorough analysis of Art – 'that strange business, the experience of our senses . . . It is apt to burst like a bubble and leave one without any firm conception,' he wrote for *A Canvas to Cover*. 'I do not possess the kind of mind which can sort out each single thread in such a tangible skein of thought but, having got hold of one thread, I am trying to follow it completely, bit by bit, and unravel it from the rest. At the same time, I am not unaware that the other threads are composed of the same fibre, that they are equally strong, that they play just as large a part in man's structure and that, in the end, it will probably be found that they are all joined together.'

The circus and the ballet had tested and proved his technique and broadened his personal perspective; the war had released his capacity to express emotion. At last he had arrived at a point when he could accept that his senses, like Constable's, were most stirred by the great expanses of sky and by moving clouds and the shadow of trees reflected in slow-moving water so that he need go no further than the familiar places he had loved in boyhood, where wind and weather and the seasons offered him a new subject every day and a joy which it was his challenge to convey. He saw no need to experiment with his style of painting.

'I believe that any form of deliberate experiment is unwise and dangerous,' he wrote. 'I am old-fashioned . . . I am offering nothing new but following a great tradition.'

But he did experiment with the method, sometimes attacking his canvas with a heavily-laden brush or a palette knife. He again began to cultivate water-colour, using it, not as some of his contemporaries were doing as a hard, dry gouache, but applying it in clean, swift washes of free-flowing colour that merely hinted at the underlying drawing and was ideally suited to the tender, lyrical quality of light and atmosphere he sought to portray. The appearance of effortless ease of his post-war water-colours, sometimes reminiscent of Wilson Steer's landscapes in the same medium, give no indication that more often than not, they were achieved only after many frustrating attempts. It took years of observation, he said, to capture the elusive tonal quality created by the fleeting effects of changing light which caused objects to lose the stability of their own colour, shadows to become cool or warm and the landscape transformed to a pattern of contrasts.

When his initial excitement at recognizing East Anglia as his ideal painting ground subsided he turned in what he described as 'an endless search for explanations and discovery', to the French Impressionists whose experiments with the problem of light and atmosphere had been made in a countryside very similar to his own.

He probably felt a challenge to match his own interpretation of
landscape with theirs. But although Sisley, Pissaro and Monet had
at one time or another all worked in England and must have seen
the work of the Norwich School, none of them had portrayed the
rivers and marshes of his beloved Norfolk. So to compare his work
with theirs he must paint in their country and on a summer's day,
accompanied by his brother and Reg Bloom, he piloted *Endeavour*
down river and out of Yarmouth for his first sea-crossing in his
floating studio.

'I shall never forget the moment when we sailed out of Yarmouth
harbour and the queer feeling in my stomach as *Endeavour* lifted to
the ocean,' he recalled. 'Neither shall I forget our landfall on the
other side.'

They made for Ostend, being the nearest Continental port to
Norfolk. Through a slight navigational error they landed, as they
learned from one of the holidaymakers swimming off the shore, at a
small French seaside resort a few miles south of their destination.
But the tide was with them and an hour later they moored at
Ostend and waited for the lock to open. There, after John had re-
swung the compass, the trip demonstrated the endless possibilities
of taking *Endeavour* wherever its owner wished.

In years to come, Seago would sail to Holland and work his way
along the Dutch canals, stopping off at little towns to see the great
pictures in the art galleries. He would go to France to paint at
Honfleur where Boudin and Monet had set up their easels in the
sunshine to observe and learn about the subjects they most loved.
He would cruise between the banks of the Seine and Argenteuil and
Vernon, through the painting grounds of Corot and Van Gogh and
on to Paris, and beyond.

In time, his journeys emphasized a need to put down roots in his
native soil and he often thought of a small Tudor house near a
Norfolk river. It could just be seen above a high wall: a Dutch-style
house with mellow, red brick walls, leaded windows and a gabled
roof with black tiles. Walnut House in Ludham had been built
in 1603 after the engineers came over from Holland to supervise the
drainage of the East Anglian marshes. In just such a house Vermeer
and Rembrandt would have painted but Seago had no idea who
lived there.

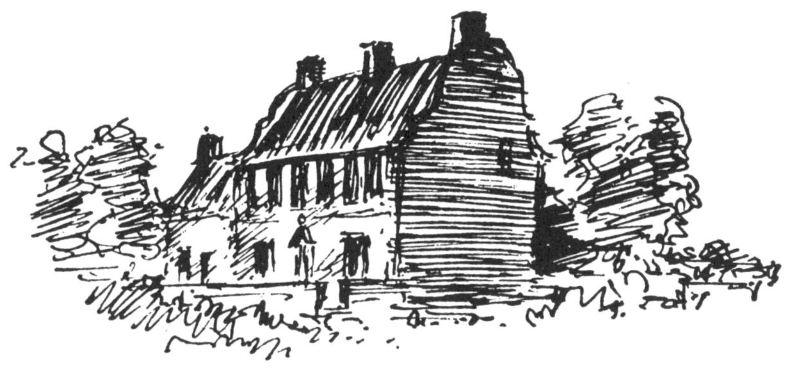

One day, walking past it with a friend he had made in the army, Bryan Gibbs, who was visiting the neighbourhood, he pointed it out as the house he had always loved. When Gibbs suggested it would be interesting to see it from the inside Seago did not want to bother the owner, but Gibbs persisted and the two men walked up the short path and knocked at the door. Gibbs explained to the daughter of the local schoolmaster who opened it that his friend was an artist who had always admired her house and wondered if she could permit them to see more of it. The lady said that she could not show them the sitting-room where her father was ill but that otherwise they were welcome to look around. Afterwards, Seago left his card saying that should she ever decide to sell her home, he would be grateful if he could have the first refusal.

Once again his innate gift for being in the right place at the right time had served him well, for within months the schoolmaster died and the house was for sale. Seago bought it with a loan from his father, changed its name to the Dutch House and found a local builder with a traditional pride in craftsmanship. The original oak staircase, hidden behind a door covered with layers of old wall-papers, was opened up; several intermediate modern fireplaces were removed to reveal the original open hearths in the hall, dining-room and sitting-room and for the back of the house Seago designed a large two-storey-high barn-like studio to join on to the original house. It was to be made of metal and asbestos and camouflaged with bricks and tiles to blend in with the old part. Most of the garden was dug up and replanned, down to the stretch of woodland leading to a dyke into Womack Water. Here the wild garden was preserved as a natural bird sanctuary where, blue as the punt lying in the jungle of reeds, kingfishers flashed by and bitterns uttered their weird, marshland call and where Seago never tired of painting.

He believed his new home would be the ideal setting where he would be free to devote his whole life to painting, but while he was waiting to move in his heart turns were occurring with almost weekly regularity. According to his brother the family had learned to accept them philosophically with a 'hard luck old man' attitude, but his mother was particularly concerned in case he had an attack while he was alone in his new house. After Peter Vanzeller had left for South Africa it was suggested that John, whose health had again broken down in the navy, might live with his brother. But John was trying to make a living decorating old furniture and firmly rejected the suggestions. He too was determined to make his own way in the world and was already considering the possibility of living abroad in a warmer climate.

Then Brian Seago learned that a similar house with a farm attached, next door to the Dutch House, was for sale and he had no hesitation in buying it and moving in. It seemed the ideal solution. Once again Mabel Seago could build her life around her younger son who lived just two fields away but far enough, the son thought, to insulate him from the inhibiting effect that his mother had on his painting, and near enough for him to discharge his filial obligations in full with the minimum of effort.

Meanwhile an unexpected and immediate advantage resulted from his new home and took the form of a new control he gained over his heart turns. When he had his first attack there the local doctor was contacted. He was a lively Scot recently demobilized from the navy. A few months previously he had read a medical article on how an attack of paroxysmal tachycardia might sometimes be curtailed by pressing a thumb on the vagal nerve in the neck to induce its slowing action to the victim's heart. The doctor had never seen a case of paroxysmal tachycardia until he met Seago. With some trepidation, he put one hand on Seago's pulse and with the other pressed on the nerve in his neck, exactly as the article had prescribed. Immediately he did so he felt the patient's pulse slow down.

'It's stopped,' Seago told him.

'I know it has,' said the doctor, surprised but equally relieved.

Seago insisted on learning exactly how 'the trick' worked. He discounted the doctor's warning that it was extremely difficult to apply the right amount of self-pressure and in the future he found that if he applied it at the first warning, he could invariably abort an attack. Inevitably, he sometimes misjudged the pressure and applied too much, so that he lost consciousness – occasionally at inopportune moments as when he was doing his Christmas shopping and collapsed in the doorway of a large Norwich store. More dramatically he collapsed unconscious in Paris, in the Champs Elysées, hit his head on a stationary car as he fell, and cut it so badly that his companion had to take him to hospital. A gendarme called the ambulance and when Seago regained consciousness he had difficulty in allaying the suspicion that he was under the influence of drink. But despite such incidents, for the first time in his life the painter was no longer at the mercy of his crippling disability.

Encouraged by this perhaps, for the first time he felt he ought to be meeting some of his fellow artists and not, after all, be content to spend his entire life shut away in Norfolk. He discussed this with Edward Pearce and as a result, in 1945 he was elected a member of the Athaeneum Club and the Royal Society of British Artists. In a letter thanking Pearce for putting his name forward he wrote: 'Never in my wildest moments would I consider myself a "great artist" – only one who pursues his purpose with honesty.' It was a belief he publicly reiterated in *A Canvas to Cover* published the following year. It was his most revealing book for in the text alongside the seventy illustrations he confessed his aspirations; to spend his life expressing his overwhelming love of nature in terms of light and atmosphere, and to seek for new revelations.

'I have stretched myself on the grass and gazed at up the sky and then I have shut my eyes and lain with my ear close to the earth,' he wrote with an echo of a child's sense of discovery. 'I have felt the earth tremble, as though about to speak, and I have heard a tiny murmur of sound; not of any insect or animal or tremor of grass, but of the earth and sky itself . . . I am sure the thoughts are there but they are overshadowed and obscured by those which comprise our meagre intellect.'

The influence of Constable and Wordsworth echoed through the book, again dedicated to Bernard Clegg and full of joy and gratitude and hope; but not happiness.

'I am really delighted that you think the book an improvement,' he wrote to John Gregory. 'The impression of complete happiness is scarcely real. I'm afraid I'm not blessed with that, but I do experience a certain calm due, I think, to the fact that I know at last what I want to do. Yet to come, is the realization that I cannot do it . . .' Another time he told Gregory, 'Those of us who long for the unattainable (and believe me I am one) are not of the happiest.'

His new home, he wrote to Gregory, he liked more each day. At that time his post-war paintings showed a fresh exuberance. He tackled immense pictures with a daring extravagance, as if to celebrate because the years of shortages of red paint and paper and canvas were over. There was a magnificent impression of the Bicester Hunt dwarfed by mile upon mile of rolling Oxfordshire country. In technique it was Constable. Equally ambitious was a panoramic view of Ludlow Castle painted from a high hill on the opposite side of the valley. 'View of Ludlow Castle, 1946' was priced at two hundred guineas and it dominated his first exhibition of peacetime paintings at Colnaghi's. Thirty years later, it was re-sold for ten thousand pounds.

The ebullient confidence apparent in his painting was not echoed in his private life. His new secretary, Julian Fane, then a Cambridge undergraduate at the outset of his writing career, was sensitive to the turbulent undercurrents in the painter's life. Fane believed they came from an inward fear and self-doubt and a consequent need to prove himself over and over again, not only in painting but through a physical challenge, like sailing which was the one sphere where his brother excelled over him.

Fane also saw the signs of an estrangement between Edward and his brother as well as the more deep-rooted love-hate relationship with his mother. At that time the successful painter was possibly irritated by John's admitted ill-health. Since boyhood Edward had chosen to overcome the conditions imposed by his heart trouble and he regarded illness as something to be ignored at all costs. On the other hand John, for his part, was extremely proud of his brother's success.

By the time Julian Fane had worked for the painter for five weeks, he was distressed at finding himself involved in such a 'psychological pie'. He realized, like so many of his predecessors, that he had made a mistake in accepting a job which would allow him no time to write and further his own career, or for that matter live his own life.

'I knew I couldn't supply the constant companionship he needed,' he said. 'He was afraid of being alone, he dreaded being left alone with his mother, and whenever they met there was a tense uncomfortable atmosphere. Ted was on the defensive against his parents. Yet all the time he wanted to impress them.

'He worried incessantly about the nature of his talent, and if and how it would develop. I think he knew he was a craftsman without parallel, but feared he lacked the essential mysterious quality of a great artist. He would say in depressed or honest moments that he had a picture-postcard mind. Yet occasionally, not only because of his fine craftsmanship and not only because of the terrific amount he produced, he painted pictures that were excellent by any standards.

'Work – painting – was the genuine centre of his life. He read a good deal: Laurens van der Post and Van Loon and books about people who had performed feats of patriotism, endurance and courage, for instance explorers, war heroes, spies, outsiders who managed to turn failure into success. He loved the countryside and the sea and approved of Hardy and Masefield. But he was very aware of his lack of education and shied away from anything he would call "highbrow".'

It seemed the painter would have a difficult task to find as sensitive an assistant as Julian Fane. But just as the new studio was nearing completion a permanent successor arrived on the doorstep. Peter Seymour was an art student. During the war he had served with the South African army in Egypt, Libya and Italy, and afterwards had come to England on a loan grant of £144 a year to study at Camberwell School of Art. The theatre was in his blood. He was the only child of a musical comedy actress who had married a theatrical manager, a nephew of the actor Godfrey Tearle. They emigrated to South Africa soon after their son was born.

In England, Peter Seymour tried to find a job to supplement his meagre allowance and a mutual friend told him that Edward Seago needed a new secretary and suggested he should apply. Within a fortnight, he was installed in the Dutch House, with no salary but on the understanding that he would receive art lessons and his keep. The promised tuition materialized, regularly and remorselessly and regardless of whether the recipient had either the time or the inclination so that, after some weeks, he found it embarrassing and irksome. By then his only wish was to help to organize the life of the painter who had charmed him irrevocably at their first meeting, and to take over the smooth running of 'the most gracious and romantic home' he had ever known. At his request the lessons ceased, to the detriment of an undoubted talent.

He stayed at the Dutch House until the end of Seago's life although, after two years, he asked if he could have three months' leave to prove to himself that he was capable of earning his own living. Seago arrogantly discounted such a suggestion for although he gave Peter no financial remuneration he had come to rely on him to bring order and happiness into his life. The painter was afraid a realistic salary might give Peter independence so that one day he might leave and for Seago that was an intolerable thought. Eventually he opened a bank account for Peter and, from time to time paid a moderate sum into it but he always paid for all Peter's requirements with unstinting generosity.

—— XI ——

Royal Recognition

Seago's need for a reliable understanding companion, sensitive to all his moods had never been greater for as his peacetime career gained momentum, his energy seemed inexhaustible. Following the success of his early exhibitions at the Colnaghi galleries, it had been decided to take the unusual step of showing only water-colours at his exhibition in the autumn of 1947. Its success set a pattern for the alternate oil and water-colour exhibitions there over the next twenty years.

While he was working for the exhibition he discussed with Masefield plans for an ambitious three-volume collaboration as a sequel to *The Country Scene*. It was to be called *The English Landscape*, to be published by Collins and each volume would contain four parts reflecting, in prose and pictures, different aspects of the countryside. There would be ten pictures to each subject and the first volume would cover Bridges, Earth-works (including ancient Roman sites, etc.), Marshland and Flat Country, Windmills and Watermills. However it transpired that Masefield was reluctant to leave his wife, because she was not well and would not travel to East Anglia to refresh his memory about the subjects for the second part of the volume, so that the whole project was abandoned.

Meanwhile, Seago had drafted his ideas for the three volumes, painted seventy water-colours for his exhibition and had written

Tideline, a collection of memories and impressions in words and pictures, dedicated to Bertram Priestman.

'What a loyal friend you are. I am greatly touched by the dedication,' the eighty-year-old Priestman replied. 'I can't see any sign in your work today, that you have been influenced by my particular style of work and that I am glad of. It does me credit too, to a slight degree and I am glad to say it applies to almost all the many pupils I have had altogether . . . I envy your ease (apparently) of handling paint and the technique is, generally speaking, so very suitable . . . I am so glad to see (as does not surprise) that you have an eager set of clients which I expect will grow rapidly, so it can't matter much to you that the absurd treatment at the RA is such. Irritating as it naturally was, like Wilson Steer and W. Nicholson, you can ignore it till they beg of you to send. I don't want you to think I am disloyal to the RA – *far from it*, but it is because I am devoted to it as an institution that it hurts one to see it going the wrong way it is at present and to be able to do nothing personally.

However, 'the absurd treatment at the RA' (when they had rejected three of his pictures) did matter to Seago. It reopened a scar which festered for ever, although 'the eager set of clients' multiplied more rapidly than even the foresighted Priestman could have dreamt. Before the opening of Seago's annual London exhibitions, queues of potential purchasers camped in Bond Street from first light so that exclusive neighbouring tradesmen protested at the unprecedented sight. When Colnaghi's doors opened at nine o'clock the scene inside the normally quiet, elegant galleries was an undignified scramble, comparable to the first day of a sales week. Genuine collectors were enraged when they saw the pictures they wanted snatched from under their noses while speculators bought anything on which they could lay their hands. By the end of the first morning it was indeed rare for any picture to be without a red dot indicating its sale.

The annual free-for-all was a growing embarrassment and eventually the directors of the gallery devised a routine whereby numbered catalogues were issued when the doors opened. One hour later, a member of the firm stood in the centre of the gallery, called

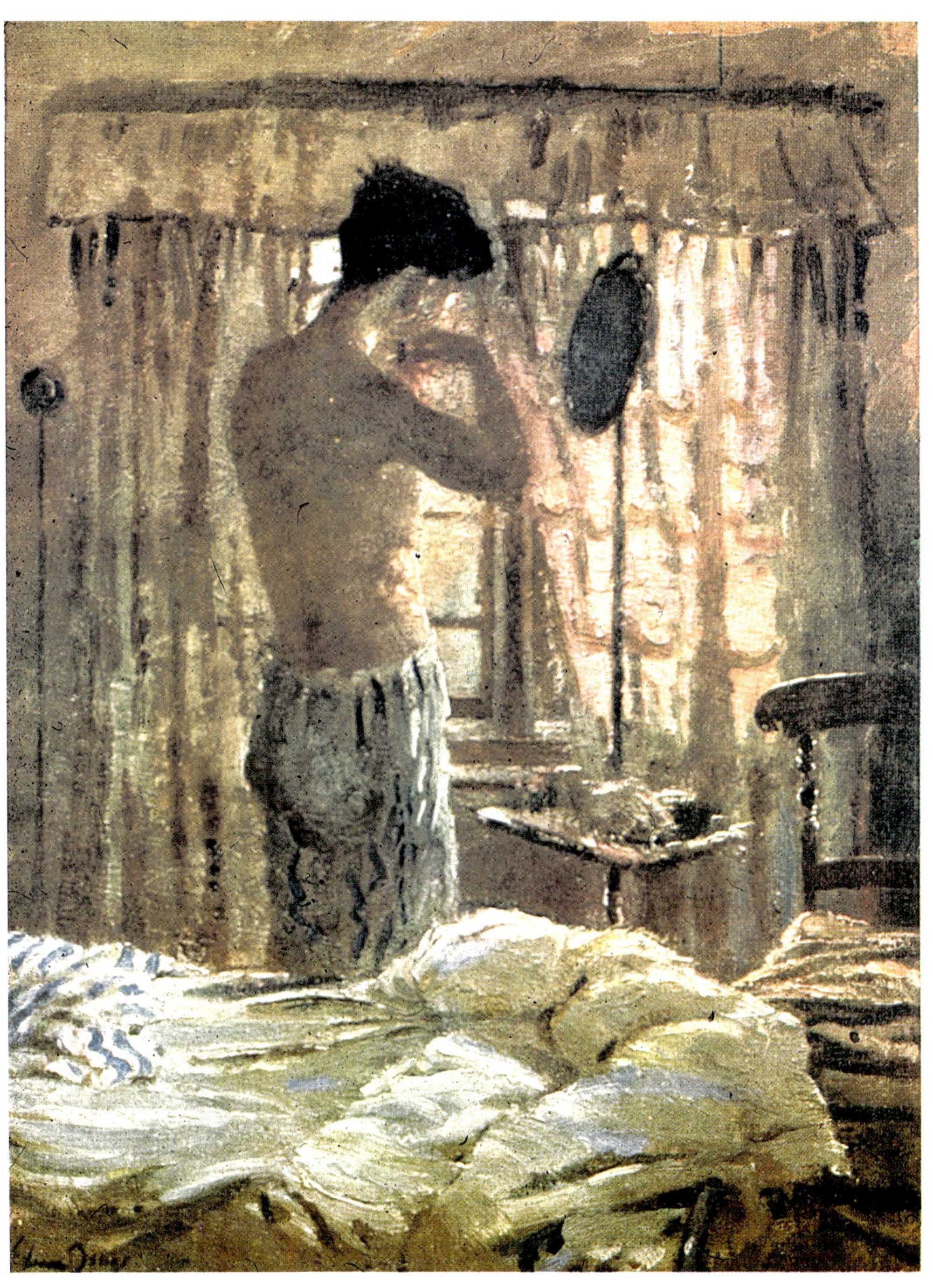

12 The East Window
Seago believed this picture of Vernon Russel Smith, a young pilot who
had been invalided out of the R.A.F., was the best he had ever painted.

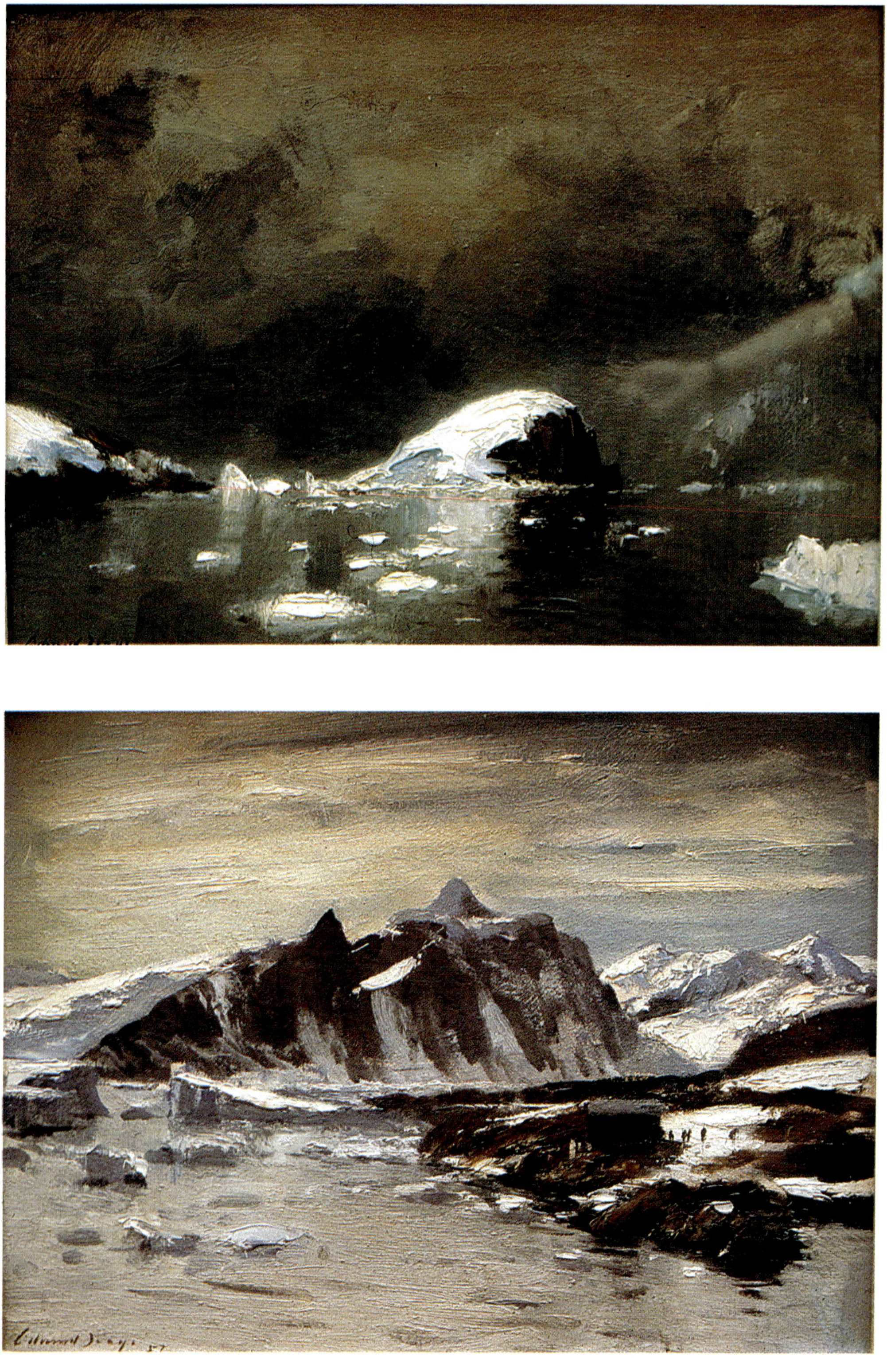

13. Two studies of Antarctica

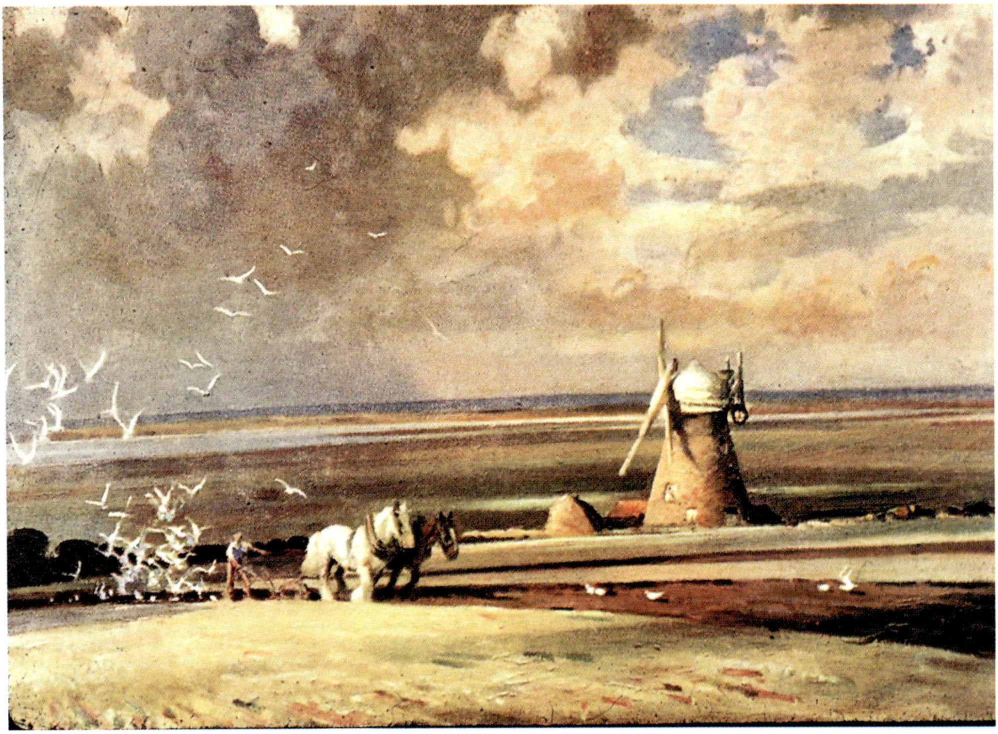

14. The Landmark

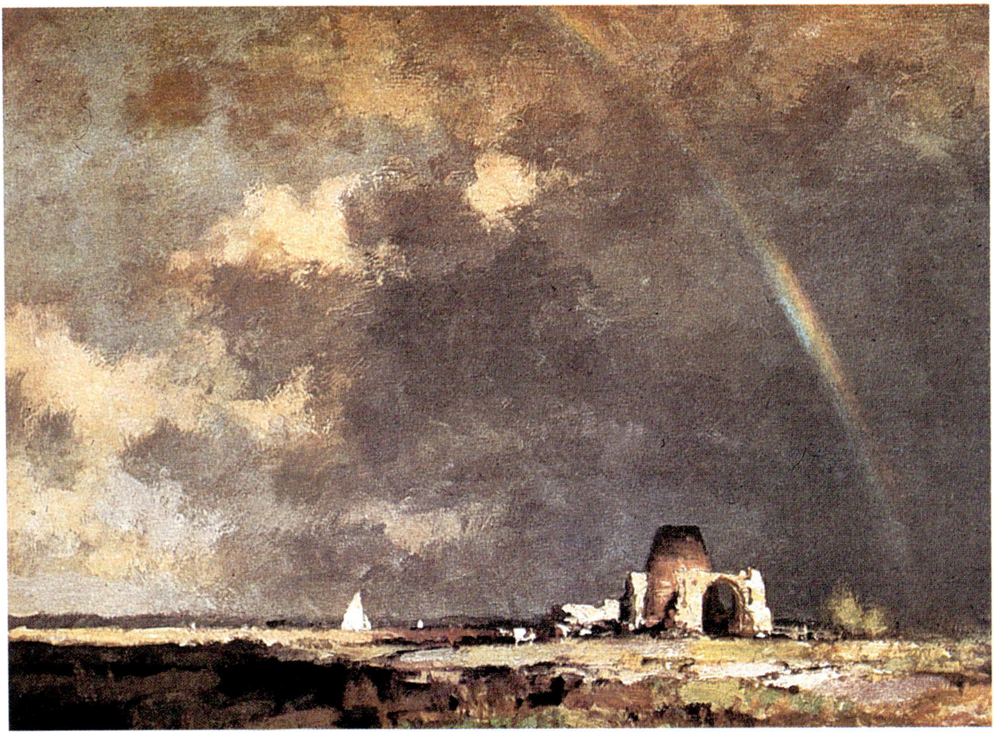

15. Rainbow at St Benet's Abbey

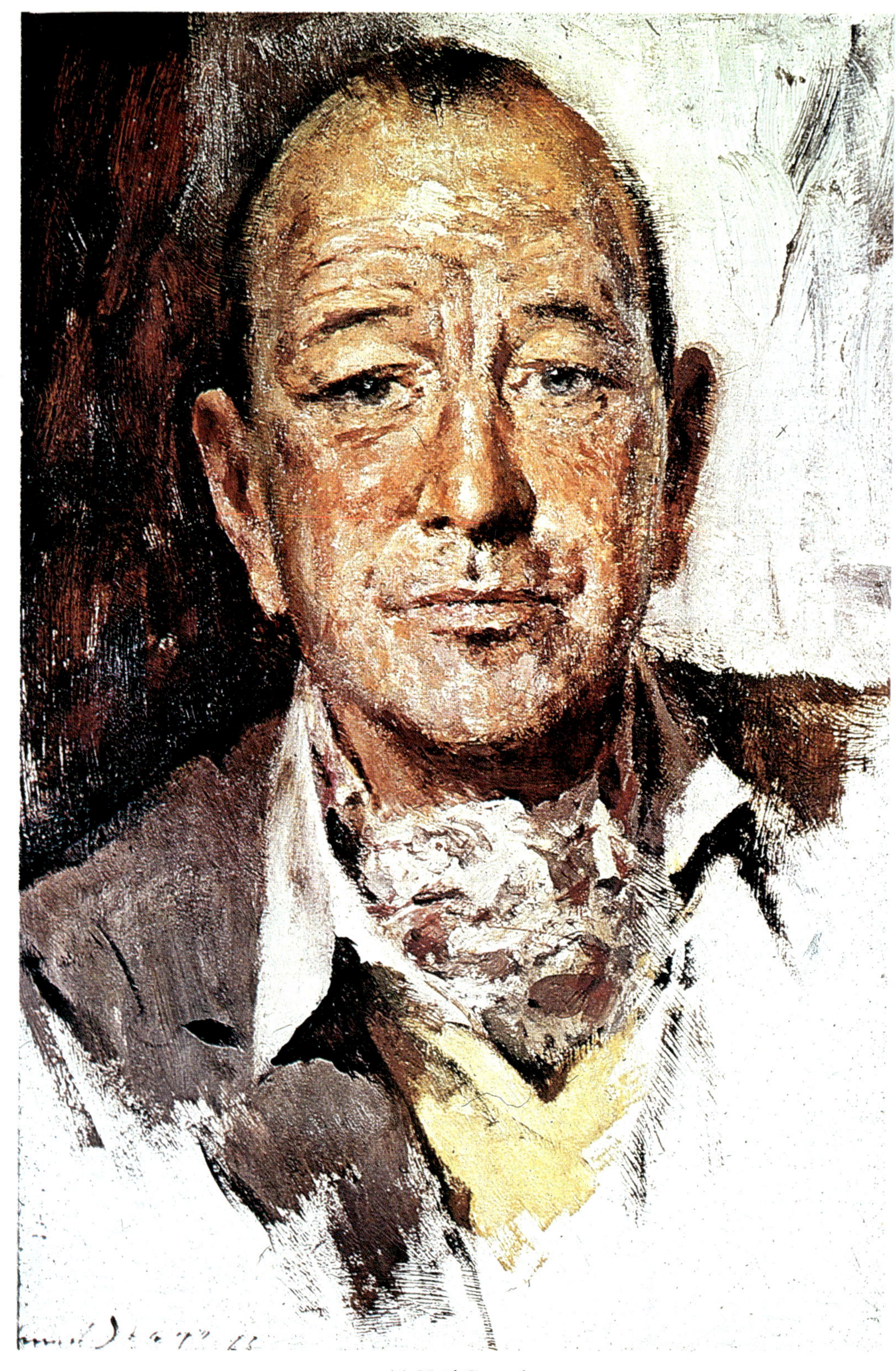

16. Noël Coward

out the catalogue numbers in sequence and took an order for one picture only from each holder. Still the queues formed long before opening time and sometimes several members of one family could be recognized there as well as representatives of an agency which had been commissioned to obtain numbered catalogues. The painter who was the cause of all the rivalry would have been far happier to see critics from some of the national newspapers at his exhibitions but, after the early years, almost without exception, they stayed away.

For the newspaper reporters it seemed the annual success story had become repetitive; for the critics the pictures rarely varied in style and content. Edward Seago rated attention only when he was lured away from his beloved landscapes to apply his craftsmanship and personal idiom, like the great topographical artists of old, to the pageants and personalities of the time. At the wedding of Princess Elizabeth and Lieutenant Philip Mountbatten he made three impressions of the Royal procession turning into Parliament Square, paintings in which the scarlet and gold uniforms were startling in their effect in contrast to the sombre day and the dim greyness of the crowds. With such scenes of light and movement the painter's unrivalled gift of a photographic memory, painstakingly trained, came into its own. With landscape he had a total recall for up to seven years, he estimated and yet curiously, with portraits, this gift did not apparently always apply.

'I am having an anxious time painting a portrait of the King,' he wrote to John Gregory. 'Not enough sittings – they are too far apart and one works under difficult conditions. He is very helpful and, on the whole I don't think it's going too badly.' There were three sittings in a small room in Buckingham Palace and afterwards Peter Seymour borrowed the King's RAF tunic and 'stood in' so that Seago could work on the painting in his studio. The portrait had been commissioned by the Royal Air Force Association and it was the first time the King had been painted in RAF uniform. There were two versions of the picture, one showing the King standing and the second, destined for the RAF College, Cranwell, seated. The former was acclaimed 'the picture of the year' in the 1948 summer exhibition of the Royal Society of British Artists and at the time was considered by some to be the best portrait of the King ever painted.

Only the painter's close friends could notice that the King's expression in the picture bore an uncanny resemblance to that of Peter Seymour.

Later that year Seago painted a companion portrait for the Royal Air Force which seemed to cause him far more difficulty than the King's portrait.

'I'm stuck in the studio trying to work on a portrait of the Queen which is really getting me down,' he complained to Gregory and admitted: 'I don't really like doing them, but as things are I dare not refuse the commission.' Invariably he seemed to be less successful with women's portraits. He was at his best in his next commission, a life-size portrait of Sir Ian Fraser for a commemoration gift from St Dunstan's to mark the sitter's twenty-five years chairmanship of that organization. The fine painting captured the sightless MP's characteristic look of sympathetic intensity as no camera had succeeded in doing.

Portraits were not the only paintings that caused Seago despondency.

'Don't be depressed about your work,' Masefield wrote. 'It is done in the mood of creation, and looked at in the reaction from that mood, after the life has been given.'

At that time Seago often signed his pictures with the initial 'S' or 'E.S.' but the directors of Colnaghi's advised him to use his full name so that in years to come there would be no confusion about identity. Their wisdom was emphasized when Julian Fane's wedding present to Princess Elizabeth of a small Seago landscape signed 'S', was described in the official gift list as 'A painting by Wilson Steer'.

The Royal family, it appeared, were as united in their interest in Seago's work as the critics were in ignoring it. Queen Mary visited his exhibition on the eve of the birth of her great-grandchild, Prince Charles, to see the portraits of the King and Queen, while the Duke of Edinburgh's first public engagement after his son was born was to visit the annual exhibition of the Royal Society of Portrait Painters. In it were two portraits by Seago including the first of many studies of Peter Seymour. It was an easily-painted likeness of a sensitive, mischievous, unusual young man. He wore a beret and a cigarette dangled from his lips. Obviously there had been no tension between artist and sitter and through the years Seago portrayed him time and again in a variety of situations but always looking young, relaxed and fun-loving.

The Queen also visited the exhibition and soon afterwards Seago was invited to stay at Sandringham House for the first of a series of bi-annual visits in January and July, when the Royal family were in residence. It seems that he established a particular rapport with Queen Mary; in a letter from Sandringham in her flowing handwriting, dated 11 January 1950, Queen Mary warmly thanks Mr Seago for his book, expresses her pleasure in meeting him and in watching him sketching so quickly. Afterwards he sent Queen Mary his painting of Old Babingley Church. His gift was reciprocated by a book of drawings of Windsor by Paul Sandby which Queen Mary thought he would 'find attractive'. As a result of that first visit, Seago also designed the mascot for Princess Elizabeth's and Prince Philip's car – a silver statuette of St George and the Dragon. Afterwards he usually sent gifts of paintings to Queen Elizabeth (later the Queen Mother) at Christmas and just before her birthday, on the occasion of his summer visits to Sandringham over the next twenty-two years.

The allegations that Seago deliberately sought Royal favour and in so doing dropped some of his old friends were refuted by many Royal letters over the years. For instance, he declined the Queen Mother's suggestion that he might like to spend a few days with her in Caithness to see if he felt like painting her some pictures – she thought it would be so delightful to show him the strange landscape and wonderful skies. Later, he refused Prince Philip's invitations to stay at Balmoral or to join him for two months on the Royal Yacht for a winter cruise to the Far East.

Sandringham, however, was conveniently a part of his familiar Norfolk while the Royal approval of his work was the much-needed antidote to his perpetual insecurity. Phrases like: 'I cannot thank you enough for giving me yet another glorious addition to my Seago collection . . .' were the encouragement he never tired of receiving and he responded with generosity.

Painting was his life's obsession and he resented being separated from his favourite working ground. In 1950 he refused a final appeal from Alexander, then Governor-General, to go to Canada for his first one-man exhibition there in the Laing Gallery in Toronto. 'I

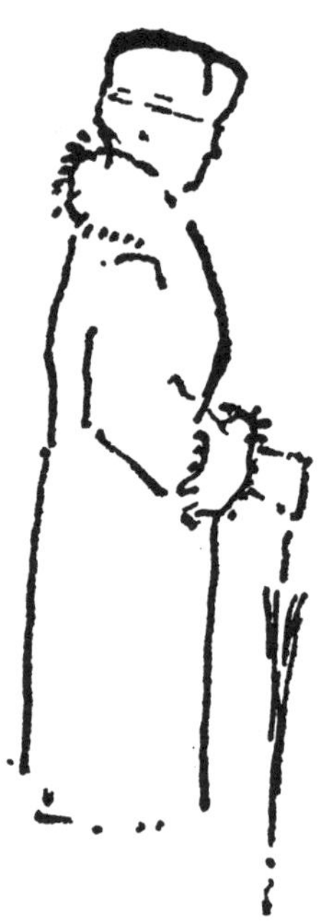

Sketch of Queen Mary from one of Edward Seago's letters

wish I could get you here. It will be a real tragedy if you can't take this opportunity of paying us a visit before we leave.' Alexander wrote after he had opened the Canadian exhibition, not in his official capacity, but as an artist and friend.

At that time Seago's output was prodigious. Simultaneously with the Canadian exhibition of fifty pictures there was his one-man show at the reopening of the newly-restored Norwich Assembly House as a cultural centre, and in London his annual exhibition at the Colnaghi galleries where he showed seventy oil paintings. He also again tried his hand at designing for the theatre and his first professional attempt was scenery for the pantomime *Mother Goose*, at the Cambridge Arts Theatre, produced by and starring his old friends, Cyril Fletcher and his wife, Betty Astell. The friendship dated from 1942 when the actor gave a recital of Masefield's poems and, to commemorate it on their first wedding anniversary he bought his wife a copy of *The Country Scene*. The illustrations in the book enchanted the Fletchers and prompted an appreciative letter to the painter which led to a long friendship.

Seago painted sixteen exquisite water-colours for his first professional stage commission. 'It was unbelievably difficult to get him to paint commercially and limit his imagination,' Fletcher recalled, 'but I was immensely relieved that he never complained about the terrible effect the stage lighting had on his sensitive work.'

The actor was even more impressed by the painter's remarkable ability to analyse stage problems and in the course of many technical discussions his respect grew. Seago designed sets for more pantomimes and his early fascination for the theatre was renewed. It was to culminate in 1958 in a set for *The Brass Butterfly* by William Golding, a comedy directed by and starring Alastair Sim. When the curtain rose at the Strand Theatre, London, the audience burst into spontaneous applause.

Meanwhile, apart from occasional trips to London and the visits to Sandringham, the only time Seago spent any time away from home was to live on his boat. At sea he became more ambitious and exchanged *Endeavour* for a younger, more seaworthy craft, *Capricorn*, a thirty-ton auxiliary ketch, built at Grimsby in 1939 which he equipped as his ideal floating studio.

Even her name fired his romantic imagination. It had been chosen because she was registered in the month of December and Seago learnt with satisfaction that those born under the zodiac symbol of the goat were headstrong and brave of heart. Further investigation revealed that the symbol should, in fact, be a sea-goat – half goat, half fish. He interpreted it in a pair of frolicsome creatures with long scaly tails which he had cast in brass, covered in gold leaf and fixed to either side of the bow of his boat's blue-green hull. Instead of a burgee, a red pennant held by another golden capricorn streamed from the top of the main mast.

Capricorn was a splendid sight. A set of brown sails showed off the unique blue hull which was repainted every year. Her owner mixed the colour to a shade he thought looked perfect against sunlit water. Gold flashed from her symbols, the name on her hull, her lifebelts and from an extravagant thin gold line just above the rubbing rail. But despite her romantic appearance, below decks no sailing man could have created more ordered efficiency. The engine room was large for the size of the boat so there was ample room to get round the 75 h.p. diesel to cope with any engine trouble. Every corner was utilized in the two white-painted double cabins, saloon and galley. Drawers were fitted between each step of the companionway leading to the wheelhouse to provide extra stowage space. In the lavatory twin racks held two dozen wet canvases and as many panel boards without danger of them being smudged in transit.

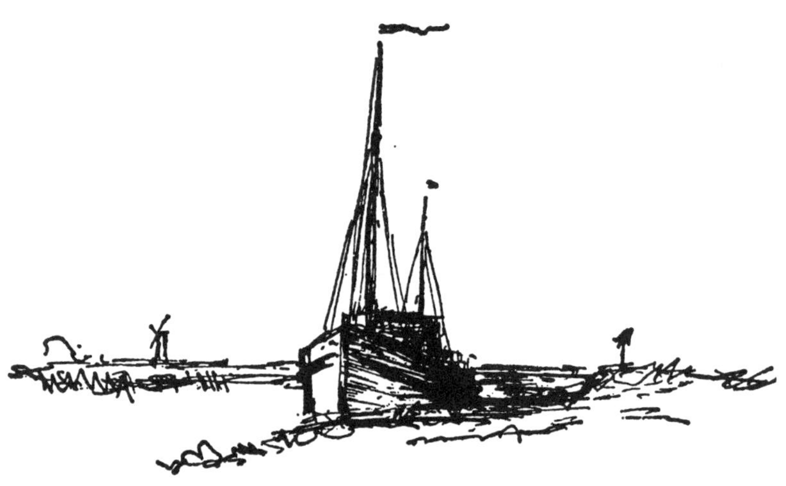

Accompanied by Peter Seymour and an old friend, Leonard Rushon, nicknamed 'Boots', who had been brought up with boats, Edward Seago set sail to paint with the minimum of discomfort wherever his mood took him.

Within a year, *Capricorn* was headline news when she was shipwrecked late at night two hours out of Yarmouth. John Seago and Reg Bloom had joined the regular crew of three for a trip to

Rotterdam and Bloom described how they were coming out of the harbour with the owner at the helm when they met a strong cross-tide and an easterly wind. John Seago, who had his Master's certificate, felt he should take charge but his brother was equally anxious to show what he could do.

Bloom recalls telling John: 'For God's sake let him manage the show and don't argue,' before they both went up front to hoist sails. Bloom suddenly spotted a lighted buoy coming towards them which Edward could not have seen.

'We rushed back to the wheelhouse,' Bloom said, 'and I shouted "Hard to starboard" and John shouted "Hard to port". Ted was completely confused. We hit it on the starboard side and started to fill with water fast. Peter appeared from the cabin with a picture in one hand and a briefcase in the other. All Ted said was "get the lifeboat off". I said, "if you wait a minute she'll float off on her own".' She did and eventually they sent out SOS signals on a hand lamp, started *Capricorn*'s pumps and turned her towards the shore. Gorleston lifeboat was called out and members of the local Rocket Life-Saving Company took their apparatus to Corton Beach, but *Capricorn* just managed to make it on her own. Next day the newspaper photographs showed the beautiful boat lying pitifully on her side and her crew carrying salvage ashore.

Seago immediately arranged for *Capricorn* to be made seaworthy again. Meanwhile, as reported in all the newspapers, he made another cruise, this time on inland waters.

'The Queen and Princess Margaret took a trip on the Norfolk Broads which lasted an hour and a half,' *The Times* reported. 'They went to Ludham to take luncheon with Mr Edward Seago, the artist, at his riverside home and then went with him to Barton Broad. After taking tea at Barton Hall, they returned, by road to Sandringham.'

The trip in the hired motor cruiser *Sandra* had been made on 5 February 1952. A few miles away King George VI was out shooting. That night the King died, peacefully in his sleep at Sandringham House.

A fortnight later, Edward Seago received a handwritten letter from the Queen Mother in reply to his message of sympathy. It read:

'. . . I have been longing to write and tell you what real pleasure your lovely pictures gave the King . . . I got back to Sandringham rather late, and as I always did, rushed straight to the King's room to say that I was back and to see how he was. I found him so well, so gay and so interested in our lovely cruise on the river; and then I told him that you had sent the pictures back in my car and we went straight to the Hall where they had been set out. He was enchanted with them all, and we spent a very happy time looking at them together.

'We had such a truly gay dinner, with the King like his old self, and more picture looking after dinner.

'Thank you with all my heart for giving us the heavenly pictures and particularly for the pleasure you have given the King on Tuesday, 5 Feb.

'One cannot yet believe that it has all happened, one feels rather dazed, and later on I shall write and thank you for the enchanting day that Margaret and I spent with you.

'But I did want to tell you about the King enjoying your pictures.

Yours very sincerely,
Elizabeth R.'

Only on rare occasions could Seago be persuaded to attend public functions away from Norfolk but near home he was always willing to be a guest speaker and revelled in the opportunity to express his views on modern art. 'I believe that more than fifty per cent of abstract art is pure balderdash, absolute phoney,' he told Norwich Rotary Club in 1952 when he deplored its exaggerated worship by a gullible public, even while admitting there were many sincere abstract painters to be found.

'Authentic landscape tradition,' Seago said, 'has come from this city and the surrounding country with Constable and those great painters – humble, simple men who devoted their lives to learning their job.' Like a postscript to the speech, within a few months, Seago was at last publicly compared with Constable. This was in a lavish book of paintings called *Edward Seago: Painter in the English Tradition*. In the introduction Horace Shipp wrote that Constable '. . . significantly belonged to East Anglia'. His passion was awakened,

Shipp wrote, by the water-woven landscape he was destined to immortalize. He knew that a painter could be given unending subjects by those wide and ever-changing skies, creating by their transient effects of light an infinite variation in the beauty of the familiar countryside. Constable in particular, Shipp said, brought to the art of landscape something of a scientist-naturalist's powers of exact observation and recording. Most of all he brought a romantic love of the actual countryside, a love, in his case, as in Wordsworth's, touched by the nostalgia of childhood. All these elements, Shipp declared, were at the basis of Seago's landscape work. In addition, Seago contributed one aspect of nature love which was absent from Constable and the East Anglian water-colour men. 'He is happy, perhaps most happy, by the sea,' Shipp wrote. 'There the sense of the out-of-doors is most completely fulfilled. The sense of freedom from the littleness of human affairs, the feeling that nature has taken over.'

In connection with Shipp's book, Seago had tried to trace a picture he felt should be used as an illustration. It was a Norfolk landscape which he had originally sold to a Norwich art dealer Joe Fairhurst. When Seago asked him about it Fairhurst could not recall it. To refresh his memory, Seago picked up a panel measuring 14 × 10 in Fairhurst's studio, helped himself to paints and set to work. Fairhurst lit up a cigarette and watched. 'He worked entirely from memory,' Fairhurst said, 'painting incredibly quickly. When I realized what was happening I deliberately held on to the cigarette until it just burnt my fingers and at that moment he finished the picture. I said, "Sign it and I'll buy it." So he did and I gave him sixty quid for it. He was not quite so famous in those days.'

Seago's journeys in *Capricorn* exemplified Shipp's theory that the painter was happiest by the sea. In his refitted floating studio he crossed the Channel to Dieppe for the first of a series of memorable cruises to Paris. He had never seen the port but he felt he knew it well from the pictures of Bonington, Francia and Whistler. Its character had been changed by modern features like lamp-posts, telegraph poles and traffic and he queried whether the older artists would have recognized it. But, for his own part, he often found good painting material in the evidence of modern times even when it could be considered a cause of disfigurement. In Dieppe, Seago set up his easel near the port, as Sickert had done, to sketch the ragged skyline of leaning roofs and chimney stacks and old grey-washed houses.

One year Mabel and Brian Seago crossed the Channel by ferry to join *Capricorn* at Le Havre and sail in it up to Paris. For a couple in their seventies it was an adventure – the hundred-mile journey along the Seine, through eleven locks and under countless bridges to moor *Capricorn* on the quayside within sight of the Place de la Concorde.

Capricorn cruised up the Seine in the August sunshine and the painter made notes in his sketch-book of the passing scenes. Had he stopped long enough to set up his easel and make more permanent records he knew he would have been faced with the difficulty he invariably encountered in strange places where he saw so much to paint that he did not know where to begin.

'At first, all the more obvious compositions catch the eye,' he wrote in his last book *With Capricorn to Paris*, after they had passed a chateau he longed to paint. 'If I had painted the chateau it would have been the whole chateau as I had first seen it – pink and grey against the dark trees and the cool, green pattern of the shadow-streaked pasture. Then I expect the light would change and I should want to paint it again. Only after I had worked there several days would my eye become more selective. I should find bits of the chateau – a corner of a terrace and some stone steps; perhaps only one doorway – and then I should leave the chateau and find endless subjects under the trees and along the smooth grass of the river bank where anglers sat by the hour.'

When he was not sketching Seago spent hours polishing *Capricorn*'s brasswork while his father took the wheel and his mother sat on deck and knitted. They moored for two days at the village of Petit Andely, below the ruin of the Chateau Gaillard, built by Richard Coeur de Lion.

'For me, this glimpse of it was a wish come true,' Seago wrote, remembering the first time he had seen a painting of the Chateau. It was in the book by Alfred East which, as a boy, had stirred his imagination and he had longed to visit it and other far-away places, instead of carrying his paints down to the familiar meadows behind his Norfolk home. On that trip up the Seine he painted the Chateau and the view from the top of its hill, of the wide landscape, with the river winding directly below, and a trail of barges pulled by a tug with smoke wisping from its funnel.

They passed Vernon, where Monet had painted and moored at a big petrol station at Conflans where the River Oise runs into the Seine. Seago painted there for an hour using a broad brush so that he could get in the main masses – the barges and tugs and distant bridges against the far bank of the town before the daylight failed. Afterwards the youth who had served them with petrol invited him into a small back room behind the filling station to see some of his own pictures. To Seago's surprise they showed he was a superb artist who worked very much in the manner of the early Florentine painters. He had studied in Paris and had been so influenced by the ardent disciples of the abstract school that he had been persuaded to abandon his natural style for theirs. The results were distorted and commonplace and caused the young man months of depression. During that time he lost track of his original purpose, abandoned the idea of becoming a painter, returned to his father's business and painted only as a hobby. To Seago it was no unusual story. It confirmed his belief that any form of deliberate experiment was unwise and dangerous – a view not shared, he said, by many of his fellow artists.

'This is an age of experiment,' he wrote, 'when talent must be wilfully moulded and eyes can no longer see without the brain distorting their vision. It is no longer enough, apparently, to approach nature with humility, hoping only that one's personality may stamp the interpretation. Nature must be put in her place, bent to the will of man's inflated sense of intellect. I have read much concerning this superior attitude and I have seen the bewildering products of its cult. I admit wholeheartedly that, by their standards, I am old-fashioned; I do not think that I shall receive the sympathy of the intellectual forces in the great art world for I admit that I am offering nothing new by following in a great tradition – except that I am me, and anything that I do cannot have been before. But I work in all sincerity, as I feel and as I see.'

In Paris, Seago worked in the Champs Elysées, the Place de la Concorde and the Tuileries Gardens, painting grounds that, in his circus days, he had chosen to ignore.

He had always discounted the 'plein air' method of painters who worked directly on to large canvases and returned to their subjects at the same time each day. He thought that was no way to capture the swiftly changing effect of light and atmosphere. His method was to make preliminary sketches in oil at one sitting, on either small canvases measuring 18″ × 24″ or panel boards measuring 16″ × 21″. They were larger than those he had once used and it could be that because they afforded him extra scope he was more successful in translating the immediate spontaneity of the subjects on to large canvases in his studio.

In the summer of 1952, *Capricorn* sailed up the Thames to London and moored at Cadogan Pier where for three weeks she would be Seago's home for the Coronation of Queen Elizabeth. The painter was one of twelve artists invited by David Eccles, Minister of Works, to paint an impression of the Coronation. He chose to watch the pageantry from the top of the citadel of the War Office building in Whitehall which gave an unrivalled view when the Coronation procession swept under Admiralty Arch. Before it arrived he made a pen and wash impression of the scene and had just finished it when the rain came and made further pen and wash studies impossible. He made a few small sketches – merely pencil scribbles – some colour notes and an impression in oils painted swiftly on a canvas 2′ × 18″. The result was translated into a large picture which the Queen hung in Buckingham Palace.

Later, with far-sighted generosity, Seago gave the Port of London Authority a painting of the Queen arriving by barge at the Houses of Parliament in appreciation for being allowed to anchor *Capricorn* at Cadogan Pier. After that he was allowed to moor there during many of his London exhibitions.

The visits to London allowed him to extend his interest in the stage and theatrical personalities. He saw *The Innocents* at Her Majesty's Theatre and was so fascinated and enthralled that he returned to many performances. In the dramatized interpretation of Henry James's eerie story, *The Turn of the Screw*, Flora Robson played Miss Gidden, the governess and Carol Woolveridge and Jeremy Spenser took the parts of her young charges whose souls were inhabited by ghosts. Literary experts had argued for years about the precise psychological and supernatural emphasis James intended in his story and, no doubt, Seago too tried to satisfy himself about its undertones. During the process he was impelled to paint Spenser in his role of the handsome, innocent-looking boy, proud and gentlemanly, who physically and mentally fell under the spell of an older man. His study of the flaxen-haired boy, looking brooding and sensual, hung in the sixteenth annual exhibition of the Royal Society of Portrait Painters and represented the beginning of an obsessional friendship between the painter and the sitter twenty-seven years his junior.

The following year Seago was represented in the exhibition by a portrait 'Conversation Piece, Sandringham', a clever study of Princess Margaret playing the piano in the green-draped sitting-room at Sandringham House, a painting acclaimed by many critics as the most interesting in the exhibition. It was the prelude to a royal portrait by Seago which received world-wide publicity as the first painting of the Queen on horseback. It had been commissioned by the Coldstream Guards and showed the Queen in the spectacular full-dress uniform of Colonel-in-Chief. In terms of treatment and likeness it was a controversial picture, assessed by some critics as 'a typical Royal Academy portrait' which, to Seago's mind, it definitely was not. 'After the war, I twice sent pictures to the Academy,' he told the newspapermen, 'but as they were rejected I stopped submitting them.' Two years later apparently he changed his mind. In 1958 'Lambeth Reach' and 'The Canal, Paddington' were exhibited there and the next year, 'The Thames at Millbank' and 'Ponza Harbour'.

Meanwhile, Seago painted at Sandringham, and sometimes sketched in the park. In 1956 Prince Philip invited Seago to join him on part of his world tour. He suggested that after the opening of the Olympic Games in Melbourne, Seago should join the Royal yacht *Britannia* for the trip to Antarctica. Such a journey, Prince Philip thought, would give a painter of Seago's talent a tremendous opportunity to work where no other artist had really tried to paint – with the exception of Wilson who did a few pictures on the expeditions with Shackleton and Scott.

The challenge prompted Seago to resume his pre-war habit of keeping a diary, but on loose-leaf sheets of lined paper instead of in the gold-embossed red-leather books. The first entry, on 10 December, described his flight to Melbourne followed by '. . . a very thrilling drive with a police escort and sirens going all the time . . .' to *Britannia* where Prince Philip welcomed him aboard. That night the guests for a dinner party included General Slim and Robert Menzies, the Prime Minister of Australia.

For Prince Philip the journey involved a full programme of official commitments but he obviously regarded painting as an integral part of relaxation. The next day before he flew off for a three-day visit to remote parts of the continent the Prince showed Seago the pictures he had already painted. While he was away Seago got to know three of the other five members of the Royal party: the veteran explorer Sir Raymond Priestley, one of the greatest living authorities on the Antarctic; Lord Cilcennin, former First Lord of the Admiralty and Squadron Leader Henry Chinnery, the Duke's equerry.

At first Seago found the motion of the ship made painting difficult, even after Vice-Admiral Sir Conolly Abel Smith, Flag Officer, Royal Yacht, tried to help by lowering the gyroscopic stabilizers, capable of cutting a roll of twenty degrees down to one of six. But the weather steadily improved after Prince Philip re-joined the ship at Lyttelton and *Britannia* set sail for the Chatham Isles, the first of the seven British bases she was to visit in the then Falkland Islands Dependencies Survey. On 19 December the wind died, the sea calmed and Prince Philip spent the afternoon and evening painting a portrait of Seago at work. Then Seago made a quick portrait of Prince Philip working at his easel.

During the next week life aboard ship settled into an amiable routine and Prince Philip passed the word that beards could properly be grown and set an example. Seago's influence became apparent in the number of amateur artists who suddenly appeared on the veranda deck. Prince Philip and Seago often worked together, either at separate easels or combining their efforts to produce a lino-cut for a 'Red Nose' certificate to be given to each member of the ship's company to commemorate their visit inside the Antarctic Circle.

'Prince Philip has really done the design for it although the ward-room asked me,' read the entry in Seago's diary, 'but I must admit his idea is better than what I had in mind! I am amazed at his keen-ness and energy.' This was written on the day when both men had experimented on an improvised roller to print three hundred sheets from the lino-block. 'The first pulls were not awfully encouraging,' Seago wrote, 'but Prince Philip was full of determination.' When the technical problems were resolved the Prince headed a team of shift workers who volunteered to work the roller.

One afternoon just before Christmas Seago made a study of Prince Philip sketching Priestley and wrote in his diary that later he and the Prince had a joint effort of sea and sky. Some years afterwards recalling the 'joint effort' Prince Philip said he suspected that he would have asked Seago where he had gone wrong in his picture and Seago would have come over and put him right. Prince Philip spent quite a lot of time on the trip trying to do skies and seas, but not he said with any great success. He found it always very discouraging to try and learn from Seago because one felt as if one were riding a bicycle on the ground while the painter was riding another on the high wire above. Just watching Seago at work gave him great pleasure he said, 'because while the results were fantastic, just watching the way he achieved them was even more fantastic'.

Seago wrote down a list of colours he recommended should be put on the palette and Prince Philip always kept the old envelope with the list on the back in his paint-box although he noted that Seago was far more economical in his colours than he was. Seago also had a recipe for priming hardboard using size and whiting but it never seemed to work for the Prince. Whenever he tried to use it lumps of white flaked off on to his brush when he started painting. Eventually, he wrote and asked Seago if he could let him have some of his home-prepared boards, which he did.

Prince Philip, Chinnery and Priestley used to stand around and watch Seago painting. They would criticize and joke and make comments and suggestions, but he never minded. His capacity for work was tremendous, the Prince recalled: 'He was always sketching. He always seemed to have a pencil in his hand and with just a few lines could reproduce all the atmosphere and "feel" of a place with just the smallest pencil sketch. He also had this photographic memory and if he'd ever painted anything he could always remember exactly *how* he'd painted it; not just what he'd painted but the way he'd done it.'

On Boxing Day *Britannia* encountered her first iceberg, a castellated beauty about two and a half miles long and a hundred feet high and, from then on, Seago concentrated on painting the exciting, unfamiliar scenery around him. 'It was tremendously thrilling,' he said afterwards. 'I had always expected something that was very very flat and instead of that it was mountainous with tremendous peaks and black rock. I thought there was going to be wide expanses of nothingness and now and again queer upright icebergs and of course I thought it would be colourless; a mixture of greys and blacks and whites, but instead of that the colour was tremendous. It was full of rich blues and greens and the cavities, particularly in the icebergs which one would expect to be very very dark, weren't dark. They glowed with the most rich luminous blues and greens which were tremendously exciting to paint. What fascinated me among the icebergs was the stillness, and you got this extraordinary silence except for the extraordinary little ripple of crackling ice on the surface of the water. It's not a sinister sound, it just gives a tremendous sense of space and loneliness and greatness.'

While he painted there, Seago was aware from an artistic point of view that he was in completely unknown territory. 'You see,' he told a radio interviewer when he returned home, 'we can't help being influenced by pictures we have seen by other painters of the past of various parts of the world and it was rather fascinating to go to a part of the world where you had seen no pictures at all because nobody had ever painted it. It was particularly fascinating because I live in a part of the world which has been painted over and over again and really is the teething ground of landscape painting.'

Although the sub-zero temperatures made it impossible to use water-colour, Seago found the dry cold no worse than a winter's day in England. He painted about sixty pictures on the expedition and gave them all to Prince Philip who sent most of them to Balmoral and had a particularly fine painting of an iceberg hung in *Britannia*. The Prince said it was a marvellous gift but if ever the painter wanted any pictures back for reproduction purposes or anything like that, to be sure and ask for them. 'Oh, that's quite unnecessary,' Seago replied. 'If I want them at any time I can easily remember them.'

In support of this Prince Philip told the story of a painting Seago had given the Wardroom of the ice-breaker *John Biscoe*, the research ship in which the party travelled to one of the remotest Antarctic bases. The Captain thought it was intended as a personal gift for him and when he left the ship he took it away with him, to the annoyance and disappointment of the officers. Seago did not hear about the incident until some ten years afterwards. He then painted the same picture all over again and sent it to the officers of the research ship. Telling the story, Prince Philip said if the two pictures were hung side by side it would have been impossible to tell the difference.

At the end of her two months' tour, *Britannia* docked at Gibraltar where the Prince stayed behind, for a short time, at Government House. On 6 February Seago flew back to England with some members of the Royal party, including Prince Philip's secretary, Lieutenant-Commander Michael Parker. It had been Parker's last official Royal journey. During the tour it had been announced that he was resigning his appointment for personal reasons. Worry and concern on this account made it impossible, he felt, for him to fulfil his duties as he wished. On 7 February 1957, the newspapers carried large photographs of Prince Philip saying farewell to his secretary (and also a small announcement to the effect that Edward Seago had been elected an associate of the Royal Society of Painters in Watercolours).

Every newspaper was anxious to obtain from Michael Parker the full story of his resignation, but at the time his whereabouts could not be traced. For many weeks during which time he could not be found, he was living at the Dutch House in Ludham, and eventually he left the country on *Capricorn*. The villagers of Ludham had often criticized Seago for his aloofness in playing little part in local affairs but despite considerable pressure, when the time came to show loyalty to him as one of their own, they preserved his secret.

XII

The Traveller Returns

In 1959 Brian Seago died, three years after John had settled in Kenya where he became a very respected game trapper. Mabel Seago lived on for three and a half years during which time her younger son tried to alleviate her loneliness and unhappiness but whenever she was in his studio he never felt able to paint. He wrote her long letters when he was abroad; sometimes on *Capricorn* but more often, as the years passed, he flew to remote parts and tackled the more intense colour contrasts in Portugal, Greece, Italy, Morocco, Hong Kong, Burma and Thailand. Many of his travels were reflected in a loan exhibition of his work at the Castle Museum in Norwich in 1962 which was opened by Earl Alexander. But the personal stories behind some of the pictures there were known to only a few close friends.

His early Portuguese paintings were reminders of an accident in Lisbon. He was leaving a small restaurant after lunch on a stormy day when a sailor running through the rain with his head down, collided with him, knocked him unconscious and caused a depressed fracture of Seago's right cheek. He was operated on under general anaesthetic at the British Hospital in Lisbon where he was detained for several days.

The Hong Kong pictures were the outcome of an invitation from John Kidston Swire, Chairman of the parent company of a Far

Eastern Trading and Shipping Group whose wife was a collector of Seago's paintings. His Hong Kong manager wanted six pictures for a new boardroom and local paintings by a British artist would be ideal. The Company defrayed Seago's expenses and he refunded them in paintings. He saw the trip as an exciting challenge because Hong Kong was a place where no British artist except George Chinnery had ever painted.

At first he was so appalled by the poverty he saw in Hong Kong that he could hardly bring himself to paint. When he eventually set up his easel to make the quick colour notes and pencil sketches from which, at this stage in his technique, the finished pictures would be painted in the seclusion of his studio in Norfolk, a crowd of youngsters invariably gathered round his easel. Always a Chinese boy on a motor cycle was the last to move away. He was Chan Nam Tsui and although he could hardly speak a word of English, after a few days he became Seago's unofficial guide to the city.

Seago learned that he was the son of a wealthy silk merchant and had been born in Shanghai. When he was about sixteen years old he had escaped from Communist China by swimming out to sea where he had been picked up by a fishing vessel, taken to Taipeh and from there had made his way to Hong Kong where he had an uncle. When Seago met him, he was working in a factory and sharing a room with six other boys.

Chan Nam Tsui showed Seago round Hong Kong where the painter was distracted by the overcrowding and apparently hopeless plight of the Chinese population. He felt that a positive way to do something about it would be to adopt Chan Nam as his own son and give him the best possible English education. This entailed getting a visa for which he needed accredited confirmation from an English College of Education with a place for a Chinese boy who spoke no English.

Seago approached the Principal of Great Yarmouth College of Art for help. He offered to accede to the College's persistent request for him to become a governor providing they would accept the Chinese boy as a pupil. Chan Nam spent two terms there and every evening he had private tuition in English and soon proved he was a brilliant student, if not a potential painter. He transferred to Lowestoft College of Further Education where within eighteen months he had taken his necessary 'O' Levels, gained 98 per cent in an advanced mathematics paper (two marks he learned had been deducted for untidiness) and seemed well on his way to becoming an electronics engineer. Meanwhile, as a compliment to his English godfather he changed his name to Edward Tsui.

Edward Tsui never quite achieved his scholastic ambition. However he took a management course, acquired a knowledge of French and an appreciation of English culture through regular visits to the theatre, the opera, ballet and the atmosphere surrounding him in the Dutch House. Eight years later, because he had no official papers, he went back to Hong Kong to try and get a British passport. There he found that the time he had spent in England did not qualify him for a British passport and he had to start from the beginning. He stayed there and became an executive with a British firm and was eventually appointed their representative for the Far East. Meanwhile his ties with England were reinforced when, on his marriage to a pretty Chinese girl, Seago gave him a cottage in Ludham as a wedding present. For the painter it was infinitely more satisfying than the eighty oils and water-colours that represented his three months' visit to the Far East, which had included a trip to Burma and Thailand.

He again met poverty in Morocco. He and Peter were having a drink outside a restaurant in the old quarter of Marrakesh when he saw a native boy in ragged European clothing, his shoes tied together with string. The painter realized that the cost of the meal he was about to order would buy food for such a boy's family for several weeks. He called the boy over, bought him shoes, a shirt and pair of trousers and later visited his home and met his family. They were living in two spotlessly clean rooms on the top floor of an old house where the only furniture was a cupboard, a folding coffee table and palliasses to sleep on. Seago sent the boy out to buy sugar, tea and flour.

The following year in Marrakesh there was another poorly-dressed boy. His name was Nassmi Jillali and to Seago's delight he spoke French. Seago was so impressed by this that he had a suit made for him and bought him two shirts, shoes, socks and a wallet and gave him £2 to put into it. The boy's first purchase was a news-paper to carry under his arm and, thus equipped and wearing his new clothes he got a job in a local hotel and then a similar job in Switzerland. They corresponded and Seago sent him an English dictionary. From then on Nassmi's English improved rapidly and when he visited the Dutch House, Seago presented him with an English-French linguaphone course.

Meanwhile the time had come when Seago rarely used *Capricorn*. He parted with her and in 1968 acquired a studio in Sardinia, on the Costa Smeralda, with a magnificent view of the Mediterranean from his balcony. He had, since 1960, discarded his technique of painting directly from nature, and out of doors he made only colour notes and pencil sketches from which to create the finished picture in his studio. Indoors he could portray his personal experience of places or subjects that had once sparked off his imagination and be undisturbed by superficial visual distractions which intruded when he set up his easel outside. Applying this technique, when he was in Sardinia he often painted Norfolk scenes and home in Ludham he worked on the views from his Mediterranean holiday home.

Once on his way to Sardinia, he made a detour to visit Istanbul where from his bedroom balcony at the Park Hotel he had an incredible view of the Bosphorous. He made water-colours and pencil sketches there to translate into oil paintings and then went into the streets and filled his sketch-books with meticulous drawings; street scenes where the houses were correct to the smallest window, a stretch of wall exact to every stone, crowded squares where every person was represented by a tiny pencil stroke. At a time when he had never painted more freely and with such apparent immense facility, his sketch-books represented a discipline he practised consistently until the end of his days.

The later sketch-books however represented exercises in technique rather than memory training because, by that time the image of every place or subject he had ever seen and wanted to paint was stored in his mind in complete detail. The wealth of images, he told his friend, the actor Peter Cushing, was stored in 'Seagoland' from where he drew on it at will. His challenge was to express the image on canvas. Sometimes he painted a real landscape from memory; at other times he created a composite imaginary picture which he described as a 'Seagoscape'.

Long before Cushing met Seago he had been an admirer of the painter's work and after one of the early post-war exhibitions wrote to tell him so. In reply came a pleasant, formal acknowledgement from Ludham. Four years later Cushing and his wife were visiting friends in Cromer where, on an impulse, the actor telephoned Seago to say he was in the neighbourhood and asked if he could call and see some more paintings. Seago explained that he was leaving for Portugal the following day so the visit would have to be that same evening. The Cushings came, the friendship was immediate, and it was five o'clock the next morning before the visitors left Seago's house. It was agreed that they would be back there to spend Christmas.

'It was a house that lent itself to Christmas,' Cushing said, recalling some fifteen Christmases he and his wife Helen spent there. 'It was decorated with holly and candles and a Christmas tree and there were presents and games round the fire and – always – laughter. We were usually the only house-guests but Auchinleck and his sister often joined us in the evening for Christmas dinner and Ted's parents and John were there. I remember one game we played which was a sort of charade called "How to Cheat the Customs Man" and the Field-Marshal excelled at this.'

Auchinleck was a frequent visitor at the Dutch House. After his retirement, painting was his main occupation and he enjoyed working with Seago so that, eventually, he bought a house at Beccles a few miles away, where he lived for seven years. He was perhaps lonely and enjoyed discussing painting and pictures and gardening. He sent Seago cuttings of strange plants he found on his travels in distant parts.

'I am sending you a dozen of these Iris. Hope you are not bored with this!!!!' he once wrote and clipped to the letter was an advertisement for 'Iris Kaempferl' – an unusual Japanese clematis-flowered iris. 'I am never happier than in the Dutch House . . .' he wrote, and in another letter suggested that Seago might like to paint a picture for the drawing-room of the new Master's Lodge at Wellington College – where he was a governor. The letter went on, '. . . I am sure Ted, you know I am speaking the truth when I say I am never happier than when with you.'

While Auchinleck enjoyed Seago's company, Peter Cushing was particularly sensitive to the strange charisma the painter exerted and aware of the depression that, as the years passed, lurked uncomfortably close to the ready laughter. At one time, some of the laughter was engendered by plays Seago wrote for his friends to act out with him on his tape-recorder. For many years it was his favourite toy and at Christmas he prepared the script for a play in which Cushing voiced all the female parts, Seago took the lead and there were supporting roles for everyone.

Such activities afforded a much-needed outlet for the painter in whom the tensions were building up. They were caused by his misgivings about his ability to achieve his own idea of perfection in painting, by family stress and by personal frustrations.

'He was gay and charming and one of the unhappiest people I've known,' Cushing said, identifying in Seago many of the traumas he himself endured as an actor. But an obvious difference between the two men was that Seago found it almost impossible to show emotion. Cushing, the less inhibited, once made a deliberate effort to break through the painter's suave barrier.

'Dear Ted,' he asked, 'are you happy?'

'What a ridiculous question,' Seago replied and Cushing recalled there was a feeling of ice between them for the next two hours.

However, to the Cushings as to Peter Seymour, Seago occasionally showed his real feelings. At such times he spoke of his parents and their lack of ability to understand his longing to be a painter, of his sense of filial duty to his mother and his real affection for his father. Sometimes, in bouts of deep depression, he made long telephone calls to Helen Cushing who tried to give him mental sustenance, and as a tangible sign of their affection, the Cushings presented him with a set of keys for their London flat and insisted that he and Peter should use it as their own.

The ties between the actor and the painter were strengthened by the fact that Cushing also painted and was one of the few people with whom Seago worked in water-colour, a medium which he never ceased to regard as 'a very private affair'.

'Oh, you *can* paint!' was his reaction the first time that Cushing showed him one of his own efforts. It was a water-colour of a jar of white roses and Seago laid it on the floor to study. The new perspective only endorsed his first impression.

'Peter, get out your bicycle and run over it. It's much better than mine,' he told Seymour and when, together, the actor and painter each made a water-colour painting of a bowl of syringa, Seago admired his friend's freedom of handling paint which, he said, many more experienced artists might envy. In the light of such encouragement Cushing was confident enough to offer a mild criticism when Seago asked his opinion of a painting of a church.

'Marvellous – as always,' Cushing volunteered, 'but I just wonder whether the reflection of the steeple in the water is just a shade crooked?'

Dead silence. It was reassurance the painter needed, not criticism nor constructive advice which Peter Seymour was the only person ever privileged to offer. Never again was Cushing invited to give his opinion of a Seago picture.

Seago invariably contrived that the stream of visitors to the Dutch House had every opportunity to see him paint. His desire for an audience arose, perhaps, not from vanity but from a positive need for constant reassurance and admiration, to combat the persistent feeling of insecurity that no financial reward appeared to allay. He disliked being alone and, moreover, enjoyed sharing with friends his own passionate love of painting so that, just as a great musician in the role of host might offer to entertain his guests by playing to them, Seago was also happy to display to them his own greatest gift.

Friends accepted as a matter of course that after dinner everyone adjourned to the studio to talk or watch television. After a time their host would move over to his easel and begin painting. Occasionally someone would stroll across and watch and offer not too critical comments such as those contributed aboard *Britannia* by the self-styled 'critics', Prince Philip, Chinnery and Priestley. Priestley, for instance, once insisted with mock intensity that no landscape detail of his beloved Antarctica should be omitted from a picture for the sake of composition.

Michael Denison and Dulcie Gray, two of Seago's many stage friends, recalled the first time they stayed at the Dutch House. After dinner the painter said, 'You've only seen my finished work, would you like to see me painting?' Denison watched a familiar scene on the Grand Canal in Venice re-created, with lightning brush strokes, in less than half an hour. As the picture took shape he asked if some of the smaller insignificant buildings, at the left of the church of St Maria del Giglio, were products of the painter's imagination.

'No, no, no,' Seago protested. 'They're exactly correct. I have a total mental photograph of the place.'

Invariably he used oils when painting in front of his friends. 'With oils I can be totally relaxed,' he told Denison, 'but with water-colours I'm as taut as a bow-string.' The conversation, Denison recalls, led to a discussion about their mutual professional needs. Both actors and painters, they agreed, must, in their respective professions, be able to relax. Another similarity was that both painters and actors could, through their work, reveal themselves to an extent that in private life shyness might have precluded. Seago had never considered acting as a compensation for shyness.

As an outcome of that evening's conversation Michael Denison the following morning wrote a passage for his autobiography that perhaps indicated why Seago, sensitive and diffident in manner, attracted many actors as his friends. His guest wrote:

'We are popularly supposed to be brimful of confidence and the social graces, because in learning and remembering our parts and performing them in public, we are doing things which ninety per cent of humanity would rather die than attempt. The truth is different. Many people in my profession are painfully shy, and have indeed found in acting their only antidote to this disability. A good part in a good play with a good entrance and a good exit will be a joy for any actor. For the shy it will be paradise, because they will be cushioned, in a manner impossible in everyday life, from the thousand natural shocks that flesh is heir to. They can come into a room *knowing* whom they are going to find, *knowing* that their contribution to the conversation is going to be effective and *knowing* that they will have no hesitation or embarrassment in choosing the right moment to leave.'

Such recognition of the comparable demands of painting and acting might well have contributed to Seago's affinity with many great actors. It was an affinity born out of the painter's impressive talent, his sensitivity, his love of the theatre, an enviable life-style and his brilliant conversation spiced with an ability to amuse.

With the help of Peter Seymour he was a good host and revelled in the role although he always assumed his guests would be happy to fit in with all his activities and accept him on his own terms. Only if they insisted did he leave them to their own devices. He provided an idyllic setting where it was easy to relax surrounded by fine paintings, including several Boudins, and a collection of early English water-colours. Meals were produced by the gardener's sister, the inimitable Miss Thompson, who lived in the village but as a young girl had learned to cook in the kitchens of great London houses.

In turn Flora Robson, Alastair Sim, Athene Seyler and Noël Coward were among the many stage friends who, with Jeremy Spenser, frequently stayed at the Dutch House or joined a trip on *Capricorn*. But only on the rarest occasions did Seago reciprocate their visits. From the time he saw *The Innocents* he maintained regular correspondence with Flora Robson who wrote to him from all over the world, while Athene Seyler and her husband Nicholas Hannen eventually bought a holiday cottage in the village. He painted Hannen's portrait and also one of Alastair Sim for the Garrick Club.

Seago's friendship with Noël Coward came later. They met at a Sandringham house-party in 1965 and when the following year Coward was elected to the Garrick Club, Seago – already a member – was asked to paint his portrait. Coward stayed at the Dutch House for the sittings and Seago so enjoyed painting the portrait that he made an exact copy of it to give to the sitter who had immediately become a friend.

'Painting a portrait is a very hit and miss affair and I wanted so much to paint one which would give you pleasure,' Seago wrote to him and Coward's pleasure was evident when he had the portrait reproduced for his Christmas card. The following year was Coward's seventieth birthday and Seago made another copy of the portrait to give to the newly-opened Noël Coward Bar at the Phoenix Theatre in London, as his 'little tribute', he wrote, 'to the man whose work I admire far more than that of anyone else in his art – or in several arts for that matter'.

The admiration was mutual. 'Your sort of painting is what I like best,' Coward wrote back. 'It is free and disciplined: it is completely lucid and, to me, evokes pure magic . . . You have filled me with a longing to paint again.'

Regularly they exchanged letters and sent each other books. Seago wrote that he intended to quote one of Coward's remarks in a speech he was to make at the opening of a local art exhibition. Coward had once told him, 'If you try too hard to be with it you run a risk of being without it.' Seago wrote to Coward that, in painting terms that was just what was happening. So many of the men in so-called high places seemed frightened to stand by their convictions, he wrote, because they were afraid of being left out. 'Falling over backwards to proclaim an admiration for stuff which I don't believe they really like or understand.'

Theatrical personalities were not the only friends Seago entertained at the Dutch House. The spectacular success of the annual exhibitions at Colnaghi's encouraged many artists, professional and amateur, to seek his advice. To professionals he was most reluctant to give it. 'The only way I can paint is to try and capture the picture in my own mind,' he said, 'and that is something you cannot teach to anyone.' To amateurs he felt he had more to offer as when in 1958 the Home Secretary, R. A. Butler, wrote to say he planned to be in Norfolk during the summer and as an admirer of Seago's paintings he wondered if there would be an opportunity for them to paint together.

Butler had been a keen amateur painter since boyhood. He had great feeling for, and knowledge of, pictures. His upbringing and training gave him an insight into the art world. In boyhood he spent much time with his uncle, Cyril Butler, a keen collector and patron of Wilson Steer, and a friend of Professor Tonks, MacAvoy and others and his first marriage to Sydney Courtauld, only child of Samuel, founder of the Courtauld Institute, a centre of art appreciation, had increased his interest and widened his horizons.

During his political career Butler had several times painted with Churchill who, he insisted, taught him to paint with courage. He described how, before Churchill arrived at a chosen painting place, one of his detectives squeezed an extravagant assortment of composite colours on to his glass palette until it resembled a shade-card of greens, mauve, Prussian blue and pink. Two glasses were then placed side by side on the painting table. One contained whisky and one turpentine and everyone watched carefully lest the enthusiastic artist dipped his brush into the wrong spirit. 'Some of those zinc-based colours were pretty lethal!' Butler commented. Painting expeditions with Seago he learned were very different affairs.

'That one week in August,' he wrote to Seago afterwards, 'was a real inspiration, quite apart from providing a turning point in my treatment of trees, skies, churches, rivers, boats and everything up to the sill of anatomy.'

It was a week when Alexander happened to be staying at the Dutch House and Butler drove over from Blakeney every day to join the two painters. He and Alexander were provided with stools and Seago stood behind them and worked on his portable easel. Butler was given the smallest canvas to work on and, he recalled, he felt rather nervous.

'Seago always settled Alexander in the best position,' he commented adding, with resignation, 'I think he was altogether much more hopeful of Alexander than he was of me!'

The 'turning point' referred to in his letter to Seago came when the latter demonstrated some of his own painting principles. He showed his companions his pictures of Norfolk churches and then took them to sketch a church with its tower silhouetted against the sky. He pointed out the way the light hit the darker stone tower and made it look lighter than the pale sky behind. They painted a large tree in the foreground of a landscape and learned Seago's trick of touching-in its leaves with a palette knife instead of with a brush, to make the tree 'come alive'.

Butler watched while Seago showed Alexander how to give his painting an added dimension by stretching a ray of light across the middle. It was an advanced technique which Butler did not attempt, but he was more than satisfied with the painting expeditions. Seago, he said, had shown him the real use of colour. In place of Churchill's range of composite colours, Seago used only basic ones – indigo blue and chrome yellow for the grass and trees and, surprising though it seemed, always chrome yellow in the skies. Often there was '. . . A touch of red to make the greens sing'.

It was evident that Seago, like Butler, also respected Churchill as a painter, but for different reasons. He considered him 'the amateur of all amateurs who thought he could do it and did it. He never explored: he never questioned: he never observed. He painted a house as if it were there, and if it had a red roof: right – here's the red paint: if there was a green field beneath it, right – here's the green paint. It never occurred to him,' Seago said, 'to ask "How red is the red? How green is the green? and, by putting the green against the red, does the red look brighter or turn the grass grey?" Those queries never entered Churchill's head.'

Butler also had an opportunity to observe Seago's ability to paint with great speed. After a morning's painting they were just sitting down to lunch when a telephone call came from Colnaghi's to ask if Seago could let them have a Norfolk landscape immediately for an important customer.

'Our host,' Butler said, 'begged to be excused while we ate our lunch. When we took our coffee into the studio, we saw that he had already filled a medium-sized canvas with a Broadland scene of a ship sailing across a wide expanse of water. There was a mill with sails and some trees in the background. We watched him paint in two cows on the left of the picture and, by the time we had finished our coffee, the whole thing was complete – exactly typical of his style!

'He told us, "I've done it so often that I know exactly how to paint windmills and Broads and the like." I suggested to him that, perhaps, such a facility might be considered a defect, particularly allied to the fact that he so often painted the same subjects. He agreed, but he said he found it absolutely congenial to paint in Norfolk and as there always seemed to be a market for his work, he felt he should go on painting the things he loved.

'Of course that facility of his had not been acquired all that easily. He maintained that an artist should paint every day, just as a pianist practised the piano. But it did mean that his was a quick art, with a quick return and, consequently, a quick disappearance into private collections all over the world. This means, I think, that despite his ability he was not taken sufficiently seriously as a great artist. But had the process been slowed up, I believe he might have been recognized ostentatiously, as one of our great modern painters.'

Seago invariably repudiated the criticism that he was an over-prolific painter by citing Turner's nineteen thousand water-colours and sketches and the three hundred oil paintings he left to the nation in 1851. Discounting a painting comparison between Seago and artists of Turner's calibre, the lasting influence of the Norfolk painter may prove significant in a more subtle way. Through unique qualities and unusual circumstances he was in a position to communicate personally with some of the most influential people of his time and with a younger generation who in their turn will have great influence.

The Prince of Wales recalled he had known Seago since he was a child.

'I was quite small when my father took me over to the Dutch House from Sandringham, for the first time. We called in to lunch at that fascinating house, full of interesting bric-à-brac and there was that splendid little garden leading down to the creek. His studio impressed itself on my memory. There was a smell of paint and those marvellous pictures of Venice, Portugal, Sardinia and Norfolk.

'He was a memorable person – always great fun and very kind and with lots of amusing stories. As a child, I liked him immediately. He was very good with children. I sailed on *Capricorn* and he gave me a special tie he had for those who'd been in her.

'I'd tried to paint when I was about seven or eight when my father had shown me how to do it with oils. Then, about two years before Ted died, I suddenly had a yearning to try with water-colours – firstly because it was something different and secondly, because I thought it was somehow more expressive than oils and such painting was more alive and had more texture and depth than a photograph. I struggled along and did some dreadful work. I wanted to have a lesson and took my pictures along to the Dutch House and asked Ted to criticize them and tell me where I was going wrong. He told me, for a start, I was using the wrong paper and the wrong brushes and where I could get the proper paper and brushes.* He said that with water-colours you've got to be particularly careful about those sort of things.

'I asked him if he'd give me a lesson. He'd never given lessons in his life; he said he was not a teacher and he didn't like teaching.

---

* Seago used rough, unbleached paper and sable water-colour brushes.

Then he said, "Alright, I'll give you a lesson – but only one." He sat down and proceeded to paint a picture entirely from memory. It was quite astonishing. He was talking all the time. Washes were running into each other and his hand just flowed over the paper in a unique way and in ten or fifteen minutes, there was this marvellous little picture. I thought it was just going to be sky – all sky – and then, suddenly, there were a few brush strokes and the sky ran into the water. Then another couple of strokes and there were two Thames barges. He used the side of a great thick brush to paint the masts – each mast with a single downward stroke. I tried to do the same, using the side of a thick brush but I just made a great blodge.

'I asked if I could take the picture away with me and he said "Of course!" It stands on my bedside table. It's a marvellous little picture.

'I asked him about technique. He explained about wetting the paper first and then trying to run one wash into another while it was still wet. He said that, with water-colours, one can create an impression rather than a direct representation of what is there. He explained that in order to do this he'd studied basic geology so he knew about the soil formation and what the shadows on the land meant and the various colours you got at different depths and stages. And he'd studied anatomy so he knew about the bone and structure of an animal. Once having learnt to paint the minutest details, he said, you go on painting a general impression. For instance, his cows were just dots of paint but they were the right dots. He showed me how, with one dot of paint, you can produce a cow. But if I tried to do it they would not look like cows.

'He made it look so easy – but it's not. I went away inspired but it is extraordinarily difficult. I've tried to do it and I still try and I have lessons when I'm at Windsor. I love it because I feel one can express a great deal through it – if it works. But if water-colours go wrong, that's that. Unlike oils there's nothing you can do to get it right.

'He is one of the great water-colourists: his expressiveness was so brilliant and the textures were so wonderful – particularly in the Norfolk paintings and particularly for someone like myself who loves Norfolk. I have quite a few of his pictures. He gave me one for my twenty-first birthday and my Grandmother has given me some of hers and I hung one of those in my room at Cambridge.

'He was a very kind and sensitive person – enormously generous and with a great sense of humour and all this comes out in his artistry . . . Recently, I was immensely inspired – indeed carried away – by the Turner Exhibition. I came away deeply moved, particularly by the water-colours and particularly because I'd tried and knew some of the problems he had to face.'

As the years passed and Edward Seago was not made a Royal Academician or given official recognition and his work was not bought for any National Collection, his insecurity reasserted itself. Close friends sensed the bitterness behind his reluctance to be described as 'a Norfolk artist' because, he complained, few people in Norfolk liked his paintings. This false assumption was based on his inability to recognize that any local resentment to him as a man bore no relationship to the admiration and pride his paintings engendered in his native county. The indifference had built up over the years largely because, with an ever-widening circle of friends and increasing commitments, he felt compelled to discard old, out-worn friendships and, to some extent, divorce himself from local affairs. Criticism caused by his reassessment of friendships in the light of new commitments and the long hours he set aside for painting extended far beyond Norfolk.

Nevertheless some friends appreciated his dilemma and their loyalty went deep, as a letter to *The Times*, written in 1968 by his wartime friend the MP John Hill shows. It was written without Seago's knowledge:

'Sir – Why is it that auction sales of pictures are usually news, whereas exhibition sales by living British artists seem of little account? Last week one of Bond Street's most prominent galleries put on view 50 English landscapes by a Norfolk painter. They seemed not obviously under-valued but all were bought within an hour of the earliest preview.

'Is not the immediate sell-out of a one-man show – for over £20,000 – newsworthy in itself? Yet no critic appears to have noticed this. The public's liking for simple, rural beauty, revealed

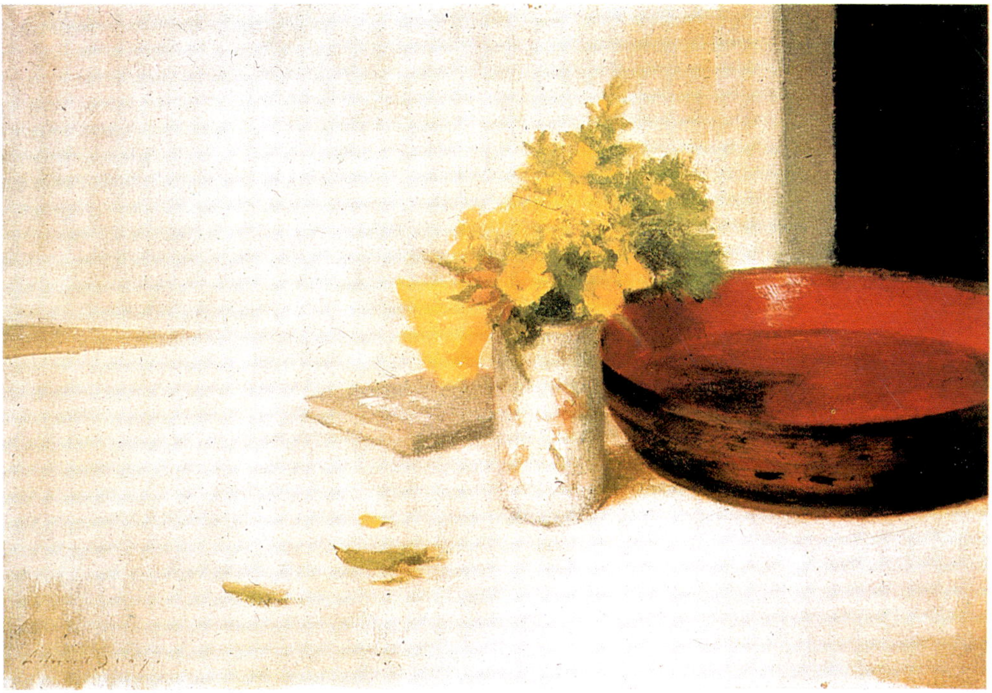

17. Still Life – Flowers in a vase

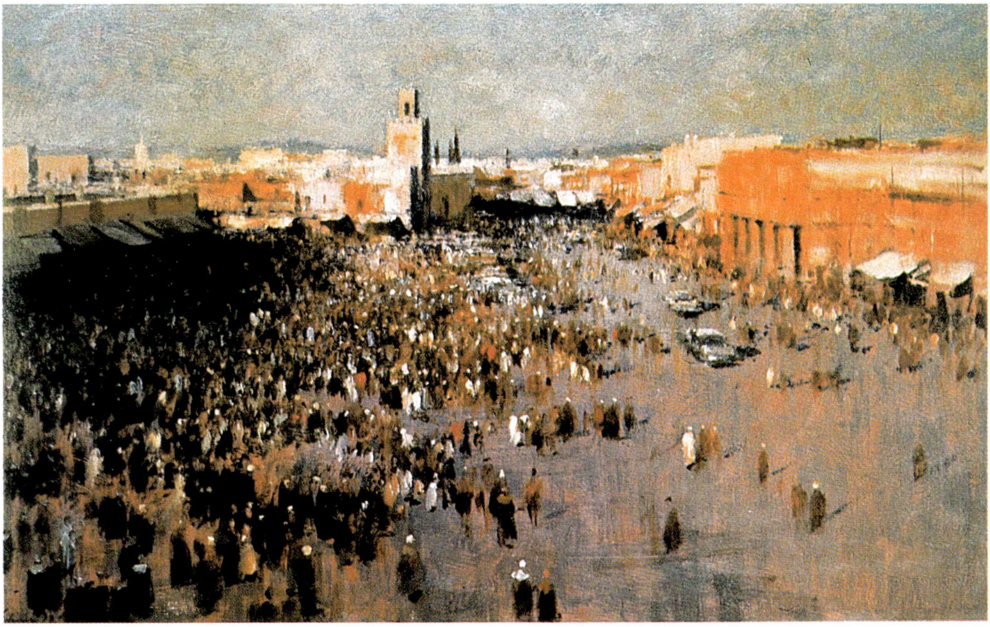

18. The Jemma al F'na, Marrakech

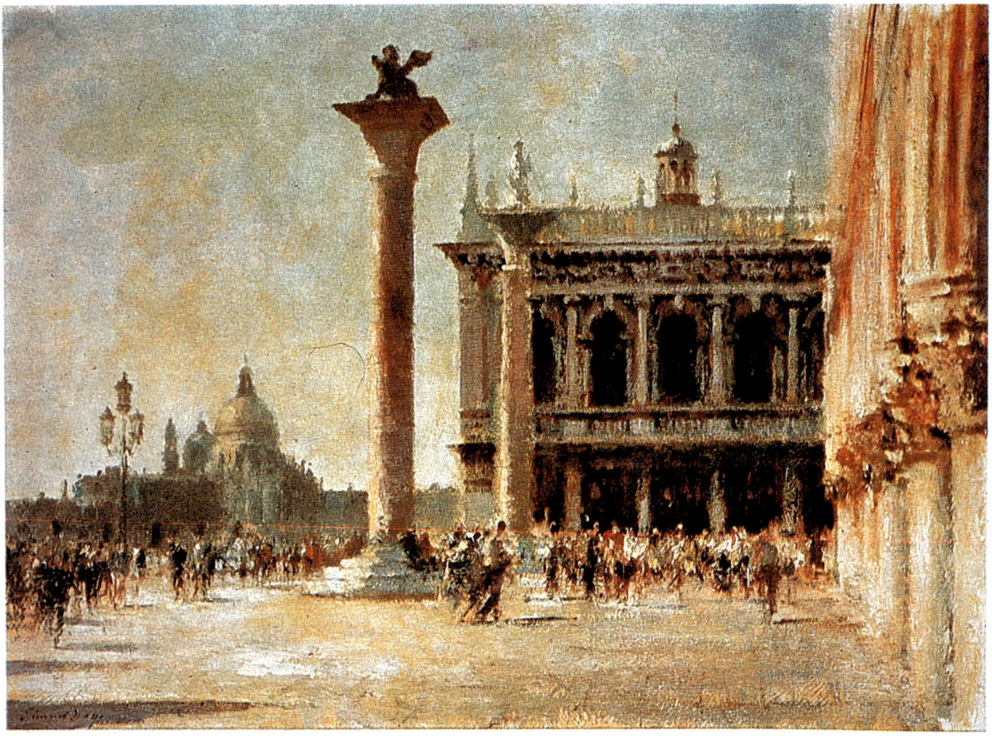

19 The Two Columns, Venice

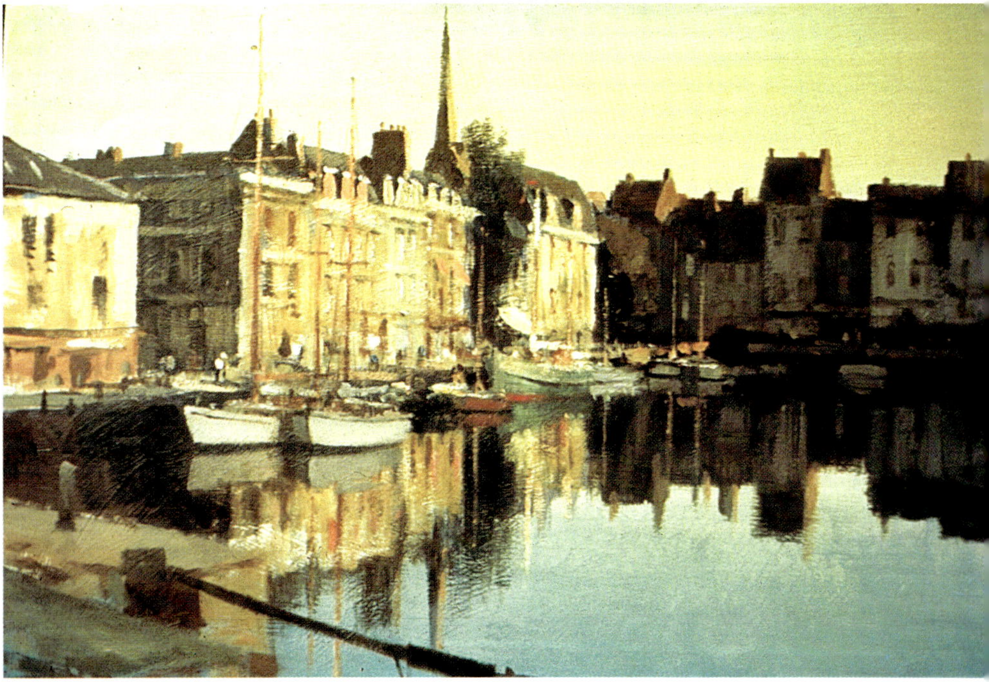

20. Amfréville, Normandy

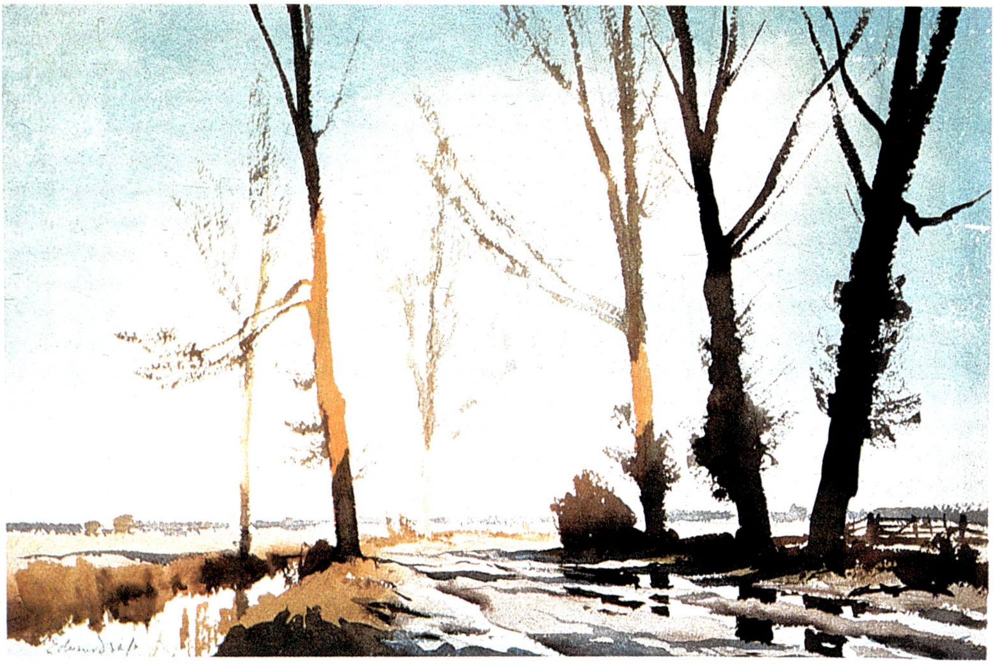

21. Winter Sunlight, Norfolk

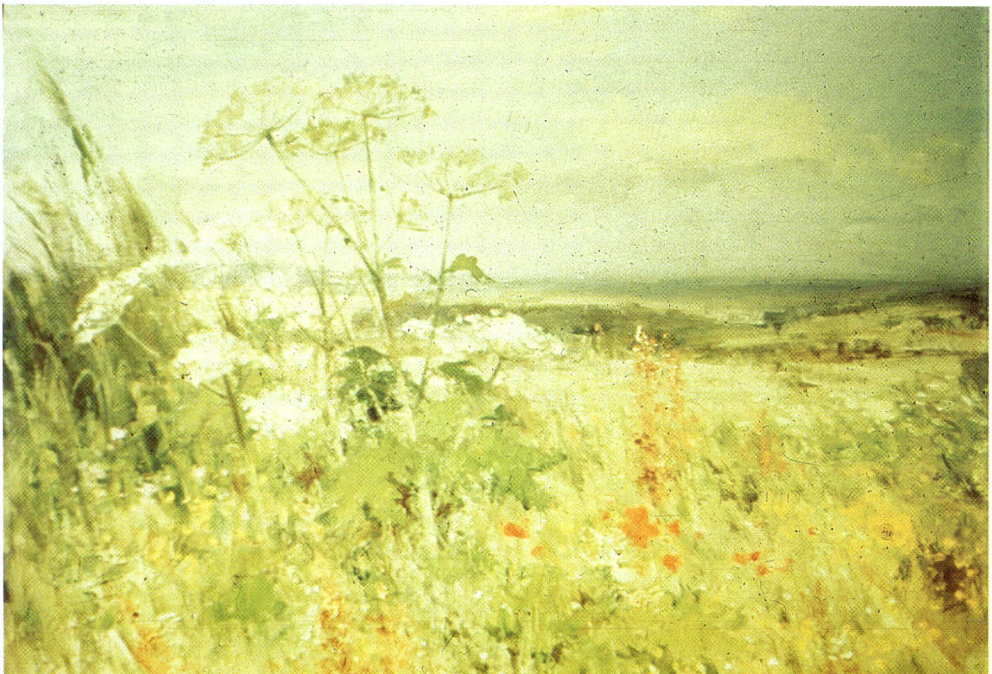

22. Summer Hedgerow

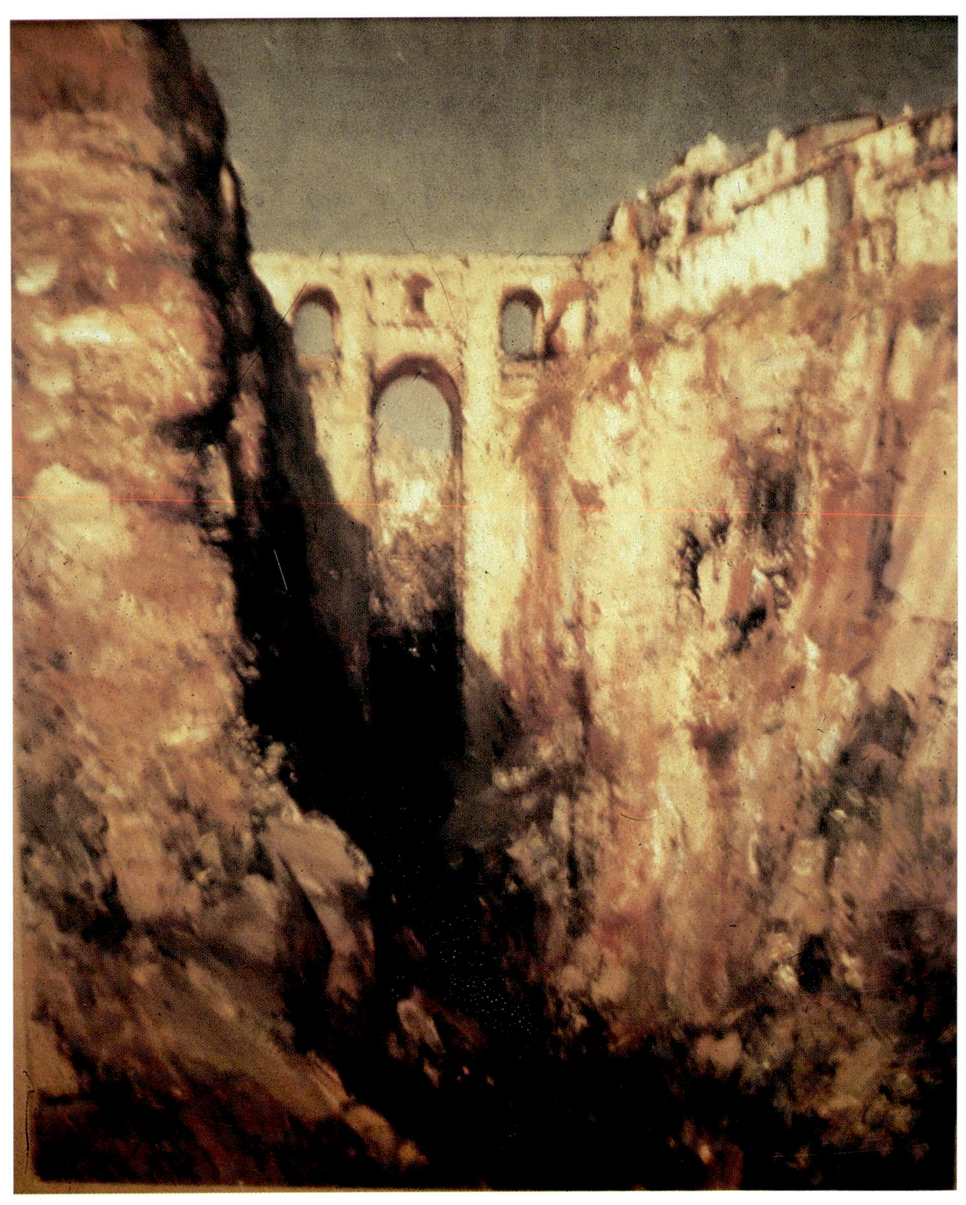

23. The Ravine, Ronda

in moments of climatic and creative truth, has met a ring of silence from those whose profession it is to inform and influence popular taste.

'Why no comment, no faint praise?

Yours faithfully,

JOHN HILL.

House of Commons, Nov, 18.'

In reply, the Editor, William Rees-Mogg, wrote that he felt it right to review the work of established and popular artists but the reason given for ignoring it was that the exhibition showed little change in the painter's development. It was the first exhibition of Seago's paintings to be held at the Marlborough Fine Art Gallery to where he moved from Colnaghi's as a consequence of the death of the director, Tom Baskett. One week after John Hill's letter was published a report of the exhibition appeared in the London editions only of *The Times*. Their critic wrote of the show:

'It consists mainly of Norfolk and East Coast landscapes with some interludes in London and on the Thames. The facility of style that has previously made his work popular in his annual exhibitions, held until now at Messrs. Colnaghi's, remains in evidence, and a typical snapshot quality may be found in paintings such as "Spritsail Barges on the Mud" and "December in Hyde Park".

'A point of present interest is how far it serves to interpret the native region of Crome. He misses something of the space of the East Anglian sky and is apt to make his clouds too solid-looking, as in "The Beach at Palling, Norfolk". The land pattern seems too little defined, for example, in a distant view of Norwich painted, incidentally, from about the same spot as in one of the Cromes in the bicentenary exhibition. But Mr Seago's touches of colour are placed with a confidently illustrative liveliness to suggest seaside life and atmosphere as in his "Beach Huts, Norfolk" and many red dots testify to the favour his paintings have with a buying public.'

The grudging review barbed with the phrase 'a typical snapshot quality' in his paintings was a poor return for a lifetime spent harnessing a great talent. Through painting Seago had shared his joy in the play of light and shadow across a landscape and his sense of delight when cloud shadows raced across the sand of a beach at Sea Palling. For him painting was the only ·true ecstasy between interludes of friendship and easy laughter and adventure, always threatened by the periods of physical disability which had dogged him from childhood.

Had the agony which he had often known in personal life intruded into painting so that his post-war pictures were created not only from a mood of exaltation, his work might have possessed a different quality which to his sterner critics could have made it less conventional and less unimaginatively predictable. On the other hand it might also have made it less appealing to his thousands of loyal admirers in many corners of the world. By painting to please himself he pleased them, and posterity alone can judge whether the critics who ignored Seago's paintings, or the collectors who loved them, were the more far-sighted.

But time will never reveal if his strange illness was the instrument which afforded the painter a freedom to wield his talent and if so, whether eventually, it exacted a toll of energy that diminished his capacity to expose himself to the soul-searching agony of seeking new challenges in painting.

Minor annoyances also sapped his creative energy. They culminated in an eight-day trial at Essex Quarter Sessions in 1971 when a hairdresser, Clifford Douce, was charged with forging five Seago paintings. Giving evidence for the prosecution Seago denied that the paintings were his.

'I do not regard them as copies,' he said. 'They are bogus pictures based on paintings of mine.' Nevertheless the jury acquitted Douce who was cleared on all five charges.

For Seago the outcome of the case was a personal affront. It contributed to his growing bitterness engendered by lack of critical acclaim or any public recognition represented by temporal honours and it struck at the very heart of his existence, for painting was his reason for living and his pictures were his most treasured possessions. He protected them by meticulous conditions in an otherwise extremely simple will which he made in August 1972.

Firstly, he instructed that one third of all his paintings in the studio at the time of his death should be destroyed by the artistic executors. This was because he accepted the fact that even a good painter could at times produce bad pictures. His executors were a solicitor, Edward Tsui and Peter Seymour, while as artistic executors he appointed Jeremy Spenser, Peter Seymour and John Erle-Drax of the Marlborough Galleries. Tsui was left a Boudin and three of Seago's own paintings to be chosen within one month of Seago's death; a week later, according to the will, Spenser was to select three Seago paintings. After that the three artistic executors were to select three more pictures for Tsui and three for Spenser, then the solicitor and Erle-Drax should each choose one painting, and finally the artistic executors should choose one for each of the painter's eight godchildren. The rest went to Peter providing he survived Seago by five years, Otherwise they would go to museums or public art galleries.

About that time Seago painted his last portrait. It was of Donald Sinden in the part of the ageing Regency buck, Sir William Harcourt Courtley, he played in *London Assurance* at the Aldwych Theatre. Again, as with *The Turn of the Screw* Seago saw the play several times and eventually wrote to Sinden whom he had met at the Garrick Club, saying he would like to do his portrait. Sinden was flattered. When the play ended he and his wife stayed at the Dutch House for a week and every morning he spent an hour putting on his stage make-up and costume. He kept it on all day and posed for an hour or so at a time.

He described how after a painting session Seago would light up his pipe, glare at him and the portrait from different parts of the studio and then study them both through a two-foot mirror to get a reverse and more objective view. From time to time, Peter made suggestions about the angle of the head or the position of a hand which Seago always accepted. In the end there were two portraits; one a full-length study of the vain, extrovert character in the play with his arms outstretched, the other a head and shoulders of the actor in full make-up and costume but sitting as he would have been after the show, not in the part he was playing.

'They were brilliant,' Sinden said, 'two completely different interpretations of the same man in the same costume. I realized while I was sitting for him that there had been no mention of what was to happen to them. My wife and I had been guests in his home for a week and I began to wonder whether he would expect us to buy one or both and for how much? When they were finished he said "I would like to present this one (the full-length portrait) to the Garrick if they'll have it and I want to give you the other".'

Sinden was in America when, in July 1973, he received a letter from Seago in which he apologized for the fact that his writing was a bit funny. 'For the last two months I have been suffering from middle ear trouble,' he wrote. 'Did you know that you've one in the middle as well as on either side?' It seemed the painter flatly refused to consult a specialist as his doctor had advised, probably because, since boyhood he had discounted the advice of doctors, to good effect, and he maintained that all he needed to put him right was the sunshine of Sardinia.

He and Peter flew there on 11 August where Seago insisted on driving the car from Olbia airport along fourteen miles of the Costa Smeralda to Porto Cervo. As soon as they started that final stage of the journey Peter realized that Seago could hardly see and he had to 'talk' him round every bend of the winding cliff-top road. But he drove the car for the next month, despite the protests of Peter, later supported by Lady Alexander and other house guests, Merle Parke, the ballet dancer, and her husband Sidney Bloch. He also ignored their insistence that he should see a doctor.

He painted two or three pleasant pictures and then, one day, a picture Peter described as 'an unbelievable horror'. It was an upright landscape on a long, horizontal canvas. Later, one afternoon in mid-September, he called to Peter, 'I think I've done a rather good picture. What do you think?'

Peter studied a small panel of a chain of barges. 'It's awfully difficult to tell 'til you've finished it,' he said. 'What are you going to do with the left half?'

'What left half?' was the answer. 'What do you mean? I have finished it.'

A fortnight later Seago collapsed. He was operated on for a brain tumour in the main hospital in Sassari. The prognosis was hopeless but two weeks later he was taken to England in a privately-chartered jet, accompanied by Peter and a leading British neurologist who had flown out to bring him back. On his return he had intensive treatment in hospital where for three months Peter hardly left his bedside. He was with him when he died there on 19 January 1974.

Once upon a time, Edward Seago had attended a gypsy funeral and, from the top of a hill he had watched the ashes of a man who had spent all his life in the open air, scattered to the wind so that the tiny particles of dust were returned to the earth and to the sky.

'I should like to think that when I die,' he once wrote, 'this body of mine will be turned to ashes and cast to the winds from a high, green hill.' Then, perhaps thinking of one person he had truly loved and who had shared his wartime home near Salisbury and crashed to death in a Spitfire he went on to qualify that wish. 'I suppose it wouldn't matter in which part of the world the hill might happen to be,' he wrote, 'but if I could make my choice I think it would be a grassy slope in Wiltshire; a strong, gentle slope which stoops to cradle a clear river winding through the dear, green, Wiltshire meadows.'

It was Peter who made the choice. One bright winter's morning he went alone and scattered the ashes of the man he most admired, over the Norfolk marshes where land and sky meet in a wide landscape such as Edward Seago never tired of painting. Just to look at such a landscape, the painter said, set his mind free.

XIII

The Prophecy

The publication of Ted's biography nearly four years after his death brought home to John how working on it had not only helped to assuage his grief but had acted as a catharsis in his own life. Sifting the facts of Ted's life had clarified and released many of his own tangled emotions. Moreover he had thoroughly enjoyed the hours spent writing down or recording his thoughts and memories.

He recalled Ted's seven books of personal reminiscences recounting many aspects of his full and varied life including painting, sailing and circus life. None, he thought, were more exciting than his own African experiences so perhaps he should do the same?

Writing about them could fill many lonely hours or the times when he was unfit for much physical activity. They would provide an endless source of material and, written as a series of episodes could be loosely strung together to form something of an autobiography.

He discussed the idea with journalist friends and publishers and with one or two writers. All were encouraging so he decided to make a start. Inevitably his thoughts flew to his first trip to Africa in 1936 and his meeting with the legendary Taffy Jones. He wrote:

'Standing before his bungalow he was a small figure in faded khaki shirt and shorts with pale sandy hair and gold rimmed spectacles; he looked about fifty-five. The impressions I've retained are of his serenity, strength of character, integrity and contentment. He was like a mystic who had discarded superficial trappings and found an inner peace. Surrounding him was a group of tall friendly Africans in colourful robes. ...

'After that first meeting when Taffy Jones told me my spirit belonged to Africa we sat with the elders watching the young people dance. The party had begun quietly but hours later the dancers were leaping wildly, their bodies glistening in the moonlight in time with the drummers intoxicated with the native beer.

'A child, looking for somewhere to sleep, climbed on my knee and settled down. The elderly headman, Ajamafuja, murmured 'damu yetu' which, I learnt, meant a matter of blood. Usually the blood of Europeans spoke only to their own people but occasionally there were ones like Reg and I, whose blood spoke to African blood and whose spirits were close to theirs. It was an indication of Jones' prophecy which, years later, would be fully confirmed.

'It was first confirmed more than ten years later when Reg and I, on Geoffrey Vever's suggestion, went to Kenya to collect a shipment of zebra for England waiting for him in Mombasa. Before we collected them we decided to take a short break in the Northern Frontier District. There we found the scenery superb, the climate perfect and we felt we were back in biblical times.

'In Masailand we met a young tribal policeman who spoke some English and with whom, with our few words of Swahili, we found we could communicate. One day he told us he wished to take us to a nice place he knew not far away. He led us along a track which wound its way among the golden brown hills under a dark metallic blue sky. After about an hour we came to a large tree which was very conspicuous in the almost treeless landscape. From there we saw a small herd of antelope and some cattle raising dust on a distant hill.

'Our guide said we should wait there and the Laiboni would come and speak to us. We had never heard of the Laiboni but learnt they held an hereditary position within a certain family and were regarded as oracles or wise men who advised the Masai people on religious and political matters and were believed to possess certain powers. They were also healers who used herbal medicines but should not be confused with witch doctors.

'We waited in the shade of the tree and I wondered why they wished to see us and on what religion they gave advice. Our guide only assured us that the Masai were a people who believed in God. As to why they wished to see us I was told sharply that it was not good to ask such questions so we sat in silence listening to the birds sing duets above us.

'After some time our companion pointed to two tiny specks in the distance and said the Laiboni were coming. About forty-five minutes later they approached and we walked to meet them. The tribal policeman bowed a greeting and seemed to say he had brought us as instructed.

'Both Laiboni wore ochre coloured cloths knotted on one shoulder, reddish brown cloaks and necklaces of coloured stones. The taller older one had a round face with the serenity of a Buddha. The other wore an expression of great intensity suggesting strong mystic powers. Both gave us friendly smiles of goodwill and held our hands. The taller one said something we learnt meant they were pleased to see us and thanked us for coming because he wanted to pass on a little message.

'For a while we stood in silence while the shorter one fixed his intense gaze on mine and held it so it became a sort of tussle between us. It was as if he saw right through me. I felt energy being drawn from me and I leaned heavily on my stick. Just when I knew I was tiring under the hot sun I felt myself being released and the intense penetrating stare relaxed into a genial smile.

'The taller one then made a little speech in which, according to our guide, he said we were very welcome and we would always be happy in this country because our spirits were close to the spirits of its people. Turning to me he said that in time I would become strong and I would eventually die here in Kenya.

'We asked our guide to thank them for coming to greet us and for the message which I believed and which I accepted as a strong staff to lean on. When this was translated to them it seemed to please them.

'As our guide bade them goodbye he placed the open palm of his right hand on his chest and bowed low. The taller and seemingly senior Laibon placed his right hand on the guide's head saying, I learnt later:

'"Please, God, I place this my son into your hands. Please protect him so his life follows a good line!" Then turning to Reg and I he raised his hand as if in blessing. From a sense of courtesy we instinctively bowed our heads. He placed his hand on Reg's head and said:

'"Please, God, I place this, our younger brother in your hands and ask you always to protect and guide him."

'With his hand on my head he said:

'"Please, God, I place this our elder brother in your hands and ask you to make him strong, as foretold, to protect him and when he is appealed to as an elder, to give him wisdom."

'We asked our guide to thank them again and convey our appreciation and then we watched the two figures walking with their springing gait away across the golden plain, their reddish brown cloaks blowing in the wind until they became two diminishing spots of colour between the gold land and the blue sky.

'People tend to associate blessings with priests but blessings from respected elder citizens are highly valued by Africans and, as we climbed into the truck, our guide told us we had been really blessed. Certainly the longer I thought about my blessing the greater became its merit and significance. For to me it had definitely confirmed Taffy Jones' prophecy, that my spirit belonged to Africa.

'That evening under the stars I told myself that I had been given the proof I needed and scolded myself for having lost the habit of prayer and Bible reading with the comfort they can give. Under the velvety sky, with no mechanical sounds to disturb me it was easy to become aware of the Almighty and resume the habit of offering a simple prayer. At the same time, alongside my serious mood and intentions I was amused to think that I had had my dormant faith revived by an African elder in the Dark Continent. Meanwhile together with my new outlook I found a heightened sense of enjoyment in the scenery, the clouds, the people and the wealth of natural wildlife all around me.

'Suddenly dark figures waving spears and shouting in a frightening way rushed at me out of the trees. I ran instantly calling out to warn the camp. Still shouting I was grabbed and held to be confronted by five laughing faces.

'"Were you really frightened?" Leshan asked, hanging on to my arm. "Do you think I'll make a good warrior?" I assured him that, for a moment, I had been very frightened and just then I thought he had been a brave warrior. The whole episode had to be re-enacted for Kaka who was waiting for us by the fire and again for two other lads when they returned. It was a typical example of the young Africans' boyish sense of humour.

'The Laiboni's prayer for me that when I was appealed to as an elder I should be given wisdom was soon called into action. Mutua, one of our lads, was a very worried young man when he came running to me while we were having breakfast. He said he was so glad I was there because he was in great trouble with the father of the girl he wanted to marry.

'Jei, another lad who was with us, pointed a finger at him and said:

'"I saw you with her last night and you carried a blanket so you could lay and play with her."

'"Yes, but only a little," Mutua replied.

'"Well, what's the problem?" I asked.

'"She says I tried to undo her apron. She told her mother who told her father and now he's very angry with me," Mutua said.

'There was general laughter, which Mutua checked immediately.

'"This is serious," he said. "I love the girl. She has nice manners and a good character and her parents are nice people. There won't be any of the trouble you get from some mothers – always asking for little presents. Her father has been kind to me because my father is dead. I've already given two goats for her and now have only to give three cows. When our first child comes, her father has promised a cow giving milk. Please, Bwana Chai, you must speak for me."

'Bwana Chai, which means Mister Tea, was the name I was given by one of our lads who realized that when I was upset tea invariably restored my equilibrium.

'Now the others urged me to speak with the girl's father. They said that because of my great age he would have to listen to me.

'"Only you can make this to lie down," Mutua said. "All people know I take you as my father." This was a convenient relationship, I thought, whereby the young man has an elder to turn to when in trouble without imposing any filial obedience. However I felt bound to help the lad because his father had been associated with us before his unexpected death. Nevertheless, I was cross with him.

'"You know quite well you should not remove her apron and enter her body until the marriage is finalised," I told him.

'"That is an old custom, Bwana Chai," he replied, "and people say it is not necessary these days."

'"Now listen to me," I said firmly. "This marriage is not just between you two people but concerns your families, your friends and your village. You must follow the old ways, bring your children up to respect their elders and to disregard those ideas from outside which are destroying your people's culture. Otherwise you had better find another father."

'His assent was given with a disarming smile.

'I knew that in some tribes an intended bride must produce a healthy child before the marriage is finalized but the Kamba, Kikuyu and Emba people require a virgin bride. With them the rule is that two young people intending to marry may only lie together and caress each other. The girl is allowed to hold the boy's penis between her thighs and, as a protection against overwhelming emotions, she wears an apron like a medieval chastity belt, securely tied by her mother. When I told Mutua he must be content with that for the time being he said:

'"You just try it Bwana Chai, I can tell you it's very frustrating."

'He told me that the girl's father was called Kithoka and he was sure he would receive me well. I was uncertain how to handle it but it was a serious matter. It is believed that by exercising restraint the young couple will have more respect for each other and the marriage will stand a better chance of success. I decided I must inspire confidence, play the dignified elder and rely on my age.

'Kithoka's compound was large, tidy and well fenced. It consisted of two round huts, a large square one and two round grain stores on stilts. The grass thatching and mud walls were in good order but there was a large plot planted with withered maize.

'We paused at the gate and called a greeting. A child ran to the larger hut. Presently Kithoka emerged and, after a pause, bade us enter, concealing his surprise. Being younger than I he received me with respect, called for chairs to be placed under a tree and offered me tea. I signalled to Mutua to wait behind.

'Courtesy did not allow me to go straight to the point. So I enquired about his own and his family's health. Then, noticing some goats, I said I hoped they were fruitful and complimented him on his compound. He nodded silently. The withered maize would be a serious loss and I expressed my sympathy and said I hoped his stores still held some cobs from the previous crop. He had a few, he said, but some people had none and for them the situation was serious.

'"We have prayed for rain", he said, "and given an offering of food but the God has not heard us."

'I said I was glad he had offered prayers according to the long established custom rather than followed the new permissive influences from outside which were destroying the ancient culture. I told him that in this respect I had spoken severely to Mutua who had assured me that he really had no bad intentions towards his daughter.

'"Is it not natural," I said, "that when laying together his blood becomes heated and that his hand should … er … er …" I was stumped and stumbled over the words "tempia kidogo" which means "walk about" which was not the decorous expression I sought.

'My verbal fumbling caused Kithoka to turn away to hide his amusement as I rounded off with a gesture.

'After a pause Kithoka said he knew Mutua called me Father and by coming I had shown my love for him. But this was a heavy matter. I agreed but said that if we could keep the matter to ourselves there would be no issue between the families. I suggested that his daughter may have been unnecessarily alarmed but she had been right to tell her mother.

'There was another pause. I reminded him that Mutua came from a respected family and congratulated him on obtaining a strong handsome son through marriage and added "Surely you will be blessed with strong healthy grandchildren."

'I then called Mutua over to make his apologies. As I watched him bowing low to kiss Kithoka's hand promising obedience and good behaviour and looking the picture of innocence I thought what a rogue he was. I then presented Kithoka with a packet of tea. I said I was unprepared and apologized for the small gift. As Kithoka seemed to hesitate I chipped in quickly saying that everything seemed now settled.

'Taken by surprise he still made no move so I placed my hands on his shoulders. He responded immediately and we embraced one another. He thanked me saying I had spoken well. We then withdrew but turned at the gate for Mutua to raise his hand in respect to the tall figure waiting to acknowledge the gesture.

'On arriving home we saw some of Mutua's friends waiting to hear the result of our mission. I was congratulated and Mutua hugged me and promised that their first boy would be called John. Then he mimed my performance to show his friends how I had tried to portray his 'hand walking about'.

'Another of our lads, Maina, also asked my help with a sexual problem.

'I had noticed that for some time, his usual cheerful nature had given way to periods of silent depression. He came to me one morning holding the palm of his left hand on the top of his head – a sign that he was both worried and in doubt. At first shyly and then with more confidence he told me that he was worried about his wife because he had been away such a long time. He looked at me steadily and said:

'"You must understand, Bwana Chai, that our women cannot wait so long. In her need she will have taken someone.

'"There is another young man she likes. He is strong, that one, and can do it six times in one night." Then, almost wistfully, added that the other lad's body had a good shape. "He is of my age," he said "and when we were bathing with the other boys he was always the best. We used to laugh and say he was lovely like a girl but in our hearts thought him good to look at. You see he is a brown one."

'A golden brown colour occurs in some of the natives and seems to be admired.

'He stood scraping the ground with one foot. His stunted body with its bandy legs was not a good shape but had a certain appeal and his cheerful affectionate nature had won him many friends. My often unreasonable anger over the mistakes he made always fizzled out when I was faced with his brown eyes and his apologetic "I say a big sorry. Please forgive a little."

'After a moment he seemed to come to a decision and said:

'"There was a day when that one and I were bathing and my wife came to the stream with her gourd. I knew she had not come for water but to look at him because I saw her eyes were attracted by the shape of his body. So, you see, I have big trouble and I ask you please for your kindness to let me go back with the next trucks."

'He glanced round to see if we could be overheard and, seemingly satisfied, said there was another matter which he could not even discuss with his father. Sensing that I was to be the recipient of his confidence, I moved to sit in the shade of the tent and waited. He followed and, after some hesitation began, at first slowly with face averted but once started he talked freely.

'He told me he was born in a time of drought when many had died, including his own mother.

'"So it was my father's mother, who fed me from her breast," he said. "Because of that I can now only do it one time in the night. My wife cannot say but I know she is not satisfied because she tried to get more from me but I cannot do it. It is a shame for me so I am also unhappy but what can I do?"

'He paused, looking at the distant hills. I felt a great sympathy for him, knowing only too well how bodies which have suffered a severe illness or starvation lack staying power.

'During another pause I reflected that it seemed unfair that because he could only do it once a night he was considered to have failed in his marriage obligations and wondered how many times were required to fulfil them. Africans consider it impolite for a young man to stand before a seated elder during a serious conversation. Maina dropped to his knees bringing his eyes level with mine. He looked at me appealingly.

'"Bwana Chai" he said. "Promise by God you will never tell of this to anyone for truly it is a great shame." Taking his hands I gave a solemn promise from which I hope the passing of time has absolved me.

'I asked him what he would do if she was already pregnant?

'"That will make it easier for me," he said. "If she wishes to stay with me I shall agree and nothing will be said if sometimes she goes to that other one at night in secret. On the other hand she must go to the father of the child and if it is the other one and he wishes to take her for his wife and she is willing I will not be difficult. I will not ask for all my dowry if he cannot pay. But if she tells her mother the real reason her father will say it is my fault and will not refund my dowry. Others would then hear about it, which would shame me. But I must have some of my dowry back so I can take another woman."

'The dowry or bride price is often criticized on the grounds that families sell their daughters but this is not really so. Although a prospective son-in-law makes a negotiated payment which he can lose through bad behaviour he also receives assistance. It is a stabilizing influence.

'Once more he paused and looked out of the tent while considering whether he should impart a further confidence. The pause plays an important part in conversation of this nature for its duration signifies the weight of the matter. After a few moments he turned to me and said:

'"You know, Bwana Chai, there are some white missionaries who say it is a bad thing to circumcise our girls and my wife has not been circumcised. Therefore her need is like that of an uncircumcised woman of the Luo people. You understand that had she been cut like our girls one time would have satisfied her and as I can do that she wouldn't have complained. It is bad luck for me."

'What Maina said so surprised me that I asked how it had come about for although some Europeans had campaigned vigorously against female circumcision, they had met stubborn resistance. He explained that his wife's father used to work for a missionary society and lived in their compound with his family. He was urged not to have his daughter circumcised and agreed for fear of losing his job. Not surprisingly, Maina had not been told about this during marriage negotiations because his bride's parents would have been afraid to disclose such a major departure from a strongly held tradition. When Maina said even his own father did not know I felt that there lay the solution. Sitting back on his haunches Maina watched me while I thought out the line of argument:

'His father would certainly be entitled to think the normal practice had been observed and because the bride's parents' failure to disclose the true situation he could rightly claim to have been misled. Then, surely, a demand for the parents to take the girl back and refund the entire dowry would be fully justified.

'They would naturally try evasive tactics because the disclosure would inevitably detract from the girl's marriage status. Then the threat of immediate disclosure of her condition would surely settle it.

'It took me several minutes to convey this to Maina with my limited Swahili. His elf-like face wore a puckered frown while he struggled to absorb my reasoning. Suddenly it clicked. His bright eyes showed he realized it was possible to preserve the secrecy of his manly weakness and not lose the all important dowry.

'When I asked if he was angry with the other lad he said that if he did not lose the dowry he would be quite satisfied. He explained that he had been his friend at school and they had been circumcised together which made a lasting bond between them. "Sisi na pendana" he said which means 'we love one another'. So it seemed the dowry was really the main point at issue.

'It was unfortunate that Maina's father had chosen an uncircumcised girl for his son. A strong lad would not have complained at finding his wife a sex partner as enthusiastic as he was rather than one who cried she could take no more and so her uncircumcised state would never have been disclosed.

'Circumcision of women means that they derive little or no pleasure from copulation, which may seem cruel and unfair. But as with all African customs there was a reason for it, dating from the days when some young men were often away from their village for several days, cattle raiding or hunting and foraging while other young warriors had to remain behind to defend the village. This would have placed a great temptation on those women whose husbands were away, had their normal desires not been blunted by circumcision. With changed social conditions the practice is slowly dying.

'Of course I arranged for Maina to go home on the next lorry but I never knew if his marriage survived; I certainly missed his cheerful laughter and his pantomime play acting of any incident that amused him. Sitting round the fire one evening I asked his friend Kamau about the girl.

'"Ah! She is not good," he replied. "She is one of those who will make trouble later. I told Maina to let her go."

'Although women do most of the manual work they are not so down trodden as I had thought at first. They have a voice in family affairs and when older can become very bossy. A scheming wife with her eyes on her husband's land can split a family by persuading one or more of the sons to side with her against their father who may be forced to leave to seek peace elsewhere and he may perhaps take another wife. At the time of writing I am trying to settle such a situation.

'The fire drew our attention and we sat looking into it, each seeing our own thoughts. After a few moment's silence Kamau continued. He said Maina's girl had once refused to dig his mother's shamba (a plot of land) when he asked her.

'"Do you know, Bwana Chai," he said, "she went to a mission school so they told her she is now educated so she has become very proud and won't work. What good is schooling if a woman cannot work?"

'I asked why it was her mother-in-law's shamba and it was

explained that the youngest son has to stay with his parents because they are old and when he marries his wife will cook for them and cultivate the shamba in place of his mother. After both his parents die the land will go to him.

'"I've found a girl, Bwana Chai," he confided gaily. "She has nice buttocks and breasts that stand up." When I commented that he was always talking about buttocks he replied.

'"Of course, we always judge them. When I see a girl I look first at the buttocks and if I like them I try to talk. But if I don't like them, well I leave. It's the same with a girl or a boy. The girl's should be nice and round but not very big; the boy's must be smaller. For the girl I like breasts that stand up and not hang down."

'Well, I suppose a good horse is judged by its quarters and Kaka once said that small buttocks might be good to look at but if a woman is to feed her child in times of drought she must have large buttocks.

'Our talk was interrupted by loud bellows and trumpeting from elephants who seemed to be very close. Obviously an almighty scrap had suddenly erupted for we could also hear the high pitched call of common zebras and lions roaring. Only the Masai lads seemed to understand what was going on. They explained that because the lions were hunting them the zebras had mingled with the elephants for protection. They told me that the elephants would attack the lions by stabbing downwards with their tusks and trampling on them. When a lion bellowed it meant that it had been hurt. The lions were obviously persistent because the angry trumpeting continued for more than an hour.'

★　★　★　★　★　★　★

'One hot and sultry afternoon we decided to take the lads to Obongi so they could bathe and buy snuff, sweet potatoes and bananas in the market. The prolonged dry season had sucked all the moisture from the surroundings of our camp and even our river was so shallow we had difficulty getting enough water for our needs.

'The market was held under the shade of some large fig trees growing near the river. Fruit and vegetables were spread out on coloured platters, people were sitting in groups idly gossiping or indulging in animated arguments about buying or selling. Others were in the river, bathing or washing their clothes and spreading them out to dry.

'I found a comfortable seat in the elbow of a tree trunk and being still too new to Africa for the customary courtesies to come readily to mind I sat down without exchanging greetings to those around me. The local people obviously hesitated to make the first move and I became aware that although I was surrounded by people, I was not yet at one with them.

'Seeking some means of contact I saw a naked young woman cradling a child against her breasts walking gracefully towards the river. Her well formed body was not yet thickened by toil and child bearing. She smiled and lifted one of the child's hands in greeting as she passed, giving me the opportunity I sought.

'I had some sweets with me and unwrapped one, broke off a small portion and held it up; she tilted the child towards me and I popped one into his mouth. At first he spluttered and then gurgled with delight. Those sitting around us shared our laughter, called out greetings or came to shake hands. The lovely young mother continued towards the river walking with that seductive swing of the buttocks acquired only by those who, as maidens, carried jars of water on their heads.

'A naked slender fishing lad followed by two younger boys came up and asked me to buy two fish he had caught. As we were more than twenty people in camp nothing less than a large Nile perch would be of any use to us. The boy told me that his father had died two years ago and he lived with his mother who was now very old.

'I bought the fishes and told the boy to wait until my friends returned. When one of them came I told him the story explaining that he must do some "mumbo jumbo" over the fishes so that the new owner took them home to his mother and did not sell them again on the way. This appealed to my friend who performed some remarkable gestures. Each time he bowed to the ground I did the same. Our antics intrigued several onlookers as well as the boys and when we thought we had done enough we begged some leaves from a woman nearby in which to wrap the fishes.

'I explained to the vendor that my friend was a great medicine man in his home-town and much respected for his powers. Solemnly I told him he had blessed the fishes so that when his mother ate them she would gain strength but he had also cursed them so that if any other person ate them they would die.

'Three rather awed boys bowed and kissed our hands, twisted their loin cloths round their bodies and set off in single file along the track led by the eldest carrying the fishes in front of him.

'We exchanged farewells with those round about us and moved to our truck. Passing the nursing mother we paused offering thanks to Allah for her ample milk and for the child. She was the symbol of motherhood with her lithe body and the child suckling contentedly at her full round breast.

'Next to her a skinny baby was sucking fruitlessly at the sagging breasts of its thin elderly mother. As we moved on we saw the younger mother take the elder mother's child in one hand and hold it to her other breast. The exasperated whimpering ceased. Turning back my companion raised both his hands saying "Thank you, Mother" and I followed his example.

'As we moved away he remarked to me:

'"You understand a little. You spoke well to the mother and they were pleased."

'I asked why he had thanked her for the child in the first place? He explained that a child was regarded as belonging firstly to the parents and secondly to the village and would grow up in a kind of extended family and would regard two or even three women as its mother.

'Grown up boys were trained to herd cattle and protect the village and defend it if attacked. The girls would cultivate the land and provide more children so both village and family might continue. It was therefore appropriate to thank a mother for her child.

★　★　★　★　★　★　★

'Living in a country where man had made only the tiniest imprint we watched nature at work without man's dominant interference. We watched elephants and giraffes feeding from trees and tall bushes, rhinos and other browsers feeding at lower levels, zebras and others cropping the grass while small duikers ate the young shoots. Often animals had to walk considerable distances to get food. We watched and learnt.

We gradually developed our own method of dealing with wild animals.

Near our encampment we built a fenced open wooden compound for our horses containing four small grass-lined pens for the animals we caught. There they had constant access to their crates lined with hay to encourage them to use them. We noticed an animal soon came to regard its crate as its own particular territory, which became a secure private home and not a prison.

'The pens were also close to the men whose companionship gave the animals a sense of security so they were soon at ease with us and would feed from our hands. When the time came to load them onto the trucks for the journey to the port of embarkation, they were so used to having people close to them that they were not in the least worried. And there was none of the desperate kicking we first had to cope with.

'We also learned how easily the metabolism and digestive system of an animal could be disrupted if it suffered much mental strain. If a wild animal was given time to feel secure and well cared for after capture and was not subjected to the stress of a journey for which it was unprepared, a steady recovery followed its capture.

'We found an animal's digestive system took as long as three months to develop the necessary bacteria to break down the dry food used during a voyage. Therefore the practice of shipping them six to eight weeks after capture coincided with the low point in their condition and the new food, however nutritious, was unable to help.

'I learnt from first-hand experience that catching wild animals can be a dangerous business. In 1966 our unit joined up with the local Kenya Game Department because they wanted to catch and move a dangerous rhino from the wild to Samburu National Park while we wanted pictures of a rhino for the film "Cowboy in Africa".

'Rhinos are valuable animals but very vulnerable. They make easy targets for skilled poachers with poisoned arrows who kill them for their horns, which Eastern peoples mistakenly believe have aphrodisiac properties. They are also very tolerant and usually recognize the herdsmen who regularly use the same areas as they do.

'For centuries these herdsmen armed only with a spear, knife and throwing stick, have led their master's cattle to graze in the early morning, returning at sunset.

'However, constant attacks by poachers will put the rhinos on the defensive so that they will charge anything on two legs and sometimes attack an innocent herdsman by mistake. When this happens appeals are made to the local Game Wardens to shoot the rhino which has the attendant attraction of providing a large supply of free meat. Game Wardens are reluctant to do this and prefer to try to persuade the animal to move off or catch it and move it to an area like the Samburu

National Park, where it can be protected. Moving the animal is a costly operation requiring specialized transport, equipment and trained men. The Game Department will therefore appeal for assistance to Wildlife Societies or professional game-catching units, like ours.

'Frequently the units used the roping method of capturing and moving a rhino but this time, because the animal was rather large, it was decided to drug it. Therefore, a vet with a miniature field unit accompanied the Game Department's two catching trucks, a Land Rover and a van carrying game scouts. We provided a truck loaded with camera equipment and I drove a five-tonner loaded with rhino crates, ropes, tackle, ramps and other gear.

'We were working in damn difficult country and my truck leapt and bounced as we followed the rhino tracks at anything from fifteen to thirty miles an hour but it was impossible to keep the animal within range. Darts had been fired but for one reason or another the animal had not received the required dose and had gone thundering on its way with us following wearily behind for four long days.

'The men were getting fidgety. The work is arduous and dangerous and tensions build up. When our unit worked on its own, these were often relieved by an almighty rumpus caused by perhaps a minor incident. This usually cleared the air and everyone felt better, but on a combined operation one had to be more careful which was not always a good thing.

'We took a break and grouped the vehicles under an acacia tree while the scouts cast about for new tracks. At the age of sixty I found it difficult to keep up with the young men who strode about all day as if Africa were too small for them so I always made the most of any break that came along.

'After about an hour the lads found new tracks and some of us moved on. I went in the warden's Land Rover with the camera man and his equipment behind a catching truck carrying some of the men. It had been decided to manoeuvre the truck beyond where the rhino was thought to be and drive the animal towards more open country. However, we lost sight of the truck during a fast chase through the bush before they found and roped the animal. When we caught up the rhino was secured by a head-rope and Tony Parkinson was trying to get a second rope on it, a tricky and dangerous operation usually carried out on foot rather than by truck to avoid the risk of the animal hurting itself by crashing into a heavy vehicle. I wanted some shots of Tony in action and approached on foot.

'The rhino was very active and was giving the men a tough time. Tony shouted a warning and the men scattered. I thought I was at a safe distance and continued filming. There was another warning and I ran back towards the truck. The rhino must have picked up my movement for he left Tony and chased me.

'I hoped the rope would tighten and the log attached to it would slow the rhino up but I had underestimated its speed and the length of the rope and I had made the mistake of running straight. In a desperate effort to increase my speed I threw away my ciné camera but to no avail. The thundering hoofs and the snorts came closer and I found myself on the ground with the rhino charging, head down, its fearsome horn directed straight at me.

'Afterwards I learned that I had been tossed several feet in the air, to the horror of my companions who saw I was going to get a second hammering before they could reach me. They were now behind the animal in relation to me and were powerless to help.

'I have heard it said that in battle soldiers do not feel the impact of wounding bullets and, in the face of danger, feel extraordinarily calm. That was my experience. I never felt the impact of the first toss that had flung me several feet in the air and, faced with the charging rhino, I could think quite clearly. I understand this is due to our built-in shock absorbing mechanism that takes care of such stress.

'My first thought was surprisingly frivolous for I saw what a super camera angle it was. Then, taking myself firmly in hand, I ordered myself to become as small as possible and lie close to the ground so the rhino's head came low down and its horn went underneath me and did not pierce me.

'I never felt the thrust that sent me flying some twelve feet through the air but I suddenly saw the ground whirling past under me and knew an immediate feeling of outrage:

'"He's tossed me," I said. "The audacity! The indignity! But don't worry, I'm alright." The thoughts flashed though my mind in seconds.

'I landed on the ground with a hell of a bang that completely winded me but by the greatest good fortune I was right against a truck and could crawl under it and lie protected while I recovered my breath.

'The last toss had sent me flying spreadeagled through the air and brought the others to a horrified standstill believing 'That's the end of him, he'll never survive that.' The two lads nearest the Landcruiser rushed at me before the rhino. They grabbed at my coat but I was still panting for breath and complaining I couldn't move. The rhino had come up to the front end and one of the lads dragged me out from the side while Tony seemed to be making mesmerizing gestures to the animal, but was in fact gathering up handfuls of dust and throwing it in its face, having no other weapon.

'The rhino seemed momentarily interested in the Landcruiser, which gave us a chance to get away. Once clear I was allowed to stand still while I tried to refill my lungs. Tony, his face grey with anxiety and looking years older came running up to say he couldn't believe I was unhurt. He played it safe and used the catching truck to put the second head-rope on the rhino. He put several men on each rope and then attached the foot-ropes.

'All I had to show for the incident was a small cut on the top of my head, which meant cutting off some of my remaining few hairs to dress it. By then I had recovered my poise enough to search for my camera and it says a lot for it that it still worked and I was able to shoot the final scenes when the animal was put into its crate.

★　★　★　★　★　★　★

'The evening bath was a ritual I always enjoyed after a tiring day and I liked to take it on the verandah of the tent so I could look across the shadowed Nile valley to the sunlit ridge beyond. Afterwards, before dinner, I rested for an hour under the mosquito net on my bed at the far end of the tent.

'One evening Tony and Alexander were so late that the mosquitoes were rising when they brought the tin bath inside the tent for their baths. Just as Tony started, the cook popped his head in to say supper was nearly ready so I got up and began to dress. Suddenly we heard the sound of a man running for his life and calling 'Bwana Chai' in a terrified voice. We recognized the voice of Jackson Kinuthia, a rough mannered unpopular lad of about twenty. Suddenly he burst through the tent flaps, rushed between Tony, who was in the bath, and Alexander waiting his turn, knocked me down on my bed and flung himself on top of me screaming hysterically. Following him were three angry-looking men with spears.

'Obviously surprised at finding themselves in our tent they hesitated for a few seconds giving Tony and Alexander a chance to grab their spears, break them and belabour the three spear holders with the shafts. From where I lay I could see Tony standing in the bath whacking the men on their heads until they collapsed moaning on the floor holding their arms above their heads to ward off the blows.

'Just as I managed to wriggle free from Jackson the tent flaps opened again and Ndezo, one of the Africans who had worked with the unit for twenty years, entered as dignified as usual wearing his little trilby hat. With a commanding gesture and a hard kick or two he motioned to the now grovelling tribesmen to wait outside. He then approached the snivelling Jackson, picked him up by the scruff of the neck and flung him after them. Then, without saying a word, he left, closing the tent flaps behind him.

'When he had gone I congratulated my companions on their remarkable performance in overcoming three armed and angry young men.

'After all, one is rarely more vulnerable than when one is in the bath.

'"What the hell has Jackson been up to?" Tony asked. I wondered what taboo he had violated and would those men have killed him had he not reached our tent? Alexander said the shouting that still persisted showed that the village people were very angry and it was a truly serious case involving us all. He thought Ndezo would try and arrange a court with me as judge.

'Some fifteen minutes later the noise had subsided and above the quiet murmur of voices I could hear Ndezo firmly giving orders. I tied my cravat, put on a jacket and waited apprehensively.

'It was Mousa who came to fetch me. He held the tent flap open and bowed me out with due ceremony. When I saw the large crowd awaiting me, I realized Ndezo was trying to establish my seniority.

'He had set the stage very well. On the far side of our compound a chair stood on a crate with a convenient step. A small platform had been placed beside it. The crowd had assembled in a semicircle leaving a clear path from the tent to the chair. I reckoned there were at least two hundred supporters for the aggressive tribesmen, compared to twelve against.

'I walked slowly up the path from our tent mustering all the dignity I could and tried to assume an air of complete composure, which I certainly did not feel, for I was really worried. A spear glinted in the darkness. I looked straight at the man holding it and got a distinct warning telling me to be careful. They were angry and meant business. I counted eight more spears on my way to the chair and each man seemed to give me the same message.

'"These people are really serious," I thought. "We must act positively and control them or we are lost."

'Ndezo stood on the platform. He was large and impressive standing above the crowd and appeared calm and dominating. He had arranged things so that when I was seated our heads were about level, proclaiming our joint authority.

'"We shall wait a little," he said to me quietly, "and just keep looking at them."

'Reg joined our little group having walked over from his tent. He made a joke about me as judge but was quickly silenced by a gesture from Ndezo. Reg just kept staring at me and whenever I looked at him he was still staring. I wondered why?

'"Dear God," I thought, "if ever I needed wisdom I need it now."

'The word "wisdom" had a significant ring to it: "Needed wisdom" ... Then came the whole sentence: "When called upon as an elder grant him wisdom." That was what Reg was trying to tell me.

'My thoughts went back over the years to our meeting with the Laiboni. Slowly the vision formed. I clung to it desperately as it changed to that face staring at me with frightening clarity. Then it smiled in the friendly manner which years ago had released me from that searching scrutiny. The blessing followed and I concentrated on it, seeking inspiration. Once again I heard my own words:

'"It will be a strong staff for me to lean on."

'It is amazing what your imagination can do. I was full of confidence and I told Ndezo:

'"We must become like witch doctors – work on their fear of spirits and witchcraft, stare them out. I'll start." He nodded.

'The three men who had rushed into our tent were on my left and I started by staring at them. It seemed a long time before the first one turned away. The second did not last much longer and the third gave in very quickly.

'"It's working! It's working!" I thought and told myself to use all my mental energy. I moved my gaze around looking directly at anyone I could pick out. Only one man offered any resistance and in a short time no-one would look at me.

'"Well done, Bwana Chai! You will make a good witch doctor. We'll set up in business," whispered Ndezo with a grin. We were beginning to enjoy ourselves as we felt we were gaining the upper hand. After another pause Ndezo said they were ready and he would speak first. This suited me, as I felt exhausted.

'He made an imposing figure standing on the platform above the crowd wearing his trilby hat and an air of command. He began by asking what was this madness to chase one of our people with spears intending to kill?

'"Now I see many others come to our camp carrying spears" he said. "In your madness do you intend to kill all of us and so bring our blood upon your heads and our spirits to haunt you?

'"Have you lost all reason and manners that you rush this upon us; we who came to you in friendliness and have given you food and money and nursed your sick children?

'"If one of our young men has done a wrong against one of yours the elders should come and state their case like well-mannered people; if compensation is due it shall be paid. But think well; did not two of our youngest men, hardly yet men and quite unarmed over-power three of yours who carried spears? Did not I and I alone kick them out of Bwana's tent as if they were cackling hens?"

'I told Ndezo he looked superb and had made a great impression. He grinned in reply and told me now it was my turn. I remained seated and spoke:

'"Truly think well on what my brother has said, and let me warn you he is much feared in his own country for his power. But he is a good man and likes to use his power to help people. But if angered he does not hesitate to put a powerful curse on a man, woman or cattle or on a place such as yours.

'"We have prepared the curse to keep away rain and if we use it you will have no rain for three years, no grass, no milk, your cattle and goats will die and your women will have to live on the fat of their buttocks and will have nothing with which to succour a child.

'"In your madness did you intend to kill us? If you succeeded our spirits would haunt you and torment you at every turn so that you would gain nothing from your labours." I stood up and pointing continued "And if my brother makes his curse you will starve. Regain your reason. This madness is for uncircumcised boys who would be whipped."

'"Good," said Ndezo, "but it is not enough." He stood up and told me to point around with a closed fist as he spoke.

'"We warn you" he said in a loud voice. "He who uses a spear or a knife on anyone will not see the setting of the sun tomorrow."

'I pointed from one side to the other.

'"Now stare at the men still standing" Ndezo whispered.

'I stared at the nearest. He was a bit stubborn so I lifted my right hand slowly, index finger extended. That was enough. He crumbled to the ground. When the last had sat down and laid his spear on the ground before him I also sat down, rather thankfully, and told Ndezo we had won and must arrange matters so they did not suffer any loss of dignity and also that we must send out good thoughts.

'Africans can transmit and send thought messages as part of their normal life but the process is foreign to most Europeans. However I tried to transmit kind thoughts mixed with firmness. Then Ndezo spoke again:

'"We came to you in friendliness" he said, "and you received us well so that we became one large family and Bwana Chai was father to us all. So let us say this to you: our eyes saw not the men who rushed into Bwana Chai's tent nor the spears they carried; our ears heard not their angry shouting. We see you are sitting soberly in our compound having come to witness a case between two of our young men. Bwana Chai will judge as a father to each one. It will be proper and polite afterwards to thank him."

'After a slight pause, murmurs of approval and I think relief came from various parts of the compound. We could relax and allow them to derive as much entertainment as possible from this exceptional opportunity. The darkness beyond the camp-lit area formed the walls of our court, the lighted branches of the enormous fig tree under which we sat were the beams and the night sky and the stars between them formed our roof.

'We told Jackson to stand close on our right and the three men to stand close on our left and to state their case and speak truly on oath. I pointed to one to begin but soon stopped him and told him to name an ancestor of his who some of the present company could remember.

He was surprised and hesitated but we pressed him and I asked for confirmation, which was given. I then asked him to swear to speak truly on oath to that ancestor spirit.

'He started to speak but I stopped him again and I told him to lick his finger, touch the ground and then lick his finger again and hold it upwards and swear to speak the truth. He hesitated a moment before taking the most powerful form of oath there is.

'"Very good you remember that," said Ndezo. "They are very impressed and uneasy."

'We took the other two through the same procedure and sensed their unease because they were now bound in a manner they did not like and did not expect. The crowd had also reacted – and were hanging on our words.

'Their evidence was consistent: two of the men were brothers and the third was negotiating to take their sister for his wife and had paid a deposit. The girl was therefore not free to dally with other men. They accused Jackson of leading her off to a secluded place and having fun with her, which they had interrupted. However they admitted he had got away before they had actually seen him with her.

'We then put Jackson on oath. His defence was that the girl had offered herself for a few shillings, which he had accepted unaware that she was bespoken. He persisted in this, even when questioned, so we both accepted it.

'However, we both thought he should have made enquiries and found out if such playing was acceptable to the local people because of differences in religious and tribal background. Many of the local people were Muslim by faith.

'I therefore pronounced him guilty of grave misconduct to the local people and fined him forty shillings to be paid to the prospective husband. At first the prospective husband said it was not enough but was told angrily that it was that or nothing and if he refused there would be enmity between us. He then came forward and accepted the money gracefully, with a bow.

'Instinctively I placed my hand on his head saying:

'"Please God! I place this, my young friend in your hands and ask you to guide him and protect him so his life follows a good line."

'He looked at me in surprise, saying "Thank you, father" and leant forward and we embraced with the customary kiss on both cheeks.

On an emotional impulse his two companions hurried forward to be blessed and embraced.

'Later I had a few quiet moments with myself and offered a prayer to the Almighty and also to Father Laibon. Reg joined me saying he was thankful it was all over.

'"I could see at first that you didn't know what the hell to do" he said. "Then I thought you must be hypnotic and then I remembered the Laiboni who stared at you so intently and I tried to send you a message. After that you were quite confident so perhaps you got it."

'When I was alone Kamau came to say that he was very sorry because it was he who had brought Jackson to us.

'"We were all very angry with him because we all might have been killed" he said. "You know Bwana Chai at first we were very frightened but you have a powerful father somewhere and he guided you. We could see it and in my heart I say thanks to him."

'The next morning the three young men came with presents of eggs and groundnuts and we gave them tea and sugar.

'Later Jackson said the girl was no good at all:

'"She didn't know how to do it and it was like lying on a mattress."

★ ★ ★ ★ ★ ★ ★

'Gradually I grew more confident in my ability to use telepathy and thought transference as the natives did. One day Reg and two of the lads went out on horseback before dawn to catch zebra but two hours later Reg and Musembe returned without Njoroge. When last seen he was going at full gallop over a ridge about three miles to the east. We three were having breakfast when Njoroge's horse limped into camp without him.

'We knew that horse would never stand still beside a fallen rider unless the rider kept a firm hand on the reins. After examining it, the probability was that it had fallen and rolled on its back and left an injured Njoroge lying anywhere within an area of twelve square miles east of the camp. This consisted of a tree-covered ridge separated by a strip of open ground from a bush covered plain.

'We decided that Reg and Musembe would cover the approaches to the camp and the ridge on horseback while I and two other lads would go to the bushy section in a truck carrying a stretcher, first aid kit and food for the horses.

'The air was still cool when we set off and riding in the truck we were able to overlook most of the scrub where a few animals grazed undisturbed. We met a farmer with his cattle who told us he had not seen Njoroge but showed us where Reg and Musembe had crossed onto the ridge. Using the strip of open country as a guideline we began a systematic search making a leg westwards and then back eastwards always turning northwards.

'The sun rose and the truck gathered heat. I noticed Kamau had sensibly discarded his shirt and shorts for a shuka; a single piece of cloth wrapped round the body with two ends knotted over one shoulder and reaching halfway down the thigh. It is open on one side so the air can circulate and the wearer has no horrid sweaty patch in the small of his back.

'As time passed I developed a worrying feeling that we were in the wrong place and asked the driver to go towards the open ground so we could contact the others. Kamau stood on the top of the cab holding his shuka high above his head to attract their attention. Soon they came trotting towards us trailing two plumes of dust. After a discussion we decided to continue the search systematically.

'I was finding the midday heat exhausting so I asked the driver to stop the truck, got off and thankfully lay down in the shade of a large bush while the driver walked about to stretch his legs. Suddenly he waved his arms in an exasperated gesture saying Njoroge could be anywhere within twelve square miles and we really had nothing to go on. The area still to be searched was too large to be covered by nightfall and after dark an injured man was easy prey for a lion, hyena or wild dogs. I knew our system of searching was logical but my hunch that we were looking in the wrong place had grown stronger and was most disturbing.

'Kamau was again standing on top of the cab, a hand shading his eyes as he studied the plain, his red shuka streaming behind in the wind. It dawned on me that his people still used thought transference as a means of communication. His sense of intuition should be stronger than mine and he might therefore have a stronger hunch. I told him I knew Africans could send thought messages and Njoroge would be trying to reach us that way. I asked him if he had any feelings in his head that might help us to find him?

'"So you know of these things and are not afraid?" he said when he understood.

'I said that there was nothing to fear, thought transference was a well-known faculty but Africans were usually better at it than Europeans. He then admitted he had tried to reach Njoroge that way but could not hear him. Clasping me round the shoulders he begged me not to abandon the search:

'"He is my friend and I love him" he said and turned away to hide the tears.

'I was sure we were in the wrong place and were wasting valuable daylight. I told Reg I was convinced we should be at least a mile further north. While Kamau fed the horses and took their saddles off to rest their backs I told Musembe what I knew about thought messages and that I was sure Njoroge was trying to reach us and asked him what he thought. Speaking softly he said he was thinking all the time about Njoroge but could not hear him. We decided to continue the search but to meet again in an hour. As the sun moved westwards our anxiety increased and Kamau was weeping openly. Every time I used the binoculars his face came close to mine as he urgently asked what I saw.

'My hunch grew stronger and seemed to pull me northwards. My head throbbed and I felt I was suffering from sunstroke and our slow zigzagging moves east and west became so exasperating that I had the greatest difficulty in controlling myself and ordering everyone to stop. With the sun low in the sky Njoroge would be feeling desperate at the prospect of the dangerous night ahead of him.

'All my thoughts were centred on him. We had not yet covered half the area in which he might be lying and with our present system were unlikely to find him before dark. The only alternative was intuition and neither Kamau nor Musembe seemed to have any hunch whatsoever. We only had mine, such as it was.

'Handing the binoculars to Kamau I sat down on some canvases lying in the truck and concentrated all my mental energy on Njoroge and tried to break free from my surroundings. Kamau bent down to speak but I brushed him aside. By the end of an hour when we met up with the others I was exhausted but confident.

'Reg and Musembe had been in the saddle for ten hours and slipped stiffly from their horses rubbing their legs.

'"I've been talking to Musembe" Reg said handing me tea and aspirin "and we think your hunch is probably right. Njoroge must be transmitting like blazes and you may be getting it; after all you've done it before. So just tell us where you want to go."

'They gathered round hurriedly eating a sandwich and gulping down hot tea.

'Pointing to a small hill I said I would like to go towards it and that we should go quickly for a mile and then search carefully. I told them I was convinced Njoroge could not walk and visualized him lying under a bush; he might have put his hat on a stick to attract attention.

'"Suits me fine" Reg said winking at Musembe.

'"So you also have a hunch" I exclaimed.

'"Sort of but not strong like yours" he said.

'When I asked him why he had not said so before he just grinned and said he didn't want to jam my reception but as we thought alike we ought to find Njoroge before dark. Telling me to keep tuned in and Kamau to cheer up he swung himself back in his saddle.

'When we had gone about a mile we slowed to a walking pace, the truck heading towards the hill and the horses weaving about on either side. We stopped frequently to allow me to search with my binoculars. The low sun cast shadows on the ground, the bushes on our left were in shadow and those on the right were brightly lit. A bush far away to our right attracted my attention. I studied it carefully. There was something odd about it. Suddenly it dawned on me. It was a hat.

'I banged on the cab roof shouting;

'"It's there on a bush." Kamau asked what was there.

'"His hat of course, over there"' I shouted. Sounding the horn we drove as fast as possible towards it. Kamau said he couldn't see it.

'"Neither can I properly but I'm sure it's there" I answered. In a minute we both saw the hat on a stick standing above the bush. Kamau leapt out of the moving truck and ran to the figure on the ground.

'He was on his knees, his friend's head cradled in his arms, smiling through tears of relief but too moved to speak when we arrived. Njoroge's right ankle was very swollen and his left shoulder severely bruised. He told us he had tried to walk with a stick but had collapsed and crawled under the bush. In the afternoon, sensing we were looking for him, he had put his hat on a stick and pushed it through the bush.

'While we tried to make him comfortable he thanked us saying he had called on us and we had heard him and back in camp he embraced Reg and I when saying "good night". Musembe and Kamau also came to say "good night" and told me how they had lost all hope of finding Njoroge, and how they had wanted to help but couldn't hear him; then realizing I was hearing him they had lost all their fear. Their emotions overwhelmed their shyness and both kissed me saying "Shauri ya damu yetu" and bade me sleep well.

'Njoroge had felt sure Reg and I would try to find him and had therefore concentrated all his mental energy on us, ignoring Kamau and Musembe who had not the practical means to make a search.

'"Perhaps it is only a small thing to you that an African called to Europeans and led them to where he lay" Kaka said, "but it is a big thing for us and we have said thanks to God." He stood looking far over the hills and then said quietly:

'"You are very close to us, Bwana Chai."

★　★　★　★　★　★　★

'When we first formed our catching unit we had been advised not to employ missionary trained men. We soon learned it was sound advice. Now, thirty years later I still think it is wrong to interfere with other people's customs and beliefs.

'This belief was shared by Dr. Igor Mann of the Kenya Veterinary Department. He was a Polish refugee from a poor family who was understood to have a close understanding of African affairs.

'"Most missionaries only want converts to their own particular creed" he said, "and they don't want to analyse the Africans' own faith which has been adapted to survive in a harsh environment.

'"Long before white people came here Africans believed in a God or a Supreme Being. Have you not heard the expression 'Santa sana Mungu' (Thank you God) or 'Mungu ta saidia sisi' (God will help us)? They were in the hearts of the Africans long before any missionary set foot here.

'"'But', says the missionary to the African, 'your God and your customs are not good. We bring you something better.' Is it better, I ask you, to put a small cross on a chain round his neck and give him different clothes, if by your teaching you replace his conception of the Almighty with one which he cannot comprehend? If you also destroy the cohesion of his family life and social structure, which are the foundations for survival in his harsh environment, and if you cut him off from the guiding influence of the elders who form the highest court for settling the manifold problems humans have to face, it is a grave disservice and will lead to trouble.

'"The trio of African life is the dead or ancestor, the living and the unborn child. They believe the spirits of the dead remain in the surroundings for a time before going to join other ancestor spirits. During this period the living will respect their huts and possessions and will sit in the favourite places of the departed to keep their spirit there.

'"I came poor to Africa" he told me, "with no racial prejudices, no wish to change people and no religion to preach. That allowed the Africans to form a link with me."

'Igor Mann was by no means the first or the last person to criticize the missionaries and the effects of their teaching in Africa. A similar view was expressed by an old friend in the Colonial Service and his wife who had provided us with a home during our first days in Kenya. We met recently when this kindly bespectacled Commissioner to the Northern Province who, it was said, could outstrip any of his men when out walking, had just returned from a trip to settle a violent quarrel between two prominent Somali families over grazing rights.

'"It was a tricky one" he told me. "It's dry there and with the poor rains, tempers flare up easily and I didn't want the quarrel to spread. It had been simmering for some time. Then two lads of opposing families had a big fight in which one lost a tooth and the whole thing came to boiling point.

'"I called a meeting and let them shout at each other for some time and then told them that the respected elders should be exchanging gifts not insults and accusations and then quoted a piece from the Koran.

'"You should have seen their faces as an infidel quoted the law of the prophets. I then ordered a sheep to be killed and said I would preside over a feast of reconciliation after the evening prayers that night when two goats would be given as compensation for the tooth. The lads and the old men embraced and all seemed glad the row was settled. It is difficult for them to settle disputes without a mediator even if they want to."

'Reg expressed surprise that this mediator could quote from the Koran.

'"My dear Dick," he was told. "Nearly half the people whom I serve in this province are Muslims and if I am to get anywhere with them I must know the sacred writ that is supposed to order their lives as well as they do, if not better!"

'I wondered whether he had had an exhausting trip?

'"Nothing like as tiring as the missionaries I found here on my return" he said. "Some of them really are rather trying. They want to build schools, educate the children of those they call 'the heathen people' up to standard four and dress them properly because they think it is quite disgraceful the way they go about half naked.

'"They looked horrified when I said that I thought these people were rather lovely as they were. Since the Christian Church teaches that God created man in his own image it is odd that so many missionaries abhor nakedness which they mistakenly associate with immorality.

'"I feel we are not yet ready for that kind of education which will come in time of course. It is not that I am obstructing the Lord's work, but the missionaries are far too ready to discard local customs which have developed over the centuries. There is a lot of common sense behind them and they have helped these people to survive."

'He had tried to point out to the missionaries, he said, that a child must learn to live in this harsh land while it is young and to take it away from the family to a central school would interrupt this. There it would be encouraged to think itself well educated and so despise its parents and the family home. Thus parental authority which is the main guiding discipline is destroyed with no replacement.

'"This life may be tough for them" he said, "but it is what they know. There is tribal unity, good fellowship, humour, family affection and a well-established system whereby the parents care for the young who, in turn, care for the aged. It would be a great disservice to upset this before we can offer a better alternative which I hope one day we will be able to do."

'He laughed at the merit of teaching the young and leaving the old and said the older people were so conservative and not willing to change their own ideas of God for those of the missionaries. He was however trying out some elementary educational schemes combined with carpentry, hygiene and animal husbandry for all age groups.'

★　★　★　★　★　★　★

'It was just daylight when I awoke. There were the first tentative calls of the birds growing into a jubilant chorus with the early dawn. An elderly rhino passed leisurely through the camp. The rain had stopped and walking towards the men's tents I saw a figure standing a little apart, dark and slender against the bright eastern sky. He made a movement with his right hand as if pouring something on the ground and then stood with head bowed and hand held slightly forward. It was Lorrok Ole Monsiro.

'Hearing me approach he turned, apparently vexed at my intrusion but, seeing me about to withdraw, he held out his hand. Having seen Africans holding hands when talking or walking, I was used to the custom.

'We stood hand in hand watching the sun rise beyond a distant ridge. I was glad to be held still to absorb this moment. Those who have smelt the scent rising from the parched earth when it is first blessed by rain after months of drought, who have seen drops of water cupped in leaves or hanging like jewels from bushes, and small yellow butterflies hovering over the puddles, know the magic of this moment when life begins again.

'Our hands were joined but were our thoughts? Were we both simply enjoying a sense of peace induced by the colourful sky and the moist-scented air of a glorious morning or with him was it a much deeper impulse that had brought him naked from his bed to stand thus before the rising sun?

'His right hand held a cup and on the ground lay a small patch of thick milk not yet absorbed by the damp earth. Did it signify an act of worship?

'Realizing I had noticed it he was embarrassed and our communion was broken. He turned and moved towards his tent. What personal devotion had I been allowed to share momentarily only to be no longer welcome when I became aware of the cup and the milk? I made an appealing gesture and he returned and took my hands in his.

'With my limited vocabulary I was unable to say that I respected the beliefs and customs of his people and did not ridicule them as some Europeans had. I could only try and convey these thoughts as he gazed earnestly into my face.

'Perhaps he got the message because when Kaka came over with a cup of tea he bounded off in leaping strides calling cheerfully to the others.

'"The Masai youth leap like antelopes," Kaka said.

'Sipping my tea and remembering Lorrok's earnest expression I knew that hasty questioning on such delicate matters would be resented and I would have to wait until a suitable opportunity occurred. A few Africans had already spoken guardedly to Reg and I about their ideas on God and it was clear to me that they had known of a God for some time.

'Now, after many questions and answers during long years of association I have no doubt that even before the coming of the white man, Africans worshipped a God. Names and concepts may differ slightly according to the tribes yet there is a common concept of a supreme spirit, all-powerful and all embracing. I wondered what particular act of worship Lorrok had performed before the sun rose?

'As we sat round the fire that evening the subject was raised, tentatively, at first. Wise old Kaka led the young men gently until it was revealed that Lorrok had performed an act of worship and thanksgiving. There came a pause and I felt my presence was causing anxiety and it seemed unwise to pursue the subject. I recalled that in some Masai encampments the unexpected arrival of a strange European was still considered a bad omen calling for prayers and perhaps an offering.

'A boy, Leshan, put more wood on the fire, which sent flames and sparks soaring into the darkness and created dancing shadows around us. Then Kaka spoke quietly again and the tall lad, Mpapai, scratched a pattern in the earth with a stick. Suddenly he looked up his eyes and teeth gleaming in the firelight. In a firm tone he said that Kaka had spoken well and they could all talk freely to me.

'This met universal agreement and they all began to talk at once, their long fingered hands moving impulsively. With Kaka's help I elicited the true facts.

'Lorrok had been praying to the ancestor spirits who had not yet passed into another body and so were living nearer to God and he had asked them to convey to God his thanks for the gift of the sun. By pouring all his morning milk on the ground he had endorsed his prayer by a small personal sacrifice.

'Leshan and another lad with wide eyes fixed on me, talking together with expressive gestures said: "How can we know about the sun and how it came to be there?"

'Another voice added:

'"It is warmth and light to us and yet we do not know anything about it."

'Turning to me Lorrok said gravely:

'"Yet it is wise and proper to give thanks for that great gift."

'The others agreed and told Kaka to ask me what I thought about a Masai allowing a white man to join him in prayer to the greatly revered ancestor spirits. Kaka's expression showed how anxious he was as he translated the question.

'I replied that Lorrok's good and strong thoughts had surely guided mine because, as we stood together and he had taken my hand and allowed me to share his time of prayer, I had known a feeling of peace and a sense of gratitude towards God for such a lovely morning.

'"So you did not laugh?" Leshan said.

'"What the hell do you mean?" I snapped at him angrily, in English, "Of course I didn't laugh." Turning to Kaka I asked him to explain to the lads that prayers were sacred whatever the religion or faith, especially when shared by two or more people. Never, at any time, were they the subject of laughter.

'Apologetically, Leshan came and took my hands in his, bowing over them. This seemed to reassure everyone and, one by one, they rose to go to bed. Another lad, Mpapai, came to bow low to me and said 'goodnight'. Instinctively I placed my right hand on his head. He looked up in surprise:

'"How do you know our custom?" he asked me and turning to the others he said "He knows us."

'They talked excitedly among themselves. Gazing into my face Lorrok said:

'"How did you know? Tell us."

'How did I know and what thought had spontaneously prompted the gesture?

'A vivid picture came to mind and from years ago I could clearly see the two Laibonis standing against a background of golden plains and gentle hills as they bid Reg and I "Goodbye" during our first trip to Kenya. I saw our guide bow low before the elder who laid his right hand on the bowed head.

'"Where have you been?" Leshan asked, peering into my face as the vision dissolved into the dark figures in the firelight. "You went away from us. Where to? I know. Can you not tell?"

'In *Out of Africa* I remember the author saying that whenever she allowed her thoughts to return to the family home the African people knew it and said she had been away from them.

'To my relief Kaka said firmly:

'"Bwana Chai wants to go to bed now."

'When they had gone I asked him what he had said to them after the tall lad who had scratched the ground with a stick had said they could talk to me. He told me that he had reminded them that I had been well received by the Laiboni when I first came to Kenya. Therefore it was not wrong for them to talk to me about sacred matters. He added that one boy had said that it was well known that our spirits were close to theirs and that was why they had joined our unit.

'I asked Kaka how the hell he knew about the Laiboni? He said that he was with us at the time.

'"But you remained here in the town and didn't even meet the Laibonis," I said. He looked at me as much to say, "When will you grow up?" bade me goodnight and left me to my thoughts.

'So there it is. You keep an incident to yourself because it is entirely personal and years afterwards you learn that many people have known about it and discussed it. Well! That's Africa for you.

'It is involvements like this which still give me a purpose and which so enrich my life in Africa. They also give me something to do now that the active days of working with animals are over.

'How I would love to have it all again. Writing about it is the next best thing for thus I can, in a way, live it all over another time.'

★　★　★　★　★　★　★

Writing about it all was not enough. As he worked on his autobiography he found living alone was a depressing business and gradually his health deteriorated. The native boys, in their huts in the grounds, constantly pestered him for money.

His closest friends were Christopher and Birgit Archer and Birgit often acted as hostess for him when he entertained. One day, no doubt overcome by loneliness, he asked if he could live with them. Although they were extremely fond of him, they refused. On 21st January 1987, at the age of seventy-eight, after going out for dinner he was found dead in bed.

He was cremated and, just as thirteen years before John Seymour had scattered his brother's ashes over his beloved Norfolk marshes, Christopher Archer scattered John's ashes over his favourite camping site at Isiola, three hundred miles away from Nairobi. It was the site introduced to him by Gilbert Sauvage at the start of a career outlined by the *Daily Telegraph* in an obituary, which paid tribute to 'his valuable work in Africa'.

He would have liked that tribute but would have found it no more satisfying than the fact that part of his own life story should be linked to his brother's biography between the covers of this book.

Sketches and Drawings

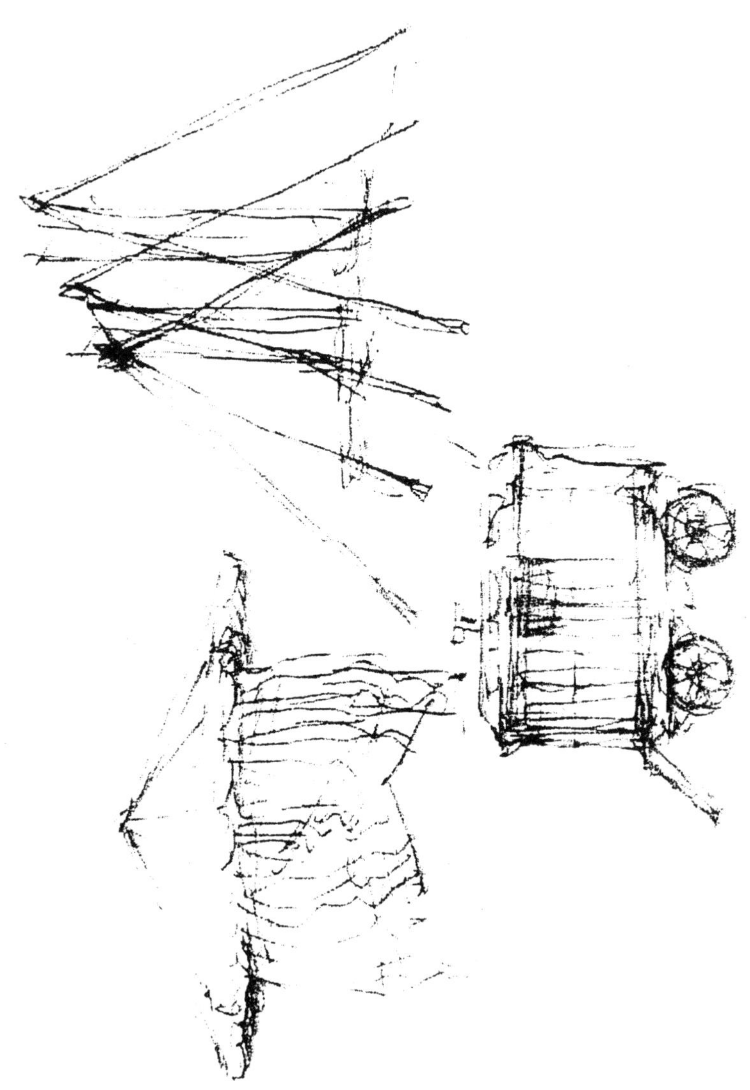

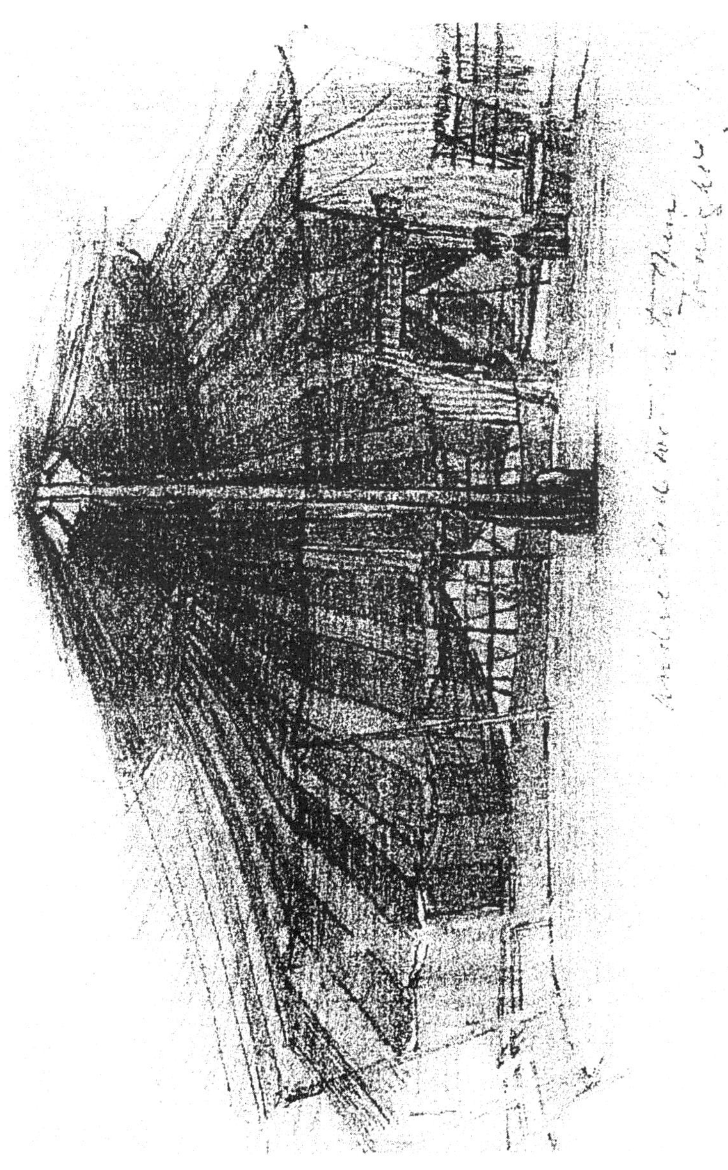

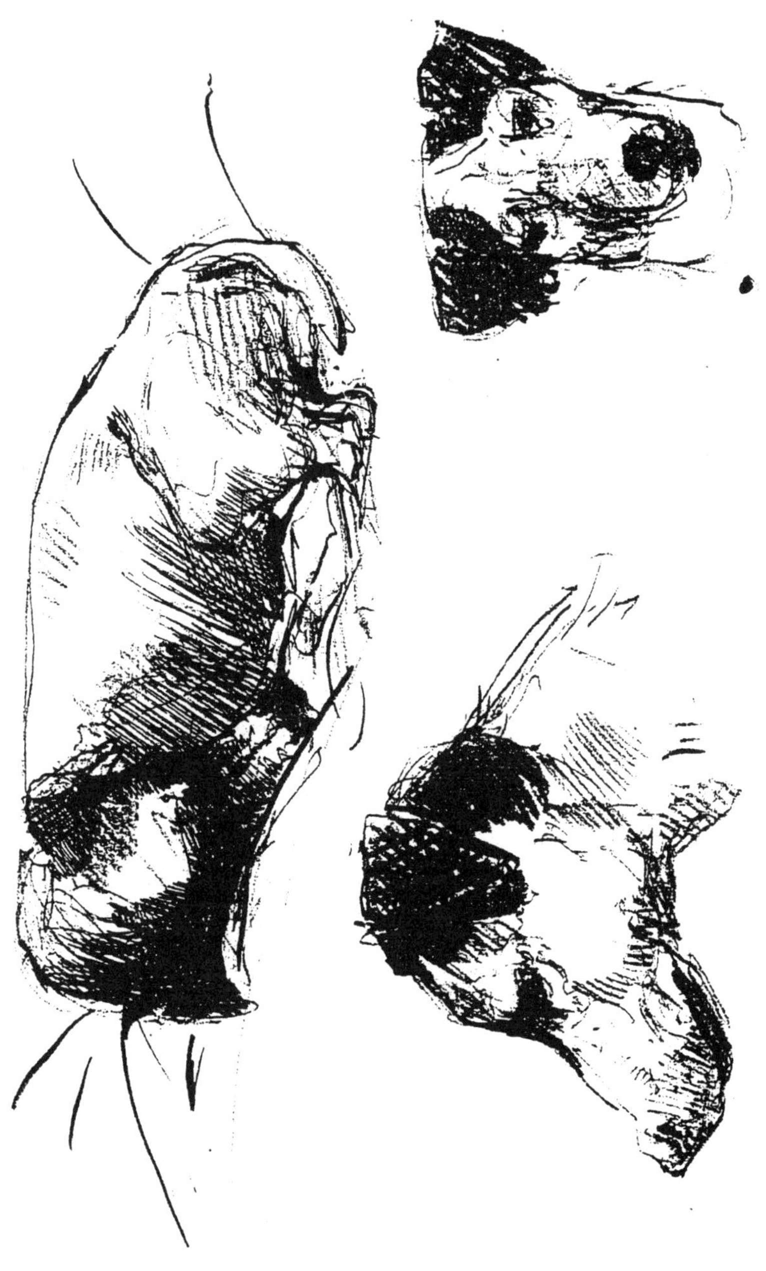

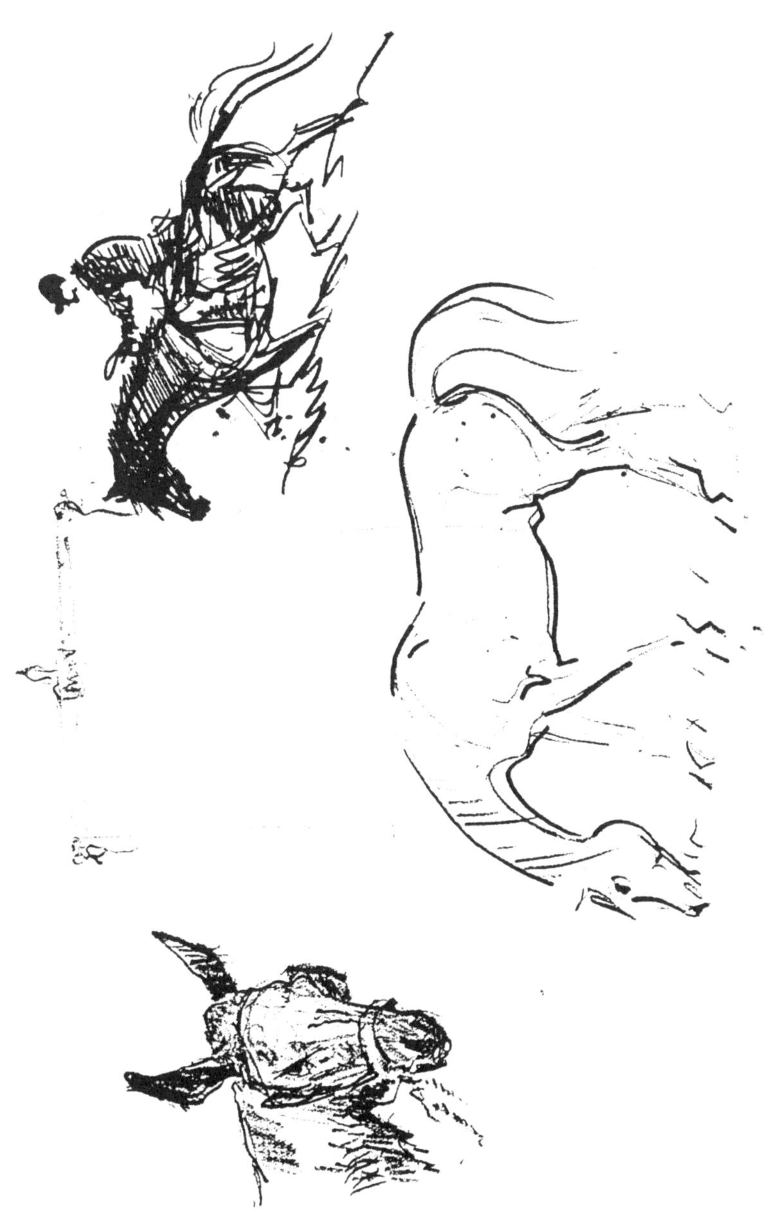

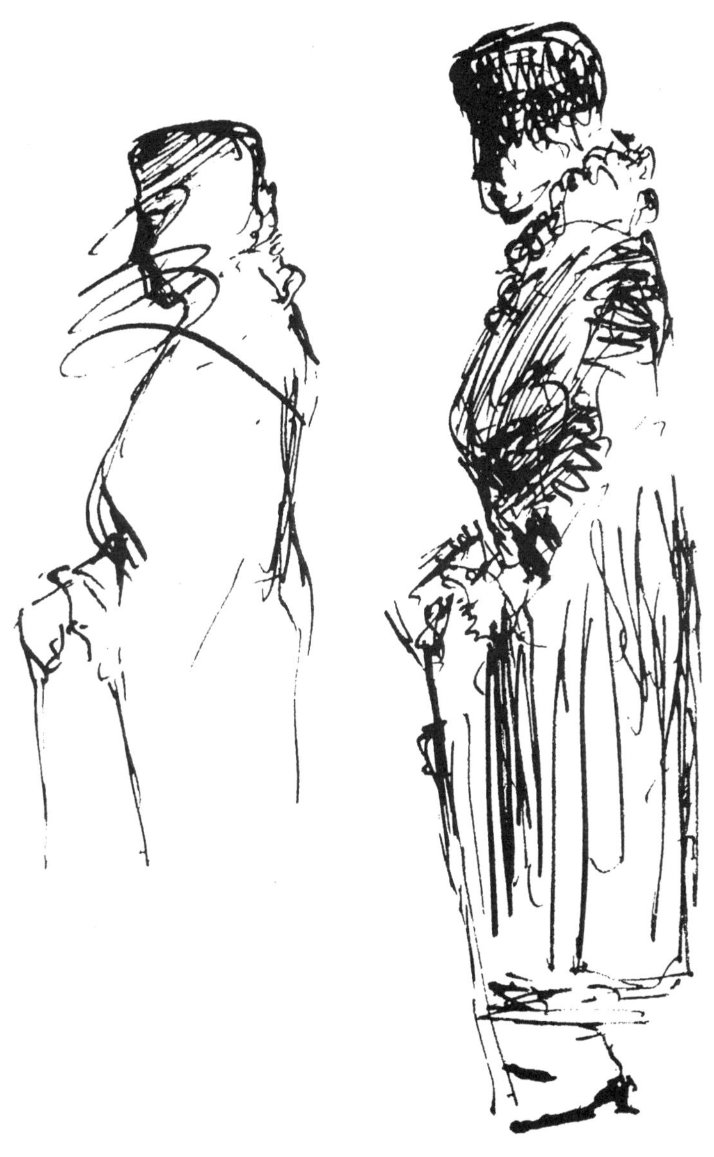

BIBLIOGRAPHY

Edward Seago's books and writings referred to or quoted in this book

Books:
CIRCUS COMPANY With an introduction by John Masefield, Putnam, London, 1933
SONS OF SAWDUST Putnam, London, 1934
CARAVAN Collins, London, 1937
THE COUNTRY SCENE With poems by John Masefield, Collins, London, 1937
TRIBUTE TO BALLET With poems by John Masefield, Collins, London, 1938
A GENERATION RISEN With poems by John Masefield, Collins, London, 1942
PEACE IN WAR Collins, London, 1943
HIGH ENDEAVOUR Collins, London, 1944
WITH THE ALLIED ARMIES IN ITALY Collins, London, 1945
A CANVAS TO COVER Collins, London, 1947
TIDELINE Collins, London, 1948
WITH CAPRICORN TO PARIS Collins, London, 1956

Other Writing:
Essay A PLACE TO PAINT in *The East Anglian Book*, East Anglian Magazine, Ipswich, 1971
Introduction to *The Paintings of Field-Marshal Earl Alexander of Tunis*, Collins, London, 1973

Book of Paintings:
EDWARD SEAGO: *Painter in the English Tradition*
    Introductory text by Horace Shipp, Collins, London, 1952
EDWARD SEAGO, *A Review of the Years 1953–1964*

Other Published Sources

Alexandra, Queen of Yugoslavia, *For A King's Love*, 1956
Bolitho, Hector, Alfred Mond: *First Baron Melchett*, 1933
Connell, John, *Auchinleck*, 1959
Denison, Michael, *Overture and Beginners*, 1973
East, Sir Alfred, *Landscape Painting*, 1911
Fraser, John Lloyd, *John Constable*, 1976
Munnings, Alfred J., *An Artist's Life*, 1950
Munnings, Alfred J., *The Finish*, 1952
Reading, Eva Marchioness of, *For the Record*, 1972
Nicolson, Nigel, *Alex*, 1973
Stokes, Hugh, *Appreciation of A. J. Munnings, R.A.* for the Munnings
    Exhibition at the Castle Museum, Norwich, 1928
Thesiger, Wilfred, *My Kenya Days*, 1994
Times, The, 1968
van de Post, Laurens, *Introduction to Catalogue* for Seago Exhibition at
    Marlborough Fine Art, London, 1972
Williamson, Henry, Essay 'Peace in War', *Eastern Daily Press*, 1943

Unpublished Sources

Family letters, narratives, diaries, letters and other personal papers in
    the possession of Mr John Seago and Mr Peter Seymour.
Letters belonging to Mr Alan Delgado.
Diaries and lettrs belonging to Mr John Gregory.
Diaries of Mr Ronald Horton.
Tape recording made by Mr Nigel Nicolson for his biography of
    Field-Marshal Earl Alexander of Tunis.
History of the Wollaston Family, W. H. Wollaston, 1960.

ONE MAN EXHIBITIONS

Arlington Gallery	London	1929
Sporting Gallery	London	1933
Sporting Gallery	London	1934
Alpine Club Gallery	London	1936
Sporting Gallery	London	1937
Carstairs Gallery	New York	1938
Medici Gallery	London	1939
Castle Museum	Norwich	1944
Colnaghi's	London	1945
Castle Museum (Italian War Pictures)	Norwich	1946
City Art Gallery (Italian War Pictures)	Bristol	1946
Colnaghi's	London	
	– Every Autumn	
Annan Gallery	Glasgow	1948
The Assembly House	Norwich	1950
Laing Galleries	Toronto	1950
Kennedy Galleries	New York	1952
Watson Gallery	Montreal	1952
	Oslo	1953
	Bergen	1953
Loan Exhibition during King's Lynn Festival	King's Lynn	1954
Kennedy Galleries	New York	1954
Cowie Gallery	Los Angeles	1954
Laing Galleries	Toronto	1954
Kennedy Galleries	New York	1956
St James's Palace	London	1957
Laing Galleries	Toronto	1957
Galerie Brughel	Brussels	1958

Kennedy Galleries	New York	1959
Laing Galleries	Toronto	1959
Galerie Brughel	Brussels	1960
Kennedy Galleries	New York	1961
Cowie Gallery	Los Angeles	1962
Loan Exhibition at the Castle Museum	Norwich	1962
Pieter Wenning Gallery	Johannesburg	1963
Russell Button Gallery	Chicago	1964
Marlborough Fine Art	London	1968
Maxwell Galleries	San Francisco	1968
Marlborough Fine Art	London	1970
Fuji Television Gallery	Tokyo	1971
Pieter Wenning Gallery	Johannesburg	1971
Marlborough Fine Art	London	1972
Marlborough Galerie	Zurich	1973
Laing Galleries	Toronto	1973
Fermoy Art Gallery	King's Lynn	1974
Marlborough Fine Art, Memorial Exhibition	London	1974
Pieter Wenning Gallery	Johannesburg	1975
Marlborough Fine Art	London	1976

EDWARD SEAGO'S POST-WAR OVERSEAS JOURNEYS

1948   With *Endeavour* to Belgium
      Ostend, Bruges, Brussels

1949   Motored to Italy via France
      and Switzerland
      Lenno, Como, Porto Fino

1950   Motored to Italy
      Chioggia and Venice
      Belgium

1951   With *Capricorn* to South
      Holland
      With *Capricorn* up the Seine
      to Paris

1952   With *Capricorn* to Boulogne,
      Dieppe and up the Seine
      to Paris

1953   Portugal
      With *Capricorn* to Holland
      Amsterdam, Delft, etc.

1954   Portugal
      With *Capricorn* to Holland

1955   Portugal
      Italy
      Rome, Porto Ercole, etc.

1956   With *Capricorn* to Paris
      Spain
      Torremolinos, Ronda,
      Granada

1956-7   Antarctica via Bangkok and
      Singapore

1957   Ponza
      Italy
      Rome and Naples

1958   Ponza
      Italy
      Rome and Naples

1959   Paris
      Holland

1960   Venice
      With *Capricorn* to Paris

1961   With *Capricorn* to Dieppe

1962   Hong Kong, Burma and
      Bangkok

1964   Greece and Paris

1965   With *Capricorn* to Paris

1966   Morocco

1967   Morocco
      France

1968   Morocco
      Sardinia

1969   Holland
      Sardinia

1970   Sardinia

1971   Sardinia and Turkey

1972   Sardinia

INDEX

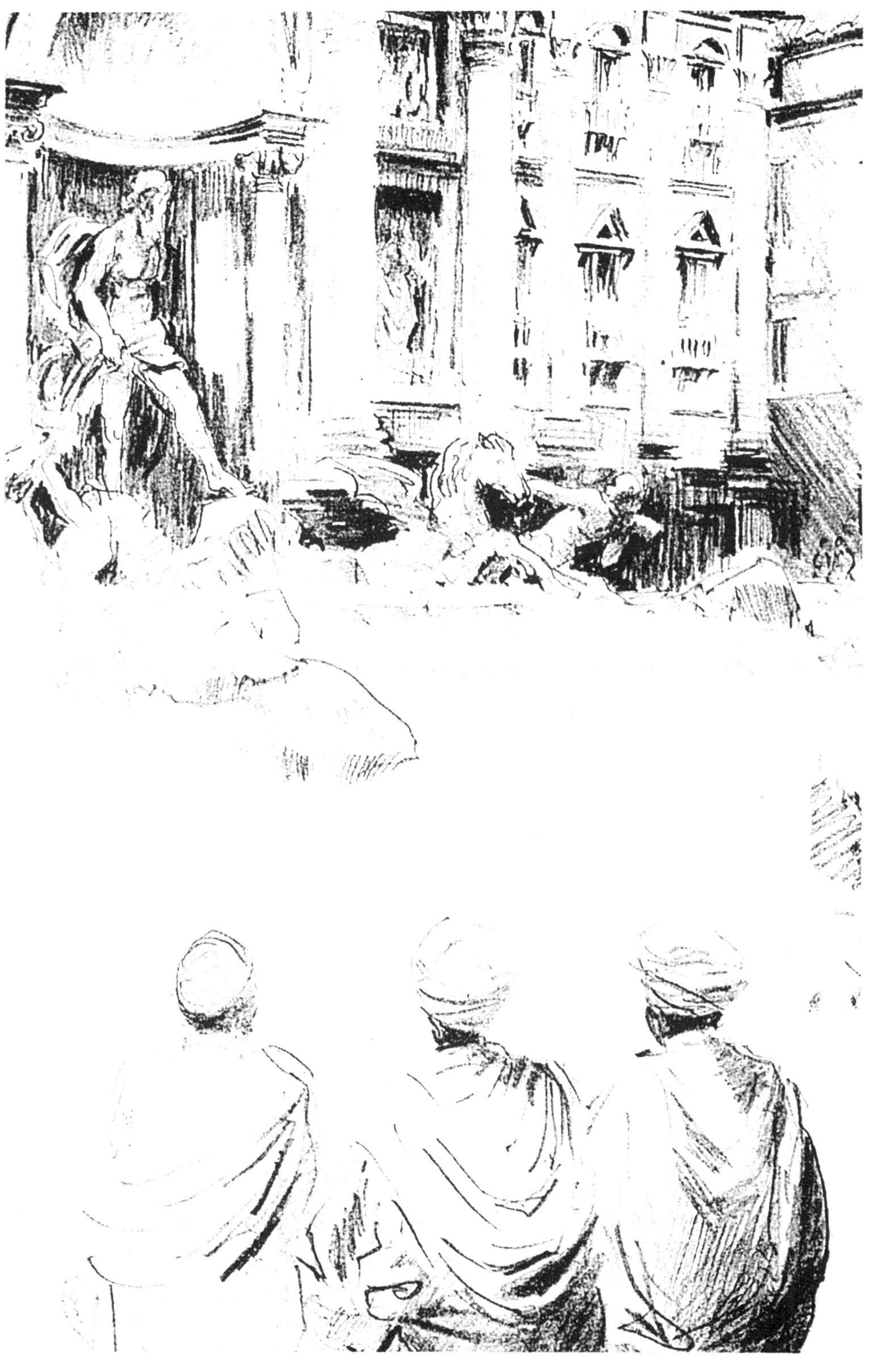

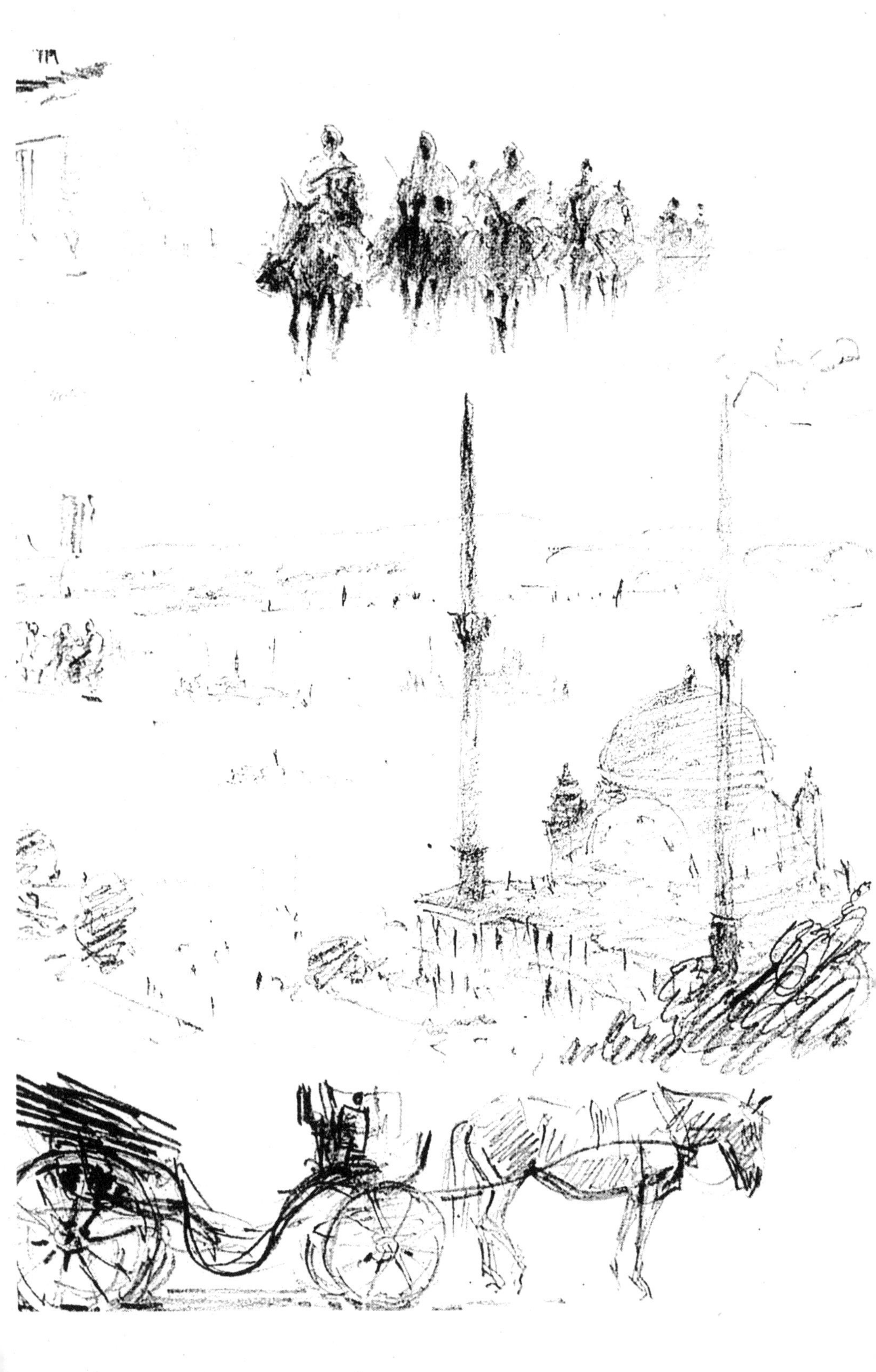